THE ART OF

SPIRITUAL GUIDANCE

THE ART OF

SPIRITUAL GUIDANCE

A CONTEMPORARY APPROACH TO GROWING IN THE SPIRIT

Carolyn Gratton

CROSSROAD • NEW YORK

1992

The Crossroad Publishing Company
370 Lexington Avenue, New York, NY 10017

Copyright © 1992 by Carolyn Gratton

Printed in the United States of America
Typesetting output: T$_E$XSource, Houston

Library of Congress Cataloging-in-Publication Data

Gratton, Carolyn.
    The art of spiritual guidance : a contemporary approach to growing
in the spirit / Carolyn Gratton.
      p. cm.
    Includes bibliographical references.
    ISBN 0-8245-1158-1
    1. Spiritual direction. I. Title.
BX2350.7.G73 1992
253.5'3—dc20

91-33505
CIP

CONTENTS

FOREWORD

W E cannot "go it alone." It has ever been thus. Standing at the brink of the third millennium, people are seeking guidance in overwhelming numbers and for reasons beyond counting. Men and women seek guidance when faced with life's complexity, when they lose grip on its purpose and meaning, or when resources to resist or endure pain and suffering seem in short supply. Sometimes guidance is called for when we are overcome by delight, thrilled by beauty and wonder, or redoubled in strength by hope, "the thing with feathers / That perches in the soul" (Emily Dickinson). Many of us are as ill-prepared for light and joy as we are for darkness and suffering.

The pace of life that too many of us keep leaves us exhausted, frustrated, indeed depleted. We are understandably prone to impatience or, worse, indifference with controversies, discussions, and chatter about the spiritual life. Those who earnestly seek God in the depths of their beings are sometimes reticent about various techniques in prayer, the use of personality type indicators as incentives to more effective prayer, or workshops on "how to" pray. Vast numbers of lay persons are diffident, feeling quite inadequate when faced with the prospect of being introduced to traditional schools of spirituality, discernment, or spiritual direction, be it Ignatian or another approach. Shelves in libraries and bookstores are crammed with practical wisdom of all sorts, whether it be that of the self-help manual, the Twelve-Step Program, or the potpourri that fits under the heading of "inspirational" writing. Where to turn? Where to begin?

Whatever course one may follow, more and more learn quite quickly that we need help along the way. The guidance provided by another is often an indispensable source of wisdom that enables us to make good in life's purposes. Be it in efforts to make sense of the meager conundrums that cause us to feel as though our world is falling apart, or in making choices that will chart our energies, time, and resources for years to come, the wisdom of someone more experienced in the ways of recognizing the working of God's Spirit is a resource both rich and rare.

Professor Gratton's earlier works *Guidelines for Spiritual Direction* (Denville, N.J.: Dimension, 1980) and *Trusting: Theory and Practice* (New York: Crossroad, 1982) had convinced me that she has an extraordinary ability to instruct both spiritual guides and those seeking guidance. In *The Art of Spiritual Guidance* she has integrated into one coherent whole a wide variety of current psychological and spiritual insights on the art of spiritual guidance. Incorporating knowledge from the human sciences and mystical theology, the present volume judiciously combines the wisdom of the Christian tradition with contemporary resources. Rather than espousing one or another of the "schools" of spirituality, Professor Gratton provides an essential and eminently readable overview and synthesis that those in the work of spiritual direction and guidance have been anticipating for quite some time.

What makes this volume so compelling is that it is a work of love. With almost twenty-five years of working experience in the field of spiritual guidance, Carolyn Gratton has told in these pages the story of the heart, the inner core of the human person, the source of wholeness wherein all dimensions of life are integrated. *The Art of Spiritual Guidance* combines traditional and contemporary resources in such a way to empower others with the confidence necessary to attend to the Spirit in that region of wound and wisdom that is the human heart.

Ministers, spiritual guides, counselors, adult educators, retreat and conference center personnel, formation directors and lay leaders from all traditions will find that *The Art of Spiritual Guidance* comes from the pen of one skilled in the art. Readers will recognize in Carolyn Gratton a sure guide along the path, summoning us to the fullness of the Mystery that bends so near to us and lures us to itself.

MICHAEL DOWNEY

ACKNOWLEDGMENTS

- To my students in the Monday morning spiritual direction seminar who kept suggesting that I try to put some of it in a book;

- To the Toronto Grail group, who have been patiently listening to this material in various forms for years;

- To Janet Somerville whose felicitous phrasing has added much needed sparkle to the text;

- To Tina Whitehead, who created order from this chaos not once, but several times;

- To Michael Downey, who insisted I write an article on spiritual direction for his dictionary, and now contributes the foreword;

- To my colleagues at Duquesne's Institute of Formative Spirituality (Adrian, Chuck, Rick, Susan, Jean, Keith, Carole, and Dennis) for their dedication to the work of integration that has brought us together for so many years;

- and to all of you who indicated that you want this book NOW; my thanks.

Here it is.

Introduction

LOOKING FOR CONNECTIONS

L IFE tends to get complicated. Or rather, we the living find our lives getting complicated, more and more so as we near the end of the twentieth century.

Most men and women I know (and I myself from time to time) look for some type of guidance when life feels overwhelming by reason of its complexity, or its pain, or its loss of meaning, or even its breath-stopping wonder. At such moments, many of us search for a trustworthy wisdom that will connect us with the larger purpose and meaning of everyday events.[1]

Purveyors of various kinds of wisdom come in crowds these days. Modern guides are not shy. Bookstore shelves are crammed with manuals explaining how we can live more fully: in our bodies, in the marketplace, in emotional and social exchanges, in all the functional dimensions of life today.

Spiritual Guidance for People Like Us

A reliable approach to spiritual guidance today must be able to integrate all these partial dimensions. At the same time, it must be able to affirm our personal capacity for participation in an ultimate mystery that is more than any of these parts. We are looking for a trustworthy way for human hearts. The "heart," in this ancient sense, is the inner core of the human person: the source of intentional wholeness that can integrate all the dimensions of life.[2]

We are beginning to realize that we cannot meet the spiritual questions of a late-twentieth-century seeker, Eastern or Western, merely by quoting the wisdom of the Sufis or the Gita or of the early Fathers and Mothers of the church, not if the modern person knows about neuropsychology, cultural anthropology, and redaction criticism of scriptural texts. But even for the most sophisticated person, a transformed spiritual awareness can be born in a moment of utter wordless simplicity. In the midst of an ordinary day the veil can suddenly tear, the light

1

can burst in upon a sleeping human heart, and life can be seen all at once for what it is: a mystery too wonderful for speech, too beautiful for thought.

"Oh, earth, you're too wonderful for anyone to realize you!" exclaims Emily in the American play *Our Town*, when she comes back from death to live one ordinary day of her life again. She adds, "Do any human beings ever realize life while they live it?"[3] It is this "too wonderful" experience of being alive and realizing it that lies at the center of the process of spiritual guidance we are going to explore.

This book is about spiritual guidance for us as we are today — with all our cultural complexity and fragmentation, with all our inner capacity for unifying the reality we live into a profound, open, vital simplicity. The approach to spiritual guidance that will unfold in this book invites us to recognize the mysterious capacities of the human heart. Human life is open, not closed. The heart can be drawn beyond itself, can hear and love other people, can receive all of creation and its creating God. There is no need to deny anything that belongs to our humanness. Between the ambiguity and messiness of our everyday lives and the invisible but energizing Mystery of holy Otherness that gifts our lives with ultimate meaning, there is an intrinsic and transcendent connection. Spiritual guidance can help us grow in awareness of that connection and that ultimate meaning.[4]

People in late-twentieth-century North America typically live in a way that dims or blots out their felt connection with ultimate meaning. In his book *Will and Spirit*, psychiatrist Gerald May muses on the poignant fact that responsible North American adults are often so concerned with doing all the jobs their commitments entail that they lose their experiential connection with the divine mystery of life.[5] They continue to do all the work to which they have committed themselves, but they lose touch with why they made the commitment in the first place. Thus, in the outward sphere of activity and work, many of us have lost the sense of connectedness with a larger purpose and meaning. We can also lose sensitivity to what is going on in the inner dimension, in our life of feeling and emotion. Even more easily, we can lose sensitivity on the spiritual level. We can cease to feel the touch of the Mystery that bends so near us in order to communicate with us. Thus, we can find ourselves still working busily, but out of touch with our feelings and closed off from the longings of our aspiring spirit as well.

So we need forms of guidance that are down-to-earth enough to take seriously the problems that we encounter in work, in relationships, and in committed responsibility, while helping us to remember and savor the Mystery that connects all these.

To be human means to be spiritual. Human beings have longings and aspirations that can be honored only when the person's spiritual capacity is taken seriously. These aspirations include but go beyond our longing to be whole, our desire for growth and development in all the dimensions of being human. The Western world, since the Enlightenment, has tended to repress the recognition of spiritual aspirations. But now, not only in those Eastern countries where it has never been repressed, but also in the Western world, there is a surge of interest in spirituality. It is emerging not only among transpersonal psychologists and purveyors of Eastern methods of meditation, but also among Christians. Many desire to live a spiritual life that embodies a receptive "yes" to a hidden Presence already there in our unfolding human lives. Such a spiritual life can be rooted in the Gospels and in the tradition of the Christian people through the ages. A great many Christians had never discovered that truth, or had forgotten it. Many are now rediscovering it. It is for them especially (though not exclusively) that this book is being written.[6]

As We Are Today

The current rediscovery of spirituality is taking place in the midst of a time of stretching and shifting in modern modes of consciousness. We find ourselves pushed toward "thinking globally" — committed to working for the transformation of the entire world. Our concern for ourselves and for our families is interlayered with concern for the human species as a whole. In our day, that means not only global justice and peace, but also a new urgent concern for other species, other aspects of creation, the entire environment. "The universe is no longer seen as a machine made up of a multitude of separate objects, but appears as a harmonious indivisible whole, a network of dynamic relationships that include the human observer and his or her consciousness in an essential way," says Fritjof Capra in his book *The Turning Point*.[7]

In an earlier book, Capra pointed out that the style of consciousness of "the new physics" is similar to the worldview of mystics in many of the great religious traditions.[8] It is, he thinks, a more relational and integrative way of seeing, allowing for "yin" (receptivity) as well as "yang" (assertiveness) insights. The "yin/yang" duality is an ancient Taoist way of describing polarity, or complementarity, in life. The more relational, interactive approach of receptive openness corresponds to "yin," the dark or feminine half of a dark-and-bright sphere. The more assertive approach of self-organizing autonomy corresponds to "yang," the bright or masculine half of the sphere. Our present North American culture continues to favor "yang" values over "yin" values, says Capra, but this is shifting as we try more relational modes in new approaches to ecology, health, psychology, and even economics.

Capra sees the growing awareness of feminine intentionality as a sign of a more receptive, open-ended approach to reality.[9]

All of this points to radical shifts in the consciousness of all people, both religious and nonreligious. What is it saying to us who are concerned with spiritual guidance for today's committed adults?

— First, contemporary people looking for assistance on the spiritual journey are probably seeing themselves more as a whole and less as a "soul" separated in some way from its embeddedness in a vital-functional body.

— Second, contemporary seekers are possibly more inclined to experience themselves as open systems, inextricably connected and interrelated with the culture and situation in which they find themselves, as well as with other persons and networks of persons.[10]

— Third, contemporary people — soaked since birth in the media of mass communication — cannot imagine themselves to be independent in their life field or in their thinking from the life fields and the thinking of thousands of other, sometimes very different arenas of thought and action that impinge upon their own. There are no more ghettos of thought or action left to hide in. We are all affected by pluralism. It may well be that the extreme and fragmenting pluralism of our time poses one of the greatest challenges to the art of spiritual direction today.

— Finally, spiritual guidance today insists on connectedness. Present knowledge, both scientific and spiritual, refuses to be isolated from the concrete realities of people's immediate circumstances. It also refuses any separation from the invisible cosmic whole that is the ultimate context of each individual life.[11]

Today's adults cannot find guidance reliable if it does not make sense in terms of their general cultural and professional formation. A religious view of life that has not kept pace with our adult unfolding cannot be trusted as a framework for reflecting on who we are and where our lives are going.

Encountering "Otherness"

The mystics and spiritual masters of old were deeply aware of an essential truth that modern minds can often confuse. It is this: the spiritual quest is about the relationship of the human person to what is not oneself — to what is ultimately Other, to a Sacred Presence, to, if you will, a divine Someone Else. We today sometimes turn spiritual guidance into concern for a merely interiorized process of growth and development.[12] Thus, we can miss out on the energy available only when we see human life as a dynamic dialogue — as the possibility for an *encounter* between our partial selves and a larger mysterious whole.

Then the aim of spiritual guidance becomes that of helping persons get the various parts of their life in tune with the larger Mystery as it flows throughout the whole.

The Sufi mystics have a story that images this process. In fact, this short legend could provide a guiding image for us as we try to imagine the role of the spiritual guide. It seems that there once were some fish who spent their days swimming around in search of the water. Anxiously looking for their destination, they shared their worries and confusion with each other as they swam. One day they met a wise fish and asked him the question that had preoccupied them for so long: "Where is the sea?" The wise fish answered: "If you would stop swimming so busily and struggling so anxiously, you would discover that you are already in the sea. You need look no further than where you already are."

The wise fish is, of course, the spiritual guide or, sometimes, the deepest part of us that is in touch with the Holy Spirit. The place where we already are is described in different ways in various great religious traditions. Their descriptions point to the invisible sea that surrounds us, the Tao for some; the Mystery of All That Is for others; Being; the divine Will; the intimate presence of the Holy Other; the flow of created and uncreated energies; the abyss of Nothingness or simply the holy Otherness of God — these and many other descriptions point to the possibilities that lie around us and within us for tapping into invisible sources of energy for loving and being loved. If we at all identify with the swimming fish, we recognize our need from time to time to encounter a wise fish. Some of us even feel the need to become one![13]

For those of us who identify with the latter need there will be another book based on the approach of this one. It will describe how a transcultural group of men and women learn within a supervised practicum to come to grips with the challenges involved in the day-to-day practice of spiritual guidance. Available in the near future, it will be an effective tool to be used in conjunction with this book.

Chapter One

WAKING UP TO FREEDOM AND WHOLENESS

THERE are all kinds of ways of waking up from the sleep of the everyday to the awareness that we are alive, and embodied, and necessarily (whether we like it or not) involved in the flow of the universe. History and art record many such moments of awakening. Often, the record includes the individual's profound recognition that in spite of the weight of circumstances and in the midst of the cosmic drama of unceasing change, he or she is inwardly free.

Yet there are millions of human beings whose hearts continue to slumber, who remain for a lifetime dozing in a taken-for-granted existence. Helping persons to wake up to the range and power of their own human hearts is one of the perennial goals of spiritual guides.

In a somewhat different way, that goal is also a perennial one for artists and writers. Recent fiction and autobiography continue to describe the entry of individuals (or their refusal to enter) into a transformed consciousness. Three well-known examples might be helpful here.

Etty Hillesum's diary, *An Interrupted Life*, gives us an intimate record of that young Jewish woman's life in Holland — of her friendships, her family, her ideas, her love.[1] Hillesum's daily routine of intellectual and sensual pleasure was shattered by the dark years of Nazi occupation (1941–43). Her diary shows her being forced to confront some of life's most serious questions as she struggles with the moral issues and the cruel realities of that time. The events burning in her life became catalysts, evoking inner resources of faith, hope and love that were "already there" but not previously in her conscious awareness. We see her transformed into a compassionate and deeply spiritual woman by the events that challenged her humanity.

Judith Guest's novel *Ordinary People* tells the story of a refusal.[2] Beth Jarrett, the central character, is an organized and efficient wife

7

and the mother of a suicidal son. She is unable to face the death of one of her sons and the mental illness of another; nor can she face her own affectional inadequacies. Beth Jarrett has built a respectable, comfortable life. But as it crumbles, her inner deformations engulf her, and she flees. She "cops out" on a classic mid-life crisis, refusing to deal with the imperfect world and limited self that are hers.

Norman Cousins's *The Healing Heart* is autobiographical.[3] The book tells us how his personal faith, hope, confidence, and will to live were the attitudes that helped him to meet the life-challenging event of the breakdown of his physical health. After his heart attack, Cousins begins gradually to see that health does not depend only on vital-physical conditioning. Emotional and spiritual questions — questions his doctors were mostly unprepared to deal with — are health issues as well.

These three crisis stories show us people in contemporary circumstances who have been forced by events in their lives to wake up from the taken-for-grantedness of their everyday routine. They must make decisions about the very meaning of their lives.

These three, and others like them, would make ideal candidates for the kind of spiritual guidance this book is all about.

Each of these three could agree, from personal experience, that the universe and life itself are in a constant process of formation and reformation, of taking a certain shape or structure and then losing that shape by being restructured. Human beings, too, receive a certain form from what happens to them in the course of their life. But as they marry, or start a new job, or get caught in a war, or have a child or a major new idea, the shape of life changes. Even their presence in a room changes when someone else enters or leaves that room.

With some formative insight, our three persons would also be able to see that although they are always part of the ongoing process of giving and receiving form, they are never totally determined by it.

Human beings are always free to respond to what happens. Not absolutely free, it is true; but really free, with a relative and limited freedom. Human persons can give form to life as it changes, even in chaotic situations like war, family crisis, or a heart attack.

Freedom Is What We Seek

This inner freedom is essential to being human, to being spirit. It is true that we also see impersonal "laws" — chemical, biological, even social "laws" — constantly operating in the universe. Nonetheless, the human spirit is able freely to choose to give form, in a way that confounds the appearance of determinism.

This assumption — that human beings have limited but real freedom — is central to our understanding of spiritual guidance.

The Christian tradition, in centuries of reflecting on the Gospel of the Incarnation, affirms that the divine Mystery has entered the process of history, the ceaseless giving and receiving of form. God's self-communicating grace is here in this process, meeting human freedom. Therefore, Christians can speak not only of formation and reformation, but also of divine transformation.[4] Those who seek guidance, as well as those who offer it are, like the fish swimming in the water of the Sufi legend, situated within this mystery. They are able to be receptive to the divine form-giving, and they are able to partake in it. In their need and in their freedom, human beings are situated in this vast open process, and there they can encounter God. An appreciation of human freedom and of its built-in directedness toward the divine Presence underlying all life events is the basis of the church's traditional understanding of spiritual direction.

We are certainly not always aware of this aspect of our reality. Like the fish, we are busy swimming and seeking. We get distracted. We get lost in routines and crises, in daily striving for power and status and possessions or even just survival. We lose touch with our desire for the "more," with our human capacity for freely partaking in the fullness of the Mystery. We lose touch with the transcendent aspirations of our searching human hearts.

We need to be reminded, often, of the hidden intentionality of those longing hearts. When they lose their way, for the moment, they need guidance. The spiritual guide is there to help seekers freely awaken to or "remember" the path along which God is leading their hearts.[5]

Starting Points for Direction

There are times when our established routines and our accustomed frame of mind seem to be able to contain the ongoing flow of life. We cope well, or at least satisfactorily. Things make sense, or at least they stay within the reach of what we might expect. Those are the seasons when people are most likely to "fall asleep" to the deeper possibilities of their own lives.[6]

There are other times when unexpected events interrupt the flow of our lives and raise sharp new questions. We have already glanced at three books about life events that question someone's whole frame of reference: a son's suicide for Beth Jarrett, a heart attack for Norman Cousins, the Nazi invasion for Etty Hillesum. In Hillesum's book, for example, we watch the author (diarist) grow and become transformed by the divine Other in whom she does not consciously believe. She is transformed not in spite of the questions presented to her by the

Holocaust, but because of them, and because there are no easy answers to the mystery of human suffering and compassion.

Life questions that arise from experience often overflow the frame of mind in which we try to receive them. Transitions force us to go deeper, to ask what this new event or loss or person means for me, in view of the larger purpose of my life.

What is this event saying? What is it asking of me as response? How shall I react when my spouse draws away from me without explanation or warning? What shall I do about my children whose ways I no longer understand? Why continue in this job or commitment in community when I can see no real result, when I'm feeling coerced and controlled, when I have lost my original enthusiasm?

Dilemmas like this push people toward ultimate questions.[7] Even very young people today are often pushed hard by such questions. They are not taking their future for granted; they are thinking deeply, often despairingly. The questions of "ordinary people" aren't so ordinary anymore. I have overheard ten-year-olds, on their way to the skating rink, talking about AIDS and death and nuclear war and environmental catastrophes. When people are being haunted by ultimate questions, functionalistic answers do not satisfy them. Neither are they interested in pious formulas or in dogmatic confrontations. At such moments, they are looking for the spiritual direction of their lives.

Where can contemporary people turn with such questions?

In traditional societies, there were usually village elders, or shamans, or other wise women and men who could be consulted during critical periods in the lives of individuals or of the tribe. Who fills that role for modern North Americans? Today the gurus for most people seem to be newspaper columnists or talk show hosts like Phil Donahue, Oprah Winfrey, or Dr. Ruth.[8] There is a certain homely wisdom there, and a fund of pop psychology. But as life guidance, the insights of today's media stars come nowhere near the calibre of the guidance given centuries ago by the desert Fathers and Mothers, or by later contemplatives in the Christian tradition.[9] Today's gurus tend to offer functionalistic solutions or ways to escape the problem of meaning altogether. Granted, some questions are merely functional, and deserve a functional answer. But many questions are not. "Who am I? Who is really in charge? Why me? Why did this happen to me?" The "who" and "why" questions often arise from the deepest part of our being.

These are questions that themselves give guidance as they lead us forward into freedom. These are questions that can free us to confront life's ambiguity instead of escaping into some authoritarian cult where all the answers are figured out ahead of time. As Rilke said to the young poet: Try to love the questions themselves; do not seek the answers now, but live the questions themselves.[10]

To seek guidance is not necessarily the same as looking for answers.

People seek guidance that can show them how to participate more deeply in the Mystery that is the underlying ground of all the questions. By being helped to listen to and to trust the events of their own lived experience, people can come to understand their problems and worries against a wider and deeper consciousness of the Mystery of All That Is.

In somewhat the same way, a Chinese painting lets us see small human figures against an obviously larger and more imposing background that reveals the cosmic reality of nature and the Tao.[11]

To get lost in Tao includes the willingness to live as part of a whole that is much larger than I am, a Whole that is mysterious, and that endows my life, too, with mystery and ultimate meaning. As Gabriel Marcel has put it, a person's life is not merely a series of problems to be solved. Someone's life is a mystery to be lived.[12] My life is a mystery to be lived in a style that integrates my gifts and resources and respects my intrinsic limits.

From this point of view, each person is a unique, limited, embodied presence to the Mystery that is the Everything. Or — since personal presence to the Mystery is a free act of being — there could be, at the core of someone's life, an absence from the Mystery. Usually, though, there is in each of us a kind of receptive consciousness that from time to time allows us to notice and reverence the interconnectedness of persons with the world around them and with its mysterious Source. From that interconnectedness flows abundance of life.

Integration in an Age of Pluralism

By itself, psychology is inadequate to hold and handle that abundance of life. Even before I had finished my doctorate in psychology, I was aware that the methods of psychological observation cannot by themselves yield understanding of someone who is seeking spiritual guidance. Techniques learned from the study of behavior and of unconscious dynamisms can teach us much. But, when spiritual guidance is being sought, psychological methods need to be complemented by a much more intuitive perception of how a particular person is living in relation to the larger Whole. I needed to explore something of the dialogue of each person's autonomous self with her or his essential rootedness in God and in the rest of creation.[13]

Spiritual guides have been aware for centuries of the spiritual seeker's need for an integrative awareness of the Whole. It used to be the case that at the heart of every great culture lay an integrated, more or less agreed upon worldview that dealt with the human person's relationship to the Whole, the Everything, and to its mysterious Source.

Western civilization, for example, used to have at its heart a more or less unified worldview based primarily on Christian revelation. That view of the meaning of life was dominant in the culture and alive in it and was in fact quite widely and deeply shared by Europeans. Then came the Renaissance, and with it a shift of consciousness that brought an explosion of sciences and philosophies. Science has not stopped exploding. Secularism has flourished, eroding the power of religion to ground people in a common spiritual frame of reference. New frameworks — including whole new sciences — multiply around us. Each new framework raises thousands of new questions. Each new science — think of bio-engineering, subatomic physics, social anthropology — offers its own set of answers. But only to its own set of questions. Those questions are not about the Whole.

It is as if each science has claimed a slice of reality. There are many brilliant slices. They complement one another in fascinating ways. But there is no longer one unified underlying vision on which people profoundly agree. This modern situation is sometimes called "pluralism."[14] It makes life more difficult for anyone attempting to offer coherent spiritual guidance. In the European Middle Ages, for example, a spiritual guide could take for granted a great deal of implicit spiritual formation that would be common to the people who sought him out — because a common horizon of deeper meaning was vividly symbolized and presented to people at every level of their inherited culture. Today, that is not the case.

People, however, still face the need to integrate their lives. North Americans often turn to psychology when they feel a need for integration. But psychology — itself offering only a "slice" of reality — exists now in many different "slivers." There is a Freudian sliver, an Adlerian sliver, a Jungian sliver, a Rogerian sliver, a behavioral or Skinnerian sliver, just to begin with. Some people boldly grasp one sliver and make it into an explanation of the whole, as Skinner has done in behavioral psychology. Others (and this is more common) are eclectic, taking a behavioral bit here and a Jungian piece there, working toward a synthesis that can hold more of their sense of the whole story.

All these currents of modern thought affect people who are trying to understand Christian spirituality and who wish to offer spiritual guidance to contemporaries. These days one can find books of spiritual guidance combining Jung and Teresa of Avila, Ignatius and the Sufi mystics, gestalt therapy and John of the Cross.[15]

Through the centuries, it has been common for people offering pastoral care to draw on current psychologies and to borrow techniques for the "cure of souls" even from disciplines that espoused contending anthropologies. This point is made in Roger Hurding's *Roots and Shoots: A Guide to Counseling and Psychotherapy*.[16] Hurding's book deals with the rise of today's secular psychologies, and also with the Christian reaction and response to each new sliver of the psychological slice. He examines how Freud's exploration of the dynamics of the vital dimension led spiritual counselors to ask what is going on below the surface of the inner life, to question the unconscious, the sexual instinct, and the developmental stages, and to be critical of an individual's need for religion itself. Hurding goes on to look at the responses to Adler, Erikson, Horney, Fromm, and Sullivan, and at Jung's archetypes as guides for the whole of the inner journey.[17] Hurding also points to the new life-shifting and transpersonal methods of guidance that are proliferating as people sense the need for still deeper change that moves one beyond the isolated self.

Two discoveries stand out here for me. The first is that any spiritual guidance that people will trust will eventually have to be in harmony with the dynamics flowing from life as a whole, not from just one layer of life. Life needs to be received in its entirety as a mystery full of meaning, not split up into parts that can be dealt with like a problem. The second discovery is that the personality theory that underlies any trustable human guidance will have to include the human person's origins in Mystery as well as the person's other dimensions and capacities — the sociohistorical, the vital, the functional, the transcendent, and also the pneumatic,[18] that deepest capacity that makes us potential participators in the life of God.

In the light of all this, one distinction that research into the discipline of formative spirituality has taught me to make is between what we might call formative counseling and formative spiritual direction.

Formative *counseling* (or guidance) is concerned with the normal questions of growth and development that belong to the sociohistorical, vital, functional, and transcendent dimensions of human life; with how the person absorbs/resists the cultural pulsations of his or her environment, with embodiment and temperament, with the person's ambitions, attitudes and skills and with how she or he employs these in the daily dialogue with the "more than" in life. Formative spiritual *direction*, on the other hand, while it is concerned with all of the above, focuses on awakening the person's heart to the larger life of participation in Mystery, as illumined by the specific revealed tradition within which the person is committed.

It is possible to have spiritual guidance or counseling that is formative for life yet is not necessarily bound to any of the great faith traditions. Spiritual direction, on the other hand, usually involves mutual adherence to a faith tradition.

How People Are Spiritual

Anyone who offers coherent spiritual guidance must be grounded in some central understanding of how human beings are "spiritual," of what the human spirit truly is.[19] There are philosophical ways of approaching this understanding, and there are more imaginative or symbolic ways. For example, Teresa of Avila imagined the human soul as a castle made of a single crystal. The poet Gerard Manley Hopkins described the soul as "immortal diamond." John of the Cross discerned within each human being a "living flame of love." None of these images is a theological definition of the soul, but all three tell us something of the soul's greatness and hiddenness.

The approach to spiritual direction that is developed in this book accepts a basic assumption about each human person: the human person is a unique, never-to-be-replicated image of the Mystery itself. This way of guidance assumes that each person's life develops as an expression of his or her emerging foundational life form, or embodied soul.[20]

"Spiritual" in this sense refers to who we are, to our distinctively human ability to express this soul personally, through our powers of mind and will. It is as spirit that we are open to "more than" the vital-functional aspects of reality. It is as spirit that we freely aspire to what is beyond or below the surface of things, and that we are able to long for "more." This longing of the human spirit constitutes the central dynamic force of human life.[21]

Spiritual life, then, refers not only to inner life, but is concerned with the entire created field in which that life unfolds. It is not confined merely to the rational-functional intelligence, but intuitively reaches out beyond the visible to the invisible.

Throughout history, people searching for transcendent meaning have developed worldviews based on this human capacity for encountering invisible Mystery. In the East as well as in the West these syntheses are called "spiritualities."

For me the word "spirituality" points to a vocational or "called" aspect of the human person that the rational/scientific viewpoint often misses entirely. Perhaps soul and spirit are best understood in terms of a relation, a relatedness to all that is. On the one hand we have the "call," given to each human person even before birth, to become a unique "diamond." On the other hand we have the life process of gradually discovering and expressing that call concretely, in dialogue with the changing appeals discovered in the world as it evokes commitments of time and energy in each person throughout life. Spiritual call cannot be understood in terms of inner life alone. Each person's call includes evocations from the life situation in which we find ourselves, with its concrete possibilities of justice, compassion, and healing, encountered at the various ages and stages of the person's development.[22]

Frederick Buechner expressed this relation of soul to its concrete expressions in real history when he wrote, "The place God calls you to is the place where your deep gladness and the world's deep hunger meet."[23] His phrase "your deep gladness" evokes the divine image that each of us interiorly is — that sparkling mysterious core of energy and life. His other phrase, "the world's deep hunger," points to the suffering in and around us that evokes our committed efforts to act. His conviction that the "gladness" and the "hunger" can "meet" points to the loving mysterious Source of our inner energy: the Source whose love embraces the whole cosmos and flows through us to heal it.

Human beings have a deep need to embody the desires of their heart by using their uniquely human power of giving and receiving form in the real world. We want to make a contribution to the world. We want our lives freely to fulfill a unique, intrinsic purpose; we have "vocational hunger."[24] One of the profound hopes of spiritual direction is to make it more possible for persons to discover what they are called to do, how they most deeply want to use their time and energy. Limited finite people also need to find out what they are *not* called to do. Both types of guidance help seekers to recognize the connection between their unique potential and what they can contribute from within their particular life field toward the transformation of the world.

It is not easy to find the link between attentiveness to one's deepest interior capacity of soul and the call to a spirit-inspired life of social commitment. Too many people try to settle for one or the other. Ignorance of the dynamics of one can seriously block the dynamism of the other. Alas, institutionalized religion often forgets this link. Church members are too often pushed into a busy doing of good works, or left in an isolated interiority and not even invited into the costly effort of living a truly spiritual life in the real world. Settling for less prevents a person from becoming a genuinely transforming presence in the world.

That is why it matters — matters for the life of the world — that we understand what it means that the human person is spirit. Both spiritual guides and those guided need to learn to dwell with gratitude on this human capacity to connect with the Mystery that embraces everything.

When we do that, we will be able to notice and to take action when the spiritual dimension of the human person is being refused or repressed — by personal fears, by institutional cramping, or by "slice and sliver" images of the human reality.

How We Co-form Our Experience

If a theory of human personality is to prove useful to someone who offers spiritual guidance, that theory must be down-to-earth and basic. It has to be foundational enough to incorporate one's constantly growing experience of persons, and subtle enough to keep us open to the many schools of thought, worldviews, spiritualities, and cultures we will work with.

How can we integrate the insights of psychological theories, medicine, pastoral care, social analysis? What about particular "spiritualities" — Franciscan, Benedictine, Ignatian, charismatic, and so on? Is there a basic, more or less simple foundation on which an integrative approach to guidance can be built?

I think there is. It is the foundational intuition that all of human life is essentially a dialogue of person and world, of spirit and infrahuman forms and processes in the human person's own organism and in his or her surrounding world. The human spirit co-forms its world as a human formation field.

In other words, human beings are a personal and social presence or openness that actually co-forms and co-creates the world they inhabit, by giving a certain form to the things, events, and persons that present themselves.[25]

Everyone is aware of this on a commonsense level. Folk wisdom tells us that people "see things differently," notice different possibilities, and "handle" apparently similar challenges well or badly.

As guides, we will become more and more aware that every person tends to dialogue uniquely with what appears to be the same reality of people, events, and things. Every time I encounter something or someone in the world — in each act of perceiving, questioning, using, organizing, explaining, or cultivating what exists — I set up an experiential dialogue with that person or thing that is my own dialogue, characteristic of me, more or less unique to me. The dialogue can be altogether unconscious or "prefocal." Questions can emerge from it, questions that can become pressingly conscious: What does this event mean to me? What is really going on? How can I cope with this? What is happening in this situation, in this society? Who am I really? In the midst of all this pain and ambiguity, what is the best direction for me to follow?

We all sense that there is more going on than meets the eye, that the dynamics of life and death, of suffering and joy are not always transparent. Our life questions point to an invisible, prefocal dialogue between ourselves (especially ourselves as human spirit) and situations that befall us in the midst of the pluralistic, disordered culture and society in which we live in late-twentieth-century North America.

There is still another set of questions that arise for Christians — for people who are trying to live the dialogue of person and world in a Gospel context. What does it mean for a Christian to live and try to love in the midst of chaos and change? How should I work for a just society or pursue peace in a world like ours?

The task of spiritual guidance lies in the attempt to make this very basic prefocal dialogue *focal*, that is, conscious and attended to. Spiritual guidance helps persons become more conscious of how they are giving a certain shape or form to their lives, at the same time as they are in the process of being formed by those very lives. Or deformed, of course; our freedom, like our world, is full of ambiguities.

Here, as always, freedom is central. Guidance aims to increase the margin of freedom, of free responsible choice, in people's lives. Good guidance helps people to make good decisions by waking them up to what is happening in their ongoing lives. To be spirit means to be able (in however limited a way) to choose more and more freely the direction in which our lives will move.

For Christians, living spiritually includes raising to consciousness the ongoing dialogue between the Gospel and the values and imperatives flooding in from society and from the culture as we seek to shape our choices from day to day.

Once we understand that there is more to the human person than the merely vital level, we could still have utmost respect for Freud's genius in exploring libidinal dynamics, or the behaviorist's estimation of the undoubted stimulus-response dimension of human behaving. But we will not take those theories as a total explanation of a person's religious or even sexual behavior. We can appreciate the truth Adler saw about human striving for power and competent functioning, but we need not always see ourselves as simply dominated by ego-oriented ambitions.

What we need is a theory of personality that can appreciate all the insights from the human sciences and integrate them into a more whole vision that gives each layer of human expressiveness its rightful but partial place within the whole. The human spirit's capacity for "more" always has to be factored in; and that can make all the difference.

Questions from Life Help Us Notice Reality

In his *Stages of Faith*, James Fowler presents a list of basic life questions that I find extremely helpful. They are as follows:

- What are you spending and being spent for? What commands and receives your best time and energy?

- What goals, dreams, or institutions are you pouring out your life for?

- As you live your life, what power or powers do you fear or dread? What power or powers do you rely on and trust?

- To what or to whom are you committed in life? In death?

- With whom or with what group do you share your most sacred or private hopes for your life and for the lives of those you love?

- What *are* those most sacred and compelling hopes and purposes in your life?[26]

As I read them, James Fowler's questions are about commitment. They are questions that speak of the underlying dialogue between the loving, thinking, acting, sensing, enculturated human heart and all that it finds lovable, thinkable, do-able, sensible, and historically "there" in the world. They are not simply problem-oriented questions that ask for advice on what one should do. They are mystery-oriented questions that flow from a heart that seeks a future for its love.

Of course, the questions of one's heart do not usually emerge as clearly as do questions in a book on stages of faith. But the guide who is paying attention will gradually learn to hear how each seeker is facing — or evading — the questions that are emerging from her or his life. Each of us lives a dialogue with various aspects of our life fields. But the dialogue is not always free, not always honest. Self-alienation, escape, denial of freedom and of responsibility are always possible. The surrounding culture can be illusion-generating. Events can be confusing. And other people can be deceiving. The dialogue with a particular aspect of one's life field can be discordant or distorted; it can need a little work.

Thus, the concealed ongoing dialogue with reality that each person lives is no shining exchange of infallibilities. Nevertheless, it is precious. Being aware of this dialogue with reality will prevent the spiritual guide (and the person guided) from getting lost in introspective attentiveness only to the inner movements of conscience, emotions, and contents of the mind. Self-knowledge is available also by looking at the self in relation to its entire life field. We find out who we are not only by looking at what happens in the time of prayer, but also by examining our commitments of time and energy through family responsibilities, friendships, work commitments, social and political efforts, and leisure activities. We also find out who we are by noticing the parts of reality to which our hearts choose to be more or less open.

An attentive guide recognizes when a person is totally absorbed in the outward impressions of sense and feeling available through the body. Or when the conscious mind is preoccupied in dealing with what the world presents to the control of the empirical ego or surface self.

An attentive guide rejoices when the person begins to become aware of her or his own heart as it relates to the underlying ground of visible, daily reality. Each day, as one's heart beats on, it is either connecting with or missing the mysterious web of meaning and connectedness, of invisible Presence that holds everything together. The human heart will never be totally satisfied until it encounters the ultimate Other as the ground of All That Is, until it wakes up to the living, flowing presence of Mystery beneath the surface of everyday life. Spiritual guidance helps us to discover or recall, not so much the exact meaning of each separate part of our lives, but rather a picture of the whole that will help us to discern and trust the loving presence of a divine Someone Else flowing through everything that is.[27]

It is not only the art of spiritual direction that is recapturing the sense of the whole of life being lived, bodily in Mystery. Religious education — especially adult catechesis — is touched by a similar vision these days. A striking example is the RCIA, the Rite of Christian Initiation of Adults.[28] Not so long ago, preparation for adult baptism was concentrated on one-to-one giving of information about the faith. Now the RCIA includes the entry into a formative community and a life-centered plan for individual growth and instruction that is primarily the sponsor's responsibility. The plan is linked to small house meetings and worship with other believers, and also to large group retreats and the Sunday celebrations of the local Christian community. Later, the "mystagogia"[29] shows the new Christian how the life of faith is responsibly linked to the lives of other people — locally and in the global church, which is the sign on earth of the all-encompassing Mystery of Christ. The paradigm has shifted — from the need to add new, truthful information to the individual mind, to communal sharing of life formation on the level of the other-centered heart.

Another related paradigm shift is under way in "official" Roman Catholic theology: the way in which that theology now describes the vocation and mission of lay Christians.[30] There is now a new definition of the particularly lay status and "charism." Lay Christians are those who, having been invited by the sacrament of baptism to enter totally into the heart of God and to accept the messianic vocation of Jesus the Redeemer, are then called by God to the world. This "call to the world" is presented as a deeply personal spiritual event, coming to each lay Christian individually from God as Creator, Redeemer, and Sanctifier. Accepting this call enables the baptized lay Christian to become a transforming presence in the world as loved and as being-saved by its Creator. Holiness — the holiness that flows from incorporation into the mystery of Jesus Christ — is fused in this description with a profound, generous, and courageous attentiveness to the world, and a readiness to act in the world. This approach will prove radically incompatible with any spirituality that attends only to interior personal dispositions and not to a person's relatedness, in faith, to the whole created and human world as it enters that person's life field.

In the last thirty years, the major concern of new publications and of research in pastoral counseling and spiritual direction has been a many-sided effort to come to terms with various developments in the field of psychology. The scores of books that have been written range all the way from fervent denunciations of psychology to enthusiastic reinterpretations of concepts of classical mysticism in terms of psychological meaning. It is a scene of confusing richness and diversity.[31]

As more and more spiritual thinkers accept the fundamental orientation I have been describing in these last two sections — that a "spiritual" life is lived in relation to a human person's whole life field, very much including his/her society and its decisions and structures — it may be that psychology will have to "move over" a little from its present place in the center of attention for writers on spiritual guidance. More attention may in the future be paid to social analysis, social theology, biblical hermeneutics that include "political readings" of Scripture, and theories of social change. There also appears to be a renewal of interest in the more contemplative thrust of spiritual living,[32] in studying how spiritual persons co-constitute their world and transform their world. They are also many ways of studying how the Spirit of holiness leads believers into that hunger and thirst for peace and justice which is transformative in real history.

A style of guidance founded on the intuition that all of human life is essentially a dialogue of person and world will certainly be able to deal with the political, social, and professional dimensions of a person's vocation, as well as with the interpersonal, interior, and intrapsychic dimensions of his or her growth. A foundational approach to guidance tends to begin with whatever questions are emerging from the lived experience of the person who comes. Anchoring themselves in the truth of a universe-in-formation, guides aim to bring this person or these persons to an awareness of how they are co-forming whatever reality they experience. The guide aims also to move toward reflectively reconnecting all the detailed happenings of a person's life field with that person's deeper longing for God. A merely psychological approach or a mainly interiorized direction will probably not be as effective, over a lifetime, in helping a man or woman to discover and live out his or her unique call.[33]

Certainly the task of helping people to listen more carefully to the unique directions emerging from within their entire life field can be enhanced by a proper use of psychological and other scientific insights. It can be enhanced, too, by critical awareness of culture, by social awareness, and by historical knowledge.

The Christian guide, who in faith wishes to assist others from within the Christian tradition, will necessarily want to go beyond those human sciences. He or she will want and need to be immersed in the vision, the key ideas, and the classic texts of that tradition. Besides the need to become a person of prudence and of practical wisdom, the one who guides will also have to become a person of prayer.

James Fenhagen observes in *Invitation to Holiness* that the movement of the Spirit in prayer is always to lead us beyond our own limited horizon to a new dimension of encounter with the world.[34] Fenhagen remarks that prayer produces in us a new set of eyes through which to view the world, and then the motivation to respond in love to what we see.[35] It is this kind of holiness that is most often the aim of contemporary people who freely seek spiritual guidance for their hearts and lives.[36]

Chapter Two

A SENSE OF THE MYSTERY

W E live surrounded by the Mystery. The mystery includes us: it is the Mystery of all that is. It includes us, and yet it eludes us. It is beyond our rational analysis, beyond the control of our powers of willing or achieving. We can live for years — indeed, for a lifetime — as if living had nothing to do with the awesome Mystery that contains us. We can feel all our lives as if we were not beloved in our very being. We can feel alone, as if the Mystery that enwraps the cosmos did not love us. Many of us do live and feel that way all our lives. All of us live and feel that way some of the time.

Yet we are, and remain, fundamentally spiritual beings. We are oriented in our depths to the recognition and love of the Awesome Mystery. There is our truest delight. To recognize and welcome the presence of the all-encompassing Mystery changes the meaning of absolutely everything that touches us. Those who live in that light are entering into a fundamental human possibility. They are saying yes in an utterly primal spiritual option with pervasive consequences.[1]

Those who say yes are also joining a particular human company. They are joining a stream of seekers and pilgrims whose presence is discernible in every age, on all the continents. One sign that a person has joined that transgenerational company is that he or she begins to feel a need for some of the skills, disciplines, ideas, and images developed by earlier pilgrims.

Today, people who choose to seek spiritual guidance and people who in fear and trembling risk offering spiritual guidance are recognizably part of this ancient human company of pilgrims into the Mystery.

They are also part of a thoroughly and specifically contemporary moment. Their spiritual thirst and openness has been prepared precisely by the triumphs, pains, breakthroughs, breakdowns, and ambiguities of this century that is now ending.

The late twentieth century is a particularly rich and a particularly

22

difficult time in which to seek, or to offer, spiritual guidance. The first chapter of this book looked briefly at the pervasive results of modern pluralism, skepticism, and fragmentation of knowledge and awareness. The decline of the social/cultural influence of organized religion is a fact of our time that both frees and weakens the personal spiritual search. For the person offering spiritual guidance, the proliferation of therapies and of explanations of human desire that abound in psychology today can be confusing and intimidating. Yet, once today's guide has found his or her own roots and reference points (and therefore knows what to look for and what to avoid), the insights coming from new psychological research can be very helpful.

This second chapter will look back at the history of spiritual seeking and spiritual guiding and into the essential resources of the Christian tradition to name some reference points that can help seekers and guides to make choices in the rich, confusing postmodern landscape of today.

Inheriting Names for the Mystery

The first thing to say about the Mystery of All That Is, the Whole that gives meaning to all the parts, is that it truly is a mystery. It cannot be comprehended or conceptualized. Nevertheless, intellectuals and mystics over the millennia of human existence have continued to try to express the profound connectedness of everything with everything else; and interrelatedness is indeed one aspect of the all-encompassing mystery of being.[2]

Thus, generations of philosophers, theologians, mystics, physicists, and biologists — and more recently biophysicists — have attempted to present a unified field theory regarding the ground of all that exists.

In Christian thought, before the great schism that divided East from West in the eleventh century, it was fairly common to view the universe as a living field brimming over with created and uncreated energy flowing from the heart of the trinitarian Creator.[3] In our time, some scientists (Heisenberg, Bohr, Einstein, Capra, de Chardin, and Prigogine are examples) present intriguingly similar explanations for what seems to be holding the cosmos together. In the terms of their particular disciplines, they are seeing both the human and the nonhuman world or cosmos as an interwoven web, a unity that builds up in patterns that suddenly regestalt on to higher levels of organization. The universe seems to them like a subatomic cosmic dance, a network of energies that intimately interconnect and form the cosmos.[4]

It is this interconnecting web of relatedness that characterizes (according to these thinkers) the way the Whole reveals itself first in the concrete. At least, such is the current scientific picture of the reality that surrounds and connects everything — including ourselves, body and mind. Physicists and biologists are alerting us to the fact that our embodied hearts participate in this unity. They cannot do otherwise. The human cannot be isolated. By its very existence as human, the whole person exists in relation to all that is. "Thou canst not stir a flower / Without troubling a star."[5]

This is by no means a new idea. But it is a very important one. And it is a happy circumstance — also for spiritual guides — that in our time it is being felt in new ways particularly by scientists, the history of whose disciplines is part of the history of our sense of fragmentation.

In converging on this insight about interconnectedness, the new scientific visionaries join a long tradition of mysticism. In every age there have been panentheistic mystics whose sense of the divine presence derives from the whole of the natural universe.[6] It is the same God, say these mystics, whom we encounter in all our transcendent experiences, whether these occur in nature or in history. Many would add that we need to notice both the cosmic and the historic epiphanies that glimmer all around us; nature grounds a cosmic epiphany, while human relations of justice and love — privately or politically achieved — can be historic epiphanies of the Mystery.

Religious symbols are not the only vehicles (as the new scientific "mystics" are reminding us) through which we inherit ways of naming the Ineffable. However, religious traditions are a particularly powerful record of historic human encounter with the Holy Other. There have always been human hearts open to the divine flow of created and un-created energies. For most human beings, the name that they give to the Mystery when they experience an encounter with Mystery is a name that they have inherited from the founders of their faith.[7]

A faith tradition becomes "inheritable" in history by a complex social process, one much studied in this century, but such a study is not the task of this book. Different people, over the centuries and in different situations, have developed a multiplicity of ways of coming into union with the mysterious Holy Otherness. These ways, which we now recognize as the great spiritual traditions, are all based on an original understanding of the human person as essentially spirit. As the founding generations· initiated new adherents, they needed to hand on the insights about human living that were derived from the original spiritual encounter. Theological doctrines would develop as people tried to clarify what they could conceptualize about the way the Mystery had manifested itself to them. Later, some of these doctrines enter the core of the faith tradition of a believing people.

But there are insights that are best carried, not by theological doctrines or by sacred scriptures, but by customs: ways of doing and of being. In all the great faith traditions East and West, we find orally or in writing the gathering of a set of customs that reflect the ways wise people have found in which they can live life from day to day in relation to encountered Mystery. In that way, a faith tradition creates a "form tradition" to help give it human, inheritable reality.[8]

Ordinary modern men and women have, perhaps because of the liberal and individualist assumptions that dominate our time, a strong suspicion of customary ways of doing things. Even when it comes to religion, "form traditions" are not granted much authority. We generally tend to be keenly aware of the conventional, numbing, and imprisoning possibilities of form traditions. We see that customs can be vehicles of both compassionate caring and of social sin.[9] And they can. But there is another side to "form traditions" when we are seeking or offering guidance for spiritual growth.

If we look at the entire history of spiritual guidance in any of the great traditions, we will find that the earliest "soul-keepers" were men and women in conscious, respectful touch with both the faith and the form traditions of the people they felt called upon to serve. Through these symbols and forms, spiritual guides of every century have struggled to connect the everyday life challenges faced by ordinary people with the deep underlying ground or "story" that can give those challenges transcendent meaning. That has always been the task of the sages and pirs and gurus, the prophets and priests of old, the desert mothers and fathers, the starets and monks; and it is the task of pastoral workers today. Faith and form traditions have a lot to do with this task.[10]

The meaning of what happens to us every day needs to be illumined, somewhat in the way that a full sentence illumines the meaning of one word.[11] Without the ground of faith in some epiphany of the Mystery, it is difficult to make full sense out of the isolated figure of a human life, even if that life is one's own. When someone has "lost the faith," as we used to say — that is, lost vital contact with an underlying faith and form tradition — he or she may still experience a spiritual awakening, still live through a personal encounter with Mystery. But the process of interpreting such an experience and of investing it with rich, enduring meaning will be very difficult to sustain. That process is not at its best when it is "solo." The meanings proper to spiritual experience are deeper than can be accumulated in one generation. There are riches of meaning that have to be inherited; one lifetime is not long enough to develop them. This is why persons often need a spiritual guide who is able to raise to consciousness the dialogue that is being lived on a prefocal level between the daily thought and actions of the person who comes for guidance, and the underlying faith and form traditions that give them spiritual meaning.[12]

Our Complex World

In the Western world today, so many people are spiritually "tradition-less" that we have become used to the consequences. We expect most people to be materialistic, to be victims of consumerism. We plan society that way. We can count on advertising, for example, to have great social power, because so few people possess the awakened consciousness, the kind of life context that would render Madison Avenue nearly irrelevant. We can confidently assume that money will weigh most heavily in the life plans of most citizens. How can it be otherwise? Most North Americans today have only the most tenuous link with those cultural traditions that once nourished an alternative consciousness.

A great faith tradition, freely and consciously and vitally adhered to, is a powerful resource for a human being in search of meaning.

With the coming of the Christian epiphany, for example, a transfigured horizon of meaning appeared for those who came to faith. With the Mystery's manifestation in Christ, members of the human race found themselves in a completely new situation. They called it a "new creation." A fresh potential for perceiving people, events, and things opened up at the coming of Christ. A new view of the world's destiny, a glimpse of the divine possibilities of human life as a whole, of the human body's new dignity, of the unity of the human race — became apparent for those with eyes to see. And they could see these possibilities precisely in their own limited lives. The taken-for-granted world of those who could look at themselves in this new Christian light (i.e., of those who could make the connection of figure to ground) was lit from within. Everyday events could "flame out like shining from shook foil" because the world in which they occur was "charged with the grandeur of God." Spiritual guides were the ones who showed how one's marriage and family, one's work and service to others, and one's prayer and sacramental life could house the redeeming presence of the Lord, for those who opened the eyes of their hearts to the presence of hidden Mystery embodied in Christ.

All of that is wonderful past words. It is joy unbounded. But, of course, we never experience such consciousness in its pure state. Neither did the early Christians. The Christian consciousness — for that matter, the consciousness proper to any great faith tradition — exists only in us, in sinners, only in real time and real history, mixed in with many other meanings and influences and blockages that are not itself. We inherit many things besides our faith tradition. It is not only the faith tradition that influences how we tend to see the world.[13]

Human culture is a thoroughly mixed bag. Every group in the world carries, unconsciously and partly consciously, countless shared assumptions about reality. Not all of them are even remotely connected with their idea of eternal life. Beneath the conscious thinking of North Americans, for example, are hidden currents of thought about individualism and competitiveness, about democracy and women's rights, about money and science and gender and what not. Some of them, but not all of them, would be compatible with Christian traditions if we looked at both rigorously. All of them are influential, compatible or not.

These hidden convictions come forcefully into play when we come up against any significant life question. The convictions are part of a wheat-and-tares mixture; human culture cannot be sterilized. And we need our culture. No spiritual guide can afford to despise a person's actual, functioning culture. When life events force people to deal with the burdens of time and limitation, with helplessness in a crisis, or with fears about decay and death, guidance will usually involve helping them to draw from the wisdom of their whole human culture, as well as from their faith. All human beings have to struggle, of course, with the distortions as well as the wisdoms that they have inherited. There is poison as well as nourishment in every human heritage. But we are human. We belong in that struggle with ambiguity, and we need the solidarity that a culture is. In challenging moments, we can draw from our cultural roots the reassurance that other human beings like ourselves have found ways to dialogue with all of life's tasks, without losing touch with the Mystery's overall direction of their lives.[14]

That is why a spiritual guide must be in respectful touch with a person's whole faith and form tradition. Each person, of course, faces a lifelong task of criticism as well as of receptivity, of purifying as well as being fed by what he or she has inherited. But that task should be undertaken respectfully. The guide's own respect for each person's felt sense of his or her faith and form tradition will be important.[15]

That bit of advice might not have been necessary in an earlier generation, except perhaps in a cross-cultural context. But today, many individuals have lost respect for, and indeed lost contact with, their roots, including their faith and form traditions. As a result, some people feel rootless. Many are searching for a sense of belonging to something trustworthy. They search for some group or entity that represents a depth of meaning and human commonality. These folks travel from group to group, longing for understanding and union and permission just to be and belong. Often they find untested psychospiritual collectives, lack of depth, and other folks who are just as lost and unconnected as they are. Such groupings cannot deal with the deep longing people bear, the longing that includes being searched for by the Mystery.

Only a great religious tradition — entered deeply and faithfully — can provide a "story" great enough to speak to that immense longing.[16]

And only a guide personally moved by deep delight in and love for the Mystery can be much help in the process.

Traditions in Today's Pluralistic Context

From the beginning of human time there have been multiple ways of naming the Mystery and of preparing oneself to encounter the Mystery and live in daily awareness of its presence. People have found themselves present in awe and wonder to Yahweh and the gift of His law; to Allah and the divine will revealed for all time to the prophet Mohammed; to all-pervasive Being in its human, social, or cosmic dimensions; to the Trinity and its epiphany in Christ. Countless sensitive and responsive hearts have questioned the sense-perceptible and the invisible aspects of life and have passed on the resulting myths and stories of their prophets and saints to the younger generations.[17]

Until fairly recent historic times, most human beings really met only one of the great faith traditions: their own. Life used to be much more local and rooted. Mobility was strictly limited. People knew that other cultures and other religions existed; there were, after all, empires and trade routes and migrations and other multicultural facts. There were conversions and missions and mixed marriages long, long ago. But the context in which these things happened had a kind of fixity and stability that it is now difficult for us to imagine. One identified with the wisdom (and the limits) of one's people in ways that are no longer possible for us.

Needless to say, the whole intellectual horizon was different in the generations that saw the founding and spreading of the world's great faiths. For many pervasive reasons — convictions about the nature of knowledge and the accessibility of truth were among those reasons — a twentieth-century type of course in comparative religion would have been unthinkable. Not just imprudent, but literally unthinkable.

From that point of view, we today live under an entirely different sky. One of the main challenges for spiritual guidance today lies in our routine, unavoidable, unprecedented exposure to the pluralism of great (and sometimes not so great) religious faith and form traditions.[18] For us, that exposure takes place in the context of a secular society, which continually compounds this "interfaith" pluralism with its own multiple, competing, nonreligious explanations of human life in the world.

That is our unavoidable daily context. It offers its own mix of dangers and advantages. It offers us opportunities for learning both to respect the great variety of spiritual ways, and at the same time to deepen our appreciation for the unique gifts of our own tradition. It offers us a chance to participate in the historic grace/charism of the ecumenical movement and of profound interfaith dialogue. There are deeper ways, too, in which this context can purify us and hasten our growth toward waiting for God in the darkness of faith, beyond formulas, ideas, and images. Those are some of the potential advantages of our present context.

Its dangers are even better known. They are, I think, too well known to need listing here. We have only to glance around us, at the state of religious awareness in any North American city now.

For our limited purpose here, we need to draw attention to only one aspect of this enormous theme — only the practical question that confronts persons who seek or offer spiritual guidance in today's pluralist context.

How can a spiritual guide learn to be alert to the advantages and avoid the traps that are specific to contemporary pluralism? What kinds of openness and what kinds of faithfulness best meet the needs of the seeking human heart?

The question is huge in the abstract. It might be easier to deal with through one example. Let's look at how guides can help seekers deal with their tendencies to block their human openness to the Mystery. Then I will point to a few of the endless ways in which guides can draw on skills and disciplines from other traditions, without compromising the necessary rootedness in one great underlying revealed "story."

The Related Problem of "Blockages"

Spiritual guides, of course, have the task of helping human spiritual beings to welcome into their daily lives radiations of peace and joy from the Mystery. Once the awakening heart has tasted the sweetness of the presence of awesome invisible Otherness, the process of guidance can help the seeker to allow that Otherness to shine through the visible happenings of ordinary life. Most of us, most of the time, live in ways that make these radiations, these shinings-through, quite unlikely. We block them. We screen them out because of fear, because of desire for control, or because we cling to our ego-self and its reign.

How do we recognize these blocks, these limitations that put a leaden curtain between ourselves and the divine light? How do we blind ourselves to its rays? Spiritual masters tell us that much of the time we act in ignorance. Desiring what is wrong for us from early childhood on, we live in the illusion that our emotional reactions to life, our desperate clinging to the masks and roles we habitually assume, and our refusal to grow in acceptance of baptismal possibilities all conspire to cut us off from the loving energy poured forth into our hearts by the Spirit dwelling within. Some theorists put the blame squarely on the family of origin,[19] on the educational system that teaches us to do and have rather than to be and admire. Others point to evil in the world and in human hearts that isolates us from our origin and resists its initiatives in our life.

In any case, we all can recognize a common dynamism arising from our investment in false energy centers, in our compulsions to feel secure, approved of, or in control.[20] We see its effects not only on our interiority, but also on the socio/cultural relational self, as well as on the psychological or personal dimension of our life with others and with God. Resistances to the flow of grace characterize not only ourselves, but our culture as well.

Here is a major reason — recognized or unrecognized — why people seek guidance. We have other sources for learning functional techniques — how to handle professional commitments, how to be more skilled as parents and homemakers, how to work for social change, and so on. But who will care about our entanglement with the Ultimate? Who will help us to let go of the patterns that block us from participating in the life of the Trinity?

People seeking guidance face this question of "blockage" on many levels. Some levels of blockage have to do with our whole lifestyle. They involve the problems of receptivity built in to the entire life field of persons living in a consumer society and in a fast, affluent city.[21]

It seems to me that spiritual guides in the Far East are more in touch, in a general way, with people's whole life field. They speak about body posture and breathing and nutrition, as well as the more transcendent dimensions of that field. What van Kaam calls the "receptivity dynamics" of each great spiritual tradition seems to include methods of approaching and dealing with the ways in which out of fear or desire to control people block the flow of life energy in their life field. They also point to different styles of facilitating openness toward the mystery on all dimensions and in the entire surrounding field of human hearts. Some of the skills and disciplines cultivated in Indian or Chinese form-traditions can be singularly useful to hurry-hurt Westerners. For example, I know a high-strung parish priest in a big Canadian city who has used Yoga exercises nightly, for the past twenty years, as part of his effort to make more room in his life for contemplation. I know an experienced nurse on the staff of a large cancer hospital who teaches Tai Chi to anxious outpatients awaiting chemotherapy or other cancer treatments. No doubt similar examples come to mind as you read of these two.

A contemporary spiritual guide should feel at home in offering a suggestion, of Yoga or Tai Chi, for example, whose origin is in a non-Western and non-Christian tradition. And since most people do not want to wade through volumes on the relevant Indian philosophy to grasp the whole context of, for example, his or her favorite Yoga exercises, a spiritual guide needs to be a skilled translator. People need to have guidance in the language of their own actual life state, whether they are academics or steelworkers, teenagers or senior citizens.[22]

At the same time, people need more than hunches and exercises. The "blockage" problems built in to the modern Western lifestyle — or built in to someone's personal unharmonious lifestyle — are part of the much larger picture of human evil. The Christian tradition has a great deal to say on the subject of human evil. What it says about freedom, fallenness, sin, grace, and the processes of redemption forms a crucial dimension of its coherence. It would be impossible to achieve a nourishing understanding of the Christian tradition without grasping the centrality of its account of sin and freedom, sin and grace.[23]

So a Christian spiritual guide who recommends practices, disciplines, images, or stories from other faith traditions should do so in a way that respects both the integrity of what is "borrowed" and also the integrity and coherence of the (Christian) seeker's underlying faith tradition.

Again, this is not to say that everything is pure and perfect in what we think of as the Christian tradition. Receptivity and detachment, gratitude and critical freedom — both poles are necessary for anyone seeking to deepen her or his heart's commitment. Tradition does get mixed up with incidental rules and regulations. Often the core of truth is covered over and misunderstood. Tough work has to be done to make room for the fact of cultural change. Our traditions do need to be examined frequently to make sure they are facilitating the Gospel message in a humanly livable way. They could be enshrining accretional customs or even superstitions from the past.

Nevertheless, the more common temptation in our time is to undervalue (not to overvalue) the spiritual importance of the tradition. In Tibet it used to be customary to ask a visitor not about his or her country of origin, but from what "deep tradition" she or he came. The assumption behind this custom is that a background of tested experience and interpretation concerning the purpose of life and the most liberating ways to live life is what shapes our inmost being. It constitutes what we have to offer to others.[24]

Tilden Edwards, in whose book *Spiritual Friend* I found this last bit of information, goes on to uphold the value of traditions even in our time of what he calls "broken and abandoned inheritance." He says,

Perhaps most of us inevitably are a little more "outsiders" to any exclusive tradition, given our vastly greater awareness of other possibilities than were known in the past, and the individualism of our time. Yet, however tenuous our ground, we can stand in but one place at a time. That is only human. Moving from particular depth to mature universality seems to be the human way. Trying to shortcut this by starting out everywhere is likely to lead to shallow watering holes that dry up or never go deep enough in sweat and commitment to find the deep ground whose hidden depths nourish all.[25]

The guide might keep this warning in mind also in dealing with our secular pluralism today. Particularly in psychology, many attempts to include the dynamism of human longing for transcendence have developed outside, or parallel to, the great religious traditions. Thoughtful writers are seeing how the age-old yearning for meaning and fulfillment beyond the self has emerged in the middle and late twentieth century in a variety of transpersonal psychologies. Some of these are linked to different spiritual traditions, as well as to traditional psychological disciplines. A useful discussion of them can be found in Roger Hurding's *Roots and Shoots*.[26] Hurding reflects on the limited scope of these disciplines, as well as on their usefulness and appeal for our generation. The Human Potential Movement spawned "new therapies" such as cognitive, transactional analysis and gestalt. Maslow's self-actualization theory and Assagioli's psychotherapy are examples of secular transpersonalism. They go some distance, but not far enough, Hurding thinks, in responding to the ultimate questions that human beings have — indeed, that human beings are.

For some people, however, these disciplines have become substitute faith traditions, providing them with a life context. In fact, today's seekers and guides live in a kind of wrap-around reference library, stocked with bits of information, including some deep and illuminating studies, regarding the great world traditions and the contemporary therapeutic movements. Granted, not everyone needs to or should become a specialist in comparative religion or psychology. But any guide, or any interested seeker, should be informed enough to be able to appreciate how the structure of a variety of great spiritual founders' contemplative encounter with Mystery has continued to satisfy longing hearts and provide a context of meaning for their adherents' lives and actions during succeeding centuries. Today's spiritual guide, besides having some idea of the healing possibilities of contemporary therapeutic movements, should also be clear not only about the richness of world traditions, but also about how these traditions tend to structure human existence in certain directions.[27] For instance, offering guidance within the Christian tradition, he or she should understand something of how this unique spiritual tradition, beginning with baptism, also structures human existence in the direction of incarnation and embodiment.[28] He or she should also begin to have a handle on the way the fish in this particular "sea" are encouraged and even driven to block out or ignore its presence all around them — how in need they are sometimes of guidance from a prayerful and experienced and knowledgeable "wise fish."

The Human Person in the Christian Worldview

While we are talking about traditions in their modern context of pluralism, it is good to remember that every worldview — religious, psychological, or philosophical — carries an implicit or explicit anthropology. That is, each coherent tradition of thought assumes its own definition or description of the nature of human being, the reality of a human person.

There is, of course in this sense a Christian anthropology, and any reliable guide in the Christian tradition will have a practical, commonsense understanding of this Christian image of the human person. Perhaps he or she will have a philosophical grasp of the issue as well, although that is not always necessary.

This wisdom, however, no longer comes as standard equipment, even among practicing Christians. In our general society, there is fragmentation and skepticism around any understanding of "human nature," because there are so many competing opinions, descriptions, and theories. Many educated people end up concluding that it is hopelessly naive to think that we know what a human being is. Even among Roman Catholic thinkers, the precise and confident analyses of the nature and powers of the human creature — which mediaeval theologians so enjoyed — are mostly ignored these days. Having lost our philosophical uniformity, we are more grateful than we used to be for the symbolic ways in which the biblical writers celebrate what it means to be a divinely created, embodied, limited-yet-free spiritual person.

As the psalmist tells it, we are mysteriously chosen and fearfully, wonderfully made by God in our mother's womb.[29] We are made, "male and female, in the image and likeness of God." We are weak and mortal and infinitely precious. Our true identity is mysterious, even to ourselves. "We are already the children of God; but what we are to be in the future has not yet been revealed" (1 John 3:2). When our struggle is completed there will be for each of us "a white stone, with a new name written on the stone which no one knows except the one who receives it" (Rev. 2:17). We are wounded now, and in the dark now, and we already carry in our bodies seeds of unthinkable glory, seeds of transformation. We are being drawn toward the Light by an intrinsic attraction, by the affinity or homing instinct of the light already created in the depths of our being.

In spite of all this wonderful biblical imagery, many modern Christians have only a dim view of what it means to be embodied human hearts, bearers of a life form, and potential sharers in the life of the Trinitarian mystery.[30] Modern Christians may be very much aware of their vital-physical dimension, with its sea of emotions and feelings; of the social/historical pulsations that co-form our presence to reality;

of their powerful ego-functional capabilities, so prized by our achieving society; and even of the (usually more neglected) aesthetic and transcendent dimensions of being human. But many are almost totally ignorant of the spiritual or "pneumatic" dimension of our hearts.[31] A divine inner direction, a personal call unique to each person's created being, is the heritage of every person. It is divinely intended to unfold so that human (and mystical) self-realization flows from the unique address of the Mystery to each one of us individually.

True self-knowledge includes an adequate understanding of the call inherent in all of our created possibilities — our "human form potencies"[32] that undergird our capacities for loving, thinking, choosing, admiring, creating, working purposefully, and the like.

Christian thought has always had a "high," awe-filled conception of the created grandeur of the human person. It includes the conviction that the Holy Spirit can be present in human persons and can influence their growth and development, their capacity as human spirit. At certain gifted moments of life, human beings become aware that in our human state of sinfulness and impotence, we need this Spirit — we need grace — to realize the transcendent longings of our own hearts. That is the pneumatic dimension of human beings: their capacity to be receptive to grace, to cooperate with divine grace. Being open to the presence of God is a permanent capacity of the human heart.[33]

When we believe that about being human, we need more than a psychological or psychotherapeutic approach to the capacities of the heart. Each one of us is so much more than a bundle of instinctual, biological, physical processes. Traditions like behaviorism and psychoanalysis just do not deal with the intrinsic spiritual capacities of the human person. Maslow, Jung, Freud, and Rogers are shrewd and fascinating. What they have observed is important, and their hypotheses can stretch our minds, can teach us to notice a great deal about human reality. But there is more to people than those theories have room for.

Since I am a psychologist by training and by trade, I have more than a passing interest in the development of modern psychological theories and psychotherapeutic practices. And since I work regularly as a counselor, I am continually confronted with people's deep life questions. Therefore I very often have the concrete experience of being forced to recognize the limits of merely humanistic theories. I am compelled to go beyond them, precisely by the weight of the questions being raised/embodied by the seeker who has come to me for counseling. I am compelled to call on a wider and deeper anthropology. I must be in touch with a worldview that is solid enough to ground these questions, wide enough to admit their reality. That worldview must have room for this seeking person's whole life field, and also for God, the mysterious and originating ground of all that is. If I did not have access to such a worldview, I would somehow have to "amputate" living dimensions of the persons I see as a counselor.

Yes: it is important for anyone offering guidance in the Christian tradition to have a working, rooted sense of that tradition's teaching on the human person.

As a kind of footnote to that point, let me acknowledge that there are different levels and different goals in various guidance situations. We do not always need the whole weight of the Christian synthesis; sometimes what we need is more limited, more immediate, more intuitive. Every "client" embodies particular and different questions.[34]

Christian anthropology suggests some specific principles that Christian guides assume and respect.[35] Here are a few of them. Always the underlying dynamism, the basic energy of the emerging self flows from the foundational life form, the person's "soul." The soul always remains a mystery to itself and to others throughout the whole of life. It was created capable of a specific, personal fulfillment that is greater than we are able to grasp or describe under the conditions of our present life. However, throughout our present life we struggle with incompleteness, sin, limited vision, distortion, and various kinds of darkness. In a guidance situation it is the human desires, feelings, hopes and ideals, imaginings, and anticipations embedded in the person's life project that need to be (respectfully) explored. Every person carries primordial feelings of trust or distrust of the Mystery; these feelings need to be built on, or questioned, when priorities have to be ordered and when turning points are reached.[36]

Christian faith nourishes specific expectations for a person's inner growth. The message of baptism includes the certainty that this person is divinely chosen, personally loved and called by name into union with God. That vocation to the delight of intimacy with the Mystery is primordial; it comes first, and it grounds the person's vocation to mission. Going forth to bear fruit becomes the natural result of having been chosen. That scriptural image of the vine and the branches comes alive when contemplative presence overflows into action. The image speaks of the human heart, made to abide in Love, to stay united to the Vine, yet at the same time invited to bear fruit, to move out from its "dwelling" stance into service of others. Moreover, this image is of fruit destined "to remain": it points to the Eschaton, the mysterious Kingdom of transformed existence that awaits the whole of creation at the end of time.

Joy in the Mystery

In this chapter, we have been concerned with the function for spiritual guidance of the great faith traditions: how problematic they are, and how essential they are if someone is to achieve human depth in exploring the meaning of encountered Mystery. It is probably clear by now that I do not believe anyone can be a reliable spiritual guide unless he or she is rooted in, and faithful to, one of the great faith and form traditions.

However, a faith tradition is only a way of inheriting meanings that seekers in earlier generations have developed after they themselves lived an encounter with the Mystery. The Spirit of God (Christians believe) can shape such a tradition, can protect it, too, from being utterly destroyed by human distortions. But the tradition is not the Spirit.

It is the Spirit, the Mystery, that the seeking human heart longs to encounter. That gives life and joy. The tradition (at its best) can only structure the interpretation of the encounter in a humanly sustainable way.

Without the element of personal encounter with the Mystery — which gives deep spiritual joy — a great faith tradition is merely spiritless religion.

Many people who look for spiritual guidance are already in contact with institutional religion (with, for example, their local church) and are dismayed by it. They find little relationship between their personal spiritual quest and the seemingly "spiritless" character of the tradition as they meet it in their parish. They find that it has no living heart, no contemplative and relational core.

Most modern people are just not willing to stay in a church that never opens them up to abundance of life. People want to discover a love that casts out fear of abandonment, fear of vulnerability, fear of loss of control. If the local church has become an unquestioning part of the culture of control and efficiency, how can it lead anyone to such a love? If church membership dulls instead of quickens someone's sense of an invisible sacred center of all that is, why bother?

In *The Color Purple* the heroine, Celie, had never been introduced to any image of God other than the old white man with a beard, legalistic and authoritarian.[37] Her friend Shug is much more awakened. Celie is astonished: she says to Shug, "You telling me God love you, and you ain't never done nothing for him? I mean, not go to church, sing in the choir, feed the preacher and all like that?" But Shug's God is a lover who is "always wanting to share a good thing," who is "pissed if we walk by the color purple in a field and don't notice it."[38]

These days, the Celies of the world are a lot less patient. Indifference and fear are the typical responses to a church that does not know spiritual joy, that has lost the dynamism of its tradition.

What is true for the church is true for spiritual guides. Guides who are going to reach spiritually awakening women and men in our times must be awake themselves. A guide who has lost her or his experiential connection with the Mystery will not long be credible. Guides must be people who are moved by "the dynamics of delight."[39] They must have tasted for themselves and seen "how good is the Lord." They must be faithful to the inviting joy of that encounter. And they must be willing to share that delight with others.

There is a tiny parable in the Gospels (Matt. 13:44) about someone who finds treasure hidden in a field, then "in his joy, goes and sells all that he has and buys that field." Paul Ricoeur remarks that the structure of that little story explains "the dynamics of delight" that are foundationally important for the whole spiritual process. There are three moments in the story: finding the treasure, selling what one has, buying the field. It is the attractiveness of the treasure — the delight of the finder in discovering it — that sets the other two steps in motion. As Ricoeur points out, it is our delight in experiencing the Mystery that makes us willing to sell other things in order to have more of it.[40]

Spiritual guides find that the dynamics of delight indeed come first. They need to learn to help people reflectively uncover what has drawn them, fascinated them in their experience of the Mystery. Only then are we ready for "selling" and "buying" — for detachment, for repentance and metanoia, for decision and commitment. Christian discipline and detachment do not make sense except as a result of having already been captured by love.[41]

The structure of the following of Christ in the Gospels fits this pattern. The first apostles, the women like Mary Magdalene and the woman at Jacob's well, and then later Paul — all of them grounded their lives in their initial meeting with Christ. "I have found him whom my heart loves," says the bride in the Song of Songs...(Song of Sol. 3:4). There was a moment of unaccountable attraction, and they went from there.

That is the experience that guides and seekers should begin examining when they meet for spiritual guidance. In a Christian continuity, it does not make sense to begin with the "oughts" of the tradition but on the person's grounding in positive experience of the Mystery. It will be different for each person — like Shug's color purple in a field, or perhaps only a vague sensing that there is more going on in life than meets the eye.

When a person's life is grounded in the Mystery, a certain manner or style goes with that grounding. It fosters a more open lifestyle that avoids excessive busyness, includes time for silence and solitude, seeks nourishing reading and continued growth in a spiritual approach to life. Such a life enjoys leisure for contemplation and loses some kinds of fear — fear of what other people might think or say, fear of questioning one's own actions and motives, fear of insecurity or aloneness. When someone approaches religion in terms of delight rather than of duty, that someone becomes willing to pursue what provides the delight even if the pursuit becomes painful, as inevitably it does along the way.

This is what the earliest Christian guides had in mind when they fashioned the process of Christian initiation around appreciative delight in the risen life — as a leisurely, careful preparation for Easter and the mystagogia. The Pasch of the Lord was the great mystery to be handed on to the new believers, the "newest of the lambs." This was the dynamic treasure whose unseen flow throughout the universe was — and is — capable of changing the meaning of absolutely everything else.

Chapter Three

LIFE KEEPS HAPPENING

I N the second chapter we were thinking about some rather lofty-sounding concepts: about the world's great faith traditions (especially about the revelation/tradition that is Christianity) and how they help to structure people's encounters with Mystery. We were also noticing contemporary intellectual pluralism and how it affects our ability to receive/be free within a faith tradition. We kept pausing to think about the elements in that vast picture of meaning that spiritual guides need to be clear about.

If we stopped there in our portrait of what spiritual seekers need from their spiritual guides, the whole business of spiritual direction might seem rather intellectual and conceptual — like teaching a refined course in the history of theology. Well, it is not like that.

It is true that human beings do some of their navigating by their "stars" — by the enduring fixed points of meaning that gleam through all the generations — and by remembering their own moments of delighted awareness of the all-encompassing Holy Other. But human beings figure out somewhat more of their true direction, not by the high stars, but by stubbing their toes on things stuck in the mud they are slogging through.

Spiritual guides, as a result, do not spend a lot of time reading aloud out of books on the history of The Tradition. They spend a great deal of time listening attentively to what actually happens to people as they live their lives. Their job is to help those who come to them listen attentively to what is in fact going on in their ordinary lives.

Spiritual seekers and their guides are particularly interested in the less welcome, the messier parts of what happens to people. That is because they know that we human beings tend to defend ourselves, by various strategies, against change and growth. We hate losing our usual self-image; we do not like acknowledging that a project or relationship we were committed to has failed; we close the pores of our minds against things in life, or movements in the world, that challenge our favorite concepts. All those things are breakdowns of what we had constructed. They are little deaths. And, if we become willing to learn from them, they are most especially the occasions of new life for us. They can be perceived as God's living and dynamic presence, drawing us out of our spiritual torpor or our false and all too human security, in order to transform us from the way we are now to the way we are meant to be.

When Life Patterns Break Up

Things Fall Apart and *No Longer at Ease*. Simple, haunting phrases. Anyone could use them; they convey the uncertainty and weakness all human beings feel in the face of some kinds of change. A young African novelist, Chinua Achebe, chose those two phrases as the titles of his first and his second books.[1] In a generation before Achebe's, those two simple phrases were powerfully used, by Yeats and Eliot, in famous English-language poems. All three writers were voicing the pain of whole peoples under the pressures of forced change and cultural disruption.

Unasked-for change comes in all sizes. It can be massive and catastrophic, forced on whole populations by sheer cruel power, and it can result in pain and damage so great that the work of healing takes generations and centuries. Think of the African slave trade and its consequences. Think of the destruction of aboriginal cultures when Europeans came to South and then to North America. It is all too easy to think of scores of examples.

Unsought change also comes in personal and small-group sizes. It does not always come obviously, or violently, or as the result of any deliberate decision. Change is an ever-present reality. Persons meet it in exceedingly different ways. Three books considered in chapter 1 present persons in the grip of changed, i.e., broken patterns of life: Beth Jarrett's (fictional) mid-life crisis, Norman Cousins's heart attack, and Etty Hillesum's encounter with war and gross oppression.[2]

Changing life situations, in all their diversity and emotional impact, are the only concrete opportunities we have for discovering and unfolding the unique project each one of us is as spirit. When human beings lose their familiar life circumstances — certain ways of being and of doing with which they feel at home — the loss itself brings on self-doubts and reassessments that can go very deep. The process (when we meet it honestly and trustingly) is the path to new life.

A familiar life pattern is a kind of integration (relative and more or less partial) that satisfies some of our desire for harmony or, at the very least, for predictability. While it lasts, we may enjoy the illusion of "having it all together." When it breaks down, we are challenged to work for a new integration.[3]

People engaged in the process of spiritual guidance need to become aware that any life event, no matter how fleeting or seemingly insignificant, can be material for spiritual guidance — as long as it challenges the person to move beyond where he or she is currently living. Everyday life events already contain all the hidden growth directives and conflicts persons need to recognize if they are to begin dealing with the harmony or disharmony of their underlying dialogue with the world.[4]

There are moments when life as we have known it seems to collapse around us. Perhaps a friend dies; your spouse asks for a divorce; you are fired from your job; you take a stand on a social justice issue and are forced to confront the patterns of complicity with evil that run all through your neighborhood and your nation... and yourself. Your oldest child gets into drugs, or takes up with a cult. Life itself leads us into questions like "What did I do wrong?" "Why couldn't we reach each other?" "Why can't I change?" "Does anybody care? Is there anyone there?" John Shea puts it this way:

> No insurance policy can quite tame the future. Death and all its lesser indignities — illness, suffering and loss — all await us. All our devices to make life safe — amassing money and military might — are ultimately only stalls. Our meanings are fragile, our loves passing, our hopes precarious. When the reliability of all we have constructed is brought into question, we enter the dimension of Mystery.[5]

Usually we need such jolts from real life to be moved to want to listen to reality as it is rather than as we would have it be. There is alienation in all our relationships. There is ambiguity in all our moral activity. There is fragility in all our meanings, and unreliablity in all our commitments. With St. Paul, if we look hard enough, we find ourselves crying out: "For though the will to do what is good is in me, the performance is not.... In fact, this seems to be the rule: that every single time I want to do good, something evil comes to hand" (Rom. 7:18ff.).

People often ask for help in connecting these searing experiences of human contingency with the horizon of Mystery. In that light, we can gain courage to look honestly at what we are doing, how we are acting and reacting, not only with regard to other people and our life commitments, but also with regard to God.[6]

The changing situations of daily life disclose not only past and present personal movements. They often give hints of future direction as well. People live not just according to the convictions in their rational minds, but also by the feelings in their hearts and in their guts. Spiritual guidance can help people to anchor those feeling hearts and guts in spiritual foundations. It can help people to accept life changes, even painful ones, as doors opening on to new life: to becoming more serving, more honest, more humble, more alive.

There is a deep-rooted human hunger to believe in what we used to call "God's Providence": to believe that there is a significant spiritual reality present in the seemingly random experiences of everyday life. (Notice, for example, the current fascination with "synchronicity."[7]) And indeed the treasure is already there, already buried in the field, already in the world of our ongoing commitments and tasks. The spiritual gift we need is to become open to noticing the all-encompassing Presence. Be still, says the psalmist, and know that I am God. Taoist and Sufi writings also remind us that we are as fish already in the sea, already surrounded and supported by the life-giving waters. But we can be so busy swimming that we don't notice.

When persons relax in trust, they can be open to new life directives that can flow in on them, exactly where they are.

That is different from "getting on top of this thing." As psychiatrist Gerald May points out in Care of Mind, Care of Spirit, guides must be wary of "coping techniques" that rely on the power of psychological mastery as if that were the only good thing.[8] Such an attitude deals with change merely as a "problem." It ignores the power of God and the possibilities for spiritual growth given right in the circumstances of each person's life situation.

Formative and Transformative Change

In his book Darkness in the Marketplace, Thomas Green casts his eye — an experienced spiritual guide's eye — at the Gospel story of Martha in her kitchen at Bethany.[9] Borrowing some of Green's insights, and also using some basic concepts and categories from formative spirituality, let us consider Martha.[10]

Picture Martha busily and efficiently going about the business of preparing a company meal. In her heart are all kinds of familiar directives that helped her center her life that evening on her cooking skills and on the expectations of visitors. Martha was doing what she was good at. She was probably enjoying the work, although it would have gone better if she had had an assistant — like her sister Mary, for example.

This was Martha's self-chosen way of serving the Lord: as Green says, "Working for God." Suddenly her invited guest comes to the door of the kitchen. "Martha, Martha," he says, "you worry and fret over so many things, and yet few are needed, indeed only one. . . . Mary has chosen the better part" (Luke 10:42).

At that moment, Martha's busy complacent world of competency and serving the Lord collapses. Words have been spoken that change the whole meaning, for Martha, of what had been happening there in her house. The kitchen darkens. She is stopped in her tracks.

Differentiating circumstances have decentered Martha's world. She feels a loss of balance, of integration. Emotionally she feels torn apart by those intrusive words. Hadn't she been doing her best, doing what was expected of her? Now the whole project has a different feel about it, as Martha broods in the gloom of her "dark night."

The story doesn't tell us how Martha responded. She could have merely rallied: without wasting more than a moment, she could have gathered her usual forces together and met the challenge by increasing her efficient functioning, pushing down her self-doubts and forging ahead with dinner.

A good spiritual guide, as Thomas Green points out, would have helped Martha see this situation of lost balance and unexpected criticism as an opportunity for growth — a moment of transcendent openness to God. The guide could have helped Martha find a short period of distancing from the immediacy of the situation. Then, recollecting herself, she could separate just a little from her old way of going about her task.

Can Martha detach herself enough from her entrenched controlling Type-A style of functioning, calm her bruised ego, and accept that right in this very situation she is being called to a new level on all the dimensions of her being? Such a change might not show much on the outside, or even in the final product of her culinary efforts. But it could be a crucial change.[11]

A formative change — actually, a transformative shift — could be happening in Martha's whole outlook, in the very motivations of her heart. She could have realized, suggests Green, that Providence had given her an opportunity to make a radical shift from "working for God" in a way that she saw and that she controlled, to *doing God's work* — work that is the Other's choice and done in the manner preferred by that Other whom she loves.

With God's help, Martha's heart would be able to integrate this new way into all the dimensions of her personality. Her vital-functional life of striving would open up to the transcendent motivation of her sincere desire to serve God. The pneumatic inspiration to change her lifestyle would receive vitality and wholeness as it was integrated by Martha's freely consenting heart.

Two Dimensions of Human Willing

To understand Martha's transformation even more fully, we have to do a bit of thinking about the way human willing operates. The human will (or, human freedom, if you like) has a dual capacity. It has, to borrow a well-known Chinese image, a "yang" (active) face and a "yin" (receptive) face. Unfortunately, in Western civilization we are trained to notice only the "yang" side of human freedom. How many of us are aware of the receptivity that lies at the heart of our willing?[12]

Let's think about it. There are many human actions that cannot really be actively willed. Sleeping, for instance. We can prepare ourselves to sleep by going upstairs, brushing our teeth, putting on our pyjamas, doing some light reading, sipping warm milk, and lying down. But we cannot will to go to sleep. Sleep has to come, or not. It has to overtake us, as the book falls from our hands, our eyes fall shut and "it happens" — the gift of sleep is given and received.[13]

Sleep is not the only example, of course. We can be willing to become someone's friend, but we cannot actively will a friendship. It has to emerge, freely and mutually and a little mysteriously, between two persons. It is a gift, not an acquisition. Buying a piece of property, on the other hand, can be directly willed. We can go out and just do it, if the property is for sale. Or we can go out and chop down a tree. Or telephone our banker. All those deliberate actions belong in what the philosophers call the realm of "secondary willing."

They call it "secondary" because they think that the other kind of willing, the "yin" kind, is more fundamental: it is "primary willing." Understanding an explanation, praying, trusting, falling in love, being delighted by our firstborn child — all these belong beyond the limited, functional realm of secondary willing. On this primary level of volition, the willing self can prepare the way for an action, but not master it unilaterally. For an action like trusting, for example, to be born, what we can make available is personal receptivity. An initiative, an invitation from beyond the self must fructify our receptivity or else the desired action (trusting someone, understanding something) will not be born.

Although Scripture doesn't tell us what Martha did, we can be sure that if she chose the way of transformation out of this jolt to her complacency, it would not be easy. Transitions from one way of being and operating in the world to another are never easy.

Life is filled with disruptions of our taken-for-granted worlds.[14] Each disruption of our plans or expectations for our life has the power to shake us up, to move us beyond where we were. Any such disruption — minor or major — can represent a call from the Transcendent Other, a call that can be accepted or refused.

In the middle of transitions and crises, we are apt to feel confused and also depressed. The shape of life has somehow come unglued; it is threatening to turn into something unfamiliar. We tend to resist these challenges to our seeming control. We are tempted to try only functional, coping approaches that aim to regain our lost control. But in that case, we might be resisting an invitation to undergo a process of restructuring that would bring our hearts onto a new level of relationship with the Mystery.[15]

The Classic Crisis: Mid-Life Transition

There is one crisis with which everyone who lives past the age of thirty has to deal, one way or another. That is the so-called mid-life crisis. In our culture, people are quite expert at denying this crisis, up to a point. But eventually, we run out of ways of ignoring the decline in our vital-functional power. We begin to feel finite and contingent. Life changes as familiar people die, new ones are born, and questions about the ultimate meaning of it all surface in our consciousness. Then, as never before, the detachments and transitions that belong to this "crisis of limits" invite us into a time of questing and questioning.[16] Our former commitments weigh differently as they continue both to form and to deform our ongoing embodied spirit. Some authors are comparing this interlude to a spiritual "dark night."[17]

How should our commitments change? Mid-life limits force us to notice how our commitments to persons, priorities, and purpose have already shaped and formed us. We see how some of our life goals have been blocked by unfinished business from the past. Some of our former priorities may have to shift — perhaps because we are being inwardly invited to embrace the transcendent dimension of our life. Bits of wisdom encoded in our faith tradition — discarded or neglected, perhaps, when we were younger — begin to speak to us.

According to recent theorists, the mid-life crisis may be the moment of opening to spiritual maturity. This seems to be particularly the case in the North American context. With its tensions and anxiety over the loss of familiar ways of doing and being, mid-age forces a choice between clinging fearfully to the past and freely letting go of certainties to accept the invitation of the future. With someone who is honestly living through and reflecting on this stage of life, an alert spiritual guide can recognize a time of special responsiveness to the Mystery and to the call of the person's true self.

Men and women in mid-life can be challenged to take stock of the past, to become uniquely human persons in the present, and to prepare for a future of graceful old age and the new birth of death. The process of confronting one's ambiguous past can trigger depression and self-doubt if it is a lonely process, or if it lacks light from a deep faith tradition. A good spiritual guide can make a great deal of difference in this labor of finding maturity of motivation for the second half of life, for this transition to a transformed intentionality as the heart finds its roots in the deeper dimensions of existence.

The guide in these periods may ask what this person has already learned from his or her life experiences, and how she or he is integrating the losses and change that accompany the aging process. More detachment is possible now, more reflectiveness, more trust in life. Persons can become more uniquely themselves.

At the moment, the aging end of the life cycle is claiming a great deal of specialized attention, simply because human beings are living longer. A spate of recent books attests to that interest. We are increasingly aware that transitions and challenges never cease in human life. Many older persons are being led to reclaim and "rename" their original self and its expression within the changing circumstances of their lives. There is an increasing demand for guidance in what one author calls "the turn to transcendence" as older persons struggle to recognize and surrender themselves to the central call of their being, to the working of the Spirit in their lives.[18]

In the light of these insights, it is perhaps true to say that a radical living of central Christian commitment begins to happen for most people after the turn to transcendence has been made. This turn or shift involves an opening of self to the pneumatic dimension, to the Holy Spirit: radical transformation, after all, cannot be brought about by merely human effort.

Other Ways of Looking at Change

We are certainly not the first generation of seekers to prize the particular kind of readiness to change that is being described here. Our ancestors in faith knew and valued this possibility. The New Testament is full of images of this special openness. Perhaps the most famous one is the image in the Fourth Gospel: "Truly, truly I say to you, unless a grain of wheat falls into the ground and dies, it remains alone; but if it dies, it bears much fruit" (John 12:24). Many of the paradoxes about loving your life and hating it, being willing to lose your life in order to keep it for eternal life, and other strange sayings are recommending a willing openness to transformative change.

The idea of transformative change is also fascinating to the contemporary imagination, and not only on the spiritual or religious level.

Several years ago, I noticed a striking parallel between the process of formative change and the scientific notion of "dissipative structures." That notion was advanced by Nobel Prize–winning chemist Ilya Prigogine in 1977.[19] According to his theory, the people, events and things of life can be seen as *open systems*, involved in a continuous exchange of energy with the environment. Always in process, these open systems are formed by the movement of energy through them. They are always ready to change. When the system is disturbed or upset in some way, the parts of the system can reorganize onto a higher order. Thus the whole system reorganizes itself, usually in a direction that opposes its former entropic movement toward death. The new life resulting from the stress and disruption thus destroys the entropy of habit and stasis. Stress in the structure of a system forces a new solution.

If you enjoy the analogy, you can apply it to what we have been saying about spiritual growth. Guides can welcome the stories of stress and even of suffering when they are told — welcome them as breakthrough opportunities for opening up closed places in the heart, for waking up spiritual deadness. The breakup of old ways of living makes new life possible. Maybe a healthy spiritual life really needs some "dissipative structures" from time to time.

What is most important, if we are seeking or offering spiritual guidance, is the quality of attention we must pay to any conflict situation that is spoken of. Alert guides need to pay serious attention to whatever events, memories, or feelings of conflict the seeker wants to talk about. There is always a buried treasure. Precisely within the significant life event itself, there lies hidden the spatial and temporal past, present, and future of that person's embodied spirit. The event itself, in the concrete details of its interpersonal context, contains all that is needed to put the person in touch with his or her lived relation with self, others, and God.[20]

Here is another analogy, in case you were not inspired by the "dissipative structures" borrowed from Prigogine the chemist. The *I Ching* — the classic Chinese book of changes — has its own harmony-seeking way of looking at events in time and space.[21] With its vision of the Tao, or principle of order and harmony beneath the complex flow of all things, the *I Ching* urges us to contemplate each human event of change exactly as it exists, in all its details. It has techniques for helping us not to neglect aspects of the event we would prefer not to see or dimensions that we are personally not able to articulate.

In this ancient Chinese view, there is an already-given harmony in the total flow of life. Although at first glance someone may appear to be dominating his or her life field, the truth is that positive and negative forces are always combined interdependently throughout one's entire life field. Human freedom confronts all its life choices within the eternally given harmony of this flow. The awakened heart must learn to be aware of the alternating forces of yin and yang, male and female, heaven and earth, present in any event. The heart must not impose its own perceptions; it must learn to observe and understand, yielding to the balancing possibilities that are already, intrinsically, in the situation being considered. It is by keeping within this mysterious carrying flow that one comes to savor one's true freedom.

According to the *I Ching,* unsought change is the mysterious bearer of true liberty. Our lives are small fields of force, carried along and integrated by a much larger field.[22]

The Challenge of Openness to One's Whole Context

When a Christian guide is co-listening with a seeker to that seeker's entire life field, lived under modern conditions, they will both detect influences from a myriad of sources.[23] Like everyone else in the twentieth century, Christians find themselves entwined in pluriformity. Secular (especially psychological) faith and form traditions have been part of the air they have breathed from childhood; so have worldviews and customs from the East as well as the West, from Islamic and Chinese as well as Catholic and Protestant sources, not even to mention Madison Avenue! There is no longer a more or less uniform Christian formation field underlying people's individual fields.[24]

Yet we are called to become Christian precisely within this pluriform field. No one can possibly live outside it. We can trust, because God has become incarnate and works in the field as a whole, not only in the Christian part. Our challenge lies in empowering ourselves, and others, to appraise critically which aspects of this larger field are compatible with Christian foundations, and which are not.

Surely, counting on the Incarnate One, we can afford to be generous. It is important to be sympathetic with what is already moving the people of our own culture. We can learn from, and not reject, the elements of truth that are to be found in contemporary psychology or technology. We can be alert for the good that is in social movements and subcultures, and even in the changing orientations in family life, in personal relationships and sexuality, and in the customs and perceptions that permeate our environment.[25]

If a spiritual guide and a seeker discern together that more openness, a more generous judgment would be an appropriate goal for this particular seeker, then the kind of co-listening that they do makes it possible to work in that direction. The guide can help the person become less self-preoccupied with what he or she finds personally agreeable, with what he or she resists in terms of change. This is not done indiscriminately, but as an outflow of opening one's heart in faith to the larger field of infinite truth and mercy. Nor is this goal a separate agenda item. The guide is already listening reflectively to the person's story, to the person's emotional reactions to the events narrated in the story, to the way he or she perceives the implications of relational encounters and of more public events. The guide is striving to notice — and to help the seeker notice — how the formative Mystery has been present all along to the person's life in its entirety. The ability to reflect on the presence of Mystery in all the formative shifts, transitions, and metanoias in a person's (or a community's) life is one of the gifts of grace that can follow from the guidance session.

The art of taking people seriously as a spiritual guide includes the critical skill of taking their culture seriously. In the preceding paragraphs, we were noticing the positive side of that skill and the importance of cultivating an open, generous judgment of the social movements and cultural pulsations all around us.

But we would walk blindly into every kind of trap if we were always positive about social and cultural trends. Spiritual guides must learn how to be counter-cultural, because all spiritual seekers must at some points live and think in ways that challenge the culture. Every society has in it patterns that tend to block or to deform spiritual growth. Becoming aware of them, then learning to undo their grip on our lives, is not an easy task.

Some sociologists describe the cultural milieu as our "second body." That is an eloquent way of pointing to the radically formative/ deformative power of culture and society. Society forms our "habits of the heart," as Robert Bellah and fellow researchers would say.[26] In this sense, culture means the way of life of a group developed over a long period and manifested in learned behavior patterns, myths, symbols, rituals, and customs.

Cultural and form traditions govern language and time and space conventions. Every tradition has taken-for-granted ways of dealing with sexuality and authority and money, with problems of individuality and conformity, with health and respectability and the pursuit of happiness. Cultural conventions are surprisingly powerful. Some are tenacious and enduring. Others are "trendy," shifting from decade to decade or even from year to year.[27]

Any culture may be alive with guidelines for success and relevance that deny the Mystery and promote the seven deadly sins. Anyone interested in the work of spiritual guidance — indeed, anyone wishing to make choices that are in tune with Gospel directives — must be alert for the conflicts with Gospel directives that are patterned into the society he or she lives and works in. A spiritual guide who ignores these cultural realities is not truly dealing as an embodied human being with other concretely situated embodied spirits. Any humanly spiritual act takes place within a culturally framed life field. That is part of the principle of incarnation, which applies to all aspects of spirituality.[28]

We are all divided products of divided cultures, torn by contradictory allegiances. We are afraid to risk seeking first the reign of God; we cling to the culture's prescriptions for security. In North America, for example, we are continually being urged to find ultimate security in material consumption and prosperity. If we follow those urgings, then we must close our eyes to the injustices, exploitation, and oppressions imposed on others by North American–style prosperity. We must overlook racism, sexism, militarism, and many other uses of power that tend to make the rich richer and the poor poorer. That path leads to a spiritual crisis best characterized by the scriptural expression "hardness of heart." The thrust of Gospel metanoia puts Christians in direct conflict with these and other impediments to spiritual life that are embedded in the culture around us.

"Consumerism" may be the most famous distorting pattern in North American life, but it is not the only one. Loneliness, for example, has become a major problem. Due to a widespread loss of community and of communal decision-making possibilities, many North Americans have a sense of not belonging, of alienation from others. Alienation from others can also be reinforced by prejudice and ignorance of others on an individual and a social scale. It seems to me that isolation of human beings from a sense of solidarity with others is connected also with the modern lack of faith in a wider spiritual reality that can bind people together even beyond their individual efforts at mutual solidarity.

Overactivism is another trap that spiritual guides need to be alert to in our time. Overactivism can trivialize family life and starve intimate relationships. It can alienate from their deepest selves many well-meaning helpers of others. What is now called "burnout" can hit not only business executives, but also church-based social activists who have denied their spiritual and their vital-functional limits in their passion for social change. They have rushed or pushed beyond the actual grace granted them, beyond the limits of their actual selves. They end up in anguish and hopelessness. Their pain can hardly be dealt with unless they can somehow be reconnected with a deeper primordial "yes" to the Mystery's presence in the entirety of their life field.

Another obstacle to spiritual presence in our present culture is its emphasis on living in modes of domination and functional control. From the time we enter kindergarten — or, perhaps, the day-care center before kindergarten — we are pressured to achieve, to be efficient, to compete, to win at all costs. The only consciousness that is approved of and cultivated is an action-oriented alertness useful for dealing with problems in the world of work. If we want to become a bit more passive, more receptive to the Beyond that is simply given in reality, we actually have to drop out, temporarily, from the prevailing cultural atmosphere. We do not have to be mystics to recognize overactivism as a trap. Two heart specialists popularized the problem in their book *Type-A Personality and Your Heart*, which analyzed our way of living as designed to promote heart disease. I was interested to note a similar book published in 1986, *The Type-E Woman*, subtitled "How to Overcome the Stress of Being Everything to Everybody." The author, Harriet Braiker, describes a cognitive-behavioral syndrome common among contemporary women that combines anxiety, excessive self-reliance, ego confusion, and a need for excellence into a health-destroying "everything-to-everybody" package.

Consumerism, loneliness, overactivism — these are three common traps built into our North American context about which the great faith and form traditions have much to say, much guidance to offer. But there are other cultural distortions, perhaps more recently perceived and described, in which the great religious traditions seem to be immersed as uncritically as the rest of us. The most burning current example is sexism. Traditional norms regarding human encounter with the Mystery are now seen by feminist analysis as exclusively male norms, describing and reflecting the experience of men and ignoring or misrepresenting the experience of women. The Christian church, with its symbol system rooted in the Bible, seems more unrepentantly patriarchal than any of our secular institutions when examined from some feminist perspectives.

Feminist consciousness is an enormously important phenomenon for spiritual guides to understand. The implications for spirituality are widespread as the new awareness emerging from the women's movement penetrates different cultures around the globe. Some cultural layers of sexism are fairly easy to discern and to criticize. For example, if a society tends to see its women as second-class citizens, not only do expectations of oneself as a female person tend to take a downhill course, but opportunities for a wholesome human existence may be denied as a matter of course to whole groupings of women in that society. If the bearers of a faith and form tradition hand on a symbolization of women as humanly inferior to men, then strange things will happen to the spiritual growth of women — and also of men — in that faith and form tradition. At present, however, there is passionate disagreement over what symbols humanly denigrate women, what forms of language exclude the acknowledgment of women and what religious traditions perpetuate a casting of women into subsidiary, exploited, and derivative roles. Some contemporary seekers have developed a feminist consciousness that has led them to mistrust or reject all traditional codifications of the human encounter with the Mystery, since all of them have been conditioned by traditional patriarchal culture. To be able to co-listen to reality with such a person, a spiritual guide will need to have reflected deeply on feminism and on the whole contemporary struggle over the meaning of gender.

The struggle over the meaning of gender is a burning example (but only one example) of what a difficult task it is for human beings to find truthful ways of relating to their society and culture, their "second body." People often need guidance in appraising the underlying spirit of current sociohistorical pulsations. They need critical sensitivity to the signs of the time and an ability to pick up the patterns that may be deforming even spiritual people and institutions — whether those patterns are ancient or new.[29]

There are social scientists who point out that traditional religions themselves have been shaped, and re-shaped, by the culture and its accretions.[30] That is certainly true. But do we therefore dump the traditional religions? After so many thousands of years, where are we going to find equally tested worldviews, emerging from lived experience and capable of lifting us beyond the limits of current cultural conventions? With good reason Christians have always regarded the Gospel as providing just such a liberating challenge. Gospel directives, well integrated and understood, can free us to think and to live beyond the determinisms of our culture. They can enable us to risk a series of conversions in the midst of our ongoing lives, in spite of our natural resistance to what is new and "other."

For strength to say no to the false security advertised in one's culture by the proponents of militarism, fundamentalism, or pragmatism as ultimate solutions, I think one needs somehow to belong to a community of resistance. If a man or a woman is to escape "letting the world around you squeeze you into its own mold,"[31] he or she needs faithful others who are finding their security not in consumerism or uses of power, but in trustful abandonment to the Mystery itself. For a full life that is "counter-cultural" when it needs to be, we need the help not only of a culturally critical spiritual guide, but also of long-term comrades whose solidarity is grounded in a deep, peaceful alternative vision.

Self-Knowledge through Listening to What Happens

We have been thinking about a method of reflecting on life events in the confidence that those concrete events hold directives for increased self-knowledge and for choosing the right direction in one's unfolding life. This method is simply a way of helping people discover who they really are by means of uncovering their hitherto unconscious dialogue with the world of people, events, and things.[32] When this method is used as part of spiritual guidance and in the light of a shared faith tradition, both seeker and guide can begin to discover the inward meaning of circumstances and events, that is, what they mean from the point of view of interior motivation and the wisdom of the heart. It is, by the way, a thoroughly "andragogical" method of learning about oneself.[33] An adult who has a certain emotional distance helps a fellow adult to learn more from the person's own experience, rather than from some index file of solutions that may be lurking in the guide's mind. This way, both may become more alert to the disguised dynamics, both formative and deformative, that permeate their response to the events of daily life.

As co-listeners, guides can be alert for possible onesidedness, for spiritual opportunities that might otherwise be overlooked, and for the attunement or disharmony they sense in this person's resistance to messages coming from the various polarities of the life field.[34] As a guide, I might wonder whether this person really is an open system. Perhaps he or she is closed to certain possibilities and opportunities as well as limitations and ambiguities of that field. Or maybe he or she has become so open to the dynamism of one dimension, the achieving of merely functional ambitions, for instance, that his or her heart is almost closed to transcendent and pneumatic aspirations and inspirations. Moreover, this person may be unaware of the obstacles or defenses he or she has personally set up (or their culture has set up in him or her) in order to avoid the risk of newness and growth. This person may be closed off in dispositions of distrust of God and others, in a rigid set of safety directives and hang-ups, in fear of sex, or in a rigid profile of pride from which he or she needs to become detached.

It is when life gets stressful that the personal reaction to events will reveal most clearly the underlying conflict between self and others (or self and God) that a particular woman or man has been struggling with. We do not discover ourselves by examining only the interior movements of heart or mind, although these do represent one area of our responsive selves. We come to know ourselves truly in and through our relations with others, and in and through the commitments we make to what is other. In those ways we "catch ourselves in the act" of responding and reacting to Otherness itself.

The truth about the self is not found in the ideal self, nor in the culturally isolated self, nor even in the defensive walled-in self of failed development and sin. The wise guide looks first at the real-life event or circumstances that made this person stop and think and finally become attentive enough to ask for assistance.

The emphases being put on *events* at this point may tempt us to confuse spiritual guidance with pastoral counseling. We may realize that the potential significance of such real-life events (often called "limit situations") is the basis of the developing movement of pastoral counseling. The task of the pastoral counselor — besides providing spiritual comfort for people — lies in helping them deal with whatever concrete situation is troubling them.[35]

People seek pastoral counseling for assistance with problems they have encountered with family, with aging, with women's issues, with being handicapped, and so on. Pastoral counseling aims to cope with problems in specific settings: in the parish setting, in hospitals, in prisons, and in universities. Some specialized pastoral counselors offer service to specific segments of the community, for example, to people struggling with divorce or separation, or suffering from drug addiction or from bereavement. Within the discipline of pastoral counseling, the accent seems to be situation-related. The persons served are invited to come because they are suffering from a change happening between themselves and one of the outer polarities of their lived situation.

Spiritual guidance, on the other hand, though it may get its impetus from the changes required by a particular life situation, does not usually aim at dealing with the situation itself. Spiritual guides are more interested in how people connect their living of certain situations (perhaps difficult ones) with their inner desire to live a loving relationship with the divine Other whose call the situation represents.

Some personality disorders and neurotic patterns of relating can make that connection seem difficult or impossible. When there has been a failure, over the years, to authentically work through certain conflicts or challenges, those conflicts can be stored up interiorly and can lead to defensive survival strategies that tie up a person's energy in a neurotic pattern or style. There may be a rigid set of defensive strategies for survival, hang-ups regarding sexuality, or encapsulation in willful or will-less orientations that can block further growth in wholeness. However, situated neurotic patterns, no matter how powerful, are never powerful enough to prevent a person from being open to God's gifts of grace and true holiness. With the proper type of guidance, people can be helped to perceive these painful relics of past conflicts as difficult but real opportunities for maturing.[36]

It can be hard slogging. Despair often tempts the spiritual seeker. It is necessary for a guide to have a deep understanding of hope as she or he helps seekers to come to a more relaxed and trusting style of life, to build up their courage and confidence, and to reach a metanoia of their image of God.[37]

Sometimes it might help to remember Shug, Celie's companion and guide in *The Color Purple*.[38] Shug understands where Celie got her incongruous image of the God who gave her "a lynched daddy, a crazy mama, a lowdown dog of a step'pa and a sister she probably won't ever see again." Yet it is Shug who talks with Celie about the God who is "always making little surprises for us," who loves everything Celie loves, who really wants to be loved by us. And Celie, in a radical redefinition, lets go of the indifferent old white man in her head and begins the novel's final letter: "Dear God. Dear stars, dear trees, dear sky, dear peoples. Dear Everything. Dear God."

Chapter Four

GUIDING THE HUMAN SPIRIT

EVERYONE who works for a long time with fellow human beings —
as a parent, as a teacher, as a counselor or healer of any kind —
develops a kind of mental diagram of the human person. By experience and reflection, we build a kind of inventory of the powers and
vulnerabilities that seem to be part of the created structure of any
member of our species. Most people develop their diagram mainly
on the commonsense level. They express it, when they do speak of
it, through evocative symbols, through traditional descriptions, sometimes through proverbs or fragments of poetry. Christians often express
it in the haunting language of the Bible.

People who work professionally as counselors, therapists, and in
other "helping professions" usually take courses to develop their diagram of the human person: their "theoretical anthropology," to give it
a technical name. They study various theories and schools of thought.
Often they "adopt" one theory, adding elements from other theories
when these prove useful.

People who minister as spiritual guides in the Christian tradition
discover that they too need a theoretical anthropology.[1] It helps them
to organize and to develop their insights and experience with actual
human beings. It gives them a language in which to explain what they
are doing and what they are hoping for. And it gives them a necessary
kind of professional shorthand when they consult with other guides.

Also, since we live in a time when there is all around us a lush
growth of competing psychological accounts of the human — all of
which influence us and influence the seekers who come to us — it is
essential to develop for ourselves a clear diagram of the human person
that has room in it for the great claims Christian faith makes for the
human creature.

Over my years of working and reading as a psychologist and as a
teacher of spiritual formation, I too have had to develop such a working
diagram for myself. I have found Adrian van Kaam's theory of forma-

55

tive spirituality to be the most inclusive practical synthesis between
the contemporary psychology of personal growth and the church's rich
traditions of ascetical-mystical theology. I have been working within
this growing theoretical framework ever since I began to teach graduate students who want to be able to think systematically about the
ministry of spiritual guidance.[2]

In this chapter I want to talk about how the human mind works
from the point of view of what spiritual guides need to know and to
work with. So I will need to use some specialized words and concepts
from this newly developing theoretical anthropology to set out what
I want to say. I find that when I work in this frame of reference, I
can incorporate a great deal of the important work now being done
by secular psychologists and therapists and by spiritual guides in other
schools of thought, both Christian and non-Christian.

The language I have chosen may not be entirely familiar, but it is
not difficult to understand. You will quickly recognize where it "fits"
in your own frame of reference if you are using a different one —
or if you remember the rich language of our faith-ancestors about the
human person.

How Our Minds Deal with What Happens

In the familiar Hindu tale of the six blind men examining one elephant,
the creature is a fan if I am holding its ear, a rope if I am feeling its
trunk, a temple pillar if I am hanging on to a leg. The perceiving human
mind has a powerful co-formative effect on whatever it apprehends.[3]
So, when we say that reflection on experience is at the heart of any form
of spiritual guidance and that it is important for us, in so reflecting,
to try to grasp what is really happening, we are right to suspect that it
is all going to get a bit complex.

The complexity stems from the fact that the human mind is a subtle
and powerful processor of the world it lives in and perceives. What is
important for the guidance project is to learn something about how we
can discover, not only what events have been happening exteriorly in
a person's life field, but also what has been contributed by the interior
co-happening that takes place in the mind, in the imagination, memory,
and anticipation, and subsequently in the will of the person who lived
through the event.[4]

We begin by recognizing that the mind of any human being is multilayered. We are usually most familiar with the mind's *functional layer* —
the practical part that operates like a calculator, or like a computer, if
we possess that degree of competence. With this functional layer we
plan and organize, figure things out, and come to decisions about what
to do after processing the information available to us.

Unfortunately, for many people in our culture that is the full extent of their use of the power called mind. Many intellectuals deny (and many ordinary people do not know) that the human mind was made to know far more than facts and figures. The mind is essentially an openness to more than the visible world, more even than the "more" of human freedom and creativity. Human minds are made to know transcendent reality. There is a layer of the mind that aspires not only to know but to participate in the transcendent reality of All That Is, in what we have been calling the Mystery.

As a complementary power of the human spirit, the will also has a transcendent layer that opens it to the Mystery.[5] We are more familiar with the functional or executive characteristics of the will, as it takes the practical conclusions of the mind and puts them into action. More of that later — and more later about imagination, memory, and anticipation: all powers of the mind that play a crucial role for spiritual guidance.

All the powers of the mind operate at different levels of consciousness, so that usually we are aware of only a small percentage of their operations. Just out of awareness (but still available to us) is the level of the prefocal consciousness. That is the level of the hidden dialogue between ourselves and different facets of our life field that sometimes needs to be raised to consciousness by means of the guidance process. There is a deeper layer of consciousness that could be called infrafocal, that is, not immediately available to consciousness. This layer consists of an unconscious accumulated sediment of past experiences, tensions, and undealt-with conflicts. It requires great wisdom and psychoanalytic skill, particularly in the realm of religious experience, to name accurately the manifestations of this infrafocal layer — for example, when people mistakenly claim their prophetic words and visionary experiences come directly from God.[6]

Spiritual guides need to be clear about the presence in all human beings of an equally profound transfocal receptivity to transcendent Mystery. Part of "basic human equipment" is a transconscious disposition of awe before the Mystery that can be apprehended (although not by the senses) as it suffuses and surrounds each person's life field and created reality as a whole. Transfocal consciousness is a capacity to receive more than the sense-perceptible aspects of any experienced event. Out of this capacity (or layer, if you like) emerge the deeper spiritual questions that people tend to ask. These are primordial questions that men and women live with. People can and do repress these questions because of the anxiety they feel about them. Or they can seek help with them — sometimes bringing them to the guidance situation. They are not merely questions that human minds *have*, but that whole human people *are*.[7]

Such transcendent questions are common to all human beings who have let themselves become present in ultimate reverence to Mystery as they may have encountered it. And that is precisely what spiritual guidance hopes to awaken in persons: the possibility of presence to Mystery in the events and encounters of each one's life.

It is this foundational capacity of the soul that has throughout the ages brought people together in shared consciousness that they can "seek the face of the Lord." The great spiritual faith and form traditions came into being around what van Kaam calls the "interconsciousness" of generations and communities around the globe.

A Few Applications

What are some consequences, some applications in therapy, for example, of the widespread insight that the human mind is a multilayered reality? And what difference does it make if we, as spiritual guides, acknowledge and wish to serve also the transcendent dimension of a person's consciousness?

Let's begin with a most useful truth, widely accepted by workers in any kind of guidance or counseling. The way we think has a lot to do with the way we feel — about ourselves and about the rest of reality.

The title of one book — *Mind as Healer, Mind as Slayer* — says it very well.[8] Its author explains the relation between mind-related or cognitive stress and four major types of illness: cardiovascular disease, cancer, arthritis, and respiratory disease. Psychologists like Albert Ellis are developing a similar approach, which they call the cognitive school of therapy, emphasizing how the ways we think affect our behavior and health. Among the many books on this topic of mind/body relationship is a popular paperback by David Burns called *Feeling Good: The New Mood Therapy.*[9] Using the cognitive approach, Burns teaches people to alter their moods by changing the way they think — thus dealing with emotional problems (including depression) without the use of drugs. Burns spells out ten deformative ways in which we use illogical pessimistic attitudes of mind to destroy our self-image, weaken our bodies, paralyze our wills, and generally defeat our hearts from attaining their goals and from reaching out to new aspirations.

What is particularly interesting for the guide in these ten distorted ways of thinking is how powerfully they affect not only a person's conscious perception of reality but also his or her emotions and actions in preconscious dialogue with it. People can suffer from a perfectionism based on "all or nothing" thinking. They can arbitrarily generalize from one negative experience to the whole of life. They (we) can mentally "throw cold water" on all the positive aspects of encounters with people, events, and things. They (we) can take negative emotions, and the reasoning that results from them, for the truth. People can be governed by impossible "shoulds" or by self-defeating labelling of themselves or of events. People can assume responsibility for negative events when there is no basis for doing so.

When people suffer from any of these (rather common) mental habits, there are consequences for the specifically transcendent dimensions of consciousness as well. Those patterns of thinking make it harder to arrive at a positive felt sense of the presence of the Mystery in one's life. They make people less able to relax and be carried by the Mystery, because according to their illusory thinking, they are entirely responsible for controlling all aspects of their formation field. Such anxiety-ridden functionalistic thinking tends to rule out the more creative and transcendent, the more human or spiritual modes, that belong to the realms of meditation and contemplation.

Let's look through a different lens at this same problem: the domination of a person's consciousness by the functional layer. Recall the traditional Chinese way of describing different aspects of reality and of consciousness: the yang and the yin.[10] We could say that the functionalistic mindset will operate out of a yang orientation. That can become the dominant orientation not only of a person's mind, but also of a whole society, a culture. North American culture, for sure, has a predominantly yang orientation. Before it was North American, it was generally the Western European orientation; and in that we can find the root of some serious deficiencies in the spiritual approaches of former times in the West.

There has been among Western cultures a totalizing of the operations of *functional* mind and will. Put into religious terms, that tends to the belief that if we just set our minds to it and exert our wills hard enough, we can become holy; we would automatically be leading a spiritual life.[11] We might call that "totalized yang" — and it brings a negative dynamic to spirituality. The dynamics of an authentic approach to the Mystery are the dynamics of receptivity, of yin. We can only discern the purposes of the Holy Other, and cooperate with them, by being open and receptive to the initiatives of that Other.

The transcendent mind (as distinct from the functionalist mindset) is open to reality, open to being formed by truth, rather than decisively pre-empting what truth will be or say. That attitude is what Plato and Aristotle meant by the dynamic of awe and wonder. Aristotle praised awe as a movement out of ignorance. Closer to our time, Meister Eckhart and Martin Heidegger speak in a similar way about the mind that "dwells," about a style of thinking called *Gelassenheit*, in which the mind releases itself to be caught up in the Mystery. Such a style waits for reality to reveal itself, rather than rushing to impose its own thoughts and come to closure on the questions of life even before they have consciously been asked.

"Dwelling," or *Gelassenheit*, is one way of describing meditative thinking.[12] Spiritual guidance encourages meditative thinking — allowing a place for Mystery in our lives, giving life a chance to shape and form us before we impose a form on it. In that stance we are open to the way of obedience and listening to the God who, beyond all symbols and images, dwells in the "cloud of unknowing."

The mind that reflects on experience in search of its mystery-dimension must be willing to cultivate transcendent self-presence. That is a mode of consciousness different from the problem-solving functional mode. Without doubt there are problems to be solved as well as mysteries to be lived. Indeed we do need to make decisions, find solutions, accomplish goals and pass judgments: but never in total isolation from transcendent possibilities. Otherwise our problem solving can deteriorate into a mechanical attempt to manipulate the flow of life.[13]

In a problem-solving framework, when the problem has been solved it makes good sense to stop and move on to something else. But if as guides we remain in a merely functional approach, we will overlook hidden spiritual ramifications. Then we will be as unhelpful as the doctors described in Norman Cousins's *The Healing Heart* — the doctors who were prepared to deal only with the physical aspects of his coronary disease.[14] They remained in a closed circuit of medical know-how. They did not ask whether a painful thought could be a more powerful trigger for arrhythmia than an injury to the heart muscle itself. Nor did they want to hear Cousins say that faith, hope, love, and the will to live were even more important for his heart's health than diet and medication. The spiritual dimension was not apprehended as part of the wholeness of this person's experience and of his recovery.[15]

"Psychological know-how" can be a closed circuit just like "medical know-how." It can be almost as technological. Some people (including some believers) find it very threatening to consider the type of self-knowledge that becomes available when they are encouraged to move beyond a merely psychological analysis of how they came to be in a particular dilemma. They might be fascinated with the idea of being a certain personality type who copes with conflict in a certain determined style. But they resist seeing themselves as also being unique, flawed, "immortal diamonds" longing for truth and love, searching for the source of Life. Yet it is precisely this type of spiritual reflection on personally significant life events that can open the eyes of the heart to the depth dimension not only of the event, but also of the human person who is freely bending a meditative mind and heart back upon the event.

The Power of Images

Imagination — the power we have to form internal images — is always at work on different levels of consciousness. Intertwining with memory and anticipation, our imagination constantly influences the working of our minds and wills, and therefore what we think and choose.[16]

Due to the influence that images and symbols have in shaping our lives, TV has proven to have more power to shape our imagination than either radio or the printed word. It is the dynamic power of this formed imagination that propels us into buying what the tube presents to us as compelling images. And because images are always more potent when supported by memory or anticipation, TV ads appeal to our sense of nostalgia, our taste for happiness, to our fondness for the smell of success and to our dreams of a better future, all by appealing to the imagination.[17]

If we are interested in freedom, it quickly becomes obvious that our imaginations need some kind of discipline. With its power to break us out of the limits of reality, an undisciplined imagination can do us great disservice.[18]

Karen Horney sees the destructive possibilities of an undisciplined imagination in her book *Neurosis and Human Growth*.[19] She speaks about the typically human "search for glory," which is, from a spiritual guide's point of view, a deformative work of imagination, channelling life energy into illusory goals and bringing about an undisciplined transfer of the soul's transcendent yearning for God.

Horney describes three false life strategies that spring from the illusory "search for glory." One, she says, is the solution of gaining mastery by an expansive or aggressive movement "against." Another is the solution of gaining love by the self-effacing movement "toward." The third is the solution of gaining freedom by a resigned movement "away from." It is a sobering book. In demonstrating how the drive for success or pleasure or power emerges from neurotic imaginings and fantasies, Horney's entire book speaks to the power of this central capacity of the human spirit to bend minds and wills.It can also deform our experience of Holy Otherness and our aspirations toward it.

We can, for example, encase ourselves in a false image of self. Instead of choosing to live with the image of self that God has loved into being, most of us are inclined to live with an exaggerated image that we have created for ourselves — an idolatrous image of the idealized self, which is often far from the actual truth of our being. Another false self image may be created from how we imagine other people want us to be — a self that is forever compelled to perform and achieve, one that is also frequently the product of deformed and thus deforming imaginative power. On the other hand, this power can also fasten us into a low self-esteem as we struggle through life with an underrated image of self, an image that is equally out of attunement with the originating image of self that, in its truth, allows the divine life energy to flow freely through all aspects of our life in the direction of its final goal.

Imaginative power can also *serve* our transcendent aspirations, in very positive ways. It can, by opening up our limited perception, allow us to create something new, even in and through the reality of "things exactly as they are."[20] A powerful imagination can creatively thrust us right into the real, contends James Lynch. In his *Images of Hope*, he speaks of imagination's power to envision what cannot yet be seen, and to help us overcome despair or pessimism as we wait for the vision that is not yet fully accomplished.[21]

That side of imagination has been noted by many contemporary guides who are making use of the "image therapy" developing around the work of Roberto Assagioli and the discipline of psychosynthesis. In his book *The Act of Will,* this founder of psychosynthesis speaks of ways in which we can direct the imagination ("mental pictures make things happen!") and make it a servant of the will.[22]

In *The Religious Imagination*, Andrew Greeley also speaks of the significance for Christian formation of this preconscious power that animates, vitalizes, and thus transforms our perceptions and conceptions. Contending that the Holy Spirit works through imagination, Greeley defends the centrality of myth and symbol in religious life. It is the transcendent power of the imagination that allows us to image God not as a distant authoritarian who compels from an external position of power and control, but rather as a dynamic movement of the Holy Spirit within ourselves, within all people, and within the world.[23]

There is no doubt that spiritual guides can and do make use of the human power to create internal images, to assist themselves and others in imagining something new. In helping others become more aware of the repressed and infraconscious images that continue to shape their lives, they can aid people heal memories, change habits, and build an atmosphere of prayer and hope. We can even be helped to put our old ways of thinking about God into the "cloud of unknowing" as advised by the anonymous author of that famous book.[24] However, at a certain point the level of imagination and reasoning must be left behind. When directees are ready to drop to a deeper level of attentiveness to spiritual nature and its values, the unknown God of pure faith becomes the center of spiritual attention. On this level of consciousness, self-reflection is meant to decrease or disappear as transcendent perception in faith, hope, and love illumines the way for the searching human spirit.

A New Heaven and a New Earth

There is an added opening onto human possibilities to be discovered in the human spirit's power to anticipate a future.

Operating at various levels of emotional intensity and of consciousness, the dynamics of anticipation are capable of providing a certain strength to human motivation, or of draining it away.

The question for us as guides will be, How is this person using his or her power to anticipate: creatively or destructively? What is the underlying sense or feeling about the future that this person has incorporated? Are this person's anticipations permeated with a sense of abandonment by the Mystery, or does she or he dare to risk abandonment to the Mystery?

We should not underestimate the importance of this intuitive feeling about one's life project, about the inner directedness one sees in it, and of the inner strength one derives from feeling confident, able to do something about making it happen.[25]

However, in North America confidence can run into a complication. The commercial aspect of our culture — which is its overdeveloped aspect — discovered long ago that it is "confidence" that makes a good salesperson. Or a good executive. Since Dale Carnegie and before, every North American has grown up bombarded with messages and techniques that package and sell optimism and self-confidence. These can indeed turn us into very efficient hucksters. But they are a very, very long way from the relaxed, nonmanipulative, humble, and trustful positive anticipation that comes from trust in the Mystery. Some TV evangelists have yet to notice the difference. Their widely watched programs, which fit so well into the commercialized shape of the North American social imagination, have sown widespread misunderstanding about deep, authentic Christian hope and anticipation.

Yet there does need to be something in the goal of life that attracts our efforts, that moves our hearts. Otherwise all there is to anticipate will be dry-as-dust duty. In such a case, people tend to become willful, relying on exterior willpower instead of being open to the inner attractiveness of a goal that motivates.[26]

This is a crucially important area, misunderstood or not. Without hope there is no future. Anxious, fear-filled people are no longer available for the future. Only men and women with hope can summon the energy and purpose needed to bring about good change. Martin Luther King had a dream, and his people came alive with hope. I remember being filled with negative expectations on the way to that march in Washington in 1963. I remember the joy when all my negative anticipations proved wrong.

Perhaps guides have to become more adept at questioning people about their future hopes and teaching them to use their imaginations to conjure up more positive possibilities — but in peace, not in the aggressive self-hypnotizing style that sells us power lunches, power dressing, and the like. That style forces us to become willful, relying on willpower instead of being open to the inner attractiveness of the goal, which indeed "draws us."

From the point of view of someone seeking or offering Christian spiritual guidance, this human potential to anticipate with hope is a particularly important one to nurture. The structure of biblical revelation is a rich structure of memory, but even more radically it is a structure of anticipation (the memory is for the sake of the anticipation). It is in the nature of our faith to expect "a new heaven and a new earth" and to encounter One who says, "Now I am making the whole of creation new" (Rev. 21:5).

That has been the structure of this faith tradition since its earliest beginnings, in Abraham. Those called into it are called to taste the goodness of the Lord (as Ps. 34 puts it) so that they can learn to anticipate as yet invisible, as yet unimaginable goodness "in the fullness of time." This difficult lesson is learned "under the eyes of my enemies" (Ps. 23:5) — in the middle of conflict, ambiguity, and very dim light. The path is one of steadfast hope for "realities that at present remain unseen" (Heb. 11:1) — hope that is "firm" because "the One who made the promise is faithful" (Heb. 10:24). Thus, our built-in human powers of anticipation get "stretched" toward their transcendent pole by the shape of life in this faith tradition.[27]

The Interpretive Stance of a Spiritual Guide

So far in this chapter we have been implying that a spiritual guide's view of the human person as spirit includes recognition of the given-in-creation powers of cognition, imagination, memory, and anticipation.[28] Because the human person is multidimensional or many-layered, all these powers can work on more than one level. And a guide or counselor or therapist can try to be helpful to the person perhaps only on one level (the vital-functional), if that is the only level the counselor cares about. Or perhaps on two levels, if the counselor is respectful of the transcendent powers of the human person as well as the vital-functional energies.

If we aspire to be a spiritual guide, then we are aspiring to be helpful to seekers also on a third level: in the depth dimension of the spiritual or pneumatic self, whose origin and goal is God. In fact, that is the heart of our task.

One consequence of living in our secular and psychological century is that most people are barely aware, or not aware at all, that there is a spiritual or pneumatic self to be uncovered and strengthened. But most people are vividly aware of the other layers of the self and of the work that can be done to move toward health or effectiveness on those layers. We read about all of that, in books and magazines or in news reports, from our youth. In our culture, psychiatrists and psychologists and other mental health workers are considered quite indispensable. What they do is seen as exciting. It filters through to school systems, management training programs, sales training, all kinds of self-improvement books, innumerable seminars and workshops, and into popular fiction on film or in print. It is, if anything, rather too visible.

By contrast, the specific service that a spiritual guide has to offer is practically invisible. At least, it is invisible within the terms of the current secular culture. Even if we are attracted to it (as a seeker or as a potential guide), it is hard for us *to see what it is*.

The rest of this chapter will try to talk about what it is, and what it is not.

True self-knowledge is of the self as uniquely called by Another. It is a recollected, prayerful (albeit limited) awareness of one's entire life project, of all one's potential for loving, creating, and achieving in the light of its mysterious Trinitarian horizon.

It is good to discover one's coping patterns, defense mechanisms, and other psychological traits. But the disclosure of those traits may leave me quite unaware of the depth dimension of self and situation, of that spiritual or pneumatic self whose origin and object is God. In other words, I may through diligent reflection get back in touch with the bio-spiritual in-built tendencies of my vital feelings. I may know how my heart tends to orient itself toward, away from, against, or simply with what is other. I may discover something about the ways I tend to prefer using my mind and about my fruitful or deficient styles of imagining, remembering, or anticipating. I may even have a handle on the natural willful, will-less, or willing stance of my heart. It is possible, however, that with all this self-knowledge I may still be living in ignorance of *myself in relation to transcendent Mystery*.

The heart of Christian spirituality (and therefore of Christian anthropology) lies not in feelings nor even in knowledge about feelings. Neither temperament nor even character comes first here. Rather, the uniqueness of the human person lies, for faith, in the fact that the whole person has been created, redeemed, and destined to live forever in union with a divine Other.[29]

This call is personal, and it is transcendent. It is not to be confused with the many different challenges and situations it gets embodied in during the varied course of a person's life.[30] This call is unique, it is one call, and it "returns" at different stages of a person's growth. It is the call that Jesus was always responding to as he sought throughout the course of his life to do the will of his Father.

The living out (or ignoring) of personal call always takes place in an ordinary, messy, limited, and historically shaped situation, more accurately, in a series of such situations. We could get endlessly fascinated with the colorful space-and-time features of all those situations, with the blocks and challenges each one presents. But as a spiritual seeker or spiritual guide, what we must long to become attuned to is — to use technical language — the pneumatic context that permeates both the field and the intending hearts living within it.[31]

When we look (in faith) and listen within that context of Holy Otherness, everything undergoes a change. What we notice about human persons changes, too. The uniquely sensitive and conscientious freedom of each heart is revealed as profoundly known and loved into existence. It is revealed as fallible and weak and wounded, yes, yet redeemed and oriented toward a destiny of abundant life and love. Male or female, "slave or free," aware or unaware of this universal call to participation, all human beings are called to become far more than they can imagine. Eye has not seen, nor ear heard, nor has it entered into the human heart to know what awaits those who freely respond to this calling love (1 Cor. 2:9).

Becoming and remaining in touch with this divine inner direction of our life is not at all easy. Most of us are more developed on other levels of the perceiving heart, not on this pneumatic level. Although there is in every human heart a primordial orientation toward union with God — one that is "given" in the creation of that person — we don't *feel* that already-there orientation. Coming to discern it, in any kind of reliable way, is a work of faith that takes a very long time and that goes through many stages.

Spiritual guides in the past, in our faith tradition, took it for granted that the soul's spiritual journey must go through the stages of purgation, illumination, and union. That three-stage language may make us somewhat uncomfortable today, but it recognizes realities that every spiritual seeker encounters. It recognizes that in everyone's heart and life, there is much that is not in harmony with the person's true and unique calling by God. Parting with all those things is generally painful, even while it is liberating. It also recognizes that the human self that emerges, through trial and error and choice, needs more than the wisdom of experience; the human spirit needs illumination by the Holy Spirit of God, on the way toward union with God.

That old language of the purgative, the illuminative, and the unitive way also leaves room for the various kinds of struggle and resistance spiritual seekers go through on their route. Sin is as multilayered as we are. At each stage of "progress," our sinful tendencies find ways to isolate us from our true relatedness to the cosmos, to one another, and to God.

Trouble at the Root of Our Being

The Christian idea of sin is somewhat in eclipse at the moment. Many people have experienced the churches' emphasis on fallenness as placing an overemphasis on sin and guilt. So there is a backlash against that language in the tradition.

On the other hand, I doubt if there is a human being anywhere who has not at some time identified with Paul's complaint in Romans: "I do not do what I want to do but what I hate. . . . the desire to do right is there, but not the power. What happens is that I do, not the good I will to do, but the evil I do not intend" (Rom. 7:15–19).

Paul Ricoeur, in *Fallible Man*, speaks of a "secret rift" in our nature, a fissure in the human intending heart.[32] Yet in the midst of that "sadness of the finite," we continue to be a hunger for the infinite — for "the joy of yes," as Ricoeur puts it.

The biblical images of sin suggest that since "the Fall," human beings are inclined to live in forgetfulness of who we truly are. We tend to develop a false self, a counterfeit of the deeply buried image of God (or Christ-form) that remains in the depths of our souls. Each of us grows up imprisoned in this false self. The false self can be understood in many ways. From one point of view, the false self is always a kind of pride that keeps us preoccupied with self (as psychologists might say, with narcissistic defensive needs and drives for power and control). The false self steers us toward a preference for living in illusion, denying the split between what we are (a unique mixture of authentic spiritual presence and inauthenticity, or refusal of grace) and the ideal self of our own making. It is this denial of our actual self that prevents us from living a spiritual life. Because of it we can deny what we most deeply long for in terms of our divine life call, and we can render unconscious what we wish to ignore about ourselves.[33]

That makes for captivity of the energies of the soul that could be flowing freely in tune with the larger whole. We find ourselves blocked off from our own good intentions, stranded in the midst of untruth, pursuing impulses and ambitions that somehow "miss the mark" of what we originally wanted to be and to do. The abundance of life that might have been ours in fullness drains out in counter schemes and activities that only appear to be in harmony with who we are.

Sinfulness tends to structure our life by absolutizing our greedy, grasping, clinging, manipulating tendencies, and by setting us up for partial pseudosatisfactions that can bottle us up in a prison of our own making.

As we have seen, distorting or sinful patterns in the society we live in (our "second body") can warp our human development. But as spirit, we can never be totally determined by our situation. We are always somewhat free even in the midst of a sinful situation. What does us in, frequently, is that the dehumanizing attitudes built into our sinful society are paralleled by our own personal dissonant aspirations and impulses. Human persons give form to, as well as receive form from, their culture. We are free to make a move. It is sin that isolates us from dialogue with others and with the Mystery and that locks us into the pretense of self-sufficiency.

Spiritual guidance must aim first of all at gently acknowledging the vulnerability of all human beings, the knowing and unknowing complicity with the destructive sinful principle that so often succeeds in counterforming our life. We all need compassion, both for ourselves and for others, as we attempt to wake up from the torpor and the blindness that make our hearts sluggish.

Sluggish hearts need to be awakened from sin-induced sleep. Persons living in a world that represses and denies such knowledge need to learn about the spiritual capacity and destiny that is theirs. Spiritual guidance begins with this awakening. It is a particular kind of consciousness-raising. It aims to help people pay attention to what is happening in their ongoing dialogue with all aspects of their actual situation, in the light of a peculiarly full hope. Most of us waste energy in striving to make ourselves the center of the universe, in anxiously closing ourselves off from unpredictable "otherness" through fearful security measures, and by building walls of pride between ourselves and others, ourselves and God. With the liberating awareness that can come from spiritual guidance, it is possible to retrieve both time and energy for fruitful investment in deeds of love and commitment.

True spiritual life begins in awareness of our weakness, of the inner and outer chaos that situates us in what early Christian writers called "the land of unlikeness."[34] Although our personal dialogue with reality is unceasing, it often fails to be an honest, open dialogue. Thus it can tend to be a deformative dialogue with reality, a process of self-deception, most of which happens outside our conscious awareness. That is why we sometimes need another person, an objective outsider, to help us raise these tensions within our divided self to focal consciousness. Only then are we free to choose an alternative course. Spiritual guides in all great religions, East and West, have throughout the centuries seen this task of helping persons to reach accurate self-knowledge — in their actual, broken circumstances of family, work, and society — as their central responsibility.

No human being, no matter how skilled in co-listening to the life of another, can deliver fellow human beings from their captivity to pride and selfishness. As Paul insists, it is only Christ Jesus who can save us from our sinfulness. However, an alert spiritual guide, familiar with the typical dynamics of sin and its effects on the human spirit, may be able to spot the unique sinful patterns of the dialogue with reality in a man or woman as they show up in particular empirical expressions.

For example, let us imagine a well-meaning idealistic Christian from the West — let's call her Lucy — who has heard from Scripture that she is called to be holy, but has inherited mostly privatistic and pious images of what holiness is all about. Lucy may privately decide to cultivate "a spiritual life," without knowing much about her baptismal invitation to participate in the larger Trinitarian life that runs through the whole of created reality. She will gradually begin to totalize the dynamics that belong to spiritual living. She will perhaps isolate herself from several other polarities of her life field — perhaps from all of them. This could mean cutting herself off from her own vital-functional body, from the presence of other (presumably less spiritual) people, from her work and family and recreational interests, or from the energies of her society and culture. Lucy will build an idealized "spiritual" image of herself and of her life. If she is single-minded and determined, that image might come to possess her. It will drain energy away from all the other dimensions of life and make her a "holy floater," not seriously connected with real-life people and ordinary, life-sustaining events.

Poor old Lucy. By now she is stuck in spiritual egoism, whose roots lie deeper than the scope of psychological analysis. She has an exalted need for control and dominance, and she can be freed from her growing pride only if she is awakened from her protective idealizing dreams to the falseness and imbalance of this counterfeit version of transcendent aspiration. She needs to discover that the demands of committed love are not confined to the interior dimension, but must overflow into the interpersonal and social spheres as well. Lucy needs a good spiritual guide.

When a person begins to place exaggerated emphasis on any one polarity of the life field (in Lucy's case, the "intra" pole) or on any one dimension of the human heart (even if it is the transcendent dimension), reformation can take place only when there is an accepting return to the real self as a whole in all its dimensions. To overcome a mistaken notion of love that ignores the reality of otherness, people need to learn how to live in more or less consistent interaction with *all* the people, events, and things of their life field. Then there will be less danger that sin and egocentricity will be able to shrink a human life, walling it off into one patterned set of responses. *All* of our life is the gift of God — not only those parts of it we can control and predict by rigid acts of will.

Sin, by and large, is love gone wrong. An insightful book on that theme was written in 1978, not by a theologian but by a journalist, Henry Fairlie, whose book is called *The Seven Deadly Sins Today*.[35] Fairlie looks at the personal and social results of pride, envy, anger, sloth, avarice, gluttony, and lust, seeing them all as disorders of love and of the sense of belonging that is frequently missing from our collective experience of life and justice in society. Yet each of us retains a personal drive to bestow love. Fairlie concludes that unless this love is informed by a concern for the whole — "for the long travail of the human race, and at last for the unknowable wonder and mystery of the created universe" — we cannot hope to set our egocentric loves in order.

Spiritual guides tend to agree with Fairlie. Real love invites the heart's gaze outward into all of life, as well as inward into the depths of one's soul. Here, too, openness to our intentional wholeness includes free acceptance of undenied defects and limitations, as well as attention to the unique glory to which the Mystery calls us. Settling for less than the whole, and staking out a turf that excludes parts of reality, is always a style of sinfulness. It is a willful attempt to control the Mystery, to use faith to accomplish one's own aims instead of allowing oneself to be used by the Mystery to accomplish its aims in "ways that are not our ways" (Isa. 55:8), by trusting a wisdom that is not our own.

Blocks to our growth are often associated with that powerful human drive which is the search for security.[36] Self-preservation makes us want to be in control of all the unpredictable otherness that is not ourselves. Some of us (like our fictional Lucy) flee large parts of reality and hunker down in the absolutized self, finding our security in a sort of transcendent spiritualism. But there are many other escape routes. Some of us flee for security into a life of mere sociality, making contacts and using others to take care of all needs for self-esteem and power. Others of us flee into addictive overabsorption in work or family, or even recreation. Even religion can become a consumerized substitute for encountering self or others at any depth. So, alas, can social concern; we can become totally absorbed in the larger societal picture, with its issues and causes and ideologies — and end up fixated in a social image that has become another evasion of the varied demands of an incarnated commitment.

In all these ways, and more, we can pattern a refusal to live the fullness of the life that is offered to us. Of course, it's not all our fault. Our parents weren't perfect, our job is dehumanizing, our education force-fed us on all the illusions of our society. But we remain alive and free, and our responsibility begins with us. As Menninger says, realistic acknowledgment of personal sin provides us with "the only hopeful view." Otherwise there can be no guilt, and thus no repentance nor forgiveness: no joyful re-entry into loving solidarity with others and with the Other.

Guilt, as this generation knows very well, can certainly be neurotic.

It can be an illusion-filled, paralyzing form of anxiety. But spiritual guides can help us move out of illusory guilt and toward a kind of transcendent conscience that can experience genuinely enlightening, spiritual guilt. This guilt is a kind of regret for not living to one's deepest potential. It opens a person to discovering a new transcendent direction for the future. It sharpens our appetite for learning to love more fully in the actual field of our concrete life. It opens the ears of our heart to the message embodied in the events we have lived through. True guilt is a kind of light in the midst of weakness; far from being rigidity or self-hate, it walks hand in hand with hope.[37]

What the Spiritual Guide Has to Offer

The type of listening we do as spiritual guides depends on what we believe is there to be heard. That is why I care about our "theoretical anthropology," as well as about our sense of what the revealed Tradition is saying.[38] Listening is the major form our ministry takes.

A recollected type of listening helps people learn to focus. It helps them to pay attention to their feelings, to their deformative habits of mind and heart, and to the ways in which they may be blocking the healthy flow of energy in their lives. But all this is much more likely to aid spiritual aliveness if we as guides are also attuned to *listening for God's call in this person's life*. That call sounds in the seeker's deepest self. We do not have access to the person's deepest self. So we must listen for echoes or hints of that call in the concrete aspects of the person's life situation.

There are so many other less transcendent messages present in significant life events that everyone is liable to get caught up in them and miss the underlying confrontation with the spiritual direction of life that may be hidden in that particular event. What we as spiritual guides must be sensitive to is the spiritually formative and deformative potential in every happening.[39]

As a Christian guide, we are listening to a human person who is also a baptized member of the church. The significance of baptism matters to us. This person's life field has been incorporated into a larger, older field: that communion called church, that ancient gathering of the tribes of the Lord. Baptism has ritually linked the most profound depths of that person's being — her or his capacity for the infinite — *with* that Infinite. And it has mandated that person to become lovingly involved with "the joy and the hope, the grief and the anguish of the people of our time, especially of those who are poor or afflicted in any way."[40]

That is a particular, and blessed, kind of participation in reality. How do we take it seriously in this seeker's life? Can we take it as seriously as we take the interpersonal questions, the insights and crises that define the other areas of concern that we share with this seeker?

As guides, we are looking for ways in which God's spirit is addressing the persons who come to us. More accurately, we are helping them to look for those ways. Therefore we share an interest not only in their times of prayer, but also in their work, their leisure, and their relationships with the friends, spouses, children, relatives, colleagues, and work partners and opponents in the various communities where they daily find themselves.[41]

Seekers find themselves daily not simply in their local communities, but wrapped around by the secular culture that dominates their continent. We, as guides, find ourselves in that spot too. As fellow-products of that culture (and, probably, fellow-dissenters from it), we need to develop some relevant skills both of cultural criticism and appreciation. We will be on the lookout for ways in which deformative thought patterns derived from the culture are doing people in. On the other hand, if we are encouraging the person to read some of the classic spiritual masters of the past, both of us will encounter there occasional images or patterns of thought that are jarring, even shocking, to the modern conscience. At those moments we might be more grateful for our brash, egalitarian, free-spirited cultural values.

There is another level that calls for alertness. Under almost any cultural sky, there are some neurotic tendencies that spiritually minded people seem more prone to than are less self-conscious people. For example, they are more likely to get caught up in idealizing tendencies that result from totalizing their capacity for transcendent aspiration.

Karen Horney's psychological work can help us understand how variations of this "comprehensive neurotic solution" can come to have a hold on deeply religious people.[42] Often they drive themselves too hard in order to please an inner voice that demands perfection. Often they push themselves away from being the person they actually are into some version of what they think they should be. Of course, they "should" be able to endure everything, to like everyone, to be unfailingly understanding, and always to be productive! "The tyranny of the shoulds," Karen Horney calls this state of mind.

If we find a spiritual seeker thinking this way and projecting that thinking on to self, on to authority figures (like their pastor, or superior, or the pope), or on to God, we might try to offer an alternative stance for the person to consider. Later on we will look at some other compulsions and fixations that typically block the minds or wills of spiritually minded people.[43]

And remember: don't hunt for neurotic or deformative patterns from the first conversation, or in the abstract, like some doctor checking for common communicable diseases. We are not out to prove a theory of what's wrong with (or right with) religious people. We are meeting someone concrete and unique. So encourage concrete, unique reflection. It is guided reflection on personally significant life events that can encourage us, as little else can, to examine our vocation to harmony with the divine Other.[44]

Chapter Five

CHALLENGES AND PRACTICES FOR TODAY'S SPIRITUAL GUIDES

W E live our lives today in a world of the most dizzying pluriformity. And we are challenged, as historical beings, to remain generously open to our whole context. Yet we also inherit deep and enduring norms and insights in the light of which we can choose to resist some of the more illusory trends in the culture around us. In their light we can also choose to move away from personal internal compulsions and fixations that often block the paths of spiritually minded people. Illusory ideas beckoning from outside, in the society; blocks rooted inside, in the heart: these are among the challenges faced by seeker and guide when they converse together.

New Spiritualities

It is ironic that this most secular of centuries has produced a whole range of new spiritualities. They are multiplying in confusing ways, in the absence of a strong doctrinal or critical dimension in our present culture. Some of the recent spiritual movements are cult-like new religions. Some are new ways of relating to traditional religions, particularly Christianity and Islam. Perhaps the biggest numerically is the amorphous but powerful movement known as New Age spirituality.

Though it is hard to say exactly how many North Americans believe in which parts of the New Age, this movement as a whole is growing steadily. New Age books, radio stations, magazines, crystals, candles, and health stores are still multiplying. It seems very attractive to big business: it has had impacts on management training, personnel programs, the stock market, even the military. Huge and expensive workshops are attended all over the country by people willing to pay big dollars to find out how to be whatever they want to be.

Along with believing that everyone and everything is God, New Age spirituality includes belief in astral travel, shamans, Lemurians, and tarot card readings. It is also alert to new thinking about nutrition and to preventive medicine, both of which combine with its sensitivity to the very important cultural development of ecological awareness. Its psychology tends to be Jungian, with an emphasis on the individual's intuition.

In all this we can recognize a vague connectedness with both Christianity and the major faiths of the East, plus pantheism and some sorcery, plus up-to-date sensitivity to new science. It is the mix that makes it confusing — and attractive at the same time.[1] In many ways it seems to resemble the gnostic movements that caused such tension and conflict in the first generations of Christianity. What is similar to gnosticism is the conviction of many New Agers that there is a secret knowledge of the mystery of life — a "gnosis" (wisdom) that provides a mysterious shortcut, for initiates only, to happiness and health.[2]

Some critics — not all of them from fundamentalist or orthodox Christian circles — are very worried about the New Age movement. One sees it as "a barometer of the disintegration of American culture. Dostoevsky said that anything is permissible if there is no God. But anything is permissible also if everything is God."[3]

If, as spiritual guides, we are trying to help someone who wants to be a committed Christian, then the images and ideas popularized by the New Age movement will be distinctly confusing. The New Age approach is not grounded in the incarnational and sacramental spirituality of the Bible. It is far from being able to deal with "dark nights" and with the struggle involved in opening oneself to the working of the Holy Spirit. The Christian search is centered on the knowledge of Jesus, crucified and risen, as God's incarnate message to humanity. Remember Paul's ardor on this point in his letter to the Corinthians (1 Cor. 2) where he wrestles with the gnostics of his time, speaking of a wisdom about God's intentions that is discernible only by mature believers who, under the leading of God's Holy Spirit, have begun to "have the mind of Christ."

Nevertheless, the New Age movement is an eloquent product of our own time and culture. It probably deserves the label of "pseudo-spiritualism," but it also has much to tell us — at least about our consumer culture and the needs of people in it. How do we help people to develop an appropriate critical consciousness in the face of this and so many other current phenomena? We can only strive to share formative insights that, in bringing us to a certain depth of self-knowledge, put a priority on the unique call of the Mystery. I remain convinced that to achieve this depth, we must be rooted in the essentials of one of the great faith and form traditions. They can provide us with inner transcendent/pneumatic standards that can help us appraise the relevancy to us personally of the huge variety of ethical and spiritual messages and lifestyles in the midst of which we live.

There is no way, after all, of not being involved with our own time. Spiritual life does not happen somewhere else; it happens here and now, within the intertwining presence that we are to others, to ourselves, and to God.

False and Compulsive Types of Attachment

In case this section on new religions has given the impression that spiritual guides are dealing most of the time with problems that come from novel or flawed religious ideas, let me set the record straight. Most of the time, the problems of spiritual seekers who come for guidance are the same old problems people have always had, including all the people who do not come for guidance. Human beings have defense mechanisms that make them evade the truth. They have addictions — some obvious, some subtle. They have memories with a great deal of psychic scar tissue wrapped around them. They have fears that cramp their ability to welcome the future. And people cling to all these things. Thus, the abundant life to which they are invited gets blocked. None of this is new. All of it provides the daily, normal challenges faced in the work of a spiritual guide.

Personal addictions, for example, can be understood, and even treated, on many levels. There are, obviously, many addiction counselors who are not spiritual guides.[4] At the same time, there are many who, due to the depth of spiritual insight to be found in burgeoning twelve-step programs throughout the country, find themselves having to consider addiction in its relation to the realm of spirituality and grace.[5] But when someone with an addiction has in fact come to a spiritual guide, then what is relevant is the deep underlying conflict between ego and divine call, between the self and God, of which the addiction is a part or a symptom.

In addictive clinging there is the same falseness, the same illusion and self-deception that we noticed earlier when we were talking about sin and thinking, for example, about poor old Lucy and her absolutizing of "spirituality."

On this more profound level of conflict — which often comprises the hidden agenda during initial guidance sessions — the spiritual guide may catch a glimpse of the distorted loving attachment to a false center that is keeping this particular seeker from honestly relating with himself or herself and to God.[6] The kind of attachment that is involved, and the kind of self-deception that protects it, varies very much according to the temperament of the person. Some seekers, like our fictional Lucy, are rigidly willful in their search for holiness. With some other people, guidance will involve a stripping away of a false receptivity and openness, a kind of will-less illusion that is also a dishonest attitude.

Obviously, the guidance of someone whose personality inclines them to a passive and at times sinful withdrawal from creative involvement in their own life and that of their society will call for a very different approach from the guidance of a more actively aggressive person.[7]

In my work as a guide with temperamentally different types of people, I have often remembered with amusement — and have found very useful — a simple description of four basic styles of self-protection, or mistaken self-images. The description was developed by the Jungian scholar Fritz Kunkel.[8] He portrayed four ego styles: compliant, compliant/aggressive, aggressive, and withdrawn. A "clinging vine" was the image chosen for the surface ego (or false self) of compliant people. People whose egocentric reactions tended toward a mix of compliance and aggression were "stars." More purely aggressive people got the label "Nero." As for the characteristically withdrawn folks, they were cartooned as "turtles."

Kunkel managed to link the cracking of whatever egoistic shell we might be encased in with a transformative letting go of that surface self for the sake of a fuller life. Jesus said cryptically that we must lose our life in order to save it. Kunkel helped me see that we have to lose what seems to be life (but is only the surface life of the false self) in order to really live.

Since the time I stumbled upon Kunkel, I have studied phenomenology and psychology and formative spirituality, and I have acquired a somewhat more sophisticated understanding not only of these more or less typical orientations of the heart, but also of the probable ways in which they reflect a human person's consciousness of himself or herself in relation to their world. Aggressive people (Neros, according to Kunkel) are inclined to see themselves as bigger and stronger than the people, events, and things they confront in their life field. Thus, they will naturally tend to move against, taking the offensive in encounters. Less confident, more dependent "clinging" types will tend to feel that they must adjust to the world. These bridge builders will naturally move toward rather than against other people. They will be inclined to accept events and things as they are, complying for the sake of agreement rather than asserting their right to differ. "Stars" could be expected to combine aggressive and compliant modes in a constant striving to retain the limelight no matter what the cost. On the other hand, there are many folks who see themselves as smaller than the surrounding world of others, events, and things. Usually on the defensive, the "turtles" of Kunkel's ego-typography tend to move away, to withdraw from encounters, be they human or divine. What these more or less typical ways of perceiving reality have in common is that generally they give a somewhat false picture of the way things are. They also reflect a more or less sinful sense of self in relation to what is not oneself. They reflect a consciousness that is split off from its life field, that sees itself as isolated from the flow of divine energy available in the forming universe.

When rigidified into closed patterns of thinking, feeling, and behaving, these partial and deformative orientations of the heart point directly to some of the sinful dispositions we have been trying to understand. They also indicate why being sinfully disposed to aspects of our life field impels us in the egoism of isolated pride to attempt to attain fulfillment and salvation by our own efforts and in tune with our individual sinful profile, rather than entrust ourselves to the divine Other whose sustaining presence pervades and carries everything that is.

A favorite tool among spiritual guides these days is the recently rediscovered Sufi system of self-enlightenment known as the *Enneagram*.[9] Based on the intuitive wisdom of Islamic mysticism, the Enneagram is a two-thousand-year-old nine-point method for uncovering one's compulsive attraction to certain typical false attitudes of mind, instinct, and heart. Currently it is being used in spiritual retreats and guidance situations throughout the world. The thinking behind the Enneagram is clear on the essential goodness of the core self and on the strength to be derived from its participation in the wholeness that is God; but what it points to, by means of a simple circular diagram, is a set of nine one-sided possibilities that occur when these strengths are exaggerated. Each of the possibilities is based in something good and true — a participation in the wisdom of God, for example, or in the originality of God. But when a human personality becomes over-identified with any one of these strengths, the identification takes on the character of a driving force or compulsion that orients the person's entire life. It is the old situation of a good attraction gone out of balance, so that now it is a disordered passion. The Enneagram shows that if a person's passionate love for some limited value becomes an absolute for the personality, it results in a defensive strategy that then becomes a compulsion.

Once we have a compulsion, we are programmed. Even though we chose this coping mechanism originally (more or less consciously, and perhaps extremely early in life), and even though it functions as a protective security for us, it now makes us unfree. It now shrinks and distorts the fully alive woman or man we are called to be by the Mystery. The nine compulsive modes of the Enneagram are sin-types. They reflect the selfish side of oneself, seeking self-defense and self-salvation, resisting the transforming power of God's freedom. Or, to use Enneagram language, they are distortions of God's ninefold goodness, love, efficaciousness, originality, wisdom, faithfulness, joyfulness, power, and peace.

The Myers-Briggs Typology Indicator[10] and the Enneagram describe sets of personality preferences and patterns that overlap with one another. Both of them relate to the basic givens of each person's preformative inheritance. Both are currently very popular in retreat centers. By themselves, they have nothing in particular to do with faith; they can be just as useful in a secular setting, perhaps in a personnel management workshop. But because of the easily grasped way in which these two formulas describe typical ways in which the functioning of our own ego tends to limit us, they can perhaps aid a person who is beginning to probe the question of why the good gifts of the Spirit are not coming to fruition in his or her life. They may point to some needed detachments. They may even help us (in a faith context) move away from reliance on our own strategies and resources to a sense of our need for salvation.[11]

Spiritual seekers need to uncover their underlying conflicts — of egoism vs. altruism, of addictive openness vs. true receptivity, and so on. That is a step on the way to confronting the essence of sin, which lies not in the compulsions of the presenting problems, but in the underlying conflict of self vs. God that they reflect.

Guides must see and understand that this last conflict is the focus of the shift that needs to be made. An experienced guide knows that in order to accept the detachments implied in any new way of living, the person's sluggish heart with its distorted ways of apprehending and appraising will have to undergo a radical change.

In the Gospel of Matthew, after Jesus had told the parable of the sower who went out to sow seed, the disciples asked Jesus why he spoke in parables. Jesus reached back to an ancient cry of Isaiah to answer their question. The words are about listening, but not understanding; seeing and seeing again, but not perceiving. "For the heart of this nation has grown coarse...and they have shut their eyes, for fear they should see with their eyes, hear with their ears, understand with their heart..." (Matt. 13:4–23).

It is very gradually that people become ready to change the way they look and listen. It is very slowly that they approach readiness for a shift in their life field, especially if that shift demands detachment. Spiritual appraisal that opens the way for reformation emerges only gradually.

Jesus then goes on to interpret the parable for his disciples. No matter how much of the seed is lost, there is always enough good soil too. There is always the possibility of a healing shift to fruitfulness: thirty-, sixty-, or a hundredfold. Jesus says: "Mark well the parable of the sower."

Jesus might have been speaking to spiritual guides who make themselves available as co-discerners of the presence of Mystery in the lives of fellow humans. Together guide and seeker appraise what has to die in order that there will be liberation from isolated striving and fragmenting addiction. Appropriate asceticism is one fruit of this careful appraisal of one's entire life field.

Particularly in dealing with sin, guides can never absolutize any product of human effort, such as the Enneagram test. There are many, many ways in which God's Spirit can touch and enlighten a cramped or drugged conscience. Salvation is a gift found only in the Source of all life. However, at moments of dealing with people's illusory and compulsive modes of attachment, some spiritual guides are finding tools like the Enneagram very useful indeed.

Memory: Formative and Deformative

Memory enables us to participate in the mystery of our spiritual journey by allowing the past to gain access to the present. All our experiences, great or small, have left some mark on our present personality. We are much more aware than we used to be of the retentive power of our whole being, which stores (and is affected by) far more experience than there is room for in our conscious memory.[12] Now that we all handle microchip technology and have learned something of the staggering "memory bank" capacities of computers, we are acquiring new paradigms for expressing the sheer hugeness of the human capacity for memory.

One of the challenges presented by this fascinating human capacity for remembering the past lies precisely in its power to fascinate, and to lure both guide and person guided away from their concentrated attention to the present moment with all its conflicts and ambiguities, to go in search of a past that may or may not explain them. The genius and daring of the therapeutic enterprise usually entails a detailed and often painful assessment of past happenings in order that positive as well as negative memories may be brought to the surface of consciousness and dealt with in the course of the therapeutic process.

Undoubtedly this powerful human reality has to be taken into account in spiritual guidance as well. However, the center of concern in spiritual guidance is not the past as such. Spiritual seekers and those who guide them are interested rather in life as it is unfolding in the present and as it may unfold in the future. Certainly this involves interest in how one's past contributes to and forms one's present. But an exhaustive exploration of the details of a person's remembered and unremembered history can never be central to the endeavor we have been describing as spiritual guidance.[13]

As we saw with imagination and anticipation, there are two layers operating in memory also. Bodily/functional memory refers to the ability of the organism to store information learned and to make that information available for behavior in the present. Thus we "remember" how to walk, how to eat, how to ski or type, and how to negotiate social rituals.[14] Bodily/ functional memory can also embed us in bad habits of eating, or poor posture, or two-finger typing — or habits of avoiding other people because early experience warns us that people are dangerous. Thus, when children are very little, conscientious parents try hard to lay down good traces in this powerful layer of bodily/functional memory.[15]

This layer of memory is programmable and reprogrammable by various behavioral techniques. It is fascinatingly "bodily"; it can be triggered by taste or smell, and there are competing theories, ranging from psychoanalysis to "Rolfing," about where/how our bodies "store" all this. Memory on this level is crucial for one's sense of self-continuity, and for the myriad routine skills of daily life.[16]

The second memory layer, one's capacity for transcendent memory, is the one that can move beyond mere embeddedness. One of the fundamental human powers is to create a wider context, a new "horizon," in which everything that is remembered comes to exist in a new way. The results of this power can be awesome — like a re-creation of a person's whole history and origins.

Recalling that the figure gets its meaning from the larger ground,[17] we can understand the subjective nature of our present memory of past happenings. Everything from the past is being co-formed and reconstituted by appearing against the ground of present convictions, feelings, values, and other subjective circumstances.

Family systems practitioners, for example, are finding that even identical twins brought up in the same family often do not remember early family life in the same way. Or as a friend of mine remarked to one of her brothers at a family reunion after they had recalled an incident from their childhood in radically dissimilar ways, "What the hell family were you brought up in anyway?" We are seeing here the power of the human spirit to go beyond the cold facts of the past, and to rearrange aspects of the past, giving them new meaning in a new context.

Isn't this what the process of psychotherapy is based on? The patient brings out all her or his old bitter memories, and the therapist helps him or her to rearrange and relativize their meaning and even their deformative impact.

In spiritual guidance also, it may become apparent that a person has turned one bad experience from the past into an absolute. One unhappy incident with a representative of organized religion, a priest or minister, for example, may have left this person with an absolutized unwillingness to ever darken a church door again, or even worse, to avoid any openness in their hearts or lives for the Transcendent Mystery that the offending person was supposed to represent. A long past experience of an injustice done or of violence shown by an authority figure can be absolutized in memory and end up dominating a person's entire present life, making that person bitter and unforgiving, unable to get on with the future. Spiritual guides also have to know about the healing power of transcendent memory to dialogue with negative thoughts about the past. Lives can be moved beyond past bitterness through consciousness that although the past as past is unchangeable, the past as remembered can be changed. We need not be victims of negative memories, especially in light of our freedom to choose an attitude toward them. The providential meaningfulness of past events can always be rediscovered within one's present relation to the Mystery.[18] However, we are also always free to cling to bitter memories, grudges, and resentments, and without wise guidance this may be the life-constricting choice that many of our contemporaries have chosen to make.

Guides have to realize that memory can have a wonderfully grounding effect on people's feeling about their life journey. It can also have a disintegrative and uprooting effect, especially if there is no recognition of the transcendent possibility of memory as a present means of participating in the Mystery.

In the liturgical actions of the great spiritual traditions, we find a ritualization of the group's communal memory, of its sense of itself as a people with a destiny. If a community loses a lived sense of the meaning of its rituals, it is losing its roots. Its grasp of its covenant history — of where the community has been and where it is going — is slipping.

This issue of rootedness is important for everyone. In 1976, when the TV series "Roots" captured the imagination of so many in America, wasn't it partly because people in a time of turmoil were looking for a deeper contact with reality, a sense of perspective and continuity? To remember our roots gives us a sense of passing on something valuable and of raising a new generation who will remember.

That is an exceedingly big issue for civilization. But remembering is a very important dimension of prayer as well. A prayerful lifestyle is, in part, a lifestyle of remembering: of never forgetting the blessings that have been given, never forgetting what is happening all around us in the cosmos and in the hearts of people, never forgetting the mysterious "names" of God or our own blessed identity. In Christian continuity, that is why the liturgy of the hours, the "divine office," weaves the ancient biblical psalms into the present texture of life every single day. Just as did the first singers of Israel, we taste the events of each day through the remembered sweetness of the first saving acts of God on behalf of the ancient people whose present we are. We read the Gospel every day too, dipping in to the originating memory of the Christian community. In the Eucharist, we enter the great Remembering — the *anamnesis*, our ancestors called it — which brings into the present the long-ago self-gift of Jesus Christ, so that it can now include us. In all these ways we re-member the Body of Christ.[19]

The Mystery has always been present. Appreciation of the presence of Mystery is one of the major factors in the continuity of human experience. This is why spiritual guides recommend meditative reading of the classics of the faith tradition.[20] These, beginning with the Gospels for a Christian, are the collective memory of the believing, seeking community. In the Christian tradition, for example, guides down through the ages like Cassian, Gregory, Athanasius, Basil, Benedict, Catherine, Francis, Eckhart, Juliana, Ignatius, Teresa and John, and Thérèse have opened up reality in ways that have been proved by time and can enrich individual memories in a profound sense.

Keeping Track of the Journey by Writing

Keeping a spiritual journal is a common method of helping both seeker and guide to tap in to the possible benefits of the guidance encounter.[21] Journals often help people to grow in an incarnational approach to self-knowledge. Journal writing respects what is actually happening in a person's daily life; it takes the specific and concrete very seriously. At the same time, writing a journal can be an exercise in transcendent memory. It can help a person toward a transformed — even revolutionized — sense of the meaning of his or her life.

Reflective rereading of one's journal entries from the past week or month or year can be helpful in coming to a tentative appraisal of the general direction of one's life. It can also aid in getting a handle on one's actual priorities for using life time and energy. In a period of crisis journal entries can sometimes remind one of the flavor, the actual taste of one's life questions and commitments as they were occurring in the concrete. Often careful reading will reveal the core patterns and larger meaning in terms of the dynamic movement of the writer's life.

Both practitioners of the Ignatian method of discernment, who emphasize the significance of personal history in decision making, and the promoters of the rather complex Progoff method of journal keeping — a method that sees the journal as an instrument of awareness of the organic unity of one's life — exhibit a concern for the incarnational approach to self-knowledge.[22] In neither type of journaling are the writers allowed to float beyond the concrete circumstances of their daily life. Nor are they allowed to remain on the level of the surface self, to concentrate on the social and communal roles they play, which may at times obscure the deepest self. Having a written record of what actually was happening on both the good and the bad days can cure us of our somewhat illusory nostalgia for the "good old days" as well as of our pessimistic assessment that "nothing good has ever happened to me." Also when there is no one around to talk things out with, furious scribbling in one's journal can be a way of taking distance from a distasteful incident or misunderstanding, working it through on paper and perhaps getting a new perspective on ourselves and on the other person who was the cause of our distress.

When people sit down to write about the day or about the past year, or even about their whole past life, they usually remember and dwell on what is of personal significance for them. It is a different kind of effort from, say, writing an autobiography for posterity, or for any other audience that needs to be wooed and captured. Then we will write with one eye on prospective readers. The temptation to make ourselves look good will present itself under all kinds of respectable literary guises. Well, writing a spiritual journal is not like that (or shouldn't be). One must write it, not for an audience — and not for one's spiritual guide — but for oneself, with God. It is meant only to help the journal-keeper grow in self-insight, to face sometimes painful and upsetting insights of self-discovery, and eventually to recognize points of interior conflict and tension. It is not meant to be read by an audience who will be impressed by its disclosures.

But alas, nothing is guaranteed. The "audience" dynamic can also creep in during the guidance interview. When it does, it can have an influence on what is remembered and what is talked about there as well.

Processing a Critical Point

As the population continues to grow older, there is more demand for help in facing the second half of life. In the section on "The Classic Crisis: Mid-Life Transition," I noted that if nothing else in life has made them stop and think, the event of this life transition brings most men and women into a more or less conscious reflection on how their life journey has unfolded so far.[23] Forced by the circumstances usually accompanying this life stage, both men and women have perhaps for the first time in their lives to look at the physical and psychological certainties or lifestyle or religious symbols that up until this point have formed the basis for their committed adult lives. Many seek guidance at this point for either panic or depression. Finding themselves feeling overemotional or not emotional enough, perhaps questioning the comfortable roles that have been theirs and that they are no longer at home with, they tend to experience an enormous sense of having failed in the various committed roles they have taken on. There is at mid-life, especially, a sense that nothing I've done has been good enough. One is tempted to reason thus: all the attempts I made to be loving, to serve others, to be a good parent or teacher or caregiver have been mediocre, even when other people seem to think I've done all right and even congratulate me on my success. At mid-age, I know better. My anxious feelings of guilt about past failures and uncertainty about the future seem very real to me. I feel very alone in all this, tired from all the time and energy I have wasted on all sorts of commitments that do not seem to have come to much. I'm at the end of my rope. Now may be my last chance for sexual fulfillment. I guess it's now or never to make up my mind about staying or leaving my commitment. God seems very far away; the sort of mediocre prayer life I thought was mine has just vanished. It is really sad to feel like this, to feel everything I counted on just slipping away.

To feel like this, one need not be facing either a mid-life or mid-commitment crisis. Similar negatively oriented musings will be typical of many who seek guidance, because they have fallen into a self-centered despair about their ability to cope with certain aspects or even with the whole of their lives and relationships. A few years earlier, this person may have been at the height of his or her powers, proud possessor of all the answers and pragmatically in charge of his or her own life. The lives of others, their children, less efficient fellow workers, the people they served, and even the spouses to whom they were committed may have been under their control as well. Functional mind now as then impels them to continue calling the moves, taking charge, doing something, anything, to get the situation back under control. Thus, we find that the mentality described here tempts some to retreat into the past for a better understanding of what has gone wrong, of why they are so unhappy with themselves and their lives. Others just continue to try harder, moving and thinking in a willful, rationalistic mode that alienates from self, from others, and from God, controlled now as in the past by familiar but no less tyrannical "shoulds." Still others choose to live out of anxiety-producing ideas like "The others are out to do me in"; "Life is just too much for me"; "I am so needed by everybody...they'll tear me apart"; or "I'll never get anywhere...there's nothing left to hope for."

In the discussion in chapter 3 of the spiritual challenge embedded in the mid-life transition, I characterized it as a life crisis calling for a "turn to transcendence." This is true. The indicated turn does involve an opening of the self to the pneumatic dimension, to the Holy Spirit. It will also involve the inner dispositions and outer relaxing recommended in the chapters that follow.[24] Here

I want to mention one tool used by today's guides to help these and other seemingly trapped human beings to reflect on and perhaps seek help in modifying the typical ways they tend to process reality. I am speaking of the Myers-Briggs typology test, which, along with the Enneagram system for self-understanding, is performing a useful function in giving people an initial handle on how they tend to operate in their daily interactions with their world of people, events, and things.[25] A test based on Jungian personality types, this inventory is concerned with the way people naturally prefer to use their minds, with the way they tend to perceive and make judgments. Jung has noted that in each of us there are two fundamental complementary orientations, one directed toward outer reality (extraversion) and one directed toward inner reality (introversion). It seems that as a result of our genetic heritage, our psychic energy has a preformed disposition to flow more freely in one or the other direction. An extravert's energy flows more easily and naturally toward the outer world of people, events, and things, while the introvert's energy is more naturally drawn to the inner world of concepts and ideas.

Jung also indicates two modes of the functional mind — sensing and intuition. Through our five senses we perceive the reality around us directly, while by adding associations and ideas from the infraconscious, intuition apprehends the same reality by preferring to go beneath the apparent obviousness of concrete here-and-now data to discover interrelationships and meaning.

In addition, thinking and feeling in the Jungian system represent two complementary ways of coming to conclusions and making decisions about what we perceive. Thinking is a logical process aimed at objective conclusions, while feeling is a subjective appreciation seeking a personal evaluation: do I like this or not?

Finally, perceiving and judging are seen by Jung as two complementary meta-preferences. People who prefer to perceive usually gather information by sensing or intuition, choosing to leave things open-ended, going with the flow and following things in their natural unfolding rather than coming too soon to closure. People who feel more comfortable with judging like to have things decided. They prefer to come to conclusions by thinking or feeling so they can direct the flow and thus determine how their lives will unfold themselves. A healthy person's life will exhibit a judicious balance between all these types and styles in relation to the actual situation.

In any communal situation, for example, there are bound to be opposites or at least some people who prefer to operate out of one definable orientation rather than the other. Things get even more complicated when the group members have come together to live out of a specific spiritual vision or ideal. Theoretically the vision will be shared by all, but in practice clashes are bound to occur, often without the members realizing why.

Take, for example, the counsels of poverty, chastity, and obedience assented to by members of many spiritually oriented groups. Extraverts in the group may well interpret simplicity or poverty as a mandate to share everything with others, while introverts will more likely perceive it as signalling the need for trusting dependence on God. As for the counsel regarding chaste love or celibacy, an extravert would understand it as showing love through availability, while an introvert will be inclined to see it as asking him or her to love God in and through making time for increased prayer in solitude. Finally, obedience will be seen by the extravert as a call to respond to the world's needs through service, while the introvert will be more likely to consider it first as asking him or her to live by attending to God's will and the promptings of the Holy Spirit.

If a community fails to perceive the truth in both points of view, if it limits itself to one articulation of the counsels and blocks the expression of the other, there are bound to be people left out. The ones left out may even feel compelled to leave the community, though in principle they continue to believe in the community's original spiritual vision.

To prevent such dismal complications, both groups and spiritual guides must come to a deeper appreciation of the plurality of styles out of which people tend to operate and to trust and even cherish the operational styles that differentiate human beings on the level of functional preference. However, this level of functional mind and will can never represent the whole possibility of the human heart. Nor do we reach the joy of community merely by understanding each other's thought processes and emotional functioning.

To arrive at joy in the mystery of each other — or, for that matter, joy in the mystery of my own created being — we must be able to open the nonfunctional, transcendent eyes and ears of the heart. As the wise fox said to the little prince in St. Exupery's delightful book, "It is only with the heart that one can see rightly. What is essential is invisible to the eye."[26] And it cannot be measured by a Myers-Briggs indicator, either.

It is a dangerous type of spiritual guidance that stops at the level of psychological information and pragmatic problem solving, leaving the person's transcendent capacity for participation in the Mystery unattended to and ignored.

As guides and as seekers, we are in need of a new set of eyes by which to view the world and to be moved in love to respond to what we see.

Guides and "Transference"

So far in this chapter, we have been thinking about problems, blockages, sinful patterns, and life challenges that persons seeking guidance can bring to the guidance session. Or we have been looking at practical techniques a guide might offer for a seeker's use in working through to greater light.

It is not at all the case, of course, that only the person guided has problems, blockages, sinful patterns, and life challenges. The guide has them too, in full measure.

The immediate guidance situation rests on an informal contract in which one person, the guide, agrees to co-listen for the messages from Invisible Otherness as they can be discerned in the life events of the person who comes for guidance.

There is plenty of static around the process of co-listening, lots of interference with the mysterious Message. Both co-listeners, the guide and the seeker, have things in them that will transmit noise, not signal. Obviously when two people come together in a more or less intimate and spiritually oriented encounter like guidance, each brings an appearing social self as well as an invisible preformed genetic inheritance, and a transcendent inheritance too. Like any other human meeting, it will be a meeting of entire social and cultural worlds. Their encounter will encompass their present feeling, functioning, and aspiring selves, plus two quite different sets of "givens" from the past, as well as unique personal hopes for the future.

One interesting challenge in this one-to-one contractual situation of the guidance interview is that of the possibility of transference and counter-transference.

To borrow psychological language for a moment: in a therapeutic exchange between client and therapist, psychoanalytic theory suggests that the client projects onto the listening therapist a distorted sense of that other's presence. The client "transfers" to the therapist the role of someone else, usually a significant other person from the client's past, and reacts toward the therapist as if she or he were that important childhood figure. This builds up many unrealistic reactions and expectations (both positive and negative) in the mind and heart of the client. These distorted responses have come to be labelled "transference reactions."

Therapists also (they had childhoods too) can harbor a build-up of interpersonal distortions. When a therapist responds inappropriately to his or her client, that reaction is labelled "countertransference."[27]

In the spiritual guidance enterprise, no attempt is made to foster these deformative patterns of thinking about other people. But it can happen that one or the other of the persons involved will unconsciously project a false role or an illusory responsiveness onto the fellow human being who is recounting (or listening to) the events and issues of her or his life story.

For example, a woman whose mother always gave her the impression that any mention of sexual feelings or issues was not allowed might seek spiritual guidance. Without her being aware of any self-censorship, she may never be able to raise with her spiritual guide (who happens to be a woman and a rather motherly person) any mention of the sexual difficulties she is experiencing as real obstacles in her spiritual and relational life. Her memory is selective, as everyone's is, more or less. It will never dare to recall such personally significant events before such an "audience." The negative preconscious fear that such exposure threatens can be strong enough to make her "forget to mention" these very central issues. That could be the case even when her conscious desire is to confront anything in her life that may be interfering in her relationship to others and to God.

Or the shoe could be on the other foot. If we, as guides, find ourselves between sessions spending a lot of time thinking about one particular person we are seeing, if we find ourselves in this person's presence trying to elicit praise or other positive remarks, if we worry that this person may terminate the relationship, if we dream frequently about this person, or if we try to intervene in her or his life outside the guidance session, we may be caught in what therapists call "countertransference." We may find ourselves with a strong desire to discuss this person with others. We may be preoccupied with her or him during leisure and free time. She or he may suddenly seem like the absolutely right person to ask for favors or for help with nonguidance matters. If things are thus, we might suspect that we are caught in a "positive countertransference." A negative countertransference is much more uncomfortable than that; consequently, we would probably spot it in ourselves more quickly!

If that happens, we might reflectively ask ourselves: "What chord is this person striking in me? What need, or insecurity, or anxiety in me is resulting in my giving him or her this power?"

The possibility for countertransference occurring in all guides, both male and female, provides reason enough for guides to be receiving ongoing spiritual guidance themselves. In addition, guides should ask for supervision, or at least consultation, with a colleague who can help sort out possible mixed motives that may surface in the guidance relationship.[28]

Guides Are Sinners, Ministers, and Co-Sufferers

We began this chapter by looking at false spiritualities, seductive new religions, and other popular ideas that the apostle Paul might consider as belonging to "the wisdom of this world." Later we looked at some deep and painful human problems — including sin, the most painful of all human problems. We went on to consider some minor practical tools that guides can sometimes usefully offer. But anyone who has ever drawn close to human suffering knows that useful techniques seem very puny in face of the ocean of human suffering and desire that we often meet in our work as guides.

For example, what are we to do, as guides, in the face of the challenge of idolatrous spirituality?

First of all, it helps to remember that discernment of true from false spirituality has been an awesome struggle all through Scripture — at least since the book of Job. (No, since the very first protest against "the idols of the nations" and the very first prophet who noticed that unjust Israelites could treat Yahweh exactly like an idol.) Such discernment has never been easy, and it has remained central to the task of spiritual direction during New Testament times, patristic times, the Middle Ages, and the post-Renaissance centuries. A reliable guide must attain a clear vision, an insight that can distinguish between reality and illusion and between spiritual paths that lead to maturity and wholeness, and those that lead to destruction and death.

To move toward vision like that, our discipline as guides must include contemplative enrichment of our own consciousness. Our own image of God must be freed from idolatry and from false images, not only of the living God but also of what an unaided human being is able to accomplish in the way of helping another toward relationship with this holy Otherness.

Our practice of solitude and reflection should lead us to a deeper insight, not only of the Transcendent Other but also of our solidarity with the anguish of our world. The interpretive stance of a spiritual guide must be able to deal not only with personal histories and social contexts, but also with issues of faith. A guide needs theological insights gained through study and also through deep, meditative brooding on the Word of God as mediated through her or his faith tradition.

If we do not have that, people may then receive only what they tend to demand: techniques geared toward self-salvation, formulas guaranteeing instant enlightenment. Many who think they want guidance actually only want inner pacification, isolation from the world around them and from their own deepest selves.

Guidance sessions are not always happy, harmonious times. They do not always feel useful or helpful or profitable. Our own helplessness to help will often be very painful to bear. Our fear of speaking certain kinds of truth, for fear of wounding a fragile human heart, might sometimes paralyze us. And sometimes we will simply not know what to think or what to do.

There are in fact any number of painful moments that may arise during the spiritual guidance session that are not covered in the classic texts on spiritual guidance. It is the rare guide who has not had to wrestle with his or her own confusion between neurotic strategies and apparent holiness. This becomes particularly agonizing when, for instance, religious people themselves feel that they are of worth to their community only insofar as they succeed in being a functioning member of the team; or when they as adult persons continue to use perfectionistic strategies developed during an unaffirmed childhood to win the approval of "mommy" boss or "daddy" supervisor. Strategies of excessive religiosity, being a peacemaker, becoming passive aggressive, or wallowing in self-pity may characterize the hidden agenda of many who come for spiritual guidance. They are hoping, of course, that guidance will cater to the false sense of security these strategies provide. Dispelling such illusions and mistaken assumptions about self, about God, about prayer and love and sin itself, helping a fellow human to let go of the fundamentally dishonest style that has served him or her from childhood and to give up the security measures that are sinfully cutting him or her off from the Mystery, comprise a few of the goals of Christian spiritual guidance. The process is never without its moments of struggle, as deeply entrenched patterns are revealed and self-knowledge opens onto hitherto unresolved conflicts and energy-draining neurotic claims.

At a certain point, we, as guides, may have to realize that we are no longer capable of helping a particular man or woman who is in the grip of severe inner conflicts. The time for competent referral will have arrived.[29] There are moments too when even competent referral is neither appropriate or sufficient. At such an impasse the guide has to trust that sometime later in this person's life, God will break open the "hardness of heart" in which the person is embedded. At such moments there is nothing "competent" a guide can do...except pray.

Chapter Six

A GUIDE'S VIEW
OF THE HUMAN JOURNEY

W E are moving gradually toward two central issues in spiritual guidance — toward conversion and appraisal — both of which signify that a person is well on the way to what St. Paul has labeled "spiritual maturity" (1 Cor. 2). It is clear that no one arrives at this phase of his or her spiritual life without first passing through what Paul refers to sometimes as the "newborn" phase and the phase of spiritual "youthfulness." Yet we know that these phases, although they might seem radically enmeshed in the chronological stages of human development are definitely not identical with them. We should not confuse the ages and stages of our outer history of chronological growth from childhood to old age with the spiritual unfolding of the inner intentionality of our hearts. On the other hand, it can be helpful for guides and those they guide to discover the possible interrelationship between spiritual, physical, and psychological unfolding as we move toward the recovery of the mystery hidden in God that is the goal of the spiritual journey of every human person in this life.

The lifelong attempt to recover the lost freedom to be one's deepest unique self, to transcend the level of mere ego functional mastery, and to fulfill one's deepest founding life call can be looked at in terms of five overlapping segments. We will begin with the foundations of human spiritual life. Then we will see how the youthful phase of relational and spiritual development go hand in hand as one begins to project one's dream of what his or her life might be. The source of many problems in the spiritual life can be linked to the succeeding stage of social responsibility and control when for some the need for change and conversion, for going beyond or transcending, may make itself felt as never before. A fourth section will bring us to an acknowledgment of the mature desire to reassess one's life and hand on what one has learned to the next generation. Finally, there will be a short section on relaxing and letting go — essential aspects of the spiritual journey of most adult men and women who grow up in contemporary North American culture and society.

Foundations of Personality

We begin with embodiment, with our being incarnated into the flesh of a vital human body. Courtesy of our parents, certainly, but also from the beginning we are inserted into and absorb a particular culture or form tradition. The "givens" of life, the biogenetic givenness of a basic body type with its resulting temperament inherited from preceding generations, and our embeddedness in a "second body" including a certain historical time, a certain geographical space, and a particular conglomeration of customs and traditions (the way "we" do things) have a lasting impact on our personality. So do our family or tribe or ethnic group that situates us in a defined cultural, geographic, and economic "place." Together these factors combine to form in us a certain mood, a felt sense about The Way Things Are.

From infancy, then, we are inclined to have absorbed generally positive or negative feelings about the universe into which we have been born — a powerful sense of the presence or absence of the spiritual dimension of life. This originating sense of the mystery that we pick up from the group or community around us tends to remain with us for the rest of our lives, even though there are myriad changes and revisions in the course of that life. Even before we have much conscious choice, we were focused on certain ways of viewing reality, on certain ways of channeling our life energy, on certain motivating thoughts, emotions, and behaviors that originally belong to others — to parents, siblings, surrounding aunts, uncles, and grandparents, all of whom are products of the particular brand of twentieth-century culture that is the context of this phase of our lives. Sometimes this earliest period is characterized as the sociohistorical cultural phase of a human life.[1]

In this phase, we are exploring the origin of our subjective human responses to the initiatives of the Mystery. These responses always come from embodied hearts that are charged with personal feelings, interests, passion, or concerns that reflect the emotions of the responsible and sensitive human beings who make them. Guides also have to be sensitive — and not only to the more objective traditions or truths about life that underlie the guidance encounter. They must also be attentive to the more subjective thinking and feeling patterns that are moving both themselves and the other person. These affective dynamics are rooted in the temperament, the vital, genetic, preformed self that is not chosen, but given while one is still in the womb.[2]

These earliest relationships formed and deformed our emotional lives, or at the very least left their mark on the unfolding spontaneous tendencies of this small person's heart. We can see these given predispositions in the tiniest newborns who, before any nurture or learning has taken place, are inclined to be active or passive, irascible or peaceful, quick-moving or slow. This earliest inclination may later be recognized as the temperamental seedbed of the person's emotional and reactive intensity. "Yes, she was always quick tempered, even as an infant" or "I remember from the time he was a baby how contented he was — even waiting patiently for his bottle."[3]

What happens to this sensitive heart as the infant's life unfolds in relation always to the people and customs and prejudices of the environing others? Did that sensitive heart tend in the direction of moving *toward* objects of its hope, longing, or desire? Did it prefer movement *away from* others, initially rejecting encountered otherness? Or did it tend to move first *against* what it encountered in life, not in flight but in a spontaneous mood of fight, thus going counter to an opposing world? Most people are a mixture of all three encounter patterns and find that when they are in harmony we can simply and wholeheartedly be *with* what comes into our lives.[4] However, the spiritual guide needs to be alert to the ways in which these natural responsive tendencies can rigidify into more or less compulsive reactions at certain times in a person's life.[5]

In all great religious traditions there comes a moment of communal recognition of the mysteriously given identity of each human being. Whether it be in the offering of the child to the gods, in a ceremony of initiation, or in the ritual of recognizing the Buddha-nature of this child, in that gesture the spark of divine indwelling in each human being is acknowledged and honored.

For many Christians, the ceremony of infant baptism marks the day when the child is first honored by the community as a spiritual being with a mysterious vocation that will conform this child to the "Firstborn" child of God, Jesus the Christ. Other Christians who (more logically) confer baptism only later, when a person has come to believe in and to choose Christ, use a dedication ceremony to welcome a baby into life, into the community, and into God's providential care. Whether for infants or for believing adults, the rebirth of baptism marks a fresh embarkation of life in its direction toward the Trinitarian Source of all life.

In infancy, the bodily or vital aspect of development is crucial. Physical growth is rapid; satisfaction of vital needs is paramount. But these bodily issues are inseparable from relational issues and psychic needs. The baby's feeling life blossoms in the family if his or her body's impulsive strivings — to be held, to be nursed, to evoke appreciative responses — are satisfied. Relational patterns emerge. They might be positive patterns of trust, courage, hope, mutuality with others. Or they might be negative patterns of feeling abandoned and isolated from others and deprived of what one needs.

As guides we must have some knowledge, especially of negative patterns from a person's infancy. But we must also be in touch with the limits of our capacity to deal with them.

Sinful patterns of narcissism and self-preoccupation can emerge during these earliest years. The foundations of what has been called "the false self system" go all the way back to babyhood. Built around the young child's instinctual need for security and for being shielded from the fears that characterize these early years, the false or counterfeit self consists mainly of illusory thinking about the power of control and possessions or self-esteem and affection to keep one safe. This is the time when the young child attempts to focus a lot of its energy on false security centers, on gaining affection or esteem, on surviving by means of a variety of defensive strategies, or on securing power and control that it mistakenly believes will ensure happiness.

"His majesty the baby" (or her majesty, of course) tries to control it all. If the child's strategies for power, approval, and control work too well and do succeed in producing the desired effects in the surrounding significant adults, that child might be in trouble in adult life. It is then highly unlikely that the grown-up Little Goody Two-Shoes or Young Prince Charming (or whatever) will be willing to direct his or her adult energy away from similar false strategies as a grown man or woman.

Very early in life, children who are managing their fears by means of compliant strategies can become committed to a false or surface self. Interiorly, they may also image God as the one who demands perfect performance, rewards only good behavior, and withholds love from those who are displeasing. As adults, those people might still be imaging God in that way.

Sometimes children dealing with the enormous fears common to childhood are helped because they encounter well-chosen fairy tales, myths, and legends. At this young age, imagination is strong and magical thinking easily mixes fact with fantasy. Fairy tales, therefore, can be quite an effective therapy: they can help children externalize their fears. If, as guides, we meet someone whose burdensome images of God or of life seem to go back to childhood defense strategies, it is possible that good legends, fairy tales, and other imagined adventures could still help that person. I have met not a few people whose Christian imagination could be fed by tales of Aslan and the faithful Frodo whose adventures speak of the gentleness and mercy of the risen Lord.[6]

In later childhood when the world widens to include school and neighborhood and when body, mind, and will are being fashioned in the interests of predicting and controlling the environment, of ordering the world along more predictable lines, the child's increasing sense of ego competence emerges to the tune of "I can do it myself." Concrete operational styles of rational thought and industry are developing, and for a while the mythic and the literal exist side by side. Ten-year-old perfectionists begin to demand stories that allow for only black or white, either/or outcomes. The good guys have to win: life has to be "fair." Like the two-year-old insisting on establishing a separate self via the reiteration of "no," the refrain of children in this age group becomes "it's not fair," backed by the solemn conviction that it ought to be, especially where *I* am concerned. Stories at this age need to provide not only a strong sense of justice and fairness, but also, in face of the emerging separate self, children need an increased sense of belonging, of identifying with an immediate group, of being clearly related to "people like us."

All of these needs are natural attempts made by the growing human being to cope with early anxieties about the unpredictable power of "otherness." One of the most common leftovers from early childhood, then, can be seen in people's excessive anxiety about behaving as an ideal self in order to placate a God who is also unpredictable, whose power must be controlled. Originating in the child's efforts to be good and do good works in order to elicit a favorable reaction from a powerful parental figure, the banking or merit-acquiring mentality so strong in some forms of Christian religion seems to harken back to this performance pattern. Early struggles with the image of an angry God who can be related to mainly in terms of familiar self-centered strategies of security and control can often be traced to this period in a person's formation history.[7]

The Relational and Initial Spiritual Phase

During the transition from childhood to adulthood there comes a time of imaging what life is to be about — a time of skill development and the projection of one's "dream."[8] Described by Erikson as a "moratorium," by others as "adolescence," it has become (at least in North American society) a more or less indefinable period in which a young person is free to dream about the future, to consider choices of love and work, to lay the ground for marriage, career, fame, and fortune, for whatever he or she considers would constitute a meaningful life. A still youthful time, it covers the years in life when the most profound changes may not yet have taken place. However, there are in the average teenage life enough frustrations, fears, losses, and confusions to interrupt at least some of the false programs the teenagers have set up for themselves in earlier years.

We must remember never to mistake natural psychological developmental stages for moments of authentic spiritual growth. We cannot draw an exact parallel between chronological stages and spiritual capacities, which as we know may unfold any place along the curve from three to ninety-three. However, there are certain characteristics of this particular developmental phase that do seem to coincide with the beginnings of the emergence of a spiritual self.[9]

First of all, it is a time of openness to the future. For some young people in our society[10] we can say that this is the moment in life when all kinds of possibilities abound — ideals, dreams of success, lots of energy to carry them out. Not having tried much, they do not know themselves very well. Others who think they know them wrap their own expectations around the young person's personal hopes. On his or her side, the young person wants to know from others "how they are doing." They look for ways to prove themselves, to testify to their own developing sense of identity and worth.

Youth is also a difficult and often self-conscious time when puzzling experiences related to questions of identity emerge. "Who am I in this changing body with its upsurges of sexual feeling and power?" or "Whatever happened to that little kid who hated the opposite sex, whose best friends were always of the same sex, and who didn't have to worry about a God who would be angry about sex?"[11] Questions of peer pressure, drugs, and status grow in intensity. Young people who are also developing their capacity for highly rationalistic speculation may become preoccupied with more than a little intense reflection about this God whose unpredictable judgments regarding intimacy and sexuality need to be restrained somehow. As one's personal myth begins to grow and flourish one is tempted to find ways of restraining the absolute power of such a God. "Maybe God is a myth. Maybe I need to just drop out of the entire God-thing for a while...."

At the same time, still embedded in the expectations of family and others, this youthful separate self is rapidly developing into a particular type of "social self" — often a reflection of what "they" — family, school, co-workers, organizations, and environing others — have to say about them. The positive side of this development is that the young person's capacity for intimacy with significant others begins to blossom in a series of first loves, crushes, admiration of models and mentors. At such a moment of blossoming of one's capacity for intimacy, a new image of God also becomes possible. God can be imagined and related to as a divine "significant other," a personal presence in one's life. The response of the young person's heart can move from mere obedience to external authority to a more personal inner responsiveness to an appealing "Other." The dream of youth may begin to include this Other as One who calls him or her to emerge as a spiritual self. Perhaps this is the moment, at whatever age it happens, when human beings become capable of what the apostle Paul would call "newborn" spiritual response.

Spiritual guides see the resulting capacity for reflectiveness and for contact with the aspiration for "more" as marking the phase when distinctively human or spiritual life can be consciously appropriated. Often coming into focus when a young man or woman has begun to move away, either geographically or at least emotionally from what he or she has always called "home," this life passage has something to do with beginning to stand on our own feet, beginning to move in the direction of what we feel life is calling us to, and beginning to take responsibility for personal decisions and choices. It also often coincides with what James Fowler had described as positioning oneself "outside the fishtank." It includes the ability to look somewhat critically at the former assumptions that governed one's earlier world of family and familiars. It also may include a growing ability to see and acknowledge present conflicts between one's external behavior and one's inner ideals. It is the moment in anyone's life when spiritual guidance can properly begin.

Youth is supposed to be the time for getting clear about what one really wants in life. Couched in terms of "finding oneself," it should be an opportunity for giving shape or form to an identity that is in keeping with what one feels drawn to, with what one has potency for, with what one's personal spiritual aspirations actually are.

In most cultures throughout the world, this is also considered the time to prepare to make choices, of marriage, of professional career, of partnerships of various kinds, or of religious commitment, to begin leaving behind the open options that characterize adolescence. Late adolescence is full of as yet untried self-confidence and enthusiasm backed by a powerful vital-functional development. The issue becomes how one is to integrate vital-functional strengths — especially a by now powerful sexuality — into a lifestyle in harmony with who this young man or woman discovers himself or herself to be. For some, this can be the time in life when great ideals are glimpsed for the first, and perhaps only, time. A kind of intuition guides many on a congenial "path with a heart." Others are not so fortunate.

At this age, how many young people know for sure when they are "ready" to make choices that involve serious commitment? It is the rare human being who is fully conscious that he or she has successfully made the transition from adolescence to adulthood. Guides must realize that the average person probably did not have solid norms for appraising these youthful life choices. Transcultural studies have shown that in all cultures young people have to make these life-shaping decisions before they are ready, before they are sufficiently wise and mature to enter into the permanent commitments that will shape their lives.[12] Thus, many or most of these life choices and commitments are made in ignorance of who the choice-maker most deeply is, or of what will bring him or her true happiness.[13] Thus, it is generally only in the years that follow the making of a major commitment like marriage or professional career, religious or other intentional options, that truly spiritual struggle and growth actually begin.

The Phase of Social Responsibility and Control

Having made certain commitments of time and energy, young adults usually enter into a time of struggle as the life field puts up all kinds of resistance to their efforts. They run into conflicts and temptations of various kinds, and their attempts to gain control of their sometimes accepting, frequently pain-filled and difficult life fields seem to mock the hunger for the invisible "more than" they had sensed earlier in life. It is really only in the attempt to concretely live out the commitments of time and energy proper to young adulthood that one begins to meet resistance, in oneself first of all, and then in other people and in the task at hand. Amid the satisfactions and the joy as well as the frustrations and fears that accompany the demands of this phase, there is usually some stress as young adults attempt to integrate their actual limited selves with the consequences of having committed themselves to an ideal or to a permanent responsibility.

Thus, in a span that may include one's late twenties, thirties, and early forties, most men and women are eager to channel their now abundant energy into fulfilling their dreams and ambitions. There is a need now to form stable, mutually supportive relationships with others and to take on personal responsibility for social systems, institutions, and relationships as one's network of familial and professional work or responsibility increases. Living with the consequences of commitments already made and new ones continuing to be made to a variety of other persons, to work and family, and to assorted segments of society, the man or woman at this stage in life is being formed and changed by these very commitments at the same time he or she is giving form to them.

In this process, conflicts do arise as the human heart struggles to bring external behavior, activities, and attitudes into increasing agreement with the heart's deepest beliefs.[14] In the midst of all this activity and busyness, there are moments when even the hardiest type-A personality[15] may be confronted with the fact that his or her entire value system has drifted off course. Especially when confronted with life's ambiguity, questions will surface about what is motivating all the effortful striving that seems endemic to this phase of life. A message like, for example, the beatitudes of the Christian Gospel can come as a disturbing, probing shock in this life stage.

At this stage there are many temptations. In face of a sometimes desperate need to give form to one's life or family or community, committed persons may be tempted in the direction either of absolutism or of relativism. They may begin to pour all available energy into the one person or ideology or group that appears to have all the answers;[16] or they may simply opt out of all commitments in favor of open options and noninvolvement. The guide of people in this life phase may suspect that they have become fixated in an either/or position. Questions about what particular life tasks this person is evading may also arise as the guide listens to this person's story and wonders about the commitments into which life energy is being channelled.

In the race to establish a niche in our competitive society, even if the intention is to establish a platform from which to serve humanity, there is a danger that the spiritual view falls into some disuse and neglect. People both in and out of formal religiously oriented lifestyles are preoccupied with making it, with survival. The routine pressures of children and work and financial problems call for concrete actualization of performance potential. It is a time for the incarnation of dreams — but dreams are often frustrated by an unfavorable environment, by lack of opportunity, and by consequent resentment and despair. Within demands for effective coping, the emphasis falls on dependable caring and the use of power accompanied by critical pragmatic reasoning. Even during periods when things are going well, there may be an imperceptible falling away from the more intuitive and contemplative side of one's nature.

In this process of overdoing in the functional mode, young adults may gradually find themselves isolated from their originating ideals. Hypertension may accompany the stress on achieving, and burnout symptoms may be observed as all energy is channelled into what works. Communication in the spiritual realm becomes increasingly difficult. If they began as idealists, these tired or frustrated adults often come to feel that their ideals have failed. They become surprisingly critical of hitherto unquestioned values and they eventually doubt the wisdom of their own faith tradition.

In his book *The Denial of Death*, Ernest Becker reminds this age group in particular of the preference for isolating oneself in manageable "little beyonds" of family, work, diversion, even religious practices, in an unconscious desire to avoid confrontation with the Great Beyond that has never ceased to be a cause of anxiety from childhood on.[17] This stage of young adulthood, with its joys and heartaches, its rough spots and meaningful achievements, evokes a multitude of new questions.[18] What does it all mean? These shipwrecks that seem to be inherent in life itself, what are they pointing to? What does it mean to be a sexual person, to be male or female, to have become a caregiver for others?

As guides, we might suspect that underlying the presenting remarks of the majority of young adults are fresh questions about the value of earlier commitments, about present use of the power that is theirs, about the experience of feeling trapped by social roles, and about the future, especially in terms of its relatedness to the meaning of God for them now.

Sometime in the first half of their working lives, many adults, especially if they started as young idealists, may go through a period of de-idolization. People or institutions they once counted on may have betrayed their trust somehow. As guides, we might ask ourselves what has this person been through in terms of transitions and crises? What is now being demonized that was formerly idolized? How can the efforts this person is so obviously putting forth be turned toward growth and transcendence, rather than ending in disintegration and despair? Is this young woman for the first time questioning the meaning of her own life? Could this relatively young man be troubled by his own approaching death?

The guide realizes that this is the point in life at which single and/or celibate people feel acutely the loneliness of their state. Married couples also at a certain mid-commitment moment may be tempted to forsake what has become a merely functional relationship. For both this may look like the final chance for sexual intimacy and fulfillment, whether they are in a lay or religious life state. The temptation to make a change, any change, in the hope of something better, or to renew depleted resources can become extremely compelling. An alert guide will detect here as never before a crisis of aspiration, a crisis that life itself can be trusted to bring about, a series of surprises that hold possibilities not only of formation and reformation but of transformation as well.[19]

Moving Toward Reassessment and Handing On

Whether a person is twenty-five or fifty-five, at any age life can be trusted to bring significant changes in the form of challenges, disruptions, and unexpected experiences. These changes are capable of altering one's familiar life flow, of turning upside down one's sense of what can be taken for granted. At the same time, life events are capable of deepening and expanding the heart. Our problem is that very often we do not or will not perceive life events — even those of crisis proportions — as moments that open us up, slit our complacency, and invite growth. Instead, we respond to events with further frustration and despair. As guides, we must hang on to the truth that *all* of life's events, both positive and negative, *can* contribute (although not automatically) to the unfolding formative thrust of a person's life.

One case in point is that described in chapter 3 as the classic transition of mid-life. Another might be the moment when one's committed life reaches a period of unexpected change or even stagnation. Even the most seriously committed people can recall such a moment when their marriage or communal group or their service to a cause that continued to form and deform their embodied spirit just appeared to lose its intensity and power to energize them. New questions surfaced in the midst of that loss of familiar ways of doing and being.

As Scott Peck reminds us, there is always an entropic thrust to the human condition that makes us cling to familiar forms of misery rather than exchange them for unfamiliar freedom. We resist losses whether they take the form of having to let go of our images of self as young, eternal, vital, and healthy, or of being compelled to admit that our major commitments are not turning out to be as glorious as we thought they might in the beginning.[20] When it begins to dawn on us that we are not finally in control of our lives and that the ego functional willfulness that may have characterized our commitments at their inception has to undergo a shift to a more receptive form of willing, we still try to cling to our childhood boast, "I can do it myself."

A time comes when we can no longer see ourselves as the sole center of our life and commitments. At the same time, we have to give up our excessive sense of community when we discover that we are finally alone before God and responsible for ourselves. Stereotypical images of ourselves — perhaps as the competent professional or as the devoted wife — also have to be put aside, along with some of our long-held stereotypical images of God.

No one wants to face the upheaval that accompanies these small but nevertheless stressful deaths to accustomed ways of being and doing in the world.[21] Yet it is precisely these flourishing false self-systems that are jolted out into the open by the less than lovely events of this reassessment phase of the human journey.

It may be precisely one's preferential option to go on ignoring the meaning and fulfillment possibilities destined for all members of the human race. Yet these are the very possibilities that will be challenged by the enforced detachments that belong to middle and older age. It may only be when some persons are stopped in their tracks by a serious illness, a divorce, or career failure that they will pause long enough to reflect on the quality of their life roles, commitments, relationships, and religious convictions. Often, too, the spiritual guide must deal with the ordinary depression and even stressful self-doubt that can accompany still another's quiet faithful fulfillment of duties in the midst of narrowing vital-functional capacities and horizons. If ever people are going to be open to self-questioning and spiritual renewal it is in this life phase that evokes disquieting glimpses of one's own egoism and greed, one's spiritual immaturity and lack of social responsibility. For the first time perhaps, questions about the ambiguous future loom large in the midst of psychic or spiritual darkness. Spiritual guides can count on the fact that at this stage in life more and more people are rediscovering the transcendent dimension that may have become weak or even be lacking entirely in their lives.

At this point, too, it may become more possible for them to see, from an entirely new angle, the age-old wisdom handed on to them by their faith tradition. They may also feel the need in their turn to hand on to their own children or students or community something more solid than their own merely subjective opinions about life and its larger meaning. Perhaps this is the reason for the return to the churches or the serious search for rootedness in some faith tradition undertaken by couples who prior to beginning their families had neglected, or discarded as unnecessary, religious beliefs from their own and other traditions.[22]

During the years leading to middle age and beyond, both men and women are faced with a choice between fearfully clinging to the past or freely letting go of certainties in order to accept the invitation of the future. Reactions may differ, as some become overactive in the present, desperately trying to keep up the appearances of young adulthood or even regressing to teenage behavior and clothing styles. Others in an effortful striving for quasi-spiritualistic solutions for the future, may become engaged in various types of New Age and transpersonalistic cults, hoping to find a sort of magical solution to the dreaded prospect of growing old. In my opinion, spiritual guides are currently being called upon to accompany the increasing number of North Americans who are quietly accepting the challenge of this life phase, who welcome the invitation to grow in wisdom and inwardness, who want to relaxedly take stock of the past, become the uniquely human persons they are in the present, and prepare for a future of graceful old age and the new birth of death.[23]

In the midst of this phase of enforced detachment, we once again approach our freedom. Spiritually we can be open or closed to what this time of life brings in the way of unpredictable joys and sorrows. The black and white, either/or nature of our perception finally breaks down as we find ourselves involved in a series of major life shifts. These transitions may be experienced as even more jolting than the movement from childhood to early and late adolescence or the transition from the open options of late adolescence to the responsibility for children and the societal tasks of young adulthood. Gradually we become more able to recognize life's paradoxes — the death that inheres in every life, the sorrow in every joy, the pain in every pleasure, the failure in every success, the no in every yes. We may even begin to befriend paradox, to agree that "it's not always going to be fair," that the good guys don't always come out on top, and that there are opportunities for rebirth hidden in every seeming death. Here we are confronting what Adrian van Kaam refers to as the "turn to transcendence."[24] A new phase of life is underway here, one in which attention and concern move in the direction of maturity of motivation. Spiritual guides are familiar with this focus. They, too, are primarily concerned with the direction taken by the intentions and desires of the loving heart. Very much to the point here is Carl Jung's suggestions that we need special schools for forty-year-olds. The great religions, he claims, were those schools of wisdom for people in the past.[25] They existed to prepare people at this turning point in their lives for the second half of life, for old age, for death, and for the life that awaits us in eternity.

It is usually in the second or even third phase of life that the struggle to recognize and surrender oneself to the central call of one's being becomes the main issue.[26] Then we come full circle to the promises that began at baptism, when the love of God poured the Spirit into our hearts to remain with us during the entire course of our journey. In these later years it is also possible for our care and concern to reach out beyond the immediacy of our family and community, beyond even the circle of our friends. In solidarity with all others there can emerge a selfless readiness to spend and be spent for future generations, to hand on in a generative gesture of love the good things that have been freely given to us.[27]

Relaxing and Letting Go

What does relaxing and letting go have to do with the "turn to transcendence" described in this last section? Are "praying and playing," as some authors would have us believe,[28] really sources of new dynamism in the second half of life? If so, in what way does the spiritual guide understand the rhythm of letting go into the relative nonaction of the later years to be of value for the spiritual journey? Let's return for a moment to our thoughts about what happens when a person begins to move toward reassessment and handing on. We discovered that this second or third phase of life, when surrendering oneself to the central call of one's being becomes a central issue, can be accompanied by a mature generativity — a desire to relax one's grasp on life's good things, for the sake of handing them on to those who will come after us.

The openhandedness associated with such mature generativity is dependent on a certain ability to shift, to let go of the ego's clutch on what it has heretofore considered important to hold on to. As mentioned in the previous section, there comes a time in life when one may choose to let go of certain past certainties in order to more freely accept the invitation of the unknown future. One of the signs that a person is beginning to shift — to move in a transcendent direction — is a kind of flexibility. Even if the person is ourselves, we might notice it. We might be more than ever aware of our weakness and fallibility. We might be, in some significant ways, more serious of purpose. But not grim. When new life enters our soul, we sense something energizing and desirable about our future. It is as if we had glimpsed a summit and were freely letting ourselves be drawn by its appeal.

When we have been drawn closer to our ultimate self and to the Love that is its ground, negative thinking steps back, at least for a time. We are less racked by doubts about ourselves. Past mistakes, or fears about the future, weigh less when we are letting the powerful mercy of God weigh more. We are lighter.

Men or women of any age who come for spiritual direction are, at first, usually marked by a focused, striving, and somewhat tense consciousness. That, of course, has muscles to match; their bodies tend to be rigid. After they have begun to make their interior shift, their bodies often look different: more flexible, more relaxed. It happens over and over again. When men and women start letting go of their will-full, usually conscientious but ego-centered hold on projects and goals, and will to embrace the greater richness that attracts their aspiring love, it is more peaceful for the body as well as for the mind.

The reverse is also true, and meditators in many traditions have known it for centuries: when the body is relaxed, mind and consciousness will clear.[29] Certainly people are picking up on this possibility today. Even people who have no conscious desire to grow in trust of God or in consciousness of the divine presence are trying yoga, massage, Tai-chi, deep breathing, jogging, mantras, biofeedback, transcendental meditation. They want not only better health; they want to calm their consciousness.[30]

When we trust God more, we can afford to relax our self-centered worried efforts to take care of ourselves. In the same movement, we trust our own preconscious feelings and intuitions more. It becomes easier to see the good side of things. They are more available to us, anyway, once we have learned (by meditation or in some other way) to empty the mind and senses of surface strivings and noisy trivia. We have "sold" what usually fragments our attention and divides our energy, so that we can "buy" the beckoning field where our real treasure is to be found.

If we are spiritual guides, we must not be too "spiritual" to enjoy this radical connectedness between mind and body, between sympathetic and parasympathetic nervous systems, between plain old relaxing techniques and the stilling of focused consciousness. Granted that control of one's breathing (and thus of the mind) is not yet faith. Granted that breaking the closed circuit of reactive striving (wants, musts, and shoulds) is not yet holiness. But it is something, and it is precious. Relaxation of these expressions of the ego's clutch can help people move out of the mode of isolated striving and "doing it alone." Then a lot of noisy and expensive things can drop away. Most of us spend a large chunk of our lives clinging to some functionally useful things that have nothing to do with our deeper life. We might cling to bodily strength and attractiveness, energetic and "in-charge" appearance, functional cleverness and efficiency, ability for control and mastery, even to an aptitude for keeping all the rules or for being always up to date. Once we realize that we have been clinging to such things for security and even for salvation, there is hope. There is more of an opening for the emergence of faith, hope, and love — to a degree that is never possible while we are still addicted to achievement or committed to security measures that block human maturity.

What happens when someone is able to shift into this more flexible state of being? Very often, his or her lifestyle changes. There will be a slowed down pace, a better approach to diet and to exercise, more respect for the body's own stress signals. When people are in this spiritual condition, they appreciate leisure more — and it is still, after all, the basis of culture!

There is a second-level shift, which belongs more to the interior dimension. People are free to move away from habits of dependency and clinging that had become obstacles to the inflow of energy and loving directives from beyond the self. Then a fuller level of love emerges through a meditative lifestyle of prayerful commitment to the Mystery of Love that lies beyond them all.

A shift like that is a many-levelled thing. Something dies, something is born. There is the old pattern of detachment from features of one's former self in order that a new attachment, a new commitment may come into being. It is the human level of the old mystery of the seed: it must move from its encapsulation in a hard little shell, through a dark time, in order to emerge as a living fruitful plant. Whether this shift happens early or later in life, we are looking here at the pattern of the "turn to transcendence."

Chapter Seven

ON BEING A WISE FISH

I N the introduction to this book, I borrowed a Sufi legend about some anxious fish who kept swimming around looking for the sea. At last they met a wise fish who said to them that if they would stop darting about so anxiously, they would notice that the sea was already all around them; they needed to look no further than where they were.

A good spiritual guide hopes to be like this wise fish. It is certainly true that many people in our time feel a need for a wise companion as they struggle to find or re-find newness of life. In the secular marketplace, a great many people are confidently making their living by offering various programs and approaches in favor of personal growth. How are we to choose among the offered "slices and slivers"? In religious circles, the "market" is even less regulated. One well-known guide, musing about the fact that the state would prosecute as criminal anyone who took a smattering of biology courses and then attempted triple-bypass heart surgery, admitted that he knows of no way to weed out incompetent spiritual directors. "Almost anyone who is of a mind to can venture into the guidance not of mortal bodies, but of immortal souls."[1]

It is important to be clear that, in Christian terms, the Spirit of God is the true guide of God-seeking hearts. Never in the history of the church has it been considered necessary for everyone to have their own "spiritual director" (to use a traditional label). There is much that eager seekers can learn about being healthily self-directed.[2] There is so much in the ordinary Christian life of a good parish or of a good faith-sharing group that is formative. There is so much illumination in life itself.

Yet, at many turning points in a person's journey, the human heart longs for a trustable, competent guide. At moments when consciousness is shifting and groping, many serious believers feel the need for a spiritual companion: someone soundly educated, who can speak from

107

personal experience of profound and growth-producing shifts on the transcendent level. And a good guide is hard to find.

The chapters of this book so far indicate some of the challenges and integrative demands made on a spiritual guide today. There is more, especially for the director of baptized Christians whose human life direction is meant to move deeper and deeper into the Trinitarian life of love, through faith and hope.[3]

Incompetent guidance can be hurtful. What are some qualities that make a guide "trustable," especially for a Christian? What are some of the shifts of spirit that are to be expected as a person grows spiritually? What demands do these shifts of consciousness make on the co-listening guide? What are some of the ethical and spiritual ground rules of this ministry? What are some of the breakthroughs and spiritual gifts that guidance tries to encourage? What are the skills that every guide must be prepared to teach? What are the life encounters that provide an impetus for spiritual change and deepening?

Patterns of an Awakening Heart

Shifts of spirit are an ever-real human possibility. At any time I can make a decisive move toward my hidden, more authentic self. There are only two conditions. One condition is that something must invite me toward a spiritual change, either an inner restlessness or an outer incident that is disturbingly significant. And I make a response. Moments of new life always involve being open to an initiative that I do not totally control. (In the language of faith, it is God who initiates all real change of heart.) The other condition is that I let something go. There is a death to one's "current self."[4] The service of new life requires a detachment from some form of life I was previously clinging to. In the language of faith, the grain of wheat must "fall into the ground and die" to bear "much fruit" (John 12:24).

In these chapters, I have borrowed the experience of several people whom we all have access to in familiar books so that we can look together at some shifts of spirit or their possible refusal.[5] Etty Hillesum, drinking of life's delights, meets an enemy occupation, watches it darken into genocidal oppression — and she becomes a contemplative mystic. Norman Cousins has a heart attack and becomes lucidly aware of the favorite blindnesses of our overfunctional culture. Beth Jarrett, on the other hand, is visited by death and madness in both her sons, but she refuses to shift her inner ground: she chooses flight.

Messages from life encounters, welcomed as providential and listened to with a vulnerable human heart, seem to embody the common path to spiritual deepening. The encounter need not be a catastrophic one, as it was for Etty Hillesum. Sometimes it is a still-vague interior awareness that there has to be some change: "I can't go on like this." My usual, established way of working (or of relating or of praying) seems to have died on the inside. I am pushed by that into a hunger for spiritual change.[6] In the gap between what I am and what I could be, the need for change becomes apparent, at least to me.

Hearing this call of my deeper self, I find myself wanting somehow to touch again or allow to touch me whatever it is in life that I am ultimately called to commit myself to in love. I may even vaguely realize that an encapsulated life of willful, self-sufficient achievement is no longer satisfying, that my lonely efforts to make it on my own have left me feeling empty and cut off from what I sense may be my "real" purpose in life. Uneasiness may have been growing for some time, and I've been pushing it away, covering it over and concealing it even from myself. Then something happens, a small incident maybe — like overhearing a remark that rankles, discovering that I'm unable to cope as well as I used to with certain people or with unexpected changes of plans, or finding myself giving way to a sudden uncontrollable burst of anger. In the Gospel story of Martha in her kitchen, we have a talented homemaker going about her usual chores, clinging to her self-satisfying role as the one who provides those nourishing, palatable meals.[7] Then "something happens," Christ makes a remark, and there is darkness in Martha's marketplace of action. This challenge to her current self did not originate entirely from within. In fact, Martha may have been feeling quite good about herself until the moment she heard Christ's words. It would seem that Martha needed a jolt from outside before uneasiness would overtake her and she would begin to consider that something would have to change in her attitude toward the good work she was already doing. Probably the new considerations prompted by that intervention from outside were a bit gloomy. Personal changes, even shifting a little from familiar ways of being and doing, require detachment from the old way in order to live in the new way. Something has to die in order that there can be new life. Martha must have felt resistant to, as well as challenged by, this call to her deeper self.

Readiness for shifts of spirit, then, for interior shifts in attitude, can originate both from within and from outside oneself. The basic structure underlying the entire project of spiritual guidance is to be discovered right within this pattern of vague dissatisfaction with one's present style accompanied by an inbreaking initiative from life itself.[8]

If, as in the Christian tradition, life itself and divine Otherness have the primacy and are the mysterious initiative-taker, then the role of the spiritual guide takes its shape from that recognition. The guide becomes the heart's companion, a co-discoverer. He or she is there to co-perceive the ways in which life events might contain directives that are calling forth that person's freedom and "deep gladness."[9]

This presumes at least two things. It presumes that the guide has been educated deeply, at heart-level, by the faith tradition that teaches us how to expect the inbreaking love of the Holy Other as a daily possibility. It also presumes that the seeker is willing to let his or her heart be touched, frightening or painful though that prospect can be. "Oh, that today you would hear God's voice; harden not your hearts...."[10]

Every day can be the today of that psalm. Each significant initiative must be reflected on, by both guide and seeker, as a possible inflooding of divine love that the person has up till this point been unready and unwilling to allow. Why unwilling? In all of us there are closed circuits of pride, fear, and self-centeredness that block the current of grace. In dialogue with a faithful guide, a seeker can become aware (they can become aware together) of what needs to be let go of, moved away from. Sometimes, the guide can point out the possibilities of new life that can be found in this seeming death.

Needless to say, all this can come as a shock to an activist, autonomous, take-charge Western person. It can feel alienating. This is a shift — to use technical language — toward preconscious meditative presence to initiatives from beyond the self. Theoretically, the Christian way has always begun with the experience of being loved — and of letting oneself be loved — by God and God's people.[11] But in fact, not only individual Christians, but even whole local churches can be living, energetically, as if it all began some other way. And as if it all gets developed by virtuous willpower alone.

In pre-Enlightenment Christian centuries, there seems to have been a kind of felt balance between action and contemplation, at least in the religious-cultural ideal of the time. But when Europeans became the explorers, go-getters, and individualists of the world, that balancing contemplative stance was not re-appropriated in the mainstream.[12]

Asia seems to have kept it longer. The Taoist doctrine of *wu-wei* is a lifestyle of noninterference, of letting things happen or letting go of anxiety and becoming receptive to the gift aspect of existence. It includes a conscious discipline of giving up effortful control and cultivating the possibility of meditative presence.[13]

Thomas Merton's translation of a Chinese poem catches the Taoist spirit of *wu-wei* at the same time as it recalls the Sufi legend of the seeking fish.

> Fishes are born in water
> Man is born in Tao.
> If fishes, born in water,
> Seek the deep shadow
> Of pond and pool
> All their needs
> Are satisfied.

> If man, born in Tao,
> Sinks into the deep shadow
> Of non-action
> To forget aggression and concern,
> He lacks nothing
> His life is secure.
> Moral: All the fish needs
> Is to get lost in water.
> All man needs is to get lost
> In Tao.[14]

It is not that the guide is going to work at making everyone more Asian. Only more receptive. In the rush of everyday modern existence, we do tend to forget that the human heart was created precisely so that it could joyfully recognize the dialogue that already exists between itself and the love that fills the universe. It is that love that is "poured out in our hearts by the Holy Spirit who lives in us."[15] We did not bring that about. I did not personally, nor did the church institutionally. It is gift, to be received.

A spiritual guide does not bring it about, either. In fact, at those moments when a seeker becomes ready to give up some willful or fearful controlling way and actually trust more deeply the hidden dialogue with Love, the guide had better be someone who knows how to "decrease" so that Christ may "increase."[16] To be any help at such a moment, the guide would have to be someone who has interiorly learned to cooperate with the Holy Spirit as this Spirit moves in people's lives, who as a "wise fish" perceives all human life fields within the transcending "sea" of God's love.

The Guide a Christian Can Trust

Some years ago I did my doctoral research on what happens when one person trusts another. What I found out applies in an interesting way to the question of what happens when a spiritual guide comes to be trusted by a seeker.[17]

When we seek spiritual guidance, what our heart wants to do is to trust God more. What gives us the confidence that a particular person can help that to happen?

The Christian tradition has strong remarks to make about this question. It teaches vigorously that the wisdom a guide has to offer is *not* a product of his or her own cleverness or even goodness. The true guide is God's Spirit. The ministry of spiritual guidance has to do with hoping to be, sometimes, a channel of that Spirit. The deepest mystery of who I am is clear only to God. Not to me; certainly not to my guide. A guide will receive me with sincere respect, aware that what is at stake goes deeper than any diagnostic category or theological explanation. If I can trust where my guide "is coming from" (an evocative bit of slang, for this subject), it had better be because my guide is "coming from" the Ground of the Trinitarian Mystery of God.[18]

If a Christian guide knows anything, he or she knows that. The overwhelmingly necessary response to knowing that is to pray: to ask for help from beyond. This seeker is the creation, the child, the personally beloved of the Mystery. Only that Other knows this seeker's inmost heart and knows the final Christ-image it is destined to become. The guide begins to "thirst for God" like the deer in Psalm 42, so that from within may flow, not half-dead theorizing, but "rivers of living water" (John 7:38), capable of refreshing all those who trust their Ultimate Source.[19]

That is the big, difficult, transcendent truth about trust in the spiritual guidance encounter: the One to be trusted is God, and we both go from there.

However, there are some less transcendent aspects as to why I might or might not trust a spiritual guide.

One is this: We trust others who are not totally self-preoccupied. That is true in any instance of interpersonal trust. It is particularly true here. A guide who can be trusted will not be tied up with self-centered plans for appearing wise or for gaining influence over others. She or he will not be locked in to the kind of emotional thinking that makes for irrational sympathies, antipathies, or stereotypes. He or she will not intrude personal pet concerns or preoccupations into the guidance interview.[20]

Another factor of trust is this: we trust people who adhere to a value horizon we ourselves respect. In the case of a spiritual guide, this aspect is sharpened and is very specific: the guide must be a deeply faithful participant in the faith tradition that the seeker also trusts. Guidance does not mean pushing one's subjective views. It means being responsible to point beyond oneself to the coherence (doctrinally and devotionally) of a trustworthy tradition, whether it be Catholic or Methodist, Buddhist or Hindu. Anything less objective than that changes the nature of the encounter.

There are, however, more subjective factors at play in concrete personal trust. There will always be an inner appeal about someone I choose as a guide. Not a surface or quick appeal, perhaps. But that person will have an internally meaningful cluster of dispositions that I regard as potentially helpful, supportive, challenging, or inspiring for me.[21] Of course, I could also be wrong about that judgment. I could be projecting my own larger-than-life expectations on another (see the discussion of "transference" in chapter 5).

Once the seeker and the guide get to work, the seeker has to put some real weight on that trust in the guide rather quickly. He will be struggling to talk about deep and delicate things. She will be trying to express a hesitant but real desire to reach out to the transcendent Other with her whole heart. He may need to speak about how, or when, he lost an earlier sense of dialogue with the Other. She will probably soon be speaking about actual concrete mess-ups in her present situation. Yes, the person seeking guidance surely will need human trust.

A trustable guide will receive these men and women with transcendent respect and will not see them as only bundles of symptoms or a mere collection of sin and disorder. On the other hand, talking about sin and disorder will not be off limits. A trustworthy guide will (sometimes) be able to indicate what messages from the deeper self — and what bits of prudence from the revealed communal tradition — a man or woman may have been evading. Sometimes, as co-discerner, the guide will be the first to notice indications from the Spirit about things in this person's life that will have to die if God is to have more room in his or her partly-stuck heart.

They can only let these possibilities happen if, for each of them, the guide continues to emerge from a trustable ground. That ground is partly, as we saw earlier, the faith tradition within which seeker and guide are both accountable. But much more radically than that, the ground is the Mystery. It is God.

Even in the case of Jesus as guide, people could not trust him unless they could trust that he "came from God." To trust Jesus was to trust Jesus' ground, the One who sent him. When the Fourth Gospel meditates on that fact, it is to underline the tragic corollary: not to believe in the Human One was not to believe in God. It is the divine Ground that makes the figure Jesus trustable.[22]

Many of us carry a precious personal memory of a spiritual guide who proved trustworthy and faithful in our lives. I remember in particular a woman who broke in on my encapsulation. What I remember with most gratitude is her selfless interest in what was most important for me, not necessarily for her, at the time. Her patience in waiting until I moved from a peripheral topic to the more personal spiritual issue was admirable. She gently drew me out until gradually I was able to name the focus for myself. She guided my wandering descriptions into some kind of framework where they could be reflected on by the two of us together. She never intruded her own preoccupations, but instead put all her efforts into helping me become a listener to my own story. Convinced of God's purposes for the world, she was seeing the details of my unique call against a larger ground: the sacred purpose that also grounds her own life.[23] It was not her attainment of "guru" status or even her knowledge of Christian tradition that made her a to-be-trusted other for me. It was her personal commitment to becoming a Christian herself, in a Trinitarian context, that "spoke to my condition." And it made her able to be patiently present to me and my world as a trusted listener and guide.[24]

A Liturgical Model of Group Direction

When we are beginning to understand what the ministry of spiritual guidance is and what its particular responsibilities are, we might profit from some "working models" that contain all its elements in various mixes.

One good (and nonintimidating) working model is the RCIA: the Rite of Christian Initiation of Adults, as that rite has been developed since the Second Vatican Council. It embodies a straightforward, unpretentious, and serious group direction/conversion process.[25]

This group process of change of heart begins with a more or less unlimited time for hearing and discussing personal stories. There is a relaxed exchange on each participant's personal and unique awakening to the faith dimension, and lots of time for questions of personal meaning.

At a certain point, the process moves on gradually to the integration of those personal experiences. An opportunity is offered for those who wish to become Christian actually to live in small communities of faith and to become acquainted with church tradition through personally participating in it with practicing Christians.[26]

After one year or more, sometimes several years, of living such a communal experience, an intensive period of more formalized spiritual guidance and discernment is offered for those who choose to continue. Usually the six weeks of Lent are chosen for the time-frame. After full baptismal initiation into the faith, a fifty-day period begins that emphasizes celebration of the new beginning and deepening of the baptized person's sacramental life. During this period, an opportunity to choose (or be chosen for) service/ministry is offered. This period of deepening in Scripture, prayer, sacrament, and spiritual awareness is called the *mystagogia*.[27]

RCIA does not end there. The life of faith includes ongoing conversion of conscience and development of the moral sense, as well as growing sensitivity to social justice issues and the needs of the human family. The call to universal love embodied in the life of Jesus demands that those who would bear the name of Christian must also "have that mind in them that was in Christ Jesus."[28] How to make connections between love of God and love of neighbor, between Gospel values in principle and concrete action in society, are basic issues for RCIA leaders as well as for spiritual guides and guided alike. In fact, the experience of lived differences on such issues makes all of us realize that our personal project — be it a special type of theology or spirituality, or a certain social ministry — while justified in itself, must not be held up as "the" ideal. Guidance does not mean pushing one's subjective views about how to live on to someone else.[29]

Those in charge of preparing catechumens for baptism and commitment within the church in the early centuries were certainly aware of the need for an objective approach to the mystery in its entirety. In their liturgical celebrations and liturgical life as a whole they recognized the church as a spiritual director who "sets the foundation of the direction along which she will lead her people [and] in the word, sacraments, and liturgical year she realizes what she preaches and sustains her people in their direction toward the Lord."[30] In recent centuries, we have overlooked liturgical life as a communal model and inspiring source of spiritual direction for all who seek to deepen their participation in the Mystery of Christ. Both private and group Christian guidance share this aim. Seekers bring to each their questions and feelings about life situations and events, hoping for help in reflecting on and coming to some discernment regarding how the elements of their smaller story can fit harmoniously within the larger story unfolded each year in the liturgical cycle.[31]

Each Sunday a clear life direction capable of forming the collective heart of the gathered community is indicated in the texts of the lectionary. Whether the presider raises these themes to consciousness, whether this person is capable of making useful connections between the scriptural texts and the lives of the people gathered for worship and nourishment is another question. But the essence of the spiritual guidance project is here — to form the heart of this particular community by helping the people in it to discern both their own personal and the group's communal call or life direction. When texts speak to the lived experience of the people, homilies become a lively form of group guidance, especially when they reflect the speaker's personal experience of being part of that unique community. The Sunday liturgy confronts us all with the larger Christian horizon of love. It calls us to let go of our independent and separatist tendencies, to step forward into the social mystery that characterizes Christian salvation, and to meet the challenge of world transformation. In their different settings, the liturgy and spiritual guidance point us personally and collectively in the same direction.[32]

What Guides Must Be Ready to Offer

What are some of the things that we, as guides, should be prepared to offer in any of the forms that spiritual guidance might take? Here is a short list for consideration:

1. Lived familiarity with the mysterious story of how we have been claimed, redeemed, and invited into intimacy by the Holy Other whose "Face" the seeker is seeking. Yes, this does mean Scripture. It means a deep intuitive grasp of how, in the past, this Holy Other has initiated covenants with persons and with groups. It means interiorized awareness of the content of those covenants. It means a deeply personal awareness of what theologians call "eschatology": of the as-yet-indescribable future toward which we have been carried ever since Abraham and Sara left Haran.

Understanding the great "story" of our tradition does not only mean Scripture, of course. Every century, since the last dream of the seer John on the island of Patmos, has had its breakthroughs of spiritual intuition as the saints and sinners and sufferers developed the dense, rich tradition we have inherited. Autobiographies of saints in different ages and cultures, conversion accounts, writings of mystics — these are some of the layers of the tradition that have proved fascinating to spiritual guides in every generation. In their startling variety and drama, they "stretch" our capacity to understand the equally startling variety of persons who seek spiritual guidance in our generation. Also, their commonalities are important. The basic dynamics of the process of change of heart under the impact of divine grace are universal. They follow certain stages of spiritual unfolding. It is very important for a spiritual guide to know and comprehend those stages. Conversion has a complex shape. We do not do anyone any favor by oversimplifying it.

2. It is important, if we are guiding someone, not to be limited by our subjective perception (based on our own immediate experience) of what is necessary to become a fully human Christian person. Needless to say, it is crucial that we have our own personal experience and that we have reflected on it. But the way for each particular human heart — even for those who have chosen the same fundamental spiritual tradition — will differ from one person to the next. The Spirit of God is moving to evoke the unique direction written in the depths of each heart.

That is why experienced guides try consistently not to impose anything on those who come to them. Experience in this ministry tends to move us steadily farther away from anxious manipulation of anyone. For example, it is prudent to avoid expressing sentiments of praise or of blame, of enthusiasm or rejection of what the other thinks or says. Enthusiasm often turns out to be pleasure over something that conforms to our own preferred ways of thinking and acting.

3. The spiritual guide is not to be the answer-giver or the problem-solver or even the realization of this other person's expectations. The helpful guide tries to be a calm, relaxed co-listener for what the Spirit may be asking at this point in the other's sacred journey.

4. Speaking of points on a journey, it is no secret that most people who seek spiritual guidance do so at a point when they are emotionally vulnerable. The guidance interview provides regular, intimate time alone with the person chosen as guide. The seductive possibilities are endless. We need to be steadily distanced enough from our own, and the seeker's hidden drives, needs, and passions, so that we can authentically represent the demand of grace, of Otherness in the everyday life field of the person to be guided.[33]

5. Quiet honesty and compassion are the gifts a guide can offer. Our genuine acceptance of the seeker's turmoil and struggle is rooted in our radical respect for this person's right to be other and this person's birthright as a child of the Mystery.

6. The interview is no time for any guide to be a star. It is not a good time to talk about ourselves. Or even about our latest theological discovery; we might be so impressed with it that we might fail to hear the other's muted cry for spiritual help in the midst of a conversation that stays fixated on some point of doctrine. We are there to help the person to listen to her or his own life and to the Spirit breathing or groaning in that life.

7. Experienced guides grow skilled in establishing a relaxed meditative atmosphere in which individuals or groups can discover what it is in themselves that might be blocking the flow, blocking their receptivity to the presence of the Holy Other. Guides also help seekers grow skilled at finding, outside the time of the interview, their own methods of reaching a quiet and relaxed attentiveness. Gentle exercise, relaxed breathing, music, the quiet recitation of a mantra — different methods help different people.[34]

8. We will spend a long time, as guides, cultivating the gentle art of not getting in the way. Newness of life streams continually from the mysterious Ground of all being. But its initiatives are imperceptible to human ears, eyes, and imaginations. Our antennas for this newness are on another level.

Think of infrared and ultraviolet light waves. They are always around us. The average bee, flying around on stubby wings, can see infrared without any of the hi-tech instruments we have devised to glimpse it. The invisible ground that we seek to touch in our lives is, like infrared, always there, but it cannot be stared at. First we need to know of its existence. We need to decide that it is worth our effort to attend to it. But we need "new eyes" to be able to glimpse it.

Spiritual guidance might be imagined as a gradual renewal of the eyes of one's heart, so that they can reliably catch glimpses of the "infrared" foundation of our lives. It is a way of tuning in to what is already there, already radiating. The tuning-in process is a kind of relaxed (and believing) objectivity. In such an atmosphere, it is more possible to see together things that one of us has been blind to. It is more possible to agree on elements that might have been missing in someone's life and to think about priorities without their being reduced merely to things that we personally believe are important.

Both guide and guided want to be in tune with and to obey directives coming from the same Ground. The hearts of both can then appreciatively attend to what must die and what must be nourished in order that a fuller life of love may be entered into.[35]

A Whole Appraising Person Responds

A trustworthy guide believes in and knows from experience the life-long possibility there is for shifts and changes in the dispositions of a human heart. Therefore, she or he is committed to helping others bring to consciousness and make judgments about the ever-changing dialogue they are with the various people, events, and things of their world and its mysterious Ground. The guide who is truly *with* people in their struggle to live from the deeper level of their heart's responsiveness will not be content to remain on the level of merely vital reactive or even functionally intellectual insights. It is never only the emotions or the conscious mind engaged in the search for God. Like the fish in the Sufi legend, people must certainly be taught to relax their tense effortful bodies and their busy inquiring minds in order to be open to a wider view of the whole. But they must also begin to reflectively question their hitherto taken-for-granted level of awareness. To what dimension of encountered reality are they currently responding? Is there a deeper meaning they have not yet noticed? Are their patterns of narrowly focused consciousness (usually accompanied by strain and tense muscles) really helpful, or might they be adding to the conflict?

It often takes a detached outsider to draw our attention to the deformative stances we habitually take to life's critical moments, whether it be the panic reaction noted by Norman Cousins as an acquaintance confronts his heart attack, or the unfree rigidity with which Beth Jarrett refuses to get involved with her less than perfect family situation. Spiritually it is entirely possible to miss or consciously avoid the call of the Mystery to one's deeper self as we busily attempt to go on exactly as before this person, event, or thing interrupted the even tenor of our life.

For both guide and seeker, the art of appraisal lies in the ability to look for signs of "infrared" in the midst of the observable, weigh-able facts as they appear in any life field or situation.[36] It is normal to look first at pro's and con's, at the arguable elements that complicate most of life's decisions. In a guidance session, for example, we may be looking at a conflict that has erupted in a woman's family or community, or at an event that is going to play havoc with a man's financial future, or at a new work opportunity and the conditions attached to it. Both of us, guide and seeker, should be interested in the ordinary facts that are open, in this case, to the mind's apprehension. But we should both look also at what these plain facts might mean in relation to the deeper, more foundational way that the seeker may gradually be coming to know him- or herself in terms of an entire life field.

Before reaching a decision about a given life event or opportunity, people need to reflect on it not only in pragmatic ways and not only as it affects their emotions, but also on how it may influence the person they are called to be by the Mystery itself. Only when he or she includes this dialogue with the heart's deeper calling can a person be said to have freely appraised a situation and be in a position to make a wise judgment about it. The process involves mind and will, cognition and feeling. It weighs facts, as well as looks for affinity with one's life call.

In his description of the appraisal disposition, van Kaam points out that its affective dimension often does produce a feeling of affinity — an appreciation for the encountered situation as holding within itself something of what belongs to the invisible call of the Mystery "for me" in my life.[37] Appraisal may also help someone identify a lack of affinity — a depreciative feeling that this situation or this person, thing, or event is not for me, either because it does not further disclose for me a deeper call or because it simply holds out no hope at all for my future growth. In the first case, an appraisal results in a kind of love, a positive feeling of yes, I can go with this. I can imagine this being good for me, I can remember the transcendent call of the Mystery to me in somewhat similar terms, and I can freely anticipate giving time and energy to something or someone like this. A depreciative appraisal would give rise to a no, as the imagination, memory, and anticipatory powers give back negative or negligible images. There is no evident way in which a giving of time, energy, or attention to the person, event, or thing represented by these facts ties in with my dialogue with the Mystery, so I will not go along with it.

Because life in its complexity is never neat and does not lend itself to lining up clearly under "appreciative" or "depreciative" labels, the work of appraisal often takes a long time. Conflicting insights and affects from head and heart, from within and without, from various spheres of the life field must be included. Especially in major life changes or transitions, this process with its scanning of facts, its wondering about implications, its tentative reaching out for and following hunches and seeming possibilities may last for years, and then only be seen as provisional. On the other hand, a person who has really profited from guidance may even in fairly major matters be able to appraise and come to life-enhancing decisions in a matter of minutes.

The Shift to a More Meditative Style

The mind can get in the way of what the heart knows or wants to know. That is no deep secret; poets, worried mothers, and other lovers have been saying that for centuries.

How do we ever "know" the voice of God in our lives? How does the mind find its way back to the heart and learn to get out of the way of what our inmost ear might hear?

One traditional piece of advice that spiritual masters from the great traditions pass on to their disciples is that the mind must learn to let go of its absorption in outward impressions of sense and feeling. That is true, but it can be misleading. The heart's way of knowing has some kinship with the state of consciousness that is receptive to myths, images, and symbols and the subtle work of artists: poems, music, the visual arts. And artists are keenly, lovingly, freshly aware of the actual thing that their senses reach out to. Art is thoroughly "incarnational," and meditative consciousness can be rather "incarnational" too.

Another way of saying it is that meditative consciousness has to move out of the achieving, working mode that our culture admires so much. It must become aware of an already-there treasure: a treasure the mind did not make, a treasure that escapes being put into words. Analysis, calculation, and prediction are of no help in coming to grasp that treasure of meaning.

Jesus was not the first to notice that even when people's minds are filled with ideas about God, their hearts might remain far from God. It is primarily the heart that must be touched, that must be guided beyond mere conceptual knowledge of self, and of others, and of God.

A daring traditional way of putting it is that the search for God's "face" (or "voice" — the images are many) proceeds by the way of *unknowing*. Human hearts come to the knowledge of their treasure not by focusing their consciousness on what can be rationally understood or logically communicated, but by being silent and receptive to the touch of an invisible presence.

We need meditative hearts, and hearts do not get that way by conceptualizing or analyzing. Meditative hearts are closer to actually being with the life-enhancing nearness of divine Otherness in their everyday living.

In several great spiritual traditions — not only Christian ones and, of course, not only Western — there are forms of meditation that aim to empty out crowded senses and still the mind's interior life. They tend to create a space of silence within the self. They begin with practical recommendations about quieting the senses or attentive breathing accompanied by a mantra or a body movement; or they begin by simply refraining from activity and business. The hope is that meditators will let go of what disperses energy and divides attention. Then their energy will be free to wait in loving attentiveness on the ultimate treasure of their restless, longing hearts.

These recommendations in no way exclude human development on other levels. Indeed, without a strongly developed vital-functional earthy self, much would be lacking in the directedness and originality of the seeking heart.

The ancient wisdom embodied in this practice of learning to empty the mind and the senses aims simply at increasing openness to life itself and to the divine presence that is its Ground. It points to the receptive dynamics of letting go and letting be and to what may be a new area of learning and growth for contemporaries who are out of touch with their spiritual path.[38]

I once discussed this tranquil inner attitude with a Chinese friend. She commented on its likeness to the Taoist vision of the tranquil heart. Then she gave me this poem by the Chinese Taoist Lao Tzu. I, in turn, was reminded of how spiritual guides sometimes are called upon to help anxious, fragmented persons to drop some defenses, relax, and flow with a more recollected style of presence. The possibility of feeling at home in this new style resides in that point of the soul where human beings are capable of meeting, of being open to, the Ground of All that Is.

Here is the poem.

> The highest good is like water.
> Water gives life to the ten thousand things
> and does not strive.
> It flows in places men reject and so is like the Tao.
> In dwelling, be close to the land.
> In meditation, go deep in the heart.
> In dealing with others, be gentle and kind.
> In speech, be true.
> In ruling, be just.
> In business, be competent.
> In action, watch the timing.
> No fight: no blame.

Chapter Eight

LIFE EMERGING FROM DEATH

A CENTRAL focus for spiritual guidance is the human heart's desire to grow and to change — to be converted again and again in the direction of its ultimate love. The Christian guide wants to help this metanoia happen. He or she is there to be of assistance as through self-knowledge and the process of appraisal a fellow Christian's divine life direction gradually unfolds and is realized in a relationship with transcendent Mystery.

As the guide views the human journey, he or she will notice the many shifts and changes that punctuate its normal course. If we live long enough, we are eventually confronted by the need to "let go." Spiritual guides from all great traditions have encouraged the shift to a more meditative style of presence. In a sense, this shift, too, is a necessary component of the lifetime process known as conversion.

What Conversion Means for Christians

We cannot even agree on how to translate the strong New Testament Greek word, but three of the four Gospels assure us emphatically that Jesus began his preaching with the call "*metanoiete!* The kingdom of heaven is at hand!"

Repent! say the old translations as they encounter Matthew's (and Mark's and Luke's) muscular verb. Do penance! says one Catholic translation from 1956. Reform your lives! says another version. You must change your hearts and minds! says one ambitious translation. Turn from sin and turn to God! says the Living Bible, trying to get it all in at once.

The struggle to comprehend what the call to conversion means is a lot bigger than the question of how to translate it. That it does not merely mean "Stop misbehaving! Behave yourselves!" seems to be reflected in the fact that the best-behaved people in Jesus' original audience — namely, the responsible and disciplined and courageous

Pharisees — had the most trouble with the message and with the messenger. Weren't they already converted and reformed?

From Mark's point of view, the people who seemed to understand Jesus' call at that point were the impetuous (presumably) young men who quit their jobs and became the first disciples. What Simon and Andrew, James and John seem to have heard was something like this: "Drop business as usual! This is the time we have been waiting for — the time of God's revolution! Open your lives to this good news!" They do just that — and everything begins. Yet later in this same Gospel, Mark makes it perfectly clear that these same disciples have misunderstood most of what Jesus is about. They are "following" Jesus on one level, but they are also stuck in old self-glorifying ways that make them passionately resist Jesus' call to the cross and their own call to servanthood. They have as yet many turns still to make on the Way. For Mark, conversion is not just once.

The Fourth Gospel, recognizing perhaps the difficulty that the Pharisees felt with Jesus' call to conversion, refuses to use the *metanoiete!* formula, which the other three Gospels recall as being the first message of Jesus and of John the Baptizer before him. The Fourth Gospel gives a sign instead: water is turned mysteriously into wine. Into the best wine. In that Gospel, the first words spoken by Jesus are not "Repent, for the kingdom of heaven is at hand," but "What do you want?" And when the two disciples of John answer, "Rabbi, where do you live?" Jesus' next words are: "Come and see." Yes, there are different ways of understanding the process of conversion. This chapter is about the many layers and meanings of conversion, about how spiritual guides can sometimes help people in the transitions that a lifetime of conversion requires, and about what conversion is like in the later stages of life, when life itself hands us the big changes and we need to learn to surrender and be led — by the Source of life.

Baptism and Conversion

Within the Christian faith tradition, conversion, the process of undergoing a change of mind and heart, is usually connected with the notion of life call. Here call means both an invitation from an initiating other and something capable of touching the inner core of one's being, one's mind and heart. When Christians think about God's call, they include the theme of sin and repentance. Responding to God's call includes a turning away from what is of lesser value (detachment) and a turning toward God (attachment) that implies not only an interior reversal of dispositions and attitudes, but also an exterior change in practical conduct.[1]

In the church today, as we attempt to adapt the Rite of Christian

Initiation of Adults to contemporary circumstances, we are finding that the first Christians regarded the precatechumenate (time before deciding to become a Christian) as a period when Christ's demand for *metanoia* challenged the intentions of those who desired to become his followers.[2] It was only after long years of testing in community and radically reevaluating the major choices and directions of their lives that catechumens were finally admitted to the ranks of those elected for initiation. Then, in the interval between the rite of election and sacramental baptism, there was a period of "illumination," of deeper discernment of faith and acceptance of conversion that would correspond to our present celebration of the six weeks of Lent. During this time, the entire community was involved in a process of "rending hearts, not garments," of turning to the Lord in a radical revision of attitude and perspective. In other words, from the very beginning of Christianity, conversion of the intending heart to center on Christ and the priorities of God through an increase in freedom and a change in purposeful direction of life was considered to be essential in those qualifying for the privilege of baptism.[3]

Today among contemporary Christians the pattern is rather different. The majority of us do not have years of instruction in the faith and form traditions of the way of Christ before being finally admitted to the awe-inspiring mysteries of the Easter vigil and full participation in the sacramental life of the Christian community.[4] Instead of the original pattern of "conversion–instruction–baptism," most adult Christians are baptized as infants and then receive instructions during a certain number of years in parochial or Sunday school or at home. But whatever happened to the whole process of conversion? If baptism is the seal of a conversion of heart and mind involving a radical change in one's priorities, dreams, and decisions regarding the future, how are we now to understand our own baptismal commitment?

Certainly baptism continues to be a sacramental celebration of a mysterious divine gift. Baptism celebrates the fact that from the instant of our creation we are children of God as well as of our parents and of the culture into which we were born. But, in affirming this element of our "new creation," do we not need to understand our baptism as calling us to an ongoing process somewhat similar to that which confronted the original people who risked everything to follow the inbreaking Otherness of Jesus?

In reflecting on who we most deeply are, we recognized that true self-knowledge really does go back to the self as originally called into being by God.[5] We also saw that this call forms the heart of the Christian tradition regarding the uniqueness of the human person. Each intentional whole person has been called "from the womb" to live forever in unity with the divine Other. This primordial orientation toward a union "already there" in our hearts *is* who we most deeply are. Yet when we take into account the ups and downs of our developmental history, the obstacles and deformative pulsations of our current culture, and personal sin and weakness, we recognize how difficult it is to remain in touch with this divine inner direction of our lives. In the gap between what we are and what we still could or ought to be, we recognize the need for change, for an ongoing process of detachment and new attachment that will bring us beyond this given moment, that will bring us closer to the call to self-transcendence we embody.

The call of Jesus is a call to new life, to life in abundance, to life that is above and beyond the limitations of mere human achievement. The hope of this new life corresponds precisely to the human capacity as spirit to go beyond, to transcend oneself, to respond to the evocation of "otherness," to the larger realm of meaning, truth, value, and love.[6]

One's years on earth are meant to be a time of discovering within the emerging forming universe how I am uniquely called to participate in the universal vocation to holiness and transformation in the Trinitarian life.

My having been baptized, with or without my consent, symbolizes that I am personally called throughout my life to turn myself around, to rediscover and return to the original call of my deepest self — my soul, an immortal diamond. In the midst of all the limitations of my life journey, my messy disruptive life events and relationships, my particular weakness of soul and body, I am called to *metanoia*. I am called to allow the Spirit's initiating activity and uncreated energies to become the inspiring motivation of my most basic identity and commitment.

For Christians since the time of the emperor Constantine, conversion is not ordinarily the result of a new decision to join the Christian community, be instructed by it in its vision of life, and be baptized. Catechesis, baptism, and conversion have lost their "institutional" connection. Our problem is how to establish any link at all between the three in our Christian living of them.

For adult Christians in most settings, conversion usually involves repeated returns to the somewhat neglected flame of faith and love that continues to flicker beneath the surface rubble of the soul. Conversion consists in recalling forgotten aspirations and divine inspirations native to this foundational form of our life. Conversion involves reawakening in limited freedom to a fresh perception of the emerging self in a continually forming universe. This new perception is characterized by an increasing capacity to discern the invisible initiatives of God at work in self and world. As the converting human person grows in freedom to assent to his or her foundational capacity for new life, more will be bestowed. As conversion and transformation of heart proceed, he or she will begin gradually to understand the deep mystery Christ was offering to his friends at the Last Supper when he said: "It was not you who chose me, it was I who chose you to go forth and bear fruit. Your fruit must endure..." (John 15:16). Converted perception will thus see human achievement and fulfillment in terms not of self-made perfection but of God-bestowed election, not as reward for virtue but as unmerited gift to poverty. It perceives life as mystery and gift, and conversion as detachment for the sake of more appealing attachment, as simply a return to the foundations of that mysterious gift in faith and fruitful commitment.

Conversion and Transformation

It is not only the mind and its perceptions that are changed in a Christian conversion process. The human capacity to will, to say yes or no, to assert responsible freedom and make choices also undergoes change and transformation.

What I have just said is, of course, a very old Christian idea. In fact, it was already an old idea when Jesus said, "You are not far from the kingdom of God!" to the Jewish scribe who had just said to him, "To love God with all your heart, with all your understanding and strength, and to love your neighbor as yourself, this is far more important than any holocaust or sacrifice" (Mark 12:28–34).

If Christian conversion is authentic, it makes us concretely more able to love. That has always been the acid test of the reality of the conversion. We end up with a genuine felt attachment and commitment to concrete loving actions for others in the world with our heart actually turning more freely to God and our neighbor.[7]

This becoming more able to love happens in small ways and in drastic ways. Part of it has to do with slowly learning not to be blinded by our individual affinities and pro-or-con feelings. That can be one of the fruits of the "appraisal" discipline that I began to describe in chapter 7: we can aim at a balanced view of persons, events, or things, a view that is not constantly blinded by our personal preferences and prejudices. Not that we should aim to ignore entirely the warmth, flavor, and spontaneity of our emotional responses. After all, they serve a "front-line" function in pulling us out of self-enclosure to meet the world's otherness. But those reactions can also be tyrannical. It can be a relief when the process of appraisal has helped us to sort out what our feelings and emotions have been trying to tell us. In practice, this often includes being free to move from depreciative knowing of a particular person, to appreciative knowledge of him or her. In other words, becoming a bit more converted helps me concretely to love, warts and all, the "neighbor" who is already in my life.

In Christian conversion, then, we do not simply learn a new doc-

.trine about life or love (that is, merely a change in cognitive content) but through the life and love of Jesus we begin to understand the paradoxical truth that life is love. That means we will begin, as the conversion proceeds, to feel and act in a completely new way. That includes emotions and feelings — our affect and our willing affirmations. It may begin with small things, like coming to see a neighbor or family member more appreciatively. But the dynamic is a radical, even drastic dynamic — the dynamic of Jesus' own love. The only truly self-fulfilling life is the life given up — even to death — in loving one's neighbor. Because, in conversion, this truth is not being learned only by the intellect. We come to embrace this truth through a relationship with God in Jesus Christ. It is in the actual following of Jesus and in the progressive detachment from what we used to cling to and what kept us from actually following Jesus that we begin to live this truth about love.[8]

All of this may be another way of coming to understand the meaning of the cross in life. It may also shed light on that central but always puzzling message of the Gospel about those who try to save their lives will lose them, and those who are willing to lose their lives will save them.[9]

Could Jesus be telling us that as long as we resist change, as long as we hang on fearfully to a more or less effective and comfortable pattern of living, that in the end we will find out that much of our thinking, feeling, and even willing and believing, has been on the wrong track? Will we find out at the end of our lives that salvation was only able to reach us when we were jolted out of our complacent stance by a challenge from the others or the Other breaking in on us in such a way that in spite of ourselves we were converted and in the process lost the old way of life that seemed so satisfactory but in reality was already dead?

Again a central issue for spiritual guidance comes to the fore. What does this person who comes for guidance really want? Is what he really wants out of life going to be sufficient for fullness of life for him? Is this wanting in need of a deep conversion, a turning upside down, in order that merely human volition will find its true consonance and direction in the will of the Holy Other? Are this person's reasonable judgments and commitments to action rooted in a deeper ground that she may not have originally chosen (you have not chosen me), so that a larger, more perfect will (but I have chosen you) may use her efforts (that you may go forth, bring forth fruit) for the lasting good of those who are her neighbors (and your fruit shall endure)? Martha in her kitchen comes to mind as we understand how a worker for God may undergo conversion into someone whose intellect, affect, and freed will are returned to the original intentionality of her reason for being.

For this to happen, Martha would have had to let go of her own plans and ideas and achievements and simply "hang loose" in unpredictable readiness and availability to do not her own, but God's idea of her work.[10]

The central focus of Christian spiritual guidance emerges right here, in this interior shift from preoccupation with one's own isolated plans and projects to suspecting that there may be an invisible plan into which those plans may or may not fit. How this new view of the larger field of one's life integrates one's free assent will be the topic of a later section.[11] But first we will look in a little more detail at the pattern of *metanoia* as it gradually unfolds within the lifelong process of conversion of the dispositions of the human heart.

A Familiar Pattern of Conversion

In giving examples of the *metanoia* they would like to have happen to themselves (or others!), people usually speak in terms of a "from ... to" pattern.[12] They say, for example, they would like to see a change in themselves from selfishness to otherness, from superficiality to depth, from fragmentation to wholeness. Therapists I know recall examples of people they have spoken with who have moved from slavery to freedom of some sort, from a state of stagnation to newness of life, from being trapped in the idealized self to acceptance of their real self. Christians find themselves wishing for *metanoia* in terms of a shift from sinfulness to gracefulness, from despair to hope, from narrowness to breadth of vision. Some of my students at the Institute might express such moves in terms of changing one's focus from self-will to doing God's will, or from immersion in the pride form to more freely expressing the Christ form.[13] In the next section of this chapter we will consider that Christian conversion always involves a shift from preoccupation with the "I" to feeling part of a greater "we."

All the personal accounts of conversion experiences that I have come across contain or imply at least one or more of these "from ... to" pairs. Usually the one who is recounting the experience devotes considerable descriptive detail to what happened in between "from" and "to."

They will begin by telling us about the restlessness they were feeling in their "from" position, of the unhappiness and conflict they experienced in their selfish, superficial, or fragmented state. "Helping people" like therapists or spiritual directors will insist on recounting the tough struggles as their clients and directees slowly emerged from their slavery to some addiction or from a certain type of sinful behavior. Some just cannot resist giving a blow by blow description (disguised often as a "case consultation") of the painful movement involved in a client's renouncement of, let us say, riskless inertia or encapsulation in an ideal self, "through" the daily unrelenting battle to let go of familiar securities and defenses, "to" grudging acceptance of new ways of behaving and even enjoying their limited but real and actual selves.[14] To move from narrowness to breadth of vision we have to go "through" something.

As anyone grows and changes from one stage or age of life to the next, he or she inevitably finds that instead of an instantaneous magical transition, there is always a middle term, a "through." Etty Hillesum did not magically move from being a fine but untried young Dutch romantic to the strong spiritual presence evoking hope and courage in fellow prisoners at Auschwitz. She went through a harsh and trying time of testing first.[15] If, on the other hand, we look again at the fictional Beth Jarrett, we realize that it was precisely because she carefully avoided living through that middle term, because she chose not to accept the challenge offered to herself and her family by the collapse of their middle-class comfortable world, that she failed to complete the pattern of conversion. She chose to resist going "through" the painful mid-life transition. She chose instead to escape the chaos and confusion involved. She failed to follow the radical route to which her life was leading her. We wonder why this adult woman found herself unable to give a free response of her whole responsible, sensitive heart. We surmise that probably in so doing she found herself increasingly unable to move from her fear and isolation to dialogue with a larger meaning. Unable to break the clutch of her encapsulating ego, she could not allow herself to undergo a detachment "from" her familiar self-image "to" a new integration, a new loving attachment to her husband and remaining son, the significant others in her life.[16]

Even in the case of St. Paul, whose well-known conversion seemed instantaneous and complete as he was blinded by a new way of seeing God's power in weakness, "through" time had to be spent in reappraisal of all his former values and priorities as he slowly learned to shift from being motivated by his own fierce ambition and Pharisaic zeal to seeking victory only in the unearned self-gift of Jesus Christ on the cross.

At this point the pattern is clear. Conversion, shifting from one way of being in the world to another, always seems to require a middle period, a "through" that links an original state of either complacency or dissatisfaction with an appeal to grow and mature, with a vaguely sensed call to become new. This newness harmonizes with a deeper mysterious dimension of one's being that can only come to life if this entire pattern is allowed to unfold.

The underlying guidance question here might be, "How is this particular person either willfully or inadvertently resisting the calls addressed to his or her heart to move beyond where he or she is now?" Previous years of reacting to life's invitations from the merely vital-functional dimension may have fixated this person's heart in un-freedom, in a closed-off or sleepy ambiguity that encapsulates the will. Such a closed circuit of impulses, ambitions, and pulsations, of plea-sures to be enjoyed and projects to be accomplished, can actually cut a person off from transcendent values, from new ideas, from tran-scendent ideals, and even at times from the inspirations of the Holy Spirit.

We wonder how this reactive mode can be shifted, be converted to a freer response? Certainly the wisdom of all great spiritual traditions is in unanimous agreement about the need for alienated human hearts to begin to open themselves to what is other.

One basic way in which guides help seekers to become more open to what is other is by teaching them to cultivate a more receptive kind of consciousness, an idea that has recurred many times in this book. We can learn to foster a receptive presence to all levels of the unpredictable initiatives of reality, whether in the form of people, events, or things. We can build in moments of retreat and relaxation, for reflective pauses even in the midst of the day's activity.[17]

That is good, but it is not yet interpersonal. Usually, it is only in re-ceptive openness to the community of human others and to inspiration from the larger Mystery that the average person, thus feeling rooted in the love of others or of God, will be able to reach beyond the hardened boundaries of the self. True conversion heads in that direction: toward trustful solidarity and communion. It calls for a shifting of one's sense of self: from isolated "I," through a letting go of familiar boundaries, to an intensity of at-homeness on a new, more other-centered level. Like the grain of wheat, the person being converted must leave behind a dy-ing form, the broken husk of the former self, and freely welcome a kind of death along with any new possibilities of life that may accompany this change.

At times like this of mid-transition, we find it helpful to set up personal life structures that will allow whatever death may be appro-priate to happen. We may begin keeping a journal, or start meditating regularly; we may want to consult a helpful person and get enough sleep. Life as we have known it will seem to be caving in, but all that is really being put to death is some aspect of our egoistic striving and pride, of our exalted ambitions and illusions. At the same time, after a long or short period of creative waiting, we will begin to discover that concurrent with apparent death there will be a release of new en-ergy in service of the new attachment of our heart. Accompanied by an increase of self-understanding, compassion for others, insight, and ma-turity, we find ourselves facing a new kind of freedom. We are enjoying the release of rebirth. We realize that the pattern of our conversion has been that of the Paschal Mystery, from death through suffering and decision to new life.[18] The fruits of this transcendent movement of life, of this "spiritual revolution," can continue to be integrated into our hearts and minds by the dynamic of our personal assent to inner renewal.

However, as I found out myself when I worked for two years in a mental hospital, and later as a counselor and spiritual director, there is something in human nature that strongly resists freedom, that would rather remain in familiar misery than have to live with the uncertainty and unpredictability of dying to the false self and continuously assenting to the new. To consistently live out our capacity for transcendent aspiration, we humans need the help of the Holy Spirit of God. By ourselves we can obtain only a limited release from our self-groundedness, from our closedness to the wider vision of a Christian worldview, from the deep fear of the freedom that accompanies spiritual rebirth.

Reformation of the Heart's Dispositions

One of the areas where our capacity for freedom can be exercised with most effect is in the area of dealing with dispositions of our heart.[19] As Christians we are asked to become renewed in the spirit of our minds, to try to dispose ourselves in certain ways, and to deal wisely with the ways we find ourselves and our hearts already disposed. Since dispositions of the heart are internal structures that channel formative energies and power in specific ways and since these powers are not well integrated in our fallen condition, we need to attentively make disciples of our sometimes unruly dispositions.

For example, people set up the structures of certain subcultures like religious life, in the realization that we acquire certain dispositions, such as taste for certain foods, habits of sleep and prayer, ways of thinking and recreating, functional routines, and so on, from interaction with our situation. These acquired dispositions, both formative and deformative, taken on throughout the course of our life more or less freely and reflectively, are somewhat open to change if we so desire. Not so the innate dispositions with which we were born. Persons who are from birth disposed to being physically strong or weak, heavy set or sprightly, intelligent or dull, easy-going or melancholy are usually not free to change these dispositions, though, of course, they are free to take an attitude toward them.[20]

When we speak about conversion of dispositions, we are speaking about a shift in those dispositions of heart that guides have tended to recognize as being deformative, as sapping a person's life energy, as paralyzing freedom. The guide's task is to help men and women to grow in self-knowledge, in gentle self-presence to whatever dispositions, innate or acquired, may be dominating their lives.

In light of these self-discoveries as well as their forgotten identity as unique image and likeness of God expressed through their powers of mind and will, many contemporary men and women are now refinding and happily returning to their own original ways of being disposed toward the world. Their days of conforming in imitation of others and of ignorance about their own innate or even neurotic dispositions are over. Less comfortable perhaps they may be, but at the same time more self-aware and true to themselves. Moreover, they are more capable of setting up life structures for themselves and others that will foster the positive type of disposition conversion they are seeking. They are, for example, fostering a prayerful disposition in their own lives by talking with well-informed guides, by reading about it, structuring the best time in their day and week to do it themselves. They are not only seeking help with prayer, but finding suitable environments conducive to it and learning how to relax and meditate on Scripture there, all in service of their transcendent aspiration for prayer and its accompanying dispositions of heart.

Guides who understand about reforming dispositions through setting up facilitating structures can also avoid past mistakes like willfully trying to reverse old dispositions by force. They will have learned that the most profound and lasting conversion of dispositions can only be the work of a saving God who needs the cooperation of our free assent to the liberating energy of grace.[21]

Dynamics of Detachment and Second Conversion

We have come to realize that the call to conversion has to begin with attachment, with an experience of the "dynamics of delight."[22] It is only when the farmer has found "treasure" he honestly considers to be worthwhile to him that he is willing to give up all that he has to buy the field. As we noticed earlier, guides must understand that the dynamics of delight come first. They must be able to help people reflectively uncover the positive aspects of their experience of the Mystery. Only then are we ready for the selling and the buying, for repentance and metanoia, for the decision and commitments that are the fruit of discipline and of the Christian disposition of detachment.

In the great mystical traditions of guidance we find mention of the need for this freeing disposition of heart. Along with humility, both the detachment and the attachment that precede it are recognized as key. Unless people have a glimpse of delight from time to time, unless their hearts are captured by the treasure that appears in Christ's appealing love, how can they be expected to "sell" lesser treasures they have spent a lifetime collecting? How can they be converted from their attachment to these inferior yet treasured dispositions of envy, greed, pride, domination, and power unless they suspect that a greater good, a more fulfilling treasure awaits them through deeper participation in the Mystery? We cannot even begin to talk about the dynamics of Christian conversion unless we start with the joy of transcendent aspiration for "more" that is put in motion by the Trinitarian Mystery rather than by any human achievement.

In detachment that belongs to conversion, then, we are willing to let go of everything else and give ourselves without reserve to being drawn by the Mystery. Basically this detachment will be "from" the ego-istic, possessive, controlling, and self-sufficient dispositions belonging to the pride form's hold on our life. The point here is that no one willingly gives up being the center of his or her own existence without a good reason. Why would anyone want to give up even the illusion of mastery, of being in control, of our right to cling to contrived finite worlds of meaning unless we were convinced that shifting one's axis from self to the divine Other would make sense and open us to a far more spacious life than what we already enjoy? Like the disciples, we must know Christ, must see where and how "he lives," and must have faith in him as a person before we will be crazy enough to leave all and follow him (John 1:35–39). Thus, the dynamics of detachment flow in two directions. They move us away "from" the desire for pleasure, possessions, and power that are not in tune with his purposes. At the same time they attract us "to" flowing with the Mystery as it appears in our daily lives in ways we often as not fail to understand.[23]

Here is where life itself not only forms but reforms and converts us even when, if left to ourselves, we would prefer to do nothing. Again we learn from traditional wisdom that in order to mature, we must be changed, we must undergo a kind of cleansing, a "purgative" way. At the beginning of spiritual life we may actively choose to engage ourselves in this process, dropping out of consumerism, stripping our lives of unessentials, relinquishing some dispositions that do not be-long to our Christian calling and learning to travel light. But all the great masters of the spiritual way warn us that at a certain point we must be willing to relinquish our own initiative even in the activity of detachment. Eventually, if we live long enough, life itself helps us to let go. The aging process takes over and gradually we are asked to surrender graciously (if a little sadly) to the tragic and uncontrollable facts of the human condition. Little by little our attachments to mate-rial objects, to our own plans, to what we expect from our own life, to ideas we have cherished, to relationships that have meant life to us, to projects and power and the comfortable illusion of mastery and con-trol are diminished, in spite of our efforts to retain them. Ill health and losses of many kinds interrupt our daily routine. The rituals we have grown accustomed to are disrupted and disappear along with certain dogmatic attitudes and structures we have built into our lives. Slowly our former ways of dressing, of eating, of recreating, and of praying are replaced by others not of our choice. Even our earlier image of God seems to vanish as we anxiously begin to wonder about our own survival as a person.

In former times we may have more or less freely chosen a lifestyle of Gospel simplicity. Now that simplicity begins to choose us. It just moves itself into our lives. Now, more than ever, it becomes vitally important that the conversion pattern of "from" and "through" be oriented "to" a meaningful Other toward whom we can move in trustful surrender. The ability to say yes to allowing oneself to be carried by the Mystery, by the God who has moved from the periphery of our being to its center, resides ultimately in the disposition of *trust*. This trust that God in the person of Christ and the power of the Spirit can be counted on to bring one's life to its fulfillment describes perfectly the converted disposition of the human being who finally recognizes and turns to welcome the buried truth of his or her deepest commitment to the Mystery.[24]

Most of us do not set out deliberately on the path of detachment and trust. When we are younger, we are too preoccupied discovering and establishing our identity, developing a sense of our vocation and immersing ourselves in commitments that consume most of our time and energy. However, as the authors of current books on mid-life have pointed out, in that transition we are called anew to the journey of conversion by circumstances outside of our control.[25]

Teilhard de Chardin has described this as the time of the "passivities of diminishment," when we must face both internal and external bits of ill fortune that tend to interrupt our spheres of activity, development, and life.[26] At any point in our history, we will, of course, have to cope with natural feelings, intellectual or moral weaknesses, fears and neurotic tendencies of all sorts. At a certain moment, confronted by the aging process and death itself, we find that expanding horizons and growing confidence in self and future begin to give way to unmistakable hints of the finality and fragility of this world as we have known it. We have reached the stage of "second conversion."

Prayer Guidance for a New Stage in Life

Life after (let's say) fifty can give people some very dark periods. Some people feel such inner confusion that we find them living in an escape mode: alcohol or other drugs, ceaseless work involvement or a hectic social life, sexual adventuring and other reactive patterns. Others "decompensate" by collapsing onto a lower level of psychological functioning such as depression, anxiety, or intense feelings of rage. The self-knowledge provided by some methods of counseling and psychotherapeutic care may help here. But they are not enough. A spiritual guide can perhaps help by introducing people to an integrated and gentle type of reflective prayer that encompasses God's providence and forgiveness and that provides a meditative look at the self in relation to the whole of reality.

It may not always be "gentle" reflection. Author Maria Boulding is blunt about our actual experiences of prayer in this dark period.[27] She notes that we begin to pray from a condition of chaos because that is where we are. Conversion means going down into the dark chaotic waters and allowing ourselves to be re-created by God's act: not once, but many times. It isn't always nice. Prayer often lights up the inner poverty of our lack of prayer, leading us to a global sense of the general "slum situation within." Still, prayer is the main thing we need to do, the only really creative thing human beings can do under the circumstances. That is what the guide needs to understand. Once aging persons begin to let go of obsolete modes of living, once they get in touch with their deepest identity and begin to assent freely to Love's mysterious plan for them, then their prayer will begin to change.

Thus, guides for people at this stage of spiritual growth will have to be familiar not only with vocal and liturgical prayer, with meditative reading, and with discursive meditation itself. They also have a responsibility to become a facilitator of what Teresa of Avila calls the prayer of recollection, a style of praying based on awareness of God's presence within us that introduces those who practice it into the life of the Trinity.[28] Actually this form of living in loving intimacy with God depends not only on the divine initiative but also on the sustaining powers of the mind. It takes an enlivened imagination and focused concentration for the whole human person seeking the divine Presence to remain in close contact with the God who dwells not only in the soul's center but also in the events, people, and things of that soul's entire life field.

The person who gradually learns to practice the prayer of recollection is tuning in to, consenting to, the "already there" Mystery that grounds both his or her individual life field and the field or web of interacting energies that underlies the entire cosmos. This insight corresponds to the way Maria Boulding describes our "chaos-marked efforts to pray." She, too, sees them as partaking in God's new creation as part of the Spirit's glorious, recreative act in Christ, as part of the salvation history of the renewed cosmos. So Christian tradition has noted specific signs of conversion of the heart to contemplation, to that receptive openness or loving abandonment of the person to the action of God

in faith and through the gifts of the Holy Spirit that guides should
be aware of. Among spiritual masters in the Western tradition there is
general agreement that perhaps at no other time in our spiritual journey do people need more the assistance of knowledgeable, experienced,
and discerning spiritual guides than at the transition from a discursive
way of praying to contemplation.[29]

At this transition, it is easy to obstruct God's transforming and purifying activity. An unprepared, inexperienced guide may try, as John
of the Cross warns, to force the person who is finding meditation impossible to meditate as before. The persons themselves may become
discouraged by the darkness and aridity they may be experiencing and
be tempted to abandon solitary prayer altogether. When confronted
with a person undergoing this type of conversion, disinclined to focus
on any particular object, inclined to simply wait quietly and affectively
on God, inexperienced guides may advise pseudosolutions, thus living up to John's description of them as "blacksmiths of the soul."[30]
More experienced guides, on the other hand, may wisely and sympa-
thetically encourage seekers in surrendering to the irresistible drawing
of the Holy Other, in slowing down and weathering the alternations
between turmoil and peace that accompany such changes.

Guides who have lived through a few conversion experiences themselves will at this stage recognize the inner trauma that inevitably
accompanies a definitive choice between God and self. Having been
there themselves, they will also be in sympathy with the person's anxious concern about all this change when attitudes and dispositions are
reversed as the real self continues to emerge.

Thérèse and Religious Conversion

On December 25, 1886, Thérèse of Lisieux underwent an interior conversion of heart that, in its classic simplicity and depth, gives us an
example of what guides should be alert to as they listen for the conversion pattern of "from–through–to" unfolding in the lives of the men
and women who seek them out. It seems that after midnight Mass on
this particular Christmas, Thérèse and her doting father were about to
engage in a family custom in which, for years, Thérèse opened and
exclaimed over the presents she found in her slippers at Christmas.
The Martin family expected that this happy evening would be like
all the others. However, Mr. Martin was exhausted and the sight of
Thérèse's slippers irritated him. As she went upstairs to put away her
hat, Thérèse, the spoilt, sensitive, and somewhat neurotic baby of the
family, overheard her beloved father remark that he hoped this would
be the last time they would all have to go through this childishness.
Thérèse's sister Celine, knowing how hypersensitive she was and see-

ing the tears welling up in her eyes, advised her not to go downstairs just then.

If Thérèse had come in and told the story up till this point, what would a spiritual guide have been alert for? In her autobiography, Thérèse fills in the picture of the hypersensitive childish little queen, center and star of an overprotective bourgeois French family, a rather immature weepy person who was nevertheless determined to please God as well as her family.[31] A guide would probably note her position in the family system, her sickly childhood, her history of scruples and loss of self-esteem, all of which is to be gathered from her autobiography. A guide would note also the strong Catholic faith tradition of the Martin family, the number of daughters already in religious life, and their adherence to the family custom of the slipper full of presents after midnight Mass. Typical of their socioeconomic class and religious ideology, the Martins would not have questioned the directives of their subculture for the celebration of this feast.

If Thérèse had revealed as much of her inner life to this hypothetical guide as she did in her journals, there would be no doubt that her preformation included not only a strong rootedness in French Catholicism of the time, but also that since baptism, she herself had sturdily fought against her sensitivity and near despair on the long journey of choice between self and God. The guide would know, for example, that since her mother died when she was four, Thérèse had tried for ten years to retrieve the strength of soul she had lost at her mother's death. The guide would know then something of the struggle she had been "through." He or she would have recognized the call of this young girl even at this early period of her life to "love God with all [her] heart and to stay poor in spirit."[32] He or she would also have understood the deep significance of this remark for Thérèse in view of the intensity of her relationship with her beloved father. Thus, as the person's story unfolds, the guide would listen carefully and compassionately to what is happening on all polarities of the life field.

The narrative continues, as Thérèse describes how, instead of taking Celine's advice, "I suppressed my tears, ran downstairs, and picked up my shoes. I pulled out my presents with an air of great cheerfulness. Daddy laughed and Celine thought she was dreaming!" In her own words, Thérèse had received "the grace to grow up." A major shift had taken place, a conversion of heart "to" a steadfast and mature disposition of soul and spirit that was to remain for the rest of her life. She writes from inside the experience, "Jesus, satisfied with my goodwill, accomplished in an instant what I had been unable to do in ten years."[33] As her own best and most competent guide, Thérèse saw clearly what was happening in this seemingly insignificant incident from her daily life. In detaching herself, or rather being detached, from former clinging to childish, outmoded ways of perceiving her family and her behavior in it, Thérèse cooperated in letting herself be shifted into an entirely new way of inhabiting her life field. Her mind and heart were awakened to a new level of presence to the underlying Mystery in her life. She was able to confront immaturity and egocentrism. She found herself on a new level of prayer life that would lead her directly to her contemplative vocation in Carmel. Yet, with the wisdom of an experienced guide, she realized at once that this great change was pure gift. This turning point in her life was not her work but God's.

Thérèse, like any other person undergoing a confusing and possibly anxious experience of disposition reversal, probably could have used some guidance in the days that followed this Christmas event. No doubt she still had to struggle with the temptation to revert to childish ways. In fact, later on one of her biggest struggles as a member of the religious community where her sister was prioress was to refrain from constantly going to see this "mother" to whom she was so attached. The longing was so strong that she had to hurry past Pauline's cell and "clutch the balustrade to prevent myself turning back."[34] For her, the "little beyond" of family affection often threatened to overwhelm her as did her need for being affectionately loved.[35] Like men and women today who find themselves moving toward a deeper involvement with the mysterious Other, she, too, had to work through the many different stages that belong to this phenomenon called "conversion."[36]

Prayer as Nourishing Compassionate Vision

Underlying the mystery of spiritual conversion we find the disposition of awe at the wonder of life itself, at the realization that we are already part of some ultimate cosmic process, that we are never really a separated isolated self but are already committed to participation in the mystery of what it means to be alive. Being able to say yes to that, being able to contemplate ourselves as being rooted in Mystery, being able to contemplatively use the imaginative powers of our minds to uncover the hidden beauty and meaning of reality, belongs to our capacity as spirit. People need the kind of conversion of heart and mind suggested by Paul Ricoeur, one that "implies a shift in the direction of the look, a reversal in the vision, in the imagination of the heart, before all kinds of good intentions and all kinds of good decisions and good actions."[37]

This vision of change in perception can be applied especially to people caught in the web of circumstances and limiting commitments known as mid-life. Guidance may be needed so that any practical reworking of life structures will be truly creative and in line with the transcendent potential of this person's unique spirit in the light of his or her particular faith and form tradition. The guide is there to help with the interpretation of present crises or transitions, both by stimulating the person's own imagination and empowering him or her to appraise a new vision for the future.

Guides who have been through some changes themselves, who have made the shift to a contemplative seeing of the interwovenness of life and Mystery, can help contemporary men and women make the connections they may need to make. Seeing something of the unity of all that is, contemplative guides are able to assist people in facing the sometimes negative images of self that appear in prayer and pull them away from true self-knowledge. In the context of prayer, both fears and ideals tend to surface. A compassionate guide could have helped a person like Thérèse come to terms sooner, for example, with what modern minds would call the "remnants of her childhood omnipotence." People need to have their expectations with regard to the spiritual life and relationship with God questioned. Which of their images and defensive ideals need to be let go of? Who will help them with the mourning and depression that follows this detachment? Who will be with people as they begin to discover the disparity between their life as they have already lived it and the unlived potential that begins to appear as they move deeper into a knowledge of untapped form potencies? Willfulness and despair often emerge unless there is someone who can empower them to see that their lives are part of a larger reconciling process that puts their own small contribution into perspective. The wise guide who, avoiding the "myth of the guru," relies not on his or her personal attainment of perfection, but on the unmerited goodness and mercy of God, can be a trusted companion for this person's journey. The guide who, like John the Baptist, steps out of the way so that the One who can truly save this person may appear, is the guide who can be trusted.

Moving beyond the mind and imagination, Thomas Merton recommends finding our heart, recovering an awareness of our inmost identity that implies recognizing that our external everyday self is to a great extent a mask and a fabrication.[38] It is not our true self, which is hidden still in obscurity and nothingness at the center of our being where we are in direct dependence on God. Merton later indicates that people whose prayer takes them into the darkness beyond images may need support in facing the truth of their own emptiness in a struggle with such darkness. Only guides who have been willing to move beyond their own fallen egoism, their own self-preoccupation, to lose their own lives in order to save them, will be alive enough to compassionately guide a fellow journeyer. Such helpers know from personal experience something of both the misery and the glory of the human condition.[39] They will never try to force anyone to move faster than the pace of grace nor forget that they, too, are fellow sinners needing mercy from the same God. The ultimate guarantee of the trustworthiness of the guide is the presence in his or her life of personal dependence on the Mystery's loving and saving activity. A compassionate guide, then, never is judgmental or harsh, never tries to live in gnostic forgetfulness of his or her whole humanity, and always tries to be mindful of the contextual faith that gives meaning to one's own and the other's call and desire for holiness.

Chapter Nine

BELONGING AND COMMUNION

SPIRITUAL guides from all the world's great traditions seem to agree that one of the most fruitful shifts accompanying a person's conversion or turning toward the Mystery is a deepened appreciation of the fact that other people share the life field with oneself. True self-transcendence can be discovered in making the conscious shift from living as an individualistic, isolated "I," to relaxing into a renewed sense of the communal "we."

Psychologists notice it too, and give it various names. Psychologist Andras Angyal describes it as a healthy movement from self-preoccupied "autonomy" to what he calls "homonomy" — a confident sense of human belonging.[1] He sees homonomy as the necessary complement of our longing for independence. As members of the human family, we always experience a necessary tension in life between the individual person and the surrounding others. Like the fish in the Sufi legend, we tend to become extremely busy swimming to survive and attain self-chosen goals. We may cease to be aware of the network of "already there" others in the water with us. This web that we are of interconnected persons, this essentially social nature of our embodied existence can and often does go unnoticed. Yet not one of us could have survived, or even come to be, without it.

Different cultures experience the individual vs. community tension, and propose its resolution, in different ways. Exceedingly different, sometimes.[2] Among the cultures of the human family, Western culture since the Renaissance has developed at a place closer to the individualist end of the spectrum than have most other cultures. That affects us deeply.

It is not that we (Western people) deny that other people share our life field. It is just that we tend to drift into a sleepy complacency that regards others as simply part of the wallpaper, hardly noticed on the walls of our narrow lives.

Spiritual guides in the West learn to be on the lookout for that

141

cultural bias. They learn to foster a conscious reentry into appreciative dialogue with the human others who share this planet.

Recently, the growing environmental movement has helped people acknowledge that humans belong to the rest of creation too. We are at home in the organic, biological, and geological aspects of the forming universe. Without it, we have no life-supporting home. But as human spiritual beings we experience special kinship and solidarity with others who share the distinctively human gift of being "spirit": whose mind, will, and creative imagination give them a particular relationship with the rest of creation.

Religious wisdom has always spoken of our tendency to live in ignorance not only of our own deepest life call, but also in avoidance of solidarity with human others to whom we truly do belong. Spiritual teachers add that we belong especially to those whose suffering and vulnerability call out for our compassion and also for our action. Conversion includes contemplative seeing not only of the Holy Other but also of the network of human others who are our companions in this life and through whom we encounter the communal wisdom about living handed on from one generation to the next.[3]

Others Share the Life Field

For men and women baptized into the Christian faith tradition, the essential command that summons their "yes" to human others is the command of love. It is "no new commandment, but an old one which you had from the start" (1 John 2:7). "You shall love your neighbor as yourself," proclaims the covenant mediated by Moses — but indeed it does go back to "the start," back before the question "Where is your brother Abel?" Jesus Christ only radicalized that ancient command by his Last Supper version of it: "Love one another as I have loved you" (John 13:34).[4]

That awesome command, however, does not exempt Christians from the conflict that runs through the human experience of community. Spiritual communities suffer the conflict as intensely as any other kind of community.

This conflict can be expressed simply. The others are never myself. They do not think and feel from exactly the same perspective on reality that I do. No community of people can ever be totally at one with my uniqueness. That is the way things are. And yet we are summoned to be church.

Many of the spiritual problems troubling people who seek guidance stem precisely from this dilemma. Much of the stress within the Christian community owes its origin to the simple fact that the church, like the human race, is composed of unique persons who — even if they genuinely care about unity — are not yet able to completely let go of self-interest in order to be available for the needs and service of others.

A mature life of being "with" others rather than simply tending against, toward, or away from them requires an extraordinarily open heart, mind, and will. To arrive there entails a difficult, demanding shift from sinful individualism to a stance of mutual giving and receiving.

Living this interpersonal dimension of our lives asks us to relinquish some of our defense mechanisms. It expects us to affirm the others as persons, to encourage their uniqueness and freedom, and to become concretely and intimately involved in their lives. We try it, and we constantly run up against the fallenness, the brokenness that haunts all human relationships. One way or another, we are caught in the conflict between self and God that underlies them all.

Unless we are grounded in Mystery — unless we experience both ourselves and the others as co-participants in Mystery — we find it almost impossible to live in compassionate love of one another for any length of time.[5] Unless we have "new eyes" that can see the others contemplatively, it is easy to miss the many-splendored thing that is our life together.

Many young people are seeking guidance regarding this communal dimension of their lives. They are looking for a community of others to whom they can offer their personal "yes." Human hearts seek a visible, viable community whose intentions match their own.[6] Believers seek a community whose invisible rooting in the Mystery corresponds in important ways to their own sense of call.

But we have to be aware of our personal call, of our unique stand in life, to be able to avoid entanglement with groups whose inner intentionality does not match our own. Without that kind of self-knowledge, it is easy to mistake a group's collective dream for our own.[7]

If group membership is undertaken before we are personally ready for it, we may be in danger of being swallowed up by the group — or, depending on our temperament, of becoming too quickly isolated from it.[8] When we are ready, we can choose simply to be "with" these other persons in ways that are really free. We can be "with" them in a way that touches their shared participation in the Mystery that lies beyond both group and members.

When a human heart has grown through some conversions, it is no longer isolated and alone but rooted in Mystery and in the community of others. Then it is capable of transcending itself in the shared vision of a larger plan. Then it can responsibly and sensitively decide how to act in dialogue with a larger meaning. In its newfound confidence, the converted heart can trust in the midst of ambiguity and pluralism. It can summon its functional and transcendent powers of willing in solidarity with others and with the "more than" in a way that, prior to *metanoia*, did not seem possible. A move forward in convertedness entails real differences of behaviors and of feeling; someone who, at an earlier time, was trapped in ego-protective strategies may become able to shed them. The common ground on which everyone stands simply becomes more obvious. "Common humanity" is the radical relatedness that is a bottom-line reality for all members of the human race; but it is not a personally significant and precious reality until persons have done some dying and some growing.

The Communal Nature of Commitments

Basic to the human story is the way others call us out of our preoccupation with self. As infants, we were called out of our preoccupation with self to learn about the larger world of mother and daddy, brothers and sisters, relatives and visitors and neighbors. As children in school, we were called out of ourselves by the schoolworld of "the kids in my class," the friendships and special groups, the fights and disappointments, the intimacies or lack of them that belong to this vulnerable, expansive period of life. For all of us, the teen years are colored by awakening sexuality, by the possibilities of love and the ambition to go after the dreams of the heart.

The calls of young adulthood tend to be more binding, more permanent. They are absorbing and strenuous calls: marriage and family life, a career, a project of social justice or humanitarian service or artistic achievement, service within the church, commitment to a great movement. These calls, for the young adult, mediate the deeper call to serve God and neighbor that they both evoke and imply.[9]

They are precious beyond gold, those commitments. Without them, how could anyone grow in love and courage? But of course, they also bristle with normal dangers. To be "fallen" means that we are constantly pulled toward idolatry. Spiritual guides, then, are always alert for ways in which these absorbing commitments of time and energy may subtly be lulling a woman or man into forgetfulness of the deeper self.

Not that we will try — if we are experienced guides — to pull people out of intense relatedness. We will have learned, over and again, that there is no spiritual fulfillment that does not in some way become part of a communal fulfillment.[10] We find ourselves by giving ourselves. We grow to be the persons we are meant to be by devoting ourselves to the common good, in some form. Yet mixed motives are the ordinary lot of all of us. As guides, we will be concerned about the purification of the motives, about the deeper motivation that gives a lived inner meaning to these expenditures of time and energy.

For example, one may join a community or network, or found a family, for a variety of reasons. I may frankly center all motivations on myself: on the achievement of my dream, to be realized in and through the personal power and resources I have access to within this group. A group (or spouse) can become for me protection, validation, justification. Or I may be like most people: my motives are probably mixed. Some are self-centered, some are more self-transcending aspirations that unite me with others in service of a larger good. I may be conscious of, and grateful for, a "covenant" dimension that evokes my personal call at the same time that "we" work together toward the common good.

Clarifications Needed by Groups

Groups have mixed motives too. Self-deception is a trap for groups, not only for individuals. We have a hard time sorting all that out. Guides need to deal with all kinds of unrealistic expectations regarding community. For one thing, there are variations in the sociological style of communities. If we as guides are aware of these differences, we may be able to help a seeker to ask the right questions about a community he or she is thinking of joining (or wondering about leaving!). We could ask the seeker (or, help her ask herself): Are you looking for a primary community, a family-like atmosphere where you can feel supported and cared for, where you can feel at home? Or do you desire rather a more clear-cut association where the common goal has higher priority and certain clearly stated roles are oriented toward achievement and action ?

Or do we feel a mixture of expectations that (if not sorted out) might guarantee frustrations ahead? Which comes first for us — contractual rights and responsibilities (such as might be shared by faculty members or managers in a corporation or cooperative) or the supportive relationships and patient friendships that endure in a primary commitment? Is our dearest goal to belong somewhere good? Or is our dearest goal coordinated, shared action aimed at transforming the public sphere?

These are some of the basic questions and hidden expectations that, when not clarified in a community or group, make for frustrations. Well-meaning people can assume too easily that "we all want the same thing," without doing the work to find out how far that is true. Sometimes the group as a whole has simply never done that work and would be unable to answer those questions about its collective priorities, even if an aspiring member knew how to ask them.

Guides dealing with people already in communal situations must be alert for these and other hidden expectations, because so many problems in community spring from that confusing source. Each person brings to the group or partnership his or her own set of "shoulds" and definitions regarding sharing, cooperation, authority, and leadership. Often these differences have never been acknowledged and appreciated. Perhaps no one has ever clarified the demands for being a member of that group. There may be a general fuzziness about goals that are functioning as foundations for communal efforts to participate. There may not be agreed-upon definitions of goals, tasks, and kinds of leadership. Or there may be a need for communal clarification of deeper values.

Without opportunities to share and celebrate what they hold in common — especially from their shared faith and form tradition[11] — group members may be unable to gear into serious joint action with others. Issues of powerlessness may become central as individuals fail to connect their own skills and talents with the group's thrust toward making a difference in the world. Yet the reason for membership in that community in the first place may have been the need to join with others toward the transformation of society: that is something we cannot do alone.

Religious communities and other gatherings of believers need this kind of collective value-clarification just as much as any other group.[12] What makes a faith group healthy for its members and good for the wider church? What keeps such a group oriented to the kingdom that is coming? The guide needs to find out how the persons who seek guidance are already participating in intentional groups with perhaps unrealistic expectations of what such a group might be able to offer. It seems clear from experience that certain groups can and do enliven an individual's faith, allow him or her to be more than just a designated role, and mediate that individual's deepest hopes for his or her life. What makes a group able to be so helpful?

One necessary condition seems to be this: a group must hold on tenaciously to the wider vision for which it was brought into being in the first place. When a group consciously and continuously renews its shared core story, when it repeatedly expresses afresh the ultimate ground that gives meaning to its collective figure, then the members will be able freely to make sense of their ongoing personal story in its light. As a member, I must be able clearly to articulate my community's central passion and prioritize my desires in harmony with the zeal of our corporate desire. When I cannot do that, I lose focus. When the main focus of a group or a relationship becomes confused and fragmented, my involvement becomes fuzzy also, and then remote.

What Am I Promising?

Supposing that a group's self-identity is clear in that way, the guide of a person seeking a communal commitment could go on to other questions. Some of them will be about the seeker, some about the group, many about the interface between the two. Does this person have some understanding of the emotional involvement, the hidden customs, the subtle evaluation process that applies to members of his or her intended group?[13] Would this group nourish or would it oppose the "habits" of this particular seeker's heart? Does this community help this seeker to shape a purpose for life that is "part of the purposes of God?"[14]

We are formed by, and we give form to, our communal groups and relationships. They are so important to our happiness that they can tempt us deeply. We need the respect of our community, and we need to have some influence in it, and we can fall deep into self-deception if we feel that we lack either respect or influence and are striving to gain one or the other.[15]

Joining a community is a kind of promise-making. In her fine study, *Personal Commitments*, Margaret Farley describes this type of promising as "our way of trying to give a future to our present love."[16] We can make such a commitment only if the ultimate horizon of the community (or person) receiving our commitment is compatible with what we profoundly cherish in our own life. We can remain faithful only to a larger self if it emerges for us from that horizon of Mystery that appeals to our deepest longing and faith. A group that turns out to be only a larger version of our ego is not worthy of commitment. Nor will such a group support commitment to compassion for the world through a lifetime of ambiguous human attempts to love and care for others.

Joining a Christian religious community — or entering a Christian marriage — is meant to be a public and prayed-over way of embodying my commitment to Christ. That theological and human ideal is a very ancient one. It still lives in the living tradition of the church — and it has consequences for the spouse, or the community, willing to receive someone who is making a commitment of that specifically Christian kind.

The early Christian catechumenate had a moment called the Rite of Election.[17] At this moment, catechumens were challenged to decide whether or not they wanted to actually join the motley collection of Christ's followers — to blend their priorities and their decisions for the future with this less than socially promising group. To be able to say yes, catechumens must have felt themselves captured by, intent on, Christ. Jesus Christ, the central focus of the community's shared vision, became the originating value for the catechumens personally. In committing themselves to this Christ who had given his life for them, these early Christians became one in heart with a community of others who had been similarly called and attracted. It was this call — not their affinity for one another or for any particular work or lifestyle — that drew them together.

Two thousand years later, women and men are still responding to the same mysterious call. They are still searching for like-minded others with whom they can live and work in a community that can mediate between their personal life dream and the larger world. When they find it, they hope that they are able to reach within it what one writer describes as "the maturing point of spiritual life."[18] At such a point, each is able to make a personal commitment that, like the tide, sets the ocean of their being in motion. "The tide gives a fixed and constant direction to the sea. Nothing is able to stand against it.... And that is the way it is with a true, life-orienting commitment: it sets our very being in motion along a chosen path."[19]

The Vision Handed On in Liturgy

In the immense field of divine compassion, countless small life fields are interwoven with each other. When human hearts deepen through some kind of contemplation, there emerges in them an intuition of human oneness prior to all separation. Spiritual nurturers of many traditions — Hindu and Sufi as well as Christian — convey a strong sense of humanity as a "communion of saints." In each religion's communal story, there is a way of handing on from generation to generation this transforming perception of universal solidarity in the Mystery. We do not learn such wisdom on our own. We receive it from someone else.[20]

If we are, or aspire to be, spiritual guides for others, that handing-on process will be a part of our ministry. The first necessity, of course, is the claiming and the interiorization of the faith tradition that roots us in the wider field of God and all creation. Then we, in our turn, interpret the Word. In the handing on of our experience, "the Word attains to new life."[21]

It is a complex process. As we grow in awareness of our sinful isolation from others and from God, we are also learning to dismantle the barriers of pride and selfishness that harden that isolation. As we apprehend more clearly the underlying conflict between self and others, between every self and God, we also feel more keenly the deeper unity that is already there among us. In its liturgy, the symbols and stories of our faith tradition persuasively present both the tornness and the oneness. After some radical decisions and choices, we may find ourselves — through those same symbols and stories — in living dialogue with the communal wisdom of our faith tradition and with the others who have now become a "we" for us.

Walter Conn wrote: "All personal conversions are intrinsically dependent on the quality and vitality of the symbols and stories available in one's community. Genuine mutuality, for example, will never be more than wishful thinking as long as our imaginations are dominated by symbols of control and competition, rather than lured by those of care and cooperation."[22]

One crucial source of symbols and stories of care and cooperation in the Christian tradition is, of course, the liturgy — not only the sacraments that celebrate the turning points of an individual's unfolding life, but also the yearly cycle of feasts and fasts, gestures and inspired words, that proclaim the saving action of Christ in history and in Mystery.[23]

Liturgical actions symbolize the past, present, and future dimensions of the Mystery among us. They are one of the ways in which a disparate group of individuals can enter into a common experience of time — both God's time and ours. Liturgical words and actions embody a transgenerational community's understanding of what a human lifetime is meant to be and of what enfolds it. They are implicit ways of thinking and imagining the universe. But they can also offer a hermeneutic for interpreting the key experiences of the lives of individual members of the faith and form community.[24]

Unfortunately, no matter how profound its encoded vision may be, no liturgical rite in and of itself can bring about transcendent growth in communal vision or in faith. Personal conversion is the only path toward that treasure. Liturgy can give those who participate in it an intuition of the good, a feeling for what the gifts of God might be and do, and little glimpses of what it would be like to live with others and with God in a relationship of "yes." But before any of those celebrated meanings can be incarnated in a human life, the human individual needs to move, change, be detached in some ways from his or her prior way of life.[25]

For example, a young woman may attend the wedding of a friend. Coming from a thoroughly secularized culture, she may be enchanted by the symbolic gestures and the music and ritual of the carefully planned ceremony. She may listen in awe as the bride and groom exchange vows in words that find their deepest meaning in the vision that community shares of Christ and Christ's "bride," the church. She may even feel moved to want "a wedding just like that."

But she has no way (yet) of realizing the meaning-horizon of that ceremony in its fullness. She may not even suspect the deeper concern for detachment from narcissism and egocentricity reflected in the texts she has been hearing. She would perhaps be reluctant to pledge herself seriously by the vows the bride and groom have made to each other. In other words, she does not become a committed person automatically, simply by feeling awe at a ceremony in which people commit themselves to each other. Personal conversion is required. And it is just as required for persons who have grown up "in the tribe" and are accustomed to its symbols, but in an unawakened, unconverted way.

Celebrating Wider Meanings

Spiritual guidance for men and women undertaking serious commitments with others must reflect the community's shared vision of Mystery. Whether the commitment be in marriage or in single life, in a religious group or simply to a significant task for the welfare of fellow humans, the wider meaning of that commitment in terms of human others and of the divine Other needs to be celebrated and proclaimed.

People today need guidance in making the connection between their personal existence and the larger space, time, and context to which rituals and communal prayer can direct them. Anthropologists are aware that liturgies can be a path that can carry people beyond the local, concrete situation to an experience of the universal and the Divine. As paths, rituals can be formative, changing the way we see, the way we experience reality. At the same time, the gestures and words and foods and songs that are used are always re-shaped by the particular community and culture in which the ritual action takes place. It is this aspect of local expression that helps bind people together to the family, tribe, or society.

It is no news that in industrial and postindustrial society, many rituals by which the traditions were handed on have lost their strength. We no longer know how to include the body, feelings, and imagination in religious ritual. We no longer have a complete worldview shared by the entire community. We no longer even have the enduring, close-knit communities of the past. And recently, in these days of smashed consensus over the meaning of gender, many women find themselves emotionally excluded from liturgies that they feel are based on an exclusively male view of reality.

Nevertheless, spirituality and a shared spiritual vision form the bedrock of any enduring community. Common sources of energy and common values are central to its expression of itself as a community and central to the possibility of loyal and satisfying personal membership. Thus, modern faith communities often turn to spiritual guides in their attempts to preserve — or to search anew for — a "common spirituality."

In my own experience over the past twenty years of conversation with men and women in religious forms of life, I have witnessed much pain around what they speak of as the loss of spirituality in their respective communities. They realize that the two-thousand-year-old tradition that was (and presumably still is) the bedrock of their religious commitment continues to offer a solid framework for integrating their lifetime commitment within their particular group. They find themselves dismayed by what they regard as the "infiltration" of certain partial but perhaps more current New Age faiths that are often simply a patchwork of unrelated bits and pieces from both Eastern and Western traditions, sometimes in combination with more or less passing secular fads.

At the same time, they are honest enough to admit that over the years, the tradition itself as well as the special spirituality that is theirs have taken on a certain number of deformative accretions. They also recognize a certain "stuckness" in communal rituals whose meanings have been lost sight of, or in customs whose original reason for being no longer applies.

A guide can point out that mere performance of Christian rites, if it fails to connect people interiorly with the attitudes and dispositions of Christ, will not ever be formative or reformative, to say nothing of transformative. The value of a communal celebration lies also in the aliveness of the celebrators themselves whose lived faith in the "new thing" they are doing shines out and enkindles the hearts of all who are present. This is true not only of religious ceremonies. We can see it in the enthusiasm that accompanies the solemn ceremonies of graduation, a victory parade for an Olympic champion, or the cheers for a well-deserved promotion. Everyone present who knows and appreciates what is happening gets caught up in an appreciation of the moment. There is an aliveness to the whole thing that hinges partly on the cost, the detachment from other values, the sacrifice that made this event possible. Is it this glimpse of the underlying cost that makes a ritual celebration alive? Maybe we need to dig a little deeper into seemingly dead rituals. What aspects of life did they originally celebrate? Are those meanings still alive but perhaps ignored or even repressed among us today?

Just as we will not get aliveness in a ritual celebration unless there is an originating aliveness in the celebrators themselves, so also we will not get an effective formation program in a community unless the people in charge of formation have conviction, integrity, and energy. Their personal lives and their hearts have to be coherent with what the ideals of that community are all about. If that is not the case, then all the information and instruction that might be given will not transform new community members into bearers of the true meaning of that community.

All through the ages, "novitiates" have understood that principle. They have made sure that initiates get to live with people who are already alive to the communal way. In traditional Christian novitiates, for example (and this is probably even truer of Buddhist or Hindu novitiates), initiates were not snowed under with words right away.

Instead, they were put into a concrete situation. They were expected to act like community members, in an everyday dispositional style that had emerged, over a long period, from a communal Christian way of viewing the world. The hope was that the initiates, or novices, would begin to experience the group's worldview from within. They would absorb, from this practical immersion, certain beliefs about "the way things are." Those beliefs — interiorized from the concrete examples around them perhaps even before they were presented in words — were meant to encourage passionate commitment to a coming Kingdom. Not only their minds, but also their emotional life would be influenced by this immersion in a covenant-based way of life.

Of course a life like that, as long as it is deep and whole, produces common expressions in ritual. That is not all it produces. It will also influence the way members approach hospitality, or meals, or dress, or housing. It will shape the way members handle their financial affairs, and the way they choose to be accessible to their neighbors. A common formation of such intensity will have an impact on the positions members (or ex-members) take on current social, political, and ecological questions.

Now that "novitiates" in the formal, canonical sense are rapidly becoming a memory of the past in Europe and North America, there is an anguished search in Roman Catholic circles, for example, for ways to replace, in lay terms or within parish and diocesan life, the intensity of Christian formation that religious novitiates and religious community life as a whole used to offer. The RCIA, the Christian Life Community (CLC) network, some communities that have emerged from the charismatic movement, the L'Arche/Faith and Sharing network, and the Renew program are a few of the many experiments in that direction. In Protestant circles, the diversity of efforts toward formative Christian community is just as great. Christians know that their faith demands some concrete community life. Formation in the faith lacks something essential if it lacks community. Learning to appraise our thoughts and actions in the horizon of a life-giving, shared tradition is not a solitary activity. The communal dimension of it adds a certain element of solidarity to our obedient listening to the divine Presence permeating all the polarities of the life field.

This is a constant theme of religious history: groups, not only individuals, are capable of attending or not attending to the presence in our midst of the saving God. The phrase "if today you hear God's voice, harden not your hearts" (Ps. 95) applies not only to persons but also to the blind eyes and deaf ears of a collective heart.

Like personal obeying, communal obedience is not concerned primarily with conformity to a written code. It is concerned rather with the attentiveness of everyone in the group to the living presence of the

Mystery among them. Not only in ritual moments but also in decision-making moments, the whole group needs to listen with open ears to the "signs of the times" and to the hidden Mystery that is concealed within them.

Unless group members are living within the same contemplative presence to this mysterious dimension of everyday life, their obedience tends to degenerate into legalism or ideology — or else it disappears altogether. There is a texture, a feel to each group's dialogue with its common faith tradition and with the whole of surrounding reality. We can almost touch that texture; it tells us a lot about the group's experience of trustful abandonment to the Mystery — or of forlorn abandonment by it. Usually this prefocal atmosphere echoes the feeling of the individual members of that community.

Loss of the Original Sense of "We"

The inevitability of change over the course of time touches every human relationship. That is as true of a community or group as it is of a marriage. Even groups genuinely committed to the love of neighbor and the transformation of society are bound to experience the anxiety and uncertainty that follows upon the loss of their original sense of "we."[26] Sureness about the collective dream will tend to break down as vital strength ebbs with age, and as early clarity is clouded by time.

Margaret Farley has a wise list of points on how we can keep ourselves "connected with, present to the object of our commitments — (with) what we love and have promised to love."[27] They include the importance of seeing everyday things and routines (and persons, of course) contemplatively. They include the cultivation, together, of imaginative hope. They include relaxation of heart; we do not have to strain to live committed lives.

Her last point is about co-presence, or mutuality. We need to stay faithful to it in spite of the "vast chasms," the "mountains to be crossed between us that all too often appear when we try to communicate, to meet each other in the depths of our lives."[28] Yes, and the equally pressing need is for members of a community to turn away from themselves and to focus with other members on what lies beyond the community itself. It is their commitment to a greater reality, to a loved Other or others beyond themselves that enhances the bond between the members of any human intentional community.

If we work as spiritual guides with members of a community, we learn soon not to concentrate on external circumstances — not even on the details of the committed deeds of service that are getting done. What matters in terms of spiritual reality is inner meaningfulness. What makes all the difference is the invisible dialogue that is occurring continually between the heart of a person (or group) and the "otherness" to which it commits itself in love.

Let us return for a moment to the fish in the Sufi legend.[29] They were in the same water as all other fish, busily thrashing and flailing in search of both personal and collective meaning. They could have continued like that till death, never questioning their way of dialoguing with the watery situation in which they found themselves. But these fish were not willing to let themselves thrash forever. For guidance regarding their ambiguous situation and the life question it evoked, they finally consulted a wise fish. And this old fish was wise enough to point out to them not simply a way out of their situation. Rather he revealed the internal meaning for them of the situation they were already in. Counting on the fact that they were free to follow or not to follow his suggestions for relaxing their hearts and reconnecting themselves to the wider meaning of their situation, the wise fish realized that only when they discovered the "internal" meaningfulness of their situation itself would they be able to escape being both determined and encapsulated by it.

Discovering a Group's Inner Meaningfulness

When, as guides, we are consulted by someone who is already situated in a committed community or who is wondering about joining one, our main need is not to be informed about all the details of that community's life. Of course there are facts about the rules, the finances, work, the safeguards for individual members, and the external relationships of that community that any prospective member should be clear about. But once that is clear, what we as guides are more interested in is the "fit" between that community and this seeker's heart. Guides are interested in helping human hearts recognize the internal meaningfulness for them personally of each situation in which they find themselves.

Each spiritual being is a kind of universe. Each is the co-forming context of his or her own experience. The personal significance of any group, or of any collective approach, lies not only in the public, explainable, historical meaning of that group. It lies just as much in the intending, loving embodied heart of the person who is choosing to co-constitute that community or that set of principles. The personal lived meaning comes not just from the group, and not just from the well-meaning member, but from the actual embodied day-by-day dialogue between them.[30]

Externally, members of any group may appear to be doing approximately the same thing. But it is inner intentionality that gives deeds their lived meaning. We should not be content with hearing only about external actions. We need to search for what is really motivating a person in her or his relations with others in the committed communal situation.

While we are at it, we can check to see if the group dynamic is preventing the relatively free human spirit of one or another person from emerging. We can gently probe the atmosphere of mutual respect or lack of it that constitutes the invisible atmosphere in which members of that community find themselves "swimming." Any decline in respect for the distinctively spiritual nature of one another, any occasions where people feel treated like things rather than like persons — those are problems that deserve a spiritual guide's most serious attention.

The majority of men and women in twentieth-century North America have absorbed functional encounter patterns from the culture. That is not bad when we are in a hardware store, but it is not much help in community life. Because of this learned tendency to "cope" with others, to "deal with them" in less than transcendent ways, we find it hard to relate to one another from the deeper level of ourselves.[31]

Most of us shy away from tapping in to an inner self or from allowing ourselves to be intimately known. Thus, the kind of sharing of vision that can raise an average group to the level of "communion" is rare indeed. It requires a spiritual shift to modes of intimacy and trust, within which one can dare to reveal one's inner hopes and desires. In the face of change, we are bound to suffer stress from time to time as the sea in which we swim — our life situation — unfolds in unexpected and sometimes distressing ways.

In any community, some of us are locked in to the reactive patterns typical of the Type-A personality.[32] Others feel particularly vulnerable in a certain life stage. For those and other reasons, people will tend almost automatically to resort to techniques of control; and for these the spiritual guide must be alert. What illusions about the ideal self is this person trying to preserve in this communal setting? In what kind of interpersonal situations does he or she take refuge in tactics of avoidance and self-sufficiency? Eventually, a good guide will be able to help this person understand some of the personal insecurities that plague the conflicted heart as we live with and relate to others in a stressful community life. (Are they listening to me? Do they like me? Will they try to overwhelm me?)

In our work as spiritual guides, people will often raise questions that have to do with a shift or unexpected change visible only to them, in the inner meaning of some significant person or situation. Their attempts to cope, to appear self-sufficient and on top of it all, are failing. They may have run out of options, or even out of their former sense of identity.

This is painful but precious. At such a "dissipative moment," those persons or that group are in a privileged condition of openness for spiritual guidance.[33] They are in obvious need of a horizon of meaning that offers "more" than their life experience has hitherto made available. Such a group needs to seek its deeper identity in a larger, all-encompassing horizon. This deeper identity, this renewed sense of being in communion with the divine Source, will call out to the men and women whose hearts are attuned to this Source and who recognize the congeniality between the new, deeper life of the group and their own inner identity as persons. The group can then come to new life through its painful death-experience.

Membership in such a spiritually alive group may be the only thing strong enough to resist the power of the present sociocultural system and to provide an adequate spiritual foundation for better and more humane ways of living.

After reading chapter 7, with its description of being a wise fish that a Christian can trust, and then realizing the further challenge offered by the demands of conversion in chapter 8 and of community in this chapter, the reader may be tempted to feel that being a spiritual guide is not for her or for him. We might have started comparing our aspirations in the direction of this ministry with what we know of the great spiritual leaders of different traditions and find ourselves very much lacking. They are the ones who handed on a horizon of meaning and life-giving directives in the form of stories, symbols, and counter-cultural lifestyles that succeeded in inspiring generations. They opened up for humankind the mysterious plan of God from all eternity, revealing hidden sources of power and energy available in the life field of those whose hearts are open and receptive. These outstanding "wise fish" of the ages have helped all humans to understand the futility of willfully trying to succeed in commitments to others from a stance that puts us somewhere outside the community. They are the ones who taught about the giftedness of life, which can only be saved by being given away. They were personally in touch with the "divine milieu" that surrounds and supports human beings every moment of our lives.

But they have handed all of this on. It is available to us if we make the effort to open ourselves to it. So one way of looking at our task as spiritual guides is to stop our effortful swimming for a moment and realize that the Holy Presence already fills the universe; it is the very sea in which all of us swim. It is what seekers are looking for when they come to us. For them, we merely represent the broader "we," the community of life, that with its inner appeal has captured their hearts.

Chapter Ten

VOCATION:
FINDING THE WORK OF LOVE

THE vocation of every human person is to live in a covenant relationship of intimacy with God. We are meant to participate
in God's creation by our work in the arts and sciences, in parenting
and medicine, in architecture and education, in restoring order out of
chaos, in restraining selfishness and helping others be open to all kinds
of liberating choices. Vocation does not necessarily mean only what we
do, our job, our work, our occupation, though these may be included.
Vocation is a matter primarily of *being*. It encompasses the totality of
our response to God's call. It involves our leisure as well as our work,
our relationships with enemies as well as friends, our public life as well
as our private life, in addition to all the uses we make of the vital-
functional drives and transcendent aspirations that are at our disposal
in this life. Vocation, in Walter Brueggeman's well-known phrasing,
means "finding a purpose for being in the world that is related to the
purposes of God."[1]

How does the spiritual guide help others grow in their capacity for
making commitments of time and energy that are in harmony with
the fullness of their vocational life call? People are seeking ways of
listening to the Transcendent Other speaking through all the events
and encounters that occur in their relations with spouse and children,
with co-workers and colleagues, with chance acquaintances and dear
friends, with unexpected otherness whether it appears in the form of
a disrupting event, a disquieting life question, or a disliked and even
threatening other person. How do they continue to live in a state of
prayerful presence, in touch with the inspirations of the Spirit, in a
life of fellowship with others (the "we" of conversion) when the "I"
of preconversion remains a strong contender for their attention and
choice?

In this chapter we will continue to be concerned with the inten-

157

tionality of the wayward human heart, with the love from which its decisions and actions flow. We will look at the heart's response to the Gospel demands of obedience, fraternal love, humility, and detachment. Again we have to recall that the Christian vocation is not just in terms of personal inner life, but is our *response* to the entire field of that life. So we have to look carefully not only at who we most deeply are but also who we are in relation to the world and the faith vision that is its context.

Others Evoke Our Committed Love

It is the otherness of the world and its mystery that evokes the love of our hearts. The reality of all that is not the self expands our life and being and draws us to go beyond where we already are. We commit our time and energy to objects and purposes in the world; as we give them shape and form, they in turn form us. There is a call at the deepest point of our being, personal and unique to ourselves. But it is not a call to isolated interiority. Rather it is an intentional call, purposive, able to give us a sense of what our lives are ultimately for.

The moment we allow our hearts to be open and receptive to otherness, the dialogue is underway. With it comes a series of questions, even of conflicts. There is a perennial conflict within us between self-centeredness and other-centeredness: between using one's capacities in the furthering of personal, self-chosen success, and developing one's gifts in faithfulness to one's true calling.[2] When James Fowler talks about this he see it as a conflict between issues of "destiny" and "vocation."[3] He claims that there are two quite different motivations for commitment. One is organized around the axis of self-actualization ("destiny"), and the other around the axis of community and of God's plan for the world ("vocation"). Someone's motivation can shift, over time, from one axis to the other. Such a shift involves not only the mind and its ideas, but the inclinations and desires of the sensing heart: all of those are at play in what Fowler characterizes as the heart's "hunger" around issues of vocation.

Marriage: A Gift of Love

Most people in the Western world inherit at least fragments of the Christian church's very high view of marriage. Centuries of Christian meditation on marriage as a sacrament have helped countless people take a "vocational" view of marriage and parenthood and family life. Deep in our religious tradition on marriage is the hope that the permanent self-gift of the spouses to each other will draw everything in their subsequent lives into the dynamism of deliberate, generous, delighting, and committed love. A "successful" marriage, in this traditional view, does more than consecrate a man's and a woman's sexual energies to the service of a faithful and personal love. It is intended to ground all of their daily work in the conscious experience of loving service, as they both work in complementary ways to nourish and educate and equip the children that their love has generated. It is intended to draw their entire relationship to the human future into a generative, nourishing, and responsible effort to hand on a better "world" to their children and their children's children. Everything that the spouses possess — property, authority, culture, skill, beauty, bodily energy, and health — is to be offered to each other, shared, and turned into gift for their mutual benefit and for the human enrichment of their children. As an old version of the marriage service puts it, "With this ring I thee wed; with my body I thee worship; and with all my worldly goods I thee endow." This same religious view of marriage — founded on the insight that what the Creator of all life commands is love of neighbor — took it for granted that the spousal, profoundly generative, and responsible style of love people learn in marriage would "spill over" into all their relationships. People in a generous marriage, it was assumed, would become more and more capable of caring faithfully not only for their own children but for all children, and thus for the whole social future. To this day, in most wedding ceremonies in Eastern Christian form traditions (Greek Orthodox, for example) the bride and the groom wear crowns on their wedding day. The symbol means that the adult commitment each is making, under God, to each other and to their shared children, gives them an authority and a responsibility within creation that is royal, anointed, sacred: a delegation to the married couple of the creative power of God. Their love for each other calls them into the human future as a whole with a regenerative mission, for which they will need, in this traditional religious view, the power of the cross of Jesus Christ: the power of suffering love.

There is a wealth of writing available to contemporary spiritual guides on marriage and family as the primary "school of love" for most human beings. It is not a neglected subject — especially not in Catholic Christian literature and symbolism. Other aspects of how human persons are called forth into a life of self-giving and world-forming love are much more neglected. For that reason, I will not develop the dynamics of marriage and family further in this chapter. Many books are available that do that in detail.[4]

Work: Another Gift of Love

Sometimes, as spiritual guides, we might have the opportunity to work with a young person during the period of conscious search for a job or a career or at least for an opportunity to make money. If so, we can help that young worker to become aware of this personal vocational hunger that, below the level of merely rational cognition, is moving his or her heart to seek out its treasure, its "dream." Young people may not yet have made conscious contact with that vocational hunger. It may not have been valued in their family or in their schooling. The current "job market" facing the young person may bristle with limits and structures that run counter to this thing called vocational hunger. But we can be sure that it is there, even if hidden and unexpressed. That hunger is linked with the heart's capacity for compassion, with the human need to participate in the faith, hope, and love that give lasting value to human accomplishment.

Sometimes, people are almost entirely hemmed in by functional considerations like economic survival, competition, financial need or advantage. Parental and peer approval can be heavy pressures; so can self-esteem. But there is also something in us (buried, perhaps) that makes us long to give ourselves to life-giving work, to work that would be worth giving our life for. That is a genuinely human ambition.

We make ourselves who we are by what we do. Deeds of love are essential to human life. The human community has known that throughout the ages. Beneath our interest in perfecting human achievement, in making a contribution to the planet and its people, lie transcendent instincts that the Gospel recognizes as categories of faith: we feel called upon to love the others as we have been loved. John Haughey, writing on the spirituality of work, comments on the idea of the vine and the branches in John 15 as a symbol of the deeper meaning and fruitfulness of all our decisions and actions for all others who share this world with us.[5] Frequently, though, we need to be reminded of Christ's words: "Live on in me as I do in you. No more than a branch can bear fruit of itself apart from the vine can you bear fruit apart from me. I am the vine, you are the branches."

When a guide is invited to help someone with decisions concerning work and action in the world, there is another important dimension to remember: such decisions must rest on the dynamic of delight.[6] Duty and willpower are not enough to carry our life work. Our most fruitful commitments of time and energy are evoked by an appraisal of the loving presence of the Mystery in the midst of what needs to be done.

Some persons feel this Presence first of all through their hunger for justice, their yearning to help people get what they need and have a right to as human persons. Others feel the Mystery most keenly through their deep response to beauty, and their intuitive understanding of the way beauty opens the human spirit and refines it. Some young hearts (and older ones) want to uncover the truth of things, for the sake of everyone and because truth attracts them like a magnet. Some spiritual temperaments, for whom goodness and kindness are the face of God, long for a lifework that can express their compassion. They have, from the beginning, an enthusiasm for service.

Those are four distinct ways of being drawn from the heart into a lifework of a particular kind, but they are merely variants within the one dynamic of delight. They are age-old ways in which the Source of all life attracts the striving human heart into the service of the whole human community on all its levels.

People concretely need to get in touch with these deeper levels of the meaning of their work. Only within this larger horizon of love, mutuality, and value can we suffuse the sometimes boring and often difficult details of daily work with the meaning that energizes our life. Daily work doesn't always feel like a congenial expression of our vocational commitment. We need all the vision we can get, if we are going to be able to stay with a work through its failures, changes, opaque periods, stress, and general messiness. There are severe trials built in to work. Some of them come from fellow-workers, who do not necessarily live up to our own expectations — but it is still possible to affirm the larger ground that includes them. Faithfulness to one's daily responsibilities need not be destroyed even when some aspects of the work and the setting turn out to be frustrating.

It is a fact: transcendent meanings and desires, rooted in the deeper levels of our personal human identity, are thoroughly practical and consequential realities. Work, for example, shrinks drastically in its appeal if persons are not in touch with these noncommercial, nonmeasurable human spiritual energies. A spiritual guide has the privilege of helping human workers (who, remember, are always somewhat free, even in a very limited situation) get in touch with those energies in their own hearts and in the wider field of life.[7]

There is a stunning piece of spiritual guidance for a worker in J. D. Salinger's novel *Franny and Zooey*.[8] Zooey is offering encouragement to his disillusioned actress sister. He reminds her of the times when "the studio audiences were morons, the announcer was a moron, the sponsors were morons," and nobody could see the shoes that their older brother Seymour insisted they shine anyway "For the Fat Lady." What Fat Lady? Seymour never explained. Yet for years, Franny and Zooey shined their shoes for her every time they went to the radio studio to go on the air. Now Zooey's spiritual counsel penetrates his sister's fed-upness as he says:

I don't care where an actor acts. It can be in summer stock, it can be over the radio, it can be over television, it can be in a goddam Broadway theatre, complete with the most fashionable, most well-fed, most sun-burned

looking audience you can imagine. But I'll tell you a terrible secret — are
you listening to me? *There isn't anyone out there who isn't Seymour's Fat
Lady.* . . . There isn't anyone *any* where that isn't Seymour's Fat Lady. Don't
you know that? Don't you know that goddam secret yet? And don't you
know — *listen* to me now — don't you know who that Fat Lady really
is? . . . Ah, Buddy. Ah, Buddy. It's Christ Himself. Christ Himself, Buddy."[9]

Work: Source of Self-Knowledge and Pain

One of the surest ways to discover who we are is to find out what
we really want in life, what in the world evokes our interest and our
committed action. In his book *Spirituality and Human Emotion*, Robert
Roberts offers a sort of exercise to help people notice what objects
of preoccupation most hold their emotional and active attention.[10]
There are a few things an individual stays interested in no matter who
disapproves or ridicules. There is a hierarchy in our life concerns that
we may not have consciously noticed, a few pursuits for which we
actually do make time and for which we willingly set aside competing
concerns. Roberts draws up a list of possible passionate concerns —
a playful and evocative list, ranging from antique automobiles to the
well-being of poor people, not excluding goals like making money and
becoming famous. The list might help people notice and talk about
the commitments that actually do channel their energy flow and their
emotional responsiveness.

An exercise like that is revealing. Guides, by the way, should often
look carefully at what they themselves really care about in life. People often seek the help of a guide because they want to channel the
love-energies of body, mind, and spirit to places where, in Frederick
Buechner's felicitous phrase, "our deep gladness and the world's deep
hunger meet."[11] Guides need to be attentive to such desires; if we are
not, seekers might easily conclude that it is hopeless to pay serious attention to such unconventional personal hopes. Unconventional? Well,
the "labor market" in industrial and postindustrial Western society is
not at all structured to respect human vocational concerns. Neither is
it structured to respect the health of the planet Earth. By and large,
the labor market is structured to reflect the ambitions of holders of
large concentrations of capital — and, to a lesser extent, the systematic
needs of governments as they collect revenue and supply "services." It
is counter-cultural to believe that one's way of earning a living should
conform to any sense of a person's unique place in the unfolding of the
Mystery of all that is. It is counter-cultural to hope that work will be
a central expression of our personal vocation to love. People, however,
continue to feel that hope, and to hunger for the spiritual dimensions
of work, as well as for a pay check.

Because of the tenacity and subjective importance of that human hope for significant work, we as guides will be called upon to help persons face some very painful problems in the area of work.

The most painful problem of all is unemployment. In our economy, human labor is understood as a cost to be minimized. Therefore, it is not considered a national emergency when there is no decent work for large numbers of people. It probably should be considered at least as urgent as, let's say, a major epidemic of polio. A person who has been deprived of the opportunity to work has been deprived of a way of participating in life, of becoming an adult with functional competence to participate in something bigger than oneself. That constitutes an injustice as well as a personal tragedy. Its results are all around us and they are bitter indeed. That challenge, however, probably calls for sustained social action more urgently than it calls for personal spiritual guidance.

Spiritual guides are more likely to be called upon to help face a different kind of problem with work. The majority of people in our culture have not found work that is congenial for them. They have never solved the problem of what they are called to do with their life time and energy. They work, but they feel unappreciated by the society in which they work. On the functional level and even, to some degree, on the transcendent level, their lives are enormously lacking in zest and appeal, to say nothing of channels for their love. They would probably feel that everything we have said about lifework, about vocational commitment, and especially about coming to self-knowledge through an appraisal of those commitments that attract us and carry value for us — that all that has exactly nothing to do with their own real life. Some people emphatically experience their work as part of the problem, part of injustice and fallenness. They see that their work objectively exploits the earth, that it contributes to waste and consumerism, and that rather than developing the person of the worker, it shrinks him or her.[12]

When a person feeling such sorrows comes to us as guides, there are many questions that we might ask.

Sometimes the causes of the person's problem are so massively social and systemic that there is little that we, precisely as spiritual guides, can do about it objectively. But we can help the person respect the truth of her situation, the truth of his suffering. We can look with that person for some persons and/or programs in the wider community where there might be resources to connect with further training or with other work — or with financial counseling if it seems crucial that the person stop work or work less.

It is a fact of life that some people experience joy in work or feel esteemed and recognized for their work only in their "volunteer" life and not in their waged labor. If, for example, our work as guides puts us in contact with nonaffluent congregations and parishes, we may find the ushers and choir members and thrift shop workers are finding both esteem and the joy of service in those free-time roles, and that they do not even expect to find it in the office or plant or shopping mall where they earn their income. In that case, the point to start from in developing that person's lived spirituality of work is their volunteer life, not their job.

But not everything is the fault of the marketplace. Sometimes we can become negative and cynical about work that is legitimate and worthy. Sometimes work becomes alienating and deforming partly because the worker is using it to avoid other more intimate aspects of life; or because work is reduced to a process for acquiring things rather than expressing who one is; or when, detached from the Mystery, work becomes a way of establishing control and of exerting power. Then we, as guides, might wonder how the work of this man or woman is feeding into a false self-system in isolation from the Mystery and from other people as well.

Has this person undergone an affective conversion? Is there any indication that the center of desire has moved, for this person, from an obsessive concern for his or her own needs, to self-giving love and generative care for others? Christian conversion is not merely doctrinal and moral, as we have been noticing all along; it is also a transformation of our affectivity. We shift, in orientation, from absorption in our own interests to concern for the good of others. This shift is expressed in committed love, a love expressed not only in words but in deeds. That level of conversion does need to get integrated into the work we do for a living.[13]

Even when the seeker who comes to us is not negative or cynical, even when it is clear that the main center of this person's life is already the love of neighbor within the context of the all-inclusive Mystery — even then, the person might have some real problems with work! Even in the midst of doing work that I am convinced is "for me," there is still need for detachment. Much-loved work can be served "idolatrously," to the damage of one's health, of one's other relationships and obligations, and of one's growth toward contemplative awareness.

Also: even if I am really trying to live in obedience to "ways that are not my ways" and to enter into God's work in the world, there are still some very human problematics involved, especially when the work-commitment is shared, as it usually is, with other people. Much has been written about the tension and conflict that inevitably exists between what is "my" task and is life-giving for me, in the midst of "our" task to which we as a team or as a community have committed ourselves. As the classic question puts it, "Who takes out the garbage?" Surrender to the object of one's commitment involves more than simply subscribing to its ideal description. There are many paths open for guidance in detachment and in humble love, which beckon as the guidance focus moves into the dialogue that goes on between a person's work and the larger "story" that gives the work its deeper meaning.

Guidance as a Work of Love

The ministry of spiritual guidance — as we very well know if we have tried it — is work too, with all the problems that go with any work. It is also gift.

To accompany another human person in choosing to follow the invitations of grace is an act of self-giving friendship. It is an act of profound attentiveness, since it involves acknowledging the dialogue that the other person is with the reality of all that is, as well as with that person's own most profound center. It seems to correspond with the way Sidney Callahan describes the spiritual works of mercy. She writes:

> The spiritual works of mercy are psychological acts which arise from our innermost personal selves and are directed to another's innermost personal needs of heart and mind. They are unique person-to-person transactions — demanding full attention and mindfulness of self and consciousness of others as unique selves.[14]

Companioning a seeker on her or his spiritual journey calls for a love of neighbor that is not possessive or exclusive. It means never losing sight of the fact that this person belongs to God, not to us. If we as guides tend to use them for our personal ends, or monopolize them, or impose on them our own private views and methods, or indulge in petty jealousy or vanity or authoritarianism, we will diminish the freedom that God's spirit wants them to have. We need to be able to keep our own small plans for people out of the way, so that they are free to live and act in harmony with the mysterious Plan that is not ours, but that contains "the designs of God's heart."

Yes, the people who come to us need to know that they are loved by us. But the real direction in which they must look is God. From God will come the love they need, not from their spiritual guide. Real love of neighbor — and the seeker who comes to us is emphatically our neighbor, in the Gospel sense — asks for our commitment to help that searching human being discover God's providence for his or her life. That means caring intensely. But it also means being willing to decrease, like John the Baptizer, so that Christ can increase in this person's life.

Ultimately then, we as guides will have to understand how the decisions that people who come to us for counsel make are imposing a narrative form on their lives. As they choose a spouse, join a group, embark on a career, or turn to Christ, questions will inevitably emerge — questions that reflect the ever-present conflict between person and community, between self and God that underlie all commitment. In the process of making choices, they are co-authoring their own story. But that story, whether they know it or not, is always part of a larger story: the main Story, in fact. They may need our help in finding out what is actually going on, what the intentions of that main Story are.[15] Otherwise they may not know how to bring their small story into harmony with the larger Will that is the mysterious Ground of their choices.

The Risk of Choosing to Act

The prospect of actually living this way, of being willing to respond freely as we participate with God in the transformation of the world, can be exciting and attractive. It can also be very scary. Once we let go of illusions and preordained patterns of "working for God," we find ourselves "doing God's work" — which often means making decisions about actions that are initiated by the Will of another. Allowing ourselves to be drawn into the purposes of the transcendent Other means that one's own transcendent willing must be exercised. Functional willing also comes into play as we figure out and execute the practical steps needed to make a certain commitment bear fruit. Questions begin to arise. How am I going to make up for the loss of former feelings of security? How can I continue to feel successful, powerful, or able to tap into social esteem and pleasure? Am I really willing to live with the consequences of choosing this action, of making this investment of time and energy?

The guide of persons dealing with this type of uncertainty also has questions. What has to change before this person is able to make a relatively free response in faith? What has to die before he or she can respond in a way that will have positive consequences for the reign of God, for continuity with the larger Gospel story, and for relatedness with others who share this mission? Will this anxious man or woman be willing to live with the consequences of these new choices of work or life commitment? How tempted will this person be to escape, to switch to a depreciative "no" when the work becomes too much, when the initiative is no longer that person's own? Affirmation (saying yes) requires effort and implies a future of unpredictable consequences. A certain amount of support in the form of positive imagination, anticipation, or memory is needed by people who are allowing themselves to be carried beyond where they originally planned to go. Trusting openness to the Spirit's energizing activity is called for at this point, so that the person can experience the joy of self-emergence in a spiritually meaningful direction.[16]

Even when the joy seems smothered by the anxiety that attends the decision-making process, the only way the spiritual journey can unfold and persons come to a sense of deeper identity is via the trial-and-error method of making decisions and then acting on them. Even when the result turns out to be failure and conflict and stressful consequences, there is no other way for humans to find out who they are called to be and what they are called to do in this life. If to be alive means to participate in the joyful loving self-expression of the Creator, then it must be possible to muster the faith, hope, and love needed to express that freedom and joy. Unfortunately for most of us, awareness of contingency and fear of meaninglessness drain off much of the life energy that would otherwise be at our disposal. We need to learn more about the way our willing operates. Again — how many of us are aware of the receptivity that lies at the heart of our willing?[17]

Spiritual guidance is meant to open us up more and more to the mysterious Initiative at work in the universe. Without this receptive openness much of our effortful planning, controlling, and organizing shrinks to a mere expression of our ego-functional needs. Truly life-giving decisions and actions are born, not from raw vital-functional ability, but from reflective hearts that are connected to the deepest, most energizing sources of life.

As guides we must realize that unless we recognize and support a creative synthesis of both these approaches, that the focus of guidance will remain stuck in questions about functional coping (What will I do? How can I handle this problem?) and questions regarding alternative ways of meeting and beating the challenge offered by a transcendence crisis. The rational human tendency to focus consciousness on solutions must be relaxed to allow the in-breaking of something new, of initiatives of the Holy Spirit and of reality itself. Just as in Eliot's play, Thomas Becket needed to forgo the temptation to do the right thing (martyrdom) for the wrong reason (because he was attracted to the glory of martyrdom), so too in spiritual guidance, deliberations must be appraised in such a way that the pro's and con's, the mixed motives and ambiguities are transformed by the larger context of intuitive apprehension of the Will of Another. It was only when Thomas Becket was able to lose his personal will in the wider will of the Other that he was able to implement his personal decision in tune with the larger "we." Then his action could be recognized as the act of someone who, carried beyond himself, had lost his will in the will of God. He was, in other words, a saint.[18]

Connecting with the Source

At the end of chapter 6 we promised to look again at this whole idea of putting people back in touch with their rootedness not only in humanity but also in the divine Source of life. This, after all, is the goal of spiritual guidance. This is where we come up against the end point of the from–through–to pattern that characterizes conversion. We find ourselves dealing with the deepest source of our freedom — of our capacity to say yes and to respond to what life asks from the depths of a "response-able" heart. From thinking about a life problem or decision we find ourselves being moved, being empowered to make a judgment, an affirmation of potency that says "I can respond, I am able to use my freedom to deal with whatever life is demanding of me." What is the source of this affirmation, of this ability to respond in a new release of energy?

All that we have concluded about the guidance project comes to fruition at this moment. People recognize themselves as called by the Mystery, not only out of their aloneness and isolation, but also into a fresh attachment in love.[19] They glimpse themselves not only as rooted in the "More Than," but also as firmly in solidarity with other members of the human family. Liberated by a source of energy and love originating beyond their own narrow capacities, they find themselves willingly letting go of attachments that have kept them from making a new step or deciding to act in a new way. They are able to go beyond some of the fears that have kept them from dialogue with the Mystery. They are more open and able to receive inspiration from that larger horizon. A renewed sense of participating in a larger plan, of sharing a larger vision emerges as some at least of the familiar blocks and hesitations become less strong or even disappear altogether. What has happened can be described as a mysterious in-breaking into human lives of the Holy Other, or simply as grace, the totally gratuitous confirmation by the Spirit that makes possible a response in faith that otherwise would not be attainable by the human heart.

We are speaking here in the realm of faith, the faith that permeates the Gospel of John as he points the way to decisions and actions that are not possible for us, but that are possible with God. On our own we cannot attain the newness of heart that makes this kind of response possible. We need, as Psalm 51 puts it, to be *given* a new heart. As lovers who are incarnated mixtures of spirit and flesh, we must grow in knowledge of ourselves and of the main attractions of our heart. In so doing we grow also in confidence that life will always be "a tune beyond us yet ourselves...a tune upon the blue guitar...of things exactly as they are."[20]

A struggle between life and death, between self and others, an underlying conflict between the self and God will always color our journey, will be part of all our decisions, and will test the motives behind all our actions. Yet in the midst of our multiple commitments, it is always possible to remain open and receptive to the spirit-filled ground of decision and action and to the directives that stream from this life-giving Source.

Decisions made in such openness can emerge only if we "abide in the vine," dwelling in wonder on the ongoing Mystery as it reveals itself daily in the field of our life. This attention to the deeper mystery and our connection with it, this relaxed openness to our entire life field eliminating none of its polarities or ambiguities, this receptivity to divine Initiatives, is only possible in the midst of a growing trust that God is present and working throughout all the details of our life. It is only in such faith that we are able more or less freely to begin to lay aside our illusions about the false self with its false programs for happiness. It is only in a climate of trusting love and obedient listening that we can begin freely to commit our precious life time and energy in decisions and actions that are consonant with who we are and with what we are perceiving of "the tune beyond us yet ourselves" that is in total harmony with "Things Exactly as They Are."

The converging centrality of both conversion and appraisal comes clearly into focus here. Without the radical personal transformation implied in the former, the appraisal process that translates appreciative faith into living deeds would not be an option for human beings. And without a growing surrender of our claims to absolute autonomy, without the death to self-will implied in radical trust of a loving God, we would never attain the maturity of the spiritual person, who, as described by St. Paul, has "the mind of Christ" (1 Cor. 2:16).

Here we find another way of describing the aim of spiritual guidance. It lies in the attainment of true wisdom, in a transformation that brings with it a contemplative knowing of the hidden things of God. Evidently from Paul's letters to the early Christians in Corinth, many were not ready for such wisdom. "Yet God had revealed this wisdom to them through the Spirit" (1 Cor. 2:10). Why then were they not open to God's Spirit that they had received in baptism? Why were they still living as "natural men," as "infants in Christ," unable to come to the true maturity implicit in such a contemplative presence to their daily lives? Obviously Paul is pointing here to the fact that men and women cannot hope to attain the wisdom that belongs to maturity by their own power. Their spirits must be transformed by the Spirit of God. But what he is also implying is that such wisdom and maturity is possible for *everyone*.

Each person is uniquely called by God within a forming, reforming, and transforming universe to an irresistible vocation.[21] In the life of each human being, response to this call (or hardening of heart in resistance to it) can and should be appraised. Nemeck and Coombs draw attention particularly to responses emerging at "thresholds" or distinguishable stages of a person's life.[22] Like forks in the road, each stage of the spiritual journey can be appraised as a "dissipative" structure or event that in breaking up familiar patterns of valuing and commitment leads to fresh intensity of life.

It would be impossible, I think, to find a trustworthy guide in any of the great traditions who does not advise prayer and attention to the providential Source of these mysterious life shifts. In fact, guides are unanimous in suggesting that the spiritual journey is meant to be a way of remembering that Source, of personally rediscovering our intimacy with God in the heart of our ordinary life. In his small book *Gratefulness, the Heart of Prayer*, David Steindl-Rast sums it up as follows:

> When our heart rests in the Source of all meaning, it can encompass all meaning. Meaning in this sense is not something that can be put into words. Meaning is not something that can be looked up in a book like a definition. Meaning is not something that can be grasped, held, stored away. Meaning is not something.... Maybe we should stop the sentence here. Meaning is no thing. It is more like the light in which we see all things. Another Psalm calls out to God in the thirst of the heart: "With you is the fountain of life, and in your light we see light" (Ps. 36:9). In thirsting for the fullness of life, our heart thirsts for the light that lets us see life's meaning. When we find meaning, we know it because our heart finds rest.[23]

Chapter Eleven

GUIDELINES FOR APPRAISAL

JUST as conversion is considered to be a central issue for spiritual guidance, so is appraisal.[1] More generally known as discretion or discernment, appraisal within the Christian tradition refers to the process of discovering, evaluating, and deciding to act or refrain from acting in tune with one's presence to particular aspects of one's life.

We can think of appraisal as an art, discipline, skill, or disposition of heart. Whatever we call it, this process of perceiving reality, judging its value, and deciding to act in accordance with that judgment has traditionally been associated with our human capacities for reflectivity and freedom. Appraisal provides a way of being responsible for one's choices in the full field of possible commitments of time and energy.

As a form of meditative presence to the mystery of All That Is, effective appraisal can facilitate a formative as opposed to a deformative dialogue between a person's entire life and the deepest desired ground or context that gives that life meaning. As an ongoing daily disposition in the midst of changing situations, Christian appraisal brings criteria of the reign of God to bear on choices both large and small within the life field. Attuning mind and heart to guidelines, values, or directives hidden in every situation, this inner disposition can also lead Christians to affirm the invisible presence of God's providential care permeating the visible field of everyday life.[2] Paul describes as spiritual maturity this contemplative knowledge of the early Christians that enabled them, with the help of God's Spirit, "to recognize the gifts he has given us ... interpreting spiritual things in spiritual terms" (1 Cor. 2:12–13).

There are many occasions when human beings are called upon to make consequence-laden decisions. People of faith prefer to make such choices and act in the light of trusted guidelines from a specific faith and form tradition. More generally, even when a particular decision is not front and center, they just need to be in touch with the movement of the Spirit in themselves and the daily happenings of their lives. Can we learn for ourselves and teach others what is involved in making trustworthy decisions in the midst of changing situations? Is there a way for hearts to reach out in loving attentiveness to the living flame of love that continues to burn during times of crisis as well as joy? Can a spiritual guide enhance a person's way of being in touch with the Mystery and with their own truth, even in a time of change and uncertainty?

If the notion of "appraisal" has begun to make sense, the reader will already suspect that every previous chapter in this book lays down one or another level of preparation for appraisal as the central dimension in spiritual direction. See the Appendix for a summary of how each chapter contributes to the understanding of this art or gift of recognizing the movements of the Spirit in all the spheres of a human life field.

Understanding the Appraisal Process

Some time ago, after spending five years researching the event of trust as it happens between people, I wrote, "For me, one of the most enlightening results of the research was the realization that it is often when things look most uncertain, when structures 'dissipate' and you literally must 'make the road while walking' that the trusting self or communal group can be guided in the best direction."[3] What struck me then as now is the realization that life is almost never neat and orderly. In fact, real life with all its ups and downs, its disappointments and upsets as well as its joys and satisfactions, is for most people a decidedly ambiguous enterprise. We hardly ever have absolute certainty about anything, even our own motivations, as we find ourselves challenged to make choices that we know will have unimaginable and certainly unpredictable and uncontrollable consequences for ourselves and others. Yet, it is precisely in the midst of all this uncertainty and unexpectedness, in the tough moments of having to make decisions almost in spite of ourselves, that we are most open to grow and become the persons we are most deeply called to be. How can we be more helpful to ourselves and others at such times?

First of all, we must appreciate the fact that appraisal — this capacity of ours to consider, assess, and evaluate a variety of life events and encounters with a view to making decisions and acting in their regard — is a capacity confined to specifically human beings. Our potential for freedom, even very limited situated freedom lies at the heart of what it means to be an embodied spirit. Freedom can be enhanced or inhibited by the use of the powers of the mind — memory, imagination, and anticipation. At every moment of the day, a person's power of appraisal either enhances or inhibits free choices and the consequent actions that make up the substance of his or her entire life. From childhood, we are called upon to make appraisals, to choose for example, between vanilla ice cream and strawberry, between playing one game or another. It is terribly important that parents allow children to grow in this capacity for making choices, even though while still young and inexperienced children also need parents and others to make the most consequence-laden appraisals for them. Swiftly, children become adults who must take responsibility for themselves and their own lives by using their personal powers of mind and will to evaluate meanings, values, and ideals that will give direction to the freely chosen acts of maturity.

Appraisal, as we have been noticing, has to do with acting, usually in the here and now. Therefore it also has to do with the decision making that precedes action, as well as with the anticipated consequences that follow action. No human person can live without at least some appraisal in service of her or his freedom of choice and action. "Not to decide is to decide," as the popular slogan puts it; to decide not to appraise involves a choice. Absence of action is also a choice, and, just like action, it will have consequences in the whole of one's human life. Appraisal ponders choices, actions, and consequences in terms of the ultimate purposefulness of the entire life of the one doing the choosing.

When we minister as guides, people often consult us about choices. What we do as guides must flow with the foundational importance for those persons of coming to a state of meditative consciousness regarding who they truly are, what they freely and primarily want out of life, and what they are most basically called to commit time and energy to by the ultimate horizon of that life.

This starting point differs greatly from the starting point of other types of guidance. Problem-solving guidance (like some types of pastoral counseling, for example) attempts to deal in an ad hoc, clearly limited way with the disruptive events or changes that bring people to seek help from time to time. Spiritual guidance has a contemplative and foundational origin. It assumes that the life of every person is rooted in a greater love, in a desire, explicit or implicit, for an ultimate Goal that, if acknowledged, will radically affect all choices made along the way toward it.

Great Christian guides of the past like Ignatius of Loyola and others who took the Gospel for their "bottom line" have always insisted that guidance begins with the foundation of the Good News of Christ's life. Jesus' death and resurrection reveals and lights up the true goal and end of all our lives.[4] When a person comes asking for assistance in the appraisal of questions about his or her commitment, in marriage, for example, or in religious or professional endeavors, that commitment itself and the love that inspired it needs to be brought into awareness.

For example, men or women may be facing upsetting changes in their work situation or may be having sexual difficulties. Perhaps they are forced to absorb a shift in feeling about themselves and their living or work situation. Maybe a conflicting commitment beckons or they are simply experiencing a deadening of interest at a stagnant period of their life. In such circumstances, confusion about what ultimately we want in life leads to even more confusion about the means or paths we choose to follow on the way to that goal. But if we can become aware once again (or even for the first time) of the original longing for God that we *are*, then values and priorities begin to arrange themselves accordingly. It is often up to the guide to be the one who trusts the Trinitarian Mystery present and acting in the confusing events of this person's life. Otherwise he or she has nothing more to offer than the problem-solvers who give assistance in decision making to people living outside of a faith context but who nevertheless must deal with all the same problems and conflicts as those for whom the life of faith adds color and substance to the flow.[5]

Unfortunately, not all of the guides who represent the church and its teachings on appraisal are aware of or put their trust in the presence of this powerful Mystery in their own lives or in the lives of those who seek their help. Because they have not learned to recognize the dialogue that already exists between personal life fields and the trusted Mystery, they cannot point to the ways the Holy Other may be speaking on all five polarities of that field, nor can they help hearts appraise by reaching out in loving attentiveness to that Presence pervading all of life. Christian guides must be persons whose faith has shaped their heart in a contemplative, trusting stance in face of the Mystery of all that is. If they do not themselves live in such a stance, they cannot be alert to the movement of the Mystery both within us and around us. They will lack an intuitive appreciation of what would be appropriate or inappropriate for a follower of Christ, against the horizon of meaning that the Christian faith provides.

Just as we can have "spiritless" religion, we can have "spiritless" guidance. A "spiritless" guide might, for example, produce willpower Christians whose appraisals and choices of action are distorted by an urgent feeling that salvation depends on their own effort and integrity. The Christian horizon invites us to humble dependence on an invisible Other whose love exceeds both our efforts and our imagining. But that horizon can be narrowed, or lost, by guides who put their trust in functional efforts to gain control and prediction-power over the invisible realm.

Both guide and person being guided must realize that, like life itself, appraisals are ambiguous and never completely satisfactory. During any given day, we may make hundreds of appraisals about matters large and small. We may at times be consciously aware of making deliberate decisions as a result of clear appraisals reflected on to the best of our ability. However, life being the reflective and prereflective mix it is, most of our daily appraisals are not made that way.

It is never possible to see clearly all the implications and consequences, for ourselves or for others, of the daily decisions that we nevertheless have to make. But there really are some basic criteria, or questions, that we can habitually keep in mind. Adrian van Kaam lists five basic questions that guides should ask, in the furtherance of appraisal:

- Is this choice going to be *consonant*? That is, will it make this person's life more in harmony with the Mystery of All That Is?

- Will this choice be *congenial* with who this person most deeply is?

- Will this choice be *compatible* with his or her actual life field of people, events, and things?

- Does the choice fit with the *competence* of this person?

- Is this choice a *compassionate* decision, taking into account the brokenness and ambiguity of the human condition and of this person's situation in it?[6]

Usually, only a provisional appraisal of day-by-day decisions is possible, even with these helpful criteria. But there is such a thing as being able to reach a "final appraisal" of a serious life decision or commitment. Even then, of course, there will still be questions that cannot be answered and ambiguous areas that do not become clear. It takes maturity to listen and choose in the midst of lack of clarity and ordinary human messiness.

As co-listeners, both guide and person seeking guidance must learn to respect the full life field both in its objective and its subjective details. Obviously they must listen for feelings, thoughts, and emotions, taking into account what is happening within the person making a choice. But they must also pay careful attention to the wisdom of their tradition, to what other people, society, and the church itself have to say. Especially when faced with a major decision, people can expect to grapple with the wisdom of generations who have gone before them, as well as with how they themselves prefer to process certain aspects of the immediate situation.

Human beings are able to take responsibility for their own freedom. As they do so, they become willing to live with the consequences of their choices. It is no part of human maturity to blame others or God for what happens once choices have been made. Mature persons acknowledge that their choices are real even though they cannot foresee all consequences, and even though they can only do what seems best at the time. Are the consequences unpredictable? Well, so is life. That is one dimension of our call to participate freely in Mystery, with confidence in a Wisdom that is not bound by time, even though our own prudence is indeed bound by time. We do not need to be grimly willful, since we cannot foresee or control everything no matter how much we ponder. But neither should we collapse into will-lessness; we are indeed free and responsible, within Mystery.

Whether persons are engaged in making a lifetime commitment or simply trying to decide whether to spend their money on a special meal or on a new piece of lab equipment, the maturity with which they also accept the consequences of their decisions becomes an important element in the guidance process. Naturally, less serious choices can be made without the fear of closing off important life options while the choice of lifetime commitment consists precisely in the ability, after a serious appraisal process, to come to closure even when one does not feel totally prepared to do so. In our society, only those people who are mature enough to come to closure and live with the consequences of a choice that closes off other options are able to decide in favor of a marriage or other lifetime commitment. It does take a certain maturity even to live fully, and then let go of, the stages and ages of one's developmental history. We frequently meet people in our society who have not succeeded in appraising their own need to move on from some aspects of childhood or adolescence to the newness of adulthood, or who cling to the culture and behavior of a much younger age when chronologically they should be open to the acceptance and challenge that middle and older age can bring.

It is often only when such persons, with guidance, can trustfully reflect or bend back on God's providential presence in their lives that they are able to accept in faith the new directives offered in an untried and unfamiliar life stage. It may be only after contemplating again and again their rootedness in faithful love that they are able to put aside some aspirations or ambitions or vital impulses and listen with openness and humility to what these new life circumstances may mean for them. Actually, it is only by means of a transcendent mind illumined by the Gospel values of faith, hope, and love, that today's men and women can be liberated from the oppression of our culture's appraisal of these ongoing life stages.[7] It is only with the eyes of the heart illumined by Christ's promise to be with us *all* our days, that we can see and appreciate in a personal way the value of each temporal stage as it partakes in the mystery of God's purposes in our lives. Otherwise we are at the mercy of cultural attitudes that have turned the adolescent policy of keeping one's options open into an ideal and the challenge of growing old, even gracefully, into a disgraceful ordeal.[8] The appraisal process that partakes in a transcendent view of each human life field in its ongoing journey as being always open to God can gradually give rise to counter-cultural ways of perceiving and prioritizing past as well as present and future directives. In addition, it can change our view of others in the culture, liberating us from their oppressive expectations and our own tendency toward envious comparison. To thus shift one's way of viewing people, events, and things is to undergo a conversion in the very spirit out of which we live our lives.

Three Levels of the Appraisal Process

Appraisal, which plays such a central role in spiritual guidance, can become a permanent disposition, a habitual, concrete way for human hearts to bring to awareness their hidden depth and orientation. Yet, not all occasions when people learn to use their minds to cope with dilemmas and decision making are lived out on the same level. Nor are all occasions when a sympathetic other attempts to come to their assistance necessarily equal to what we have been describing as Christian spiritual guidance. Let me try to illustrate the difference. I am a psychologist and therapist by trade, and sometimes it is as a therapist that I agree to see someone. At other times, people ask to see me as a spiritual director. Let's invent someone called Shellie and use her as an example of someone seeking assistance of several kinds.

Shellie, a very unhappy young woman, comes to see me about her work situation, which she hates. As we together look meditatively at all the polarities of her life field, I can begin to live myself into her dominant style of thinking and perceiving and start to understand why she is feeling so tense and uneasy. I may at a certain point gently begin to point out how I see the prefocal dialogue that is going on between her and some aspects of her work life. The service I offer her is one of shared reflection in which, as we together focus on directives the situation offers for her appraisal, she may be led to a health-giving self-confrontation. In the course of our meetings, I lead Shellie as empathically as I can to a depth where her heart can awaken to the limitations of her style of awareness. As time goes on, Shellie may begin to discover all kinds of new aspects to her problem, and as she grows in insight, she may intuitively shift from her former despairing attitude and begin to glimpse a possibility for hope. Together we will probably end up looking within the situation itself for some overlooked favorable elements that could be the catalyst for releasing new energy in her. On the other hand, we might equally come to the conclusion that this particular work situation, unless it changes, is no longer consonant with who Shellie ultimately wants to become. At this point she may need some help in overcoming the anxiety involved in making a new job decision and commitment, but this is decision making — it is not yet transcendent appraisal.

Now we move to another level of discourse in which this same young woman approaches me to discuss her difficult work situation. Right from the beginning of our conversation we both are fairly explicit about the faith and form traditions that are the underlying ground of our meeting.[9] Both Shellie and I are aware that beneath all the polarities of the life field lies a horizon of Mystery that somehow, somewhere gives a certain direction and destiny to our lives. For her this Otherness underlying her daily work situation may have receded far into the background so that it presently has little or no influence on what is happening in her daily encounters with the people, events, and things of her work. Nevertheless, she nods when I tentatively point to its existence as the invisible Ground against which we can appraise the directives being handed to her by the boss, co-workers, customers, responsibilities, and so on that are hers in the here and now. Once we discover this already there dialectical structure between the events of her life and this Ground, it may be helpful to explore her feelings about this Ground. How is it perceived on a continuum from "accepting helpful" to "threatening demanding"? How does its presence affect the story Shellie has been telling me about herself and her hated work? Does her entire situation become nuanced when seen against this ultimate horizon? Are we now talking not just about a difficult situation involving attitudes and choices, but also about a whole new dialectic of this human person and the ordering of her life in light of a divine direction or purpose?

If the latter is true, then my role also changes. I am no longer with her just to aid her in self-confrontation and decision making. As spiritual guide, whether this person names the "surrounding sea in which she swims" the Tao, the Lord God, Allah, Cosmic Mystery, the Great Spirit, or the Holy Spirit, I become co-listener with her to her entire situation as embodying directives or messages that point to the direction or purpose of her life in relation to this divine Otherness or Mystery. My service to her is one of shared reflection in which we together bend back on what is happening in her life in relation to the divine direction of that life. Issues of appraisal and decision making are now interpreted in the light of what her Islamic or Buddhist or Jewish or Hindu faith and form tradition may be saying, for example, about the fallacy of self-sufficiency or the evils of merely functional self-formation and individualistic attempts at self-salvation. Most great religious traditions have wisdom to impart regarding our ignorance of what would make us ultimately happy as well as about the egoistic and grasping dispositions that deform our approach to work. They also speak about a religious awakening of the heart that begins to acknowledge its limitations and shift toward a Way that is more open and vulnerable and that pays serious attention to the inner divine form or soul that founds each person's entire life.

Thus, no matter what this young woman's faith context may be, once we posit this "dialectical hermeneutic," then every appraisal she makes undergoes a shift. Meditative presence to the Mystery governs our being together. Within the crisis occasioned by a work difficulty, we are seeking the transcendent meaning of the spiritual direction of her entire life. As we reflect on what has happened, we try at the same time to be open and attentive to the "receptivity dynamics" preferred by the handed-on wisdom of her faith community.[10]

If this faith community happens to be Christian, we move our interpretation in this guidance encounter to still another level, which will encompass some specifically Christian thinking about guidance itself. For example, the Christian spiritual guide, along with a general knowledge of anthropology and human developmental stages and approaches to conflict and decision making, will also regard another human person as "image of God," destined for participation in the life of the Trinity. So, when I met with this young woman and she indicated her wish for guidance in the Christian tradition, I would be inclined to see her as a fallen yet redeemed member of the Body of Christ bearing within herself a transcendent destiny as baptized daughter of God. I hope to help her discover, along with possible flaws in her style of thinking and feeling, how she can identify weakness and sinful resistance to the Mystery's presence in her life as well.

Now let's go back to our friend Shellie. As we explored Shellie's anxious uneasiness, I would wonder about her grasp of spiritual or intuitive ways of knowing. Does the way she perceives her work situation do her in? Is she capable of imaginatively perceiving any of the aspects of her work/life situation with the eyes of faith in a providential divine Other who loves her and wants what is best for her? Or is she in a negative phase of her transcendence crisis in which all is experienced as "dark night" and she really does need some outside assistance to break through to the Christian meaning of the situation.[11]

A parenthesis: within the Christian tradition, spiritual guides are never supposed to appoint themselves. They do not as a rule come forward till they are appealed to, and even then, they do so only with caution. So, as her guide, I would approach this "spiritual friendship" hesitantly, being very aware that I must not stand in the way of God's gift to her of a free and friendly space in which to grow.

Within the scope of a Christ-centered perspective, I would try to help Shellie unmask some of her self-deceptions and come to the kind of self-knowledge needed for the work of truly Christian appraisal. In so doing, we might have to bring to focal consciousness some of her negative images of God and her inner resistance to thoughts and ways not her own.[12] Gradually, as some of the illusions of the pride form are dispelled, we would begin in light of the Christian tradition to move the entire project of guidance into what van Kaam calls the "pneumatic dimension."

The pneumatic dimension is another level of human transcendence potential. It is at this level — illumined by the Holy Spirit speaking in Holy Scripture and in living Christian tradition — that we can grasp the parameters of Christian spiritual guidance. Here, too, we can recognize where fresh appraisals need to be made in order to restore harmony between this person and his or her God-given call.[13]

It is at this level, too, that issues of conversion from sin as well as the illusions traceable to sinfulness come into focus. Shellie, whether she knows it or not, stands in need of the metanoia or change of heart that the Incarnation and Paschal Mystery of Jesus made possible. The transformation of perception, the illumination of the transcendent mind that allows us to see all things *in conspectu Dei* calls for a major shift in which persons become contemplatively present to the details of their everyday life. Before she can incarnate appraisals apprehended now with transformed eyes of the heart, Shellie will have gradually opened herself in prayerful presence to the Source of All That Is. Over the course of her spiritual guidance she will have grown slowly but surely in faith, hope, and love. There is no way that the guide can do more than suggest that she move toward dispositions of appreciation, humility, obedience, and reverence, that she come to know herself as both gentle and firm, and that she open herself to the gifts of the Holy Spirit. All is gift, and no amount of guidance expertise can produce the effects of the divine uncreated energies (grace) in the life of someone who is not open to receive them.

Every session of Christian spiritual guidance entails an openness to prayer and to the Holy Spirit's will for the person who is hoping to make some changes in his or her life. The purpose of Christian spiritual guidance parallels that of Christian baptism. It makes use of any and all life events and situations in service of the conversion of the heart to center on Christ and the priorities of God through an increase in freedom and a change in purposeful direction of life. Again we remember Martha working in her kitchen.[14] In speaking of the "disguises" that God wears when life seems to be going badly, de Caussade mentions that Martha's mistake lay in trying to please Jesus merely by working for him, by cooking nice dishes, by deciding for herself how she should serve him. This wise spiritual counselor suggests that Mary's choice of work was better in that "she was content to be with Jesus in any way He wished to give Himself to her."[15]

Perhaps one of the main tasks of the Christian spiritual guide is to help men and women discover precisely in the actual messy situations of their daily lives, the way in which, without their being aware of it,

Jesus has chosen to give himself to them, and how they are to "go forth and bear fruit" as a result of that choice (John 15:16).

This type of appraisal often operates in darkness and confusion; one does not see the path at all, and answers and decisions are not clear. One responds to inspiration and to the obscure attraction of a God whose commitment is to us, whose love is the basis of all possible appraisals and whose Kingdom is the criterion for all moral decisions especially in the midst of darkness and change.

Guidelines Fostering Christian Appraisal

Like human beings everywhere, Christians are confronted each day with opportunities for appraising various messages presented to them by the people, events, and things of their entire life field. Over a lifetime, with or without the benefit of formal guidance, Christian men and women are meant to gradually grow in the wisdom that pertains to the ultimate goal of their life. Their appraisal processes take place within a horizon of Mystery that contextualizes that life and imparts a certain direction to it. A Christian is a person who, illumined by the light of the Mystery's revelation in Christ, has matured in appreciating the value of his or her uniquely hoped-for life goal. For such a person, everything takes on meaning and purpose, as this hope bestows on the details of their day a sense of mission and larger purpose. Ideally, Christians who have meditated, who have become reflective and have prayerfully listened in depth to the daily happening of their lives, see more or less clearly where they are going and what they are living for. Throughout the ages, the fostering of this sense of ultimate, personal purpose and direction has been one of the main responsibilities of spiritual guides in all great traditions.

There is something that we should keep in mind if we minister as spiritual guides in the Western world in this generation of our history. In earlier centuries, people in the West simply inherited a Christian view of the world: not necessarily balanced or healthy, but certainly explicitly Christian. They just breathed it in with the cultural air. Nowadays, we can breathe all we like in the cultural air and we will not absorb a Christian worldview. Not unless we do some deliberate cultural work for it.

That is why it is important for contemporary guides — much more than guides in, let us say, the thirteenth century — to encourage solid reading and study. People also need to absorb imagination-stirring films, plays, poetry, novels, and visual art that evoke the Christian "story" in audacious contemporary terms. Seekers today need to reinvent as they go "the Christian way of life," as they integrate solid directives for Christian living with daily decisions demanded by their unique, contemporary life situations. Only in that way can they appraise all the dimensions of their use of time and energy in terms of how those daily choices help or hinder their participation in the Mystery dimension of their life.

Daily decisions, painful, difficult, or seemingly inconsequential as they sometimes may be, are frequently the focus of the guide's attention. The guide realizes that over the years a person's appraisal disposition will develop into a smoothly flowing habit. Eventually he or she will make appraisals in a split second, without lengthy periods of reflection or even concentration.[16] On the other hand, the guide also foresees that when a person is faced with having to make a decision that carries heavy personal or communal significance, the situation changes considerably. A spiritual friend may still assist the journey of this human heart.

Suppose, for example, that Shellie, the young woman troubled by her work situation, begins to realize in mid-appraisal that part, at least, of her problem is that her work does not "fit" the person she is basically called to be. In van Kaam's words, she finds that the work she has been devoting time and energy to each day is "uncongenial." It does not deeply evoke or express the founding form of her life. It does not really bring out the wholehearted commitment to God and others she is capable of. Because it probes the heart, spiritual guidance often does uncover personal capacities or potentials that people may have been repressing or denying for most of their lives. Viewing the human person as basically self-transcending spirit oriented toward ultimate fulfillment in Mystery, spiritual guidance aims first at the congenial unfolding and realization of that embodied spirit. Suppose also that Shellie, during this period in her life, comes across a group of Christians her age who have committed themselves to following Christ in a variety of works aimed at the transformation of society.[17] She is attracted by their energetically dedicated lives and at the same time somewhat put off by thoughts of what she would be giving up if she became involved with them. She is especially hesitant when she realizes that for her, choosing to join them might entail a lifelong commitment in celibacy. Coming as she does from a secular family and culture, such a choice would not be easily arrived at. Wisely, she again seeks guidance, this time with the particular issue of celibate commitment and its implications for her own life journey in mind.

When Shellie comes to see me, we would explore not only the possibility of this new life situation, but also how she might need to undergo a shift in her own capacities of mind, will, and emotion in order to arrive at a free and mature decision. Taking into account all of the elements mentioned in the preceding chapters, I would try to help her look deeply at herself not only in terms of her vital-functional make-up with the self-knowledge she has gathered from the concrete history of her functional ambitions and transcendent hopes and aspirations, but also in terms of what she herself now knows she wants out of life with her whole heart. Part of this stage would be helping Shellie reflect on the passionate desires of her heart.

It is only from the depth of human desire that a permanent commitment can find enduring roots. Shellie should be encouraged right from the start to ask her questions of life,[18] to put into her own words the deepest reasons for wanting and for not wanting to pursue this new course. The guide counts on her capacity as spirit to grasp and appraise these less tangible aspects of her choice.

The guide also knows that a valid decision must also emerge from the concrete field of her life as she has actually been living it from day to day. He or she will try to prevent her from making an unrealistically idealistic or "exalted" choice that, in its lack of compatibility with her real-life circumstances and environment, has little or no chance of succeeding.[19] Thus, both guide and Shellie will take time to dwell meditatively on the actuality of her vital and passionate nature, for example, as well as on the facts they can gather about the group she is thinking about joining. Written material as well as informed discussion of the group's history and purpose with people whose opinion they respect will help here. Nothing can equal actually living with the group for a time in order to experience for herself the "inner meaningfulness" of their communal life and identity.

During this provisional period of the appraisal process, it is important that there be an attitude of openness to fresh possibilities and to the unpredictable Otherness of the divine context, as this young woman asks herself "Am I called by grace to this commitment? Within the limitations of what I know about myself now, is this commitment really for me? Or, if it is not for me, how can I find a commitment that will be more congenial as my response to the commandment of love?" This concern will be her first priority — not simply deciding in terms of her functional identity as an individual who can efficiently handle details of a work more or less in tune with the demands of a certain role in the culture. A thoughtful guide would take care that in the process of making her choice, Shellie doesn't either become overly rational about its rightness, overly emotional about its more romantic aspects, overly willful in the sense of coming to a decision merely because she feels it is her duty to do so, or overly active in the sense that the choice becomes totally oriented to doing good works rather than simply to being who she is.[20] Actually an adequate appraisal would bring about a happy balancing of her potential to receive form and to give it as the openness of her yin capacity overflows into healthy and productive yang or action. Often people in the midst of a comparable appraisal process are moved along in a positive direction by reminders of possibilities (as well as limitations) stemming from past memories of God's providential action in their lives. They are also bolstered by glimpses of the future as they anticipate hoped-for goals and are given honest assurance that things can go well as they launch their somewhat shaky life project into a transforming world and universe.

Like the elect who felt themselves called to join the "people of the Way" in the early centuries of the church, young men and women today feel themselves called forth to affirm and sometimes join, either temporarily or permanently, various types of intentional communities and groups. Theirs is not primarily a privatized faith, but one that finds its unfolding and application in relation to others. At a certain point this young woman and all of us as well will feel the need to come to closure with a decision. Occasionally the appraisal for our decision simply takes more time than is available. So with all our good will, we sometimes make what turns out to have been a wrong decision. Nothing is totally certain except the faithfulness of God's love, which in the end is our only guarantee that "all will be well" in spite of mistakes and faulty appraisals and the pressure to make choices even when we do not feel ready to do so.

Certainly we are aided in the ability to respond with a confident "yes" when we find ourselves sharing a vision with others who experience themselves as also freely rooted with us in a larger plan that expresses a Transcendent Will. In solidarity with these others and with the mysterious "more than" that binds all together in faith, we are able to move beyond the isolation of our own inability to risk. We are able to move past mere thinking to a knowing that can make judgments and take responsibility for decisions. With others, our will becomes empowered. Knowing ourselves as called along with others we are able, in a new way, to love. Again we recognize the familiar pattern of conversion, especially as it affects both mind and will.

Christian appraisal, then, wakes us up to the invisible providential presence of the Holy Other in all aspects of our life field, and particularly in the groups of people who have become for us the bearers of the Christian faith and form tradition. Everything is gift. In this light, appraisals can move us from the selfish isolation of our encapsulated egos to a more relaxed appreciation of life-giving directives "already there" in both the expected and the unexpected events of life. Such grounded appraisals can also help channel life energy into positive actions that change and perhaps transform the situation from which they originally emerged.

We have here a method of appraising characterized by faith: faith in a revealed tradition shared with others. Faith like this gives those who participate in it an intuitive appreciation of their rootedness in the Trinitarian Mystery and of their innate relatedness to the rest of creation. Faith-fostered appraisals require acceptance of the fact that human beings are free to welcome or to resist transformation by the loving initiatives of the Trinitarian Mystery. Thus, part of the task of Christian guidance is to point out obstacles that keep us from being the freely responsive lovers we were meant to be. Often we discover that there are deformative patterns of thinking, false ways of looking at self, at life, at others, and at God that keep us from honestly appraising and judging what is really going on in our day-to-day life. It is to these unliberated patterns of thought and behavior that guides can turn their attention as they strive to encourage a kind of death to the old self for the sake of life in the new.[21]

Presence of the Holy Spirit

Insightful appraisals of where "love went wrong" are especially needed at mid-life, when most adults find themselves called forth from a state of crisis to what some have termed a "second conversion." Moving from thoughtful reappraisal of the first half of their lives through a time of repentance and meditative presence to their deepest Ground, contemporary adults, at times aided by spiritual guidance, at other times simply trusting in guidance provided by life itself, are ripe for making what van Kaam calls the "turn to transcendence" proper to the second half of life.[22] It may be only now, at this later stage in their lives, that these men and women are, for the first time, relatively free to admit to and appraise the futility of their lonely attempts at self-sufficient management and control of their personal destinies. They will be more able to face and perhaps alter the mistaken images of self to which they may have been clinging for so many years. Perhaps they will have reached the point of letting go of unrealistic expectations they may have projected on others and equally on themselves. Precisely because their love was not in order, they have been increasingly unable to accept and feel at home in the full field of their lives. Now as they reluctantly focus the powers of their minds and wills on the environing context of trusted Mystery, they may at last begin to sense the Holy Spirit present and permeating, with the directive force of love, all the interwoven polarities of that field.

In *Dynamics of Spiritual Direction*, Adrian van Kaam describes the outcome of this most deeply Christian level of appraisal by noting that when they reach the stage of "emergence by transcendent partic-ipation," adult Christians can finally allow the love of God to move and direct them.[23] It is this divine love that opens them in an entirely new way to their environment, to their families, colleagues, friends, and neighbors. Their surrounding life field becomes an integral part of their life call, so that "when they are presented with a perplexing set of options, they try to establish which option is in tune with the designs of God's love for [themselves] and others." These mature Christians attempt to read God's will in the signs of the times, writes van Kaam, adding that "the person who does so under the impact of the Holy Spirit grows to the graced heights God has destined for him from eternity." All spiritual writers who describe guidance as attentiveness to the Spirit's presence and inspirations in the full field of each person's life speak of the necessity of inner as well as outer quieting in order to attain the delicate sensitivity required for recognizing these directives.[24] One writer actually calls this art of transcendent appraisal the essence of mysticism in action, claiming that this constant openness to the breath of the Spirit can and ought to become a way of life.[25]

Even the little we have said above about the delicate and meditative nature of this type of appraisal leads us to conclude that guidance of ourselves or someone else in attentiveness to the Spirit's presence requires guidance also in the art of prayer. And prayer according to all the great contemplative traditions must be preceded by prayerful silence.[26] In order for people to clarify what they really want or what God may be calling them to or even simply to, get in touch with their honest reactions to both the spiritual and not so spiritual events of daily life, they need to be reassured through the experience of meditative presence about the existence, as Gerald May puts it, of "the eternal reality that undergirds and infuses our being."[27] After exposure to this reality, we are less likely to forget who we most deeply are and will be more likely to feel at home in what God may be asking of us. Thus, living in the disposition of Christian appraisal could be described as living in a state of prayerful presence to one's own life field and to the inspirations of the Holy Spirit in that field and throughout our life.

In his last conversation with them, Jesus told his followers that the Holy Spirit whom the Father would send in his name, would instruct them in everything and remind them of all that he had told them (John 14:26). They were to go on, then, trusting in the presence and action of that Spirit, connected like branches of a vine to a power greater than themselves. With hearts awake to a spiritual vision of reality, they were to appraise their decisions and actions not merely in the framework of their individual subjective experience of this Spirit, but in terms also of dialogue with the communal story of how other people of God before them had appraised similar choices against a larger Ground. Thus, inspiration has always been integrated with faith handed on among the people of God, the church. Obedient listening and co-listening to the Spirit speaking in personal experience, in the church, and in Scripture as well as in doctrine and in the community, are recognized as the to-be-trusted sources not only of Christian appraisal, but of the entire process of Christian spiritual guidance and direction as well.

At the conclusion of this somewhat sketchy look at the appraisal process, the foundational assumption that underlies this entire approach to spiritual guidance and its central focus on the appraisal capacity of human beings becomes evident.[28] This method assumes the existence of a to-be-trusted guiding Other whose directing love underlies the life field and time of every person called to participate in the human condition. It is trust in the radiating energy of this treasure that makes possible the risky commitment of allowing oneself to be led into unfamiliar ways, in directions one does not understand, by a Spirit known only in the darkness of faith. It is faith in the working of this divine Other throughout the entire universe as well as in individual hearts that underlies and sustains this approach. In *Abandonment to Divine Providence*, Jean Pierre de Caussade describes this treasure as one that "none discover because they suppose it to be too far away to be sought." He continues:

> The treasure is everywhere, it is offered to us at all times and wherever we may be. All creatures, both friends and enemies pour it out with prodigality, and it flows like a fountain through every faculty of body and soul even to the very center of our hearts. If we open our mouths they will be filled. The divine activity permeates the universe, it pervades every creature; wherever they are, it is there; it goes before them, with them, and it follows them; all they have to do is to let the waves bear them on.[29]

Well, perhaps amid the complexities of modern society we have to do something more than just let the waves bear us on. In fact, that focusing of mind, heart, and will on doing something more delineates fairly precisely the aim of this book. However, I do believe that without at least some appreciation not only of a scientific and holistic view of the universe, but also of the need for faith in the invisible providential care that permeates and upholds its visible changing forms, our search for guidance we can trust will never be illuminated from within by rays from the treasure gleaming "already there" in the midst of our everyday life.

APPENDIX

Summary of how each chapter contributes to our understanding of the art of appraisal.

APPRAISAL is the art of listening to or recognizing the movements of the Spirit in all the spheres of the human life field. From the introductory paragraphs of LOOKING FOR CONNECTIONS it is clear that today's men and women are looking for spiritual guidance that makes sense to us in terms of the larger mysterious context of our lives. Guidance we can accept must also make sense in terms of the scientific and professional competence and commitment that is ours as adult persons face to face with a changing, pluralistically challenging global environment. Under the impact of contemporary "systems" thinking about human and cosmic wholeness and of the definitive implications of the person-world dialogue, there is no way twentieth-century human hearts could be satisfied with a form of appraisal that deals only with isolated interiority.

Appraisal for us as we are today will have to help us ascribe meaning and value to the directives, events, and opportunities that emerge in the everyday concrete circumstances of our entire life fields. It will have to be available for all those occasions when we feel called upon to make consequence-laden decisions and would prefer to make choices and act in the light of trusted guidelines from a specific faith and form tradition. It will also need to bring us more in touch with the movement of the Spirit in our selves and the daily happenings we encounter. Implicit in the introduction were questions like:

- can we learn for ourselves and teach others what is involved in making trustworthy decisions in the midst of changing situations?

- is there a way for hearts to reach out in loving attentiveness to the living flame of love that continues to burn in times of crisis as well as joy?

- can a spiritual guide be helpful in leading persons through transition periods in such a way that the fruits of the Spirit are increased as those persons get more in touch with themselves and with the Mystery?

188

In chapter 1, WAKING UP TO FREEDOM AND WHOLENESS, we saw how, over time, life itself confronts every human being with questions of various kinds. Significant guidance issues cluster around our limited but nevertheless real freedom to respond to life's happenings, to give meaning to the people and events that come our way, and to live with the consequences of choices made in relation to them. The need for a form of appraisal that can empower us to participate more deeply and wholesomely in the Mystery as we listen to and trust the questions suggested by our own everyday experience was raised in the first section of this initial chapter. In the following section, the pluralism of contemporary guidance methods was contrasted with demands for an approach to both the human person and life as a whole that integrated the Mystery dimension even in cases where the persons involved do not adhere to any specific faith tradition. Already we were recognizing that the human spirit of every man and woman is called forth from the soul, from the spirit's foundation, and that this calling forth can be appraised as the central dynamic force in human life.

We also saw that any method of appraisal aiming to assist people to find and follow their unique life direction would necessarily have to take account not only of each person's human spirit but also of the given and chosen circumstances of the life field in which the spirit finds itself incarnated. Applying all of this to the practice of appraisal, we see why issues of waking up to life as mystery, of recognizing the limited nature of our freedom, and of learning to appreciate the foundational inner capacity of oneself, where one *is* immortal diamond, are vital to the process. Without reference to this deepest capacity of soul, for example, a valid link cannot be made between a person's call and appraisal of what might be the Spirit-inspired commitments of his or her life time and energy. Thus, in addition to learning to abide, to dwell with gratitude on this human capacity to connect with Mystery, on this image of the human person as spirit, both guides and those guided are warned in chapter 1 to look for and appraise directives for spiritual growth as they actually and often ambiguously emerge in the limited but real and sometimes messy events and circumstances of each human being's actual life.

The appraising guide realizes that what any event in people's life field means to them depends on the presence they bring to it in terms of the prefocal dialogue they tend to be with their world. Here, in its direct connection with appraisal, the issue of human freedom arises. If we are going to empower people to make better use of the limited but real freedom that is theirs, we must help them make a correct appraisal of the quality of presence they bring in practice to their prefocal as well as focal dialogue with various commitments in which they are involved. Guidance must also help them to value or appraise what a certain loved person or endeavor, a painful feeling or emotion, a specific job offer or promotion, or some drastic change in any one aspect of their life might mean specifically for them. Everything that happens can be an opportunity for this person to grow in self-knowledge and thus more freely take responsibility for the direction of his or her life. Effective guidance aids this reflective self-exploration not only in terms of expanding one's personal openness to various parts of reality, but also to the Whole, to the presence of Mystery beneath the visible surface of everyday life.

Chapter 2, A SENSE OF THE MYSTERY, focused on the human capacity as spirit that allows us to respond with awe and wonder as we acknowledge encounters with Holy Otherness and feel responsible to hand on to each generation the faith and form traditions they inspire. Recalling that spiritual guides from the earliest times have put forth much effort toward making a connection between people's everyday challenges and complexities and the chosen faith context that gives them meaning, we recognized the guide's responsibility to raise to consciousness aspects not only of a man's or woman's prefocal daily dialogue with reality, but also the relevant aspects of his or her trusted faith tradition as well. Perhaps due to their knowledge of various human sciences like sociology, cultural anthropology, and comparative religion, contemporary guides are even more aware than were their predecessors of the importance of pointing to the underlying cultural or form tradition that permeates the life field of the person who comes seeking help with appraisal and decision amid the challenges of twentieth-century technical, philosophical, and moral ambiguity. Today's guide needs to be rooted in both of these hidden sources of thinking as he or she stands ready to empower fellow human beings to probe not only their own felt sense of being personally in relation to the Mystery but also to recognize how they are living that relation as mediated by the cultural and societal circumstances in which they find themselves.

People want to get in touch with the flow of the Mystery, with the ways in which they themselves tend to block the flow of that energy in their own lives, and with the "receptivity dynamics" regarded down through the ages in their tradition as the best for facilitating openness toward the Mystery. In terms of helping others to evaluate their choices in the midst of contemporary religious pluralism and the bewildering variety of transpersonal techniques now available, it is crucial for Christian guides to take a clear view of the human heart's potential for receiving inspiration. He or she must be able to root appraisal of contemporary spiritual paths and techniques in a solidly Christian image of the human person. He or she must also be personally motivated by dynamics of delight in the Mystery prior to making any suggestions regarding detachment and the fostering of a more open, receptive lifestyle. Finally, in this second chapter we sensed the guide's responsibility for appreciating the Gospel narrative, the objective "story" that can evoke subjective responses in tune with preformed temperamental preference in those being guided. When we realize that chosen commitments reflect one's priorities and concerns as they channel the passionate energies of the universe in their flow through the searching human heart, we see even more clearly why appraisal of life as dialogue has become a central issue for spiritual guidance.

Chapter 3, LIFE KEEPS HAPPENING, focused on the fact that recent actual life events can indeed be the "stuff" of the appraisal that takes place both within and outside of spiritual guidance sessions. When fruitfully reflected on, the most ordinary events are found to contain all the hidden growth directives and conflicts the person has to face in dealing with the harmony or disharmony of his or her dialogue with the world. Disruptive events that challenge this person's familiar coping patterns are usually welcomed by guides, who desire to break through complacency, open up closed hearts, and restore a healing yin/yang balance. It was in this chapter that we discovered more about paying attention to the entire "field" of a person's life. In every event, all five polarities of a person's life field are involved. It is often the privilege of the spiritual guide to assist people to move beyond the narrow enclosure of their individual field and to recognize themselves as interwoven not only with the overarching Mystery, but also with the larger fields of their culture and society. As co-listener to another's story, the guide can be alert for unfree as well as free responses of this person's spirit, especially during periods of stress and inner conflict. Life events and limit situations seen from a "field" point of view can aid the appraisal process as they give access to self-knowledge derived directly from a man's or a woman's concrete response to a variety of life happenings and circumstances.

From our reading of the third chapter, we begin to see the importance for appraisal of the receptive as well as the more active types of willing, and of how the will as well as the intellect comes into play in a life event like the mid-life transition. Openness to the challenge of the pluriformity of contemporary formation fields makes critical appraisal of aspects like consumerism and feminist consciousness a serious focus for those who desire to live as Christians in both a positive and a counter-cultural stance toward the environing culture. Ultimately it is a balanced appraisal of the dialogue between what happens in a person's life and their inner response to it that is the most reliable source of self-knowledge.

Several levels of consciousness and the powers of human cognition as they are brought into play in attempts at spiritual guidance both of ourselves and for the benefit of others is the initial topic under consideration in chapter 4, GUIDING THE HUMAN SPIRIT. The way the human mind moves toward attentively perceiving a personally significant event, the mind's unique perspective on different aspects of the life field, has a lot to do with the response people are able to give to what happens in that field at any particular moment. Thus guides and those guided have to become aware of how appraisal is a power of the human mind and of how the dynamics of our imagination, memory, and anticipation profoundly influence the ways in which we choose to act and react toward, against, or away from what life hands us each day. We also have to realize that the person we think we are is not identical with the person we most deeply are called to be and that many people live in ignorance of themselves and of what motivates their choices in relation to Transcendence. Spiritual guidance and especially appraisal undertaken amid this kind of ignorance regarding the call of divine Otherness in every human life, when it fails to apprehend the depth dimension of life, would not be of much help for anyone's spiritual growth.

Since the way we think has a lot to do with the way we feel, a spiritual disposition of appraisal must be formed in a meditative receptive stance, especially in Western cultures dominated by the functional approach. Moreover, what a spiritual guide has to offer is not very apparent or appreciated in such an environment. Authentic appraisals cannot be made in ignorance of one's call to relationship with transcendent mystery, nor in ignorance of the deformative aspects of our dialogue with reality. The guide must be an alert co-listener to this dialogue.

Chapter 5, CHALLENGES AND PRACTICES FOR TODAY'S SPIRITUAL GUIDES, moved more deeply into an examination of current approaches to spirituality, to, for example, those growing out of the "New Age" movement. It is often difficult to distinguish some practices of that movement from what belongs to a Christian's view of the universe. It is equally difficult in the midst of a growing number of popular typological tools for personality and sin-type appraisal to perceive the most deeply held motivations of the human heart that reflect a person's call to more abundant life. Typologies can give a certain amount of useful information about a person, as, for instance, the categories of the Enneagram or the Myers Briggs indicator. However, they cannot substitute for a prayerful contemplative approach to another human being as redeemed child of God needing help to move beyond the underlying conflicts that keep him or her from relating in truth to that God.

Helpful in appraising the overall direction that one's life is taking can be the power of formative memory aided by practices like journal keeping, a meditatively conscious living through of the mid-life transition, and even a knowledge of one's operational preferences to be gained from the above-mentioned popular tests. However, transcendent appraisal must go beyond any of these tools, useful though they may be, in order that its truly spiritual aims may be realized. Nevertheless, awareness of their own counter-transferential tendencies and brokenness can challenge guides in a pain-filled appraisal of the truth of their own as well as others' spiritual journey.

The brief survey of life's developmental stages as laid out in chapter 6, A GUIDE'S VIEW OF THE HUMAN JOURNEY, did not in itself indicate a lot about what is going on at the deeper spiritual dimensions of a person's life. However, it is only when the guide recognizes the growth pattern typical of each developmental phase that he or she will be able to be of help to young people struggling with commitment choices and career decisions — to all who are seeking to appraise what for them will be the "path with a heart." It is usually only after one has experienced a few more or less difficult or uncongenial events and been jolted into suspecting the presence of a deeper hidden direction for his or her life that the central focus of guidance, one's capacity for discernment or appraisal, can emerge into focal awareness. Up until that moment, there may have been periods of being pushed by events to make decisions and live with the consequences. But a time arrives in everyone's life when sooner or later we are forced not only to give a perhaps unwanted form to our lives, but also and at the same time to reflect on the profound meaning of those choices — of, in fact, those lives.

Such a seemingly negative moment, of failure, loss of a friend, illness, unemployment, middle age, retirement, or old age, for example, when we catch sight for perhaps the first time of our divided self and glimpse its ultimate meaning as called forth by the Mystery, may mark the beginning of conscious recognition of the disposition of appraisal that has for years been at work in our lives. This capacity for making judgments and decisions, for responsibly giving form to our lives as we weigh and value the various directives in our life field, is certainly not confined to the second half of life. In fact, this innate capacity can, through repeated use, become a habitual disposition fairly early in one's life. However, its exercise in earlier years often lacks experience and may require more mature guidance, especially when life energy needs to be directed into career and vocational commitments or when questions of directing one's life time and energy in ways that are consonant with the purposes of the divine Mystery come to the fore. The consonant direction of life time and energy can also be influenced by obstacles other than those carried over from past unfolding. There are in-built resistances to both human and spiritual maturity detectable by discerning eyes within the culture or form tradition from which there is little or no escape. All those person seeking guidance, and those who guide as well, are products of a certain recognized or unacknowledged form tradition, which may or may not be an expression of one of the great faith traditions. Even the sinfulness or weaknesses in character to which we are addicted are not completely unique to ourselves. They are permeated by the pulsations of our culture, nourished and shaped by it, recognizable as belonging somehow to our time and the type of forgetfulness and disorder common among our contemporaries. Truly spiritual guidance might also be described, then, as a process of "conscientization" in the service of appraisal. In helping men and women pay attention to the quality of their ongoing dialogue with all aspects of their actual life field, it prepares a climate for reform and readies them for new growth as they embrace the turn to transcendence and thus begin to return to their rootedness in the divine Source of life.

Most of chapter 7, ON BEING A WISE FISH, is devoted to the attitudes and task of the trusted guide — that man or woman who is explicitly called forth by others to be with them as they reawaken to the call from their deeper self and feel the need for a shift, for a realignment of what has become an unsatisfactory and uncongenial style of life. The spiritual guide is called upon to expedite another's affectively felt need for detachment from encapsulation in no longer appropriate stages of developmental stagnation. The guide also helps with appraisal of less than wholesome cultural pulsations, vital impulses, and functional ambitions, even mediocre aspirations that no longer contribute to fulfilling ultimate commitments to loving and being loved, in such a way that detachment from them becomes possible. Whether originating from within or from outside themselves, this felt need to change or be changed signals the first step in a pattern with which all guides become familiar, the pattern of readying the entire person to move *from* current uneasiness and dissatisfaction *through* the painful or joyful living of and reflecting on a personally significant life event *to* a positive new attachment and style that is more truly expressive of that entire person's appraised capacity to love and be loved. Within the context of Christian faith, the event appraised as potentially formative brings with it a call from beyond both guide and person guided, a mysterious in-breaking of the Holy Other capable of evoking attitudes of receptivity and trust.

In this chapter, the guide who wishes to become a "wise fish" from within this faith paradigm was offered at least twenty suggestions for becoming a channel of in-breaking otherness for those he or she guides. These suggestions will help him or her be mindful of the affective as well as intellectual level of the guidance project. They will also help him or her to try to retain a relaxed, receptive, meditative style in spite of the to-be-expected tension generated by this person's attempts to shift his or her personal axis from self-centeredness to other-centeredness. Careful not to foster false or uncongenial dispositions and attitudes, a guide gradually leads the other person into a scanning dialogue of appraisal regarding the deeper meaning of pertinent aspects of his or her current life field and its mysterious ground. The question that keeps coming to the fore during this provisional dialogue will be whether or not any aspect of the field that is considered holds within itself something that belongs to the invisible call of the Mystery for this particular person. In weighing the pro's and con's of a certain person, event, or thing, are we moved to judge its value for him or her with an appreciative appraisal of "yes" or depreciative "no"? It is by gradually submitting tentative decisions to such an appraisal process that the mind and will of a person who comes for guidance are finally shifted in reflective response, not to the guide but to the Other whose call both guide and the one guided are seeking to disclose and understand.

At this point, the kind of guidance and appraisal we are describing implies a radical revision of attitude and perspective that baptized people call "conversion." As described in chapter 8, LIFE EMERGING FROM DEATH, conversion usually implies also a return to the foundational giftedness of life as initiated in God and to a response of trust in that giftedness via the spiritual capacity of willing. The focus of conversion direction is on the inner dynamic shift from preoccupation with predicting and controlling what may happen in one's isolated life field, to seriously suspecting that there may be an underlying invisible whole into which those controlled predictions may or may not fit. Appraisal in service of conversion would occur when one's judgment about what to do moves from restlessness and dissatisfaction of some sort, through a daily unrelenting struggle toward spiritual growth and maturity, toward an inner renewal that is often accompanied by exterior changes as well.

In this context of conversion, the relationship between appraisal and detachment emerges clearly. Detachment that flows naturally from attachment to the appeal of Christ's love can be enlisted in service of freedom to risk when the need for such action is appraised. As life moves on, the appraisal disposition calls us more in the direction of confidently flowing with instead of resisting the Mystery's impingements, and we find ourselves again at a new stage.

The co-appraising guide must take into account chronological age, especially if a certain man or woman has entered the second half of life. Guidance in prayer becomes more central at this point of "second conversion" when new anxieties and questions emerge and spiritual need, need for the Spirit, takes on a fresh urgency. It is only when persons come to know themselves as personally called by the Mystery that they arrive at the ability to respond freely, to say yes in trust that in the midst of all the limitations resulting from developmental deformation and from being born into a wounded and sinful situation, they can go beyond their fears and feel free enough to love others and God.

Being able to enter ever more fully into the social reality of the life field comprises still another central aim of the guidance process. As glimpsed in chapter 9, BELONGING AND COMMUNION, the communal wisdom of the Christian faith tradition recognizes the conflict that underlies the relationship of each unique human person and even the most trusted other people in their life. In this chapter suggestions are put forward for helping people reflect on their membership in groups of others and on the commitments they have undertaken communally with one or more fellow human beings. The shared vision, the central passion or collective dream, that animates and nourishes the group's present and future commitments must have a continuing resonance with the central core of expectations that animate the heart of the man or woman who would join one of these groups. Thus, the guide must be aware of and able to appraise the communal nature of commitments whether these involve interpersonal relatedness within a family, a work group, or other type of community. Much can be revealed by honestly appraising, for example, one's personal and perhaps hidden expectations regarding sharing, cooperation, authority, leadership styles, or whatever. Aware of the symbols and stories of care and cooperation in the Christian tradition, the guide in that tradition tries to hand these on as sources of that special community's shared vision. Thus commonly shared elements of the form tradition can become the solidary ground upon which the appraisals and judgments of group members can confidently rest. Even at times when this solidary sense of "we" appears lacking among group members, the guide can help focus collective attention on the inner meaningfulness that lies beyond the temporal boundaries of the community itself. Sometimes it takes an outsider to help us recall and reappreciate the greater to-be-trusted reality that evoked the commitment of "us" as a group in the first place.

An intentional group's communal appraisal of its wider shared vision as well as its central passion makes it possible for members to prioritize and thus focus their various commitments within it. Specifically Christian vocational appraisals should never be made without reference to both the individual making the commitment and the vision of the group in which that dedication to Christ will be lived. Because the liturgy provides a crucial source for the wider ground of a Christian community's spiritual vision, it becomes an essential element in that group's celebration of itself as well as of each individual member's spiritual search. Guidance in recalling communities and families to their deepest heritage turns out to be a form of group direction much needed by today's Christians, who, along with almost everyone else are experiencing the loss of their original sense of "we."

In chapter 10, VOCATION: FINDING THE WORK OF LOVE, the art of appraisal is applied to the central project that gives direction to the life of most people — the commitment of their life, time, and energy, in various life relationships like marriage or in concrete faithfulness to daily responsibilities for service to family and community. A realistic appraisal of ways of earning a living in the life-negating circumstances of our present culture is often the ground against which people's work decisions must be made. Absence of a spiritual dimension for life and work can add to the pain of failure to find meaningful work. Nevertheless, much self-knowledge can be discovered in and through a careful dialogue with one's working hours and days, particularly if one's work is that of a spiritual guide.

It is often the responsibility of the spiritual guide to recognize and bring forward the element of receptivity that lies at the heart of human willing and decision making. Otherwise the decisions resulting from co-listening for the Spirit may not at all reflect the openness of our pneumatic dimension to receive as well as give form to life. Here we become aware of the gifted nature of the spiritual life, of its gratuitousness, and of its potential in everyone. We also get in touch with the delicate nature of the art we have been calling appraisal and with our need to learn more about it.

In the introduction to chapter 11, GUIDELINES FOR APPRAISAL, I have explained that Appendix will contain a summary of how each chapter in this book contributes to the understanding of this art or gift of recognizing the movements of the Spirit in all areas of human life.

NOTES

Introduction: Looking for Connections

1. In this desire for being connected in our inner directedness toward a wider meaning, we resemble the fish in a brief Sufi legend recounted by Idries Shah in *The Sufis* (New York: Doubleday, 1971), 401. Entitled "Fishes and water," it reads: "Fishes, asking what water was, went to a wise fish. He told them that it was all around them, yet they still thought that they were thirsty." In our diligent search for "living waters" we sometimes need to find a "wise fish" who will connect us consciously with the larger invisible sea in which we are already swimming. The dynamic underlying spiritual guidance lies in this dialogue, this interior tuning in to the larger reality via letting go of limiting world-views and other obstacles that prevent our transformation into communion with the living Source of the mysterious sea in which we swim.

2. In concrete, global biblical anthropology, the heart is understood as the inner container not only of feelings but also of memories, ideas, plans, and decisions. It is truly the core of a person's being, the place where he or she is open or closed to God. See "heart" in Xavier Leon-Dufour, *Dictionary of Biblical Theology*, new rev. ed. (New York: Seabury, 1968), 228–29, for more on this biblical view of the human heart. See also Louis Bouyer's discussion of the centrality of "intentionality" in Christian spiritual life, in chap. 1 of his *Introduction to Spirituality* (New York: Desclee, 1961), 18. See also Adrian van Kaam, *Formation of the Human Heart*, vol. 3 of his series on Formative Spirituality (New York: Crossroad, 1983–87). The foundational approach of this present study owes much to the spiritual wisdom underlying these four volumes of Adrian van Kaam, with whom I have learned and worked for over twenty years.

3. Thornton Wilder, *Our Town* (New York: Coward-McCann, 1938), 83. For a similar moment of delight and wonderment at realizing he is alive, see the description in Ray Bradbury, *Dandelion Wine* (New York: Bantam, 1959), when twelve-year-old Douglas Spaulding, wrestling with his younger brother, gasps, "Tom...does everyone in the world...know he's alive?" "Sure, Heck yes," replies Tom. "I hope they do," whispered Douglas, "Oh, I sure hope they know" (7–8).

4. For historical overviews of changing models of spiritual guidance and an awareness of how, throughout all of human history, people have been trying to make these transcendent connections for themselves and have asked other people to help them do so, see "Direction Spirituellé" in *Dictionnaire de Spiritualité* (Paris: Beauchesne, 1957), 1002–1214; Louis Bouyer, *A History of Christian Spirituality*, 3 vols. (New York: Seabury, 1969); Jordan Aumann, *Christian Spirituality in the Catholic Tradition* (San Francisco: Ignatius Press, 1986); John T. McNeill, *A History of the Cure of Souls* (New York: Harper & Row, 1951); and Carolyn Gratton, *Guidelines for Spiritual Direction* (Denville, N.J.: Dimension Books, 1980).

5. In *Will and Spirit* (New York: Harper & Row, 1982), 163–64, May notes that we mean well, we all have good hearts, we begin with love and good intentions. But in the process of growing and changing, of "getting on with our lives," we miss the

199

point. We need to pay more attention to those dimly sensed flickers of restless longing for "more" that from time to time cry out to be recognized in the midst of even some very committed hearts and lives.

6. In a brief article on "Spiritual Direction" in the *New Dictionary of Spirituality* (Collegeville, Minn.: Liturgical Press, 1992), I have attempted to address the present need for a foundational, integrative approach to spirituality and guidance that makes sense in an age of pluralism and dialogue with other faith traditions. In view of contemporary discoveries regarding the different ways of knowing possible for humans and the abundance of guidance or direction sources opening for everyone, integration in our age of pluralism becomes a necessity if we are to live in any kind of wholeness and peace with one another.

7. See *The Turning Point* (New York: Bantam, 1982), 47, where Capra traces cultural evolution in East and West, pointing up the "systems view" of the universe that can also be discovered in the following: Morris Berman, *The Reenchantment of the World* (Ithaca: Cornell University Press, 1981); Thomas Berry, *Dream of the Earth* (San Francisco: Nature and Natural Philosophy Library, 1988); Larry Dossey, *Space, Time and Medicine* (Boulder, Colo.: Shambhala, 1982); Jacob Needleman, *A Sense of the Cosmos* (New York: E. P. Dutton, 1965); Daniel Liderbach, *The Numinous Universe* (New York: Paulist, 1989); and Gary Zukav, *The Dancing Wu Li Masters* (New York: Bantam, 1979). Along with the description in chap. 1 of Tilden Edwards's *Spiritual Friend* of "the spiritual sea in which we swim today," the reader will find more than enough material for reflection on how, due to the influence of science, society, and an increasingly global consciousness, we stand in need of the aforementioned integrative approach.

8. Fritjof Capra, *The Tao of Physics: An Exploration of the Parallels between Modern Physics and Eastern Mysticism* (New York: Bantam, 1977). Since then many authors have discussed similar insights.

9. A few of the contemporary authors celebrating the emergence of the genius of feminine sensibility and potential are Mary Field Belenky, et al., *Women's Ways of Knowing: The Development of Self, Voice and Mind* (New York: Basic Books, 1986); Irene Claremont de Castillejo, *Knowing Woman* (New York: Harper & Row, 1973); Elisabeth Schüssler Fiorenza, *In Memory of Her* (New York: Crossroad, 1983); Carol Gilligan, *In a Different Voice* (Cambridge, Mass.: Harvard University Press, 1982); Jean Baker Miller, *Toward a New Psychology of Women* (Boston: Beacon Press, 1976); Sandra Schneiders, *Women and the World* (New York: Paulist, 1986). The feminine awareness of the psychic weave between self and others complements our growing sense of self as a human organism fully engaged in the fields of our lives and forming a sort of web or network with the larger social and environmental organisms.

10. See notes 6, 7, and 8 as well as Ervin Lazlo, *The Systems View of the World* (New York: George Braziller, 1972), for more on this new understanding of the human person as necessarily interacting with his or her surrounding worlds. See also the work of Adrian van Kaam in formative spirituality for an explanation of how these insights along with contemporary pluralism of faith traditions impact the human capacity both to give to and receive form from the surrounding life fields.

11. This growing insight into the gradually shifting worldview of both scientists and mystics reminds me of one of the major discoveries during my earlier research for *Trusting: Theory and Practice* (New York: Crossroad, 1982), 175. Almost all of the classic spiritual masters in the Christian tradition, when they spoke about the to-be-trusted "divine will" underlying all of reality, employed intuitive terms that very much resemble those used by contemporary scientists as they describe our universe as "participating in a cosmic web of interconnecting energies to whose source human consciousness has access by means of transcendent aspiration." In spiritual guidance we are dealing with what spiritual writers call a "sacramental universe."

12. See again Bouyer's first chapter in *Introduction to Spirituality* (n. 2 above) for pertinent distinctions regarding "interiority." In his *Dynamics of Spiritual Self-Direction* (Denville, N.J.: Dimension Books, 1976), 384–85, Adrian van Kaam begins a defini-

tion of spiritual guidance by describing "a Spirit supported, prudent, educated and well-informed assistance that is dialogical," that is, in dialogue with all the rest of a contemporary adult's lived reality and commitments.

13. Some of the more recent and recommended writing, not only on the subject of becoming a wise fish for others, but also about living in responsible self-presence to the unfolding of our own lives, is to be found in the following: William A. Barry and William J. Connolly, *The Practice of Spiritual Direction* (New York: Seabury, 1982); Kevin G. Culligan, *Spiritual Direction: Contemporary Readings* (Locust Valley, N.Y.: Living Flame Press, 1983); Tilden Edwards, *Spiritual Friend* (New York: Paulist, 1980); Damien Isabell, *The Spiritual Director* (Chicago: Franciscan Herald Press, 1976); Morton T. Kelsey, *Companions on the Inner Way* (New York: Crossroad, 1983); Kenneth Leech, *Soul Friend: A Study of Spirituality* (San Francisco: Harper & Row, 1977); Thomas Merton, *Spiritual Direction and Meditation* (Collegeville, Minn.: Liturgical Press, 1960); Aelred Squire, *Asking the Fathers* (New York: Paulist Press, 1973); Josef Sudbrack, *Spiritual Guidance* (New York: Paulist Press, 1983) and Adrian van Kaam, *The Dynamics of Spiritual Self-Direction* (Denville, N.J.: Dimension Books, 1976).

Chapter 1: Waking Up to Freedom and Wholeness

1. Etty Hillesum, *An Interrupted Life* (New York: Pantheon, 1983).

2. Judith Guest. *Ordinary People* (New York: Ballantine Books, 1976).

3. Norman Cousins, *The Healing Heart* (New York: Avon Books, 1983).

4. Readers who wish to consult sources about grace as transformative are advised to refer to all volumes in the Formative Spirituality series by Adrian van Kaam (*Formation of the Human Heart*) as well as theologies by authors like Karl Rahner, his *Foundations of Christian Faith* (New York: Seabury, 1978) for example, or Panayiotis Nellas's theology of the human person, *Deification in Christ* (Crestwood, N.Y.: St. Vladimir's Seminary Press, 1987). Chap. 5, "The Presence of Grace," in Elisabeth-Paule Labat's *The Presence of God* (New York: Paulist Press, 1979), and *A World of Grace*, ed. Leo O'Donovan (New York: Seabury, 1980), also speak to the topic of this section. In their specifically Christian sense of the mystery, they all describe how human beings are capable of being transformed by the love of God that is poured into our hearts by the Holy Spirit who lives in us (Rom. 5:5). Mystical life is the full and free expansion of this life of grace that is God's free and forgiving self-communication to us. Without that gift, no one is capable of entering into this intimate relationship with God.

5. See above Introduction, n. 2.

6. Scripture is filled with references to these deeper possibilities, to the destiny as sons and daughters of God that awaits all those who are baptized in faith in Christ. It is primarily to this calling that the Christian spiritual guides desire to awaken the people who seek them out. To repeat, an appreciation of human freedom and its in-built directedness toward the divine Presence underlying all of life's events and aspirations forms the basis of the church's traditional understanding of spiritual direction.

7. I once asked my students at Duquesne to list the kinds of questions people most frequently brought to the guidance situation. The main question seems to be "What is happening? What's really going on — in society today? in the church today? in my family? among my friends? in my life here and now?"

8. These people were TV personalities on talk shows in the 1980s and 1990s.

9. Their insights do not, moreover, usually reach the heights of the legendary wise ones of pre-Christian generations whose wisdom arose from contemplative seeing.

10. As we note the phenomenal growth of cults in North America in the 1980s, we ask what the young people who flock to them are seeking. Unwilling to live the questions, they seem to need clear-cut and tidy answers with no grey areas, answers that are there sometimes before the questions are even asked.

11. In chap. 7 in the section entitled "Some Patterns of the Awakening Heart," is a translation of a Chinese poem by Thomas Merton that catches something of the Taoist philosophy of *wu-wei*. From the experience of a sabbatical in China and from conversations with Chinese friends I would venture to suggest that this classic doctrine of noninterference, of becoming receptive to the gift aspect of existence, stands at the opposite end of the spectrum from our Western stance of control and functionalism. And even though modern China is rapidly adopting many of the outward behaviors of the West, there still seems to be a shared possession among both sexes of an inner pattern of energy favoring "yin" as well as "yang" that will ultimately work for their survival as a people and as a culture.

12. See Gabriel Marcel, *Being and Having* (New York: Harper Torchbooks, 1965). To begin to see oneself as part of a much greater ongoing reality can be very helpful. It can help us avoid becoming totally taken up in our own little part of the process and can assist us in relativizing our problems against a larger horizon. There is only one ultimate mystery. It began before I came to be and will continue after I am gone. If I begin to experience my life as participating in this mystery, as capable of flowing and cooperating with the energies and laws of this more cohesive whole that is beyond the embrace of my present conscious ambitions and imaginative aspirations, I will not be as likely to view my life simply as a series of problems to be solved.

13. My doctoral research into trust between people and into the area of commitment taught me that these realities call for exploration not only of the powers of personal freedom and decision making, and of a person's vital-functional ability to use energy and incarnate decisions, but also they tapped into the Sources of the energy that carry the whole endeavor and hold the secret of who this committed or trusting person really is. Also in looking at the many ways in which human beings seek to escape trusting and protect themselves from the demands of their commitments, I found myself reaching far beyond the realm of mere psychology, into the presence to and thus possible absence from, the Mystery that each person is uniquely meant to be.

14. Pluralism refers to a situation in which a variety of viewpoints, explanations, or perspectives are offered as accounting for the same reality. Founded on the existence of a plurality of knowing subjects, pluralism is an inalienable characteristic of contemporary society and thought. It is also in evidence in the multitude of differing styles in spirituality as is demonstrated in Cheslyn Jones, Geoffrey Wainwright, and Edward Yarnold, eds. *The Study of Spirituality* (New York: Oxford University Press, 1986). Also illustrative of the human tendency toward "slices and slivers" are Denise and John Carmody, *Religion: The Great Questions* (New York: Seabury, 1983); David Fleming, *The Fire and the Cloud* (New York: Paulist, 1978); Urban Holmes, *A History of Christian Spirituality* (New York: Seabury, 1980); *Classics of Western Spirituality*, edited by Richard Payne for Paulist Press; and Ninian Smart, *Worldviews* (New York: Scribner's, 1983).

15. Even the slice labelled Christian spirituality has been cut up into different types according to different founders. So we have Anglican, Lutheran, Wesleyan, and Catholic spirituality — and the Catholics have Benedictine, Ignatian, Dominican, and Franciscan spiritualities among themselves. The Institute of Formative Spirituality where I work has devoted the past twenty-five years to developing a coherent systematic approach to this "slices and slivers" dilemma, and it is out of my interest in practical spirituality that makes sense to ordinary lay people like ourselves that this approach to guidance originated.

16. Roger Hurding, *Roots and Shoots* (London: Hodder and Stoughton, 1985).

17. Hurding looks at Adler's insights into innate aggressive striving and at his emphasis on individuation; at Erikson and Horney, Fromm, and Sullivan's explication of the links between development and culture, between anxiety and interpersonal relations; at the emphasis in Rogerian personalism on growth and organismic feeling; on Frankl's thoughts about human spirit as responsible search for meaning; at Jung's innate archetypes as somewhat questionable guides for the whole inner journey.

18. See Adrian van Kaam, *Fundamental Formation* (New York: Crossroad, 1983)

for more on these dimensions of the human person in a Christian tradition. See also chap. 2 of this present volume for further insight into the meaning of the "pneumatic" dimension.

19. In his small guide to mantra meditation called *Word into Silence* (New York: Paulist Press, 1980), spiritual writer and guide John Main speaks about the centrality of the spirit dimension in our nature and the deep importance of uncovering one's own spirit. He says, "Few generations have been so introverted and self-analytical as our own, and yet modern man's study of himself is notoriously unproductive. The reason for this, as I have been suggesting, is that it has been radically unspiritual; that is, it has not been conducted in the light of the Spirit; it has not yet taken account of that real and fundamental dimension of man's nature. Without spirit, there is no productivity, no creativity, no possibility of growth. The Christian's duty is to point this out, and to be able to do so with the authority of one who really knows what spirit is, but only because he knows his own spirit and the infinite expansion of man's spirit that takes place when it responds to the presence of the Spirit of God, from who it derives its being."

20. Labelled by van Kaam (*Fundamental Formation*) as the person's foundational life form, the soul is described by Elisabeth-Paule Labat in chap. 1 of *The Presence of God* as our eternal being, carried along in the generation of God . . . and shining in the deepest center of our life in the inviolable purity of the image of our creator (24). She notes that from the center of this most noble element of our being a source of living water springs (26). Two authors who describe how we co-form the reality we perceive as a result of this unique dynamism are Adrian van Kaam, *On Being Yourself* (Denville, N.J.: Dimension Books, 1972), and John Main, who in *The Christian Mysteries* (Montreal: Benedictine Priory, 1979) speaks of baptism as the deepest communal reality we share.

21. Basic spiritualization then is, first of all, basic humanization. The glory of God, according to an early church writer, is the human person fully alive, not only in his or her vital-functional capacities, but also in the spiritual capacity for going beyond merely cosmic processes in a concern for meaning, for Otherness, for the Whole.

22. Returning to the notion of dynamism, we can say that spiritual call is a matter of spirit dynamized by soul as it is called forth by the dialogue we are with the needs of our world. The flow of life energy, like the flow of electricity between a positive and a negative pole, requires at least two polarities, one of which exists in the life field of the person being called.

23. Frederick Buechner, *Wishful Thinking* (San Francisco: Harper & Row, 1973), 95.

24. So, in this type of guidance we take seriously the human need to express what van Kaam calls our "form potency," our divine life theme or desire, concretely in reality. Our capacity to give form to our world motivates our interest in making a contribution to it. See also John Haughey's book *Converting 9 to 5: A Spirituality of Daily Work* (New York: Crossroad, 1989), especially chap. 6, "What Work Lasts?," and also chap. 10, where we speak, as does James Fowler, about "vocational hunger." See Fowler's *Becoming Adult, Becoming Christian* (San Francisco: Harper & Row, 1984).

25. The same reality encountered by different people offers a unique experience even though objectively speaking it remains the same for all. For example, a tree for a hot tired person becomes a place of refuge. The same tree is a source of worry for a mother anxious that her child not climb too high in it. For the child, the tree is experienced as high adventure, while for an unhappy young woman it may be a reminder of inner conflicts from the past. For the biologist it is an object of scientific interest, for the poet it may be a symbol of God's creative originality, while for an accountant or a cabinet maker, the tree exists to be used and perhaps bring in some money when it is finally cut into lumber. Which one experienced the real tree?

26. These questions are found in chap. 1, "Human Faith," in James Fowler, *Stages of Faith* (San Francisco: Harper & Row, 1981), 3.

27. Some writers like Gerald Hughes in his *God of Surprises* (London: Darton, Longman and Todd, 1985) see spiritual guidance under the metaphor of digging for treasure,

reminding us of Jesus' saying that the Kingdom of heaven is like a treasure hidden in a field, and "where your treasure is, there will your heart be also."

28. For an introduction to the catechumenate as it formerly took place in the Early Church, see the revised *Christian Initiation of Adults: A Commentary* (Washington, D.C.: United States Catholic Conference, 1988). It provides a helpful text to accompany the final definitive translation of the rite for welcoming new members into the Catholic Church, and also serves as a form of spiritual guidance for those who teach it as well as for those who are there to learn.

29. This term refers to the postbaptismal period, usually coinciding with the paschal season, that is structured to help the newly baptized to articulate the deeper levels of awareness that have been touched by their recent experience. It is a seven-week period of meditation and reflective thinking about the mysteries they have experienced in the context of the Christian community.

30. This vocation and mission of lay Christians is defined in *Christifideles Laici*, the papal letter that officially summed up the 1987 synod on the laity.

31. Almost everyone in the field, including Presbyterians, Methodists, Carmelites, and Trappists, are making use of psychological language and concepts. There are books on the possible synthesis between Christianity and psychology as well as philosophical attempts to link up sacred traditions and psychological meaning. These include not only sacred traditions from the West but also Sufi, Taoist, and Zen traditions from the East. Books in the following collection have awakened life questions in several people I know personally: George Aschenbrenner, *A God for a Dark Journey* (Denville, N.J.: Dimension Books, 1984); Reginald Bibby, *Fragmented Gods* (Toronto: Irwin, 1987); Robert Kavanaugh, *Facing Death* (Middlesex, U.K.: Penguin, 1972); Kenneth Kramer, *The Sacred Art of Dying: How World Religions Understand Death* (N.Y.: Paulist Press, 1988); Peter Kreeft, *Heaven: The Heart's Deepest Longing* (San Francisco: Ignatius Press, 1980); and Robert Wicks, *Christian Introspection: Self-Ministry through Self-Understanding* (New York: Crossroad, 1983).

32. Witness the popularity of Ruth Burrows's books *Ascent to Love: The Spiritual Teaching of John of the Cross* (London: Darton, Longman and Todd, 1987), and *Fire upon the Earth* (Denville, N.J.: Dimension Books, 1981); of Thomas Merton's *Contemplative Prayer* (New York: Doubleday, 1971); and of Kieran Kavanaugh and Otilio Rodriguez's *The Collected Works of John of the Cross* (Washington, D.C.: ICS Publications, 1973).

33. In a chart depicting the main types of human guidance, Adrian van Kaam distinguished three major streams of guidance or direction. One grows out of the universal human tradition of therapeutic help that is not linked to any particular ultimate formation tradition. A second is clearly linked up with one special school or movement from which emerges what we might call classic spiritual direction in the life of prayer. A third more foundational stream of guidance partakes of both and often incorporates in addition one particular ultimate tradition of formation. He looks at each of these three from the point of view of its aim, its perspective, its sources, its methods, and the events with which it is concerned (*Studies in Formative Spirituality* 2, no. 1 [February 1989]: 142).

34. James Fenhagen, *Invitation to Holiness* (San Francisco: Harper & Row, 1985), 62.

35. Ibid., 60.

36. Perhaps this explains why so many of our contemporaries are returning to the worldview of Greek theologians of the undivided church who always saw Christian transformation as interwoven with human formation. They saw the universe as sustained by a constant flow of created and uncreated energy (or grace) that is always at work, forming and transforming everything that exists. See, for example, St. Gregory Palamas (1296–1359) whose thought is set forth by George Maloney in his Marquette lecture *A Theology of Uncreated Energies*, published by Marquette University Press in 1978.

Chapter 2: A Sense of the Mystery

1. Not all of us enter this human possibility in the same way. In his *Stories of God* (Chicago: Thomas More Press, 1978), John Shea mentions an old man who sits by the sea and knows that the waves he watches will crash on those shores long after he is gone. The old man is triggered into an awareness of the Mystery in which both he and the waves dwell. Then Shea tells of a young mother who watches her child in the park, and suddenly wonder seizes her and carries her into an awareness of Mystery. A third way to awareness may emerge when the car just ahead of us spins off the road and crashes down an embankment. We say we were lucky and wonder why, and the persistent question pushes us into the dimension of Mystery. We are, Shea concludes, inextricably related not only to the sea, the child, the highway, but also to the Mystery that both contextualizes and suffuses these environments.

2. The anonymous author of the *Cloud of Unknowing* (New York: Doubleday, 1973) speaks of mystical experience as consciousness of a beyond by means of the inward awareness of the heart. Others speak also of the experience of God touching us and of our response as prayer. See, for example, William James, *The Varieties of Religious Experience* (New York: Longman, 1902); Rudolph Otto, *The Idea of the Holy* (London: Oxford University Press, 1932); Evelyn Underhill, *Mysticism* (New York: Meridian, 1967); Dennis Edwards, *The Human Experience of God* (New York: Paulist, 1984); Andrew Greeley, *Ecstasy: A Way of Knowing* (Englewood Cliffs, N.J.: Prentice-Hall, 1974); Anne Fremantle, ed., *The Protestant Mystics* (New York: New American Library, 1964); and James Loder, *The Transforming Moment* (San Francisco: Harper & Row, 1981), to name only a few of the authors who might be consulted on this question of our experience of the Mystery and its interrelatedness with everything else.

3. See again chap. 1, n. 36, which refers to the dynamic view of the Greek Fathers in regard to God's uncreated energies. This love of God poured out was their way of speaking about grace. True spirituality consists in our response to this love, a view shared by Elisabeth-Paule Labat. In *The Presence of God* (New York: Paulist, 1979) she too sees the mystery of God's presence as a sea of grace that permeates and penetrates the entirety of our life field with its uncreated energies. See also Aelred Squire, *Asking the Fathers* (New York: Paulist, 1976), and John Sommerfeldt, ed., *Abba: Guides to Wholeness and Holiness, East and West* (Kalamazoo, Mich.: Cistercian Publications, 1982).

4. See above Introduction, notes 7 and 8, plus Ilya Prigogine *Order Out of Chaos* (New York: Bantam, 1984); Thomas Berry *The New Story* (Chambersburg, Pa.: Anima Publications, 1978); Teilhard de Chardin, *The Divine Milieu* (New York: Harper & Row, 1960); Robert Faricy, *The Spirituality of Teilhard de Chardin* (Minneapolis: Winston Press, 1981) and Kathleen Fischer, *Reclaiming the Connections* (Kansas City: Sheed and Ward, 1990).

5. It was Francis Thompson who wrote, "When to the new eyes of thee / All things by immortal power, / Near or far, / Hiddenly, / To each other linked are, / That thou canst not stir a flower, / Without troubling a star . . . seek no more."

6. Panentheistic mysticism is distinct from pantheism. Panentheistic means "all *in* God . . . ," that God as immanent is present and active everywhere and in everyone. Yet the transcendent God is not, as in pantheism, identical with matter, with these occasions of presence. For further explanation of this distinction, see Richard Woods, *Mysterion* (Chicago: Thomas More, 1981).

7. In *The Structure of Christian Existence* (New York: Seabury, 1979), John Cobb traces the period from the eighth to the second centuries before the birth of Christ, when encounters with the Holy Other seem to have happened almost simultaneously in Persia, Greece, China, India, and Palestine. Ancient wisdoms came to new birth accompanied by specifically religious consciousness and naming of the Mystery all over the world, as Zoroastrianism, Greek philosophy, Confucian and Taoist thought, Buddhism, and finally Judaism brought about a "fullness of time" prior to the event of the Incarnation of Christ. This epiphany, or appearance of the mysterious Godhead, did not cancel out

the others, as any work on the religions of the world will testify. See Robert S. Ellwood, *Many Peoples, Many Faiths* (Englewood Cliffs, N.J.: Prentice-Hall, 1976) for different ways of naming and relating to encountered Mystery.

8. A distinction made by Adrian van Kaam between faith and form traditions can be helpful here. He notes that a religious or humanist faith tradition offers basic beliefs in regard to the formation mystery and its epiphanies. These may develop into self-consistent, rational systems of an ontological or theological nature when their content is subjected to rational explicitations, explanations, and justifications by theologians and philosophers. Van Kaam sees form traditions as rooted in faith traditions, but as embodying directives for living that have been handed over from generation to generation in a specific culture, religion, or ideological movement, and that take the form of customs, styles, exercises, etc. — the routines and rituals of daily life (*Studies in Formative Spirituality* 3 [November 3, 1982]: 464). In the Introduction to *The Road by the River* (San Francisco: Harper & Row, 1987), Djohariah Toor mourns the loss of traditions, especially those of people whose lives contained an inner balance, a "spiritual holism." She complains that many of us have lost our roots and our ability to be in communion with ourselves and life around us. For the Native Americans we are a paradoxical people "who are too busy with our 'progress' to listen to the Great Spirit. We have not contemplated the mysteries of the seasons nor taken our children into the holy places....We cut off a spiritual heritage that we cannot afford to forget." She sees the Native Americans as a people who know how to hand on both a faith tradition and a precious form tradition, a heritage of customs and rituals that help the younger generation to know that "they are one with the earth."

9. Everyone is born into some tradition, some handed-on set of values and assumptions that provides guidelines for the way "we" do things. There is a "way" for the Hasidim, the Sufi, the Hopi, the Hindu, the Zen adherent, none of whom will have to begin inventing their entire set of ways of doing and being for themselves. This attempt to hand on its daily ways is common to all groups on the face of the earth. Whether we are a Christian capitalist, a Marxist scholar, a Buddhist monk, a Shiite Moslem mother of five, or an American Jewish lawyer, the way we go about our daily lives is going to be influenced, consciously or unconsciously, by our original faith tradition, the way our segment of the population tends to name the Mystery. It is also going to be shaped by the way our form tradition, the way the folks at home do things because of how "we" Christians, Marxists, Buddhists, Moslems, and Jews have been open to the Mystery and now as a result tend to perceive people, events, and things in daily life.

10. For more on faith and form traditions, see Adrian van Kaam, *The Science of Foundational Formation: Human Formation* (New York: Crossroad, 1985), chaps. 12 and 14. Also see Yves M. Congar, *Tradition and Traditions* (London: Burns and Oates, 1966).

11. Take the word "strike." In itself, what does it mean? Only when we hear it inserted into a full sentence do we know that it means a call in baseball, a labor dispute, a blow on the cheek, or what a fresh idea can do to us. Without the entire sentence, we do not perceive the full meaning of an isolated word.

12. Prefocal meanings are those that contextualize our lives without being consciously attended to. For example, for those whose lives were changed by conversion to the Christian way of perceiving reality, the unity of the spiritual life was revealed. It gradually became clear that normal human development included opening oneself to the life of grace and mystical contemplation. However, Christians do not always consciously read the text of their individual lives in this larger context. See the interesting volume by Janet Ruffing, *Uncovering Stories of Faith* (New York: Paulist, 1989), in which the focus of spiritual guidance lies in interpreting the directee's narrated life story within the larger "story" of faith or salvation.

13. The task of the spiritual guide is, for example, complicated by the personal, socio/relational, and spiritual mix that prevails in the worldviews of his or her contemporaries. The following authors provide an interesting sample of this mix. See Robert Bellah, et al., *Habits of the Heart: Individualism and Commitment in American Life* (Los

Angeles: University of California Press, 1985); Peter L. Berger and Thomas Luckman, *The Social Construction of Reality* (New York: Doubleday, 1966); Andrew Greeley, *God and American Culture* (Chicago: Thomas More, 1989); Monika Hellwig, *Tradition: The Catholic Story* (Dayton: Pflaum, 1974); John Naisbett, *Megatrends 2000* (New York: Nightingale-Conant, 1989); Alvin Toffler, *The Third Wave* (New York: Bantam, 1980); Chogyam Trungpa, *Cutting through Spiritual Materialism* (Berkeley: Shambhala, 1973); J. H. Van den Berg, *Divided Existence and Complex Society* (Pittsburgh: Duquesne University Press, 1974); and Daniel Yankelovich, *New Rules: Searching for Fulfillment in a World Turned Upside Down* (New York: Bantam, 1981).

14. For example, what has been deeply puzzling to the average American about the Moslem or Japanese soldier's apparently suicidal willingness to die in battle stems from that soldier's faith tradition that makes happy life-after-death sense for him out of what appears not very understandable or even meaningful to a person outside the Moslem or Buddhist tradition. Beneath the immediate life field of both Moslem and Japanese soldiers, of American businessmen and of the North American or Moslem or Japanese women who may be puzzled by both, are other equally hidden or prefocal sources of thinking emerging from their unique culture or form tradition. There is also the contrast between Eastern and Western views of the destiny of the individual soul.

15. This felt sense of the mystery varies considerably from person to person as well as from culture to culture. On one end of the continuum we have those fortunate individuals who seem to have been born with overall positive feelings about life. Convinced they are loved by the Mystery no matter what, they have a sense of "yes" about their lives. The Mystery will not abandon them. They can safely abandon themselves to the Mystery. At the other end of this continuum is another group whose principle sense of the Mystery is that it has abandoned them. Their lives from the beginning seem permeated by feelings of depression and sadness. Their hearts harbor a lived "no" sometimes even before they have come to any conscious decision about the way things are for them. See Adrian van Kaam, *Fundamental Formation* (New York: Crossroad, 1983), chap. 15. Most of us live somewhere in between, searching always for a way of life, a style of dialogue with reality, for a way "we" do things, for a form tradition that is profound enough to support and critique and structure our search for God in a trustworthy way.

16. Along these lines, for Walter Brueggeman, as quoted in James Fowler, *Becoming Adult, Becoming Christian* (San Francisco: Harper & Row, 1984), 93, vocation means finding "a purpose for being in the world that is related to the purposes of God." He is of the opinion that questions of identity — "who am I?" — become questions of vocation — "whose am I?" — only when men and women discover that part they are called to play in the larger story that belongs to the Mystery.

17. In the Anglo-Saxon Chronicles of seventh-century Northern England, we have an example of a guide who understands the universal aspiration for a life context that carries with it a solid sense of ultimate Mystery beyond. As he describes the flight of the little bird that flies in through a window at one end of King Edwin's great hall and flies out into the winter night through another, the guide compares its flight to the briefness of human life. He suggests that because we, like those who watch the bird, do not know what went beforehand nor what follows, the king might be wise to follow the new doctrine (Christianity) that "can speak to us surely of these things."

18. Since a working knowledge of the different spiritualities available today is essential for the guide, we suggest that guides become familiar with the plurality of "ways" and their differing dynamics of spiritual receptivity. Along with Huston Smith's *The Religions of Man* (New York: Harper & Row, 1958), guides might begin with Robert Ellwood, *Many People, Many Faiths* (Englewood Cliffs, N.J.: Prentice-Hall, 1976), or Mircea Eliade and David Tracy, eds. *What Is Religion?* (New York: Seabury, 1980). The contemporary variety of spiritual approaches is addressed also in Cheslyn Jones et al., eds., *The Study of Spirituality* (New York: Oxford University Press, 1980); Urban Holmes, *A History of Christian Spirituality* (New York: Seabury, 1980); Thomas Gannon and George Traub, *The Desert and the City* (New York: Macmillan, 1969); Thomas Oden, *Agenda for The-*

ology (San Francisco: Harper & Row, 1979); Robert Bellah, *The Broken Covenant* (New York: Seabury, 1975); and also in sections of David Toolan, *Facing West from California's Shores* (New York: Crossroad, 1987); Paul Knitter, *No Other Name? A Critical Survey of Christian Attitudes toward the World Religions* (Maryknoll, N.Y.: Orbis Books, 1985); and books written from within other worldviews such as Michael Horner, *The Way of the Shaman* (New York: Bantam, 1982), Abhishiktananda, *Prayer* (London: SPCK, 1972) and M. Carrol Bryant and Frank Flynn, eds., *Interreligious Dialogue* (New York: Paragon House, 1989).

19. See chap. 5, section entitled "Memory: Formative and Deformative," for reference to the influence of family systems theory.

20. In his *Open Mind, Open Heart* (Warwick, N.Y.: Amity House, 1986), Thomas Keating speaks of contemplation as a means of letting go of the false self, the self that in the course of a lifetime has allowed its truth to be obscured by denial, illusion, and repression. In upcoming chapters, we will look at the origin and effect of these emotional blockages to the flow of spiritual energy. The reader might consult some of the following for the relationship between emotions and spirituality. Conrad Baars, *Feeling and Healing Your Emotions* (Plainfield, N.J.: Logos, 1970); Mary Michael O'Shaughnessy, *Feelings and Emotions in Christian Living* (New York: Alba House, 1988); Robert C. Roberts, *Spirituality and Human Emotion* (Grand Rapids: Eerdmans, 1982); Eugene Gendlin, *Focusing* (New York: Bantam, 1978); John English, *Spiritual Freedom* (Guelph, Ontario: Loyola House, 1975); Thomas Hart, *The Art of Christian Listening* (New York: Paulist Press, 1980); and Ronald Knox, *Enthusiasm* (New York: Oxford University Press, 1950). Emotional blocks are not the only ones stopping the flow of grace and of prayer. A major focus of spiritual guidance is to pinpoint these and other blockages so that the water of life may flow in and through human hearts.

21. There are at the moment an abundance of books dealing with the effects of our lifestyle on our health. See, for example, Lawrence LeShan, *You Can Fight for Your Life: Emotional Factors in the Treatment of Cancer* (New York: Evans, 1979), and *Cancer as a Turning Point* (New York: Dutton, 1989). Also see Norman Cousins, *Anatomy of an Illness* (New York: W. W. Norton, 1979); Bernard Siegel, *Love, Medicine and Miracles* (New York: Harper & Row, 1987); and O. C. Simonton, *Getting Well Again* (New York: Bantam, 1980).

22. Years ago, in *The New Religions* (New York: Doubleday, 1970), Jacob Needleman remarked that we in North American have forgotten the fundamentally instrumental nature of religious forms. He suggests that this general absence in our contemporary religious forms of practical technique, methods, and discipline is one of the reasons the attention of so many people in the West is drawn to the religions and practices of the East. He also notes that practical psychological methods were always a central part of Christianity and Judaism, and that they still exist in certain settings (16–17).

23. In chaps. 4 and 5, especially in sections on "The isolated sinful human heart" and "Illusory and compulsive modes of attachment," we will attempt to deal more concretely with the sinful dimension of blockages in relation to the project of spiritual guidance.

24. See p. 235, n. 13, in Tilden Edwards, *Spiritual Friend* (New York: Paulist, 1980). Throughout this fine book on reclaiming the gift of spiritual direction, the author points to our need to learn again from our Christian tradition as "the lived and tested experience of a diverse body of people over time united by a commitment to approach the purpose and way of life through the lineage of Jesus Christ" (35), instead of simply borrowing from traditions other than our own.

25. Ibid. Here we return for a moment to the challenge of pluralism for the project of spiritual guidance.

26. See Roger Hurding, *Roots and Shoots* (London: Hodder and Stoughton, 1985), chap. 8.

27. Additional helpful overviews of classic Eastern and Western approaches to the spiritual life and guidance are *The Study of Spirituality,* Cheslyn Jones, Geoffrey Wainwright, and Edward Yarnold, eds. (New York: Oxford University Press, 1986); Kenneth

Leech, *Soul Friend* (London: Sheldon Press, 1977), and Urban Holmes, *History of Christian Spirituality* (New York: Seabury, 1980).

28. Many contemporaries have the mistaken idea that spirituality in the Christian tradition, unlike that contextualized by the new therapies, is concerned only with the immaterial and disembodied aspects of existence. Christian belief, on the contrary, is centered on the Incarnation, on the body of Christ that was crucified, died, and rose to become energizing nourishment for all. The transcending self is also an embodied spirit.

29. This intuitive sense of God's initiating presence beyond the veil of things is found not only in Psalm 139. It has, however, been clearly revealed in Christ, the witness of God's love poured into the heart of each person who comes into the world.

30. According to Adrian van Kaam, author of six volumes on foundational formative spirituality (New York: Crossroad, 1983-1992), this image of the human person derived from Revelation corresponds in detail to the actual lived potential of every human being. The tragedy, according to van Kaam, continues to be that most people in our society have a confused view (live in ignorance) of what it means to be embodied human hearts, bearers of a spiritual life form, and potential sharers in the life of the Trinitarian Mystery. Here as in many of these chapters, I am indebted to van Kaam's thought, especially for the constructs regarding human personality and the field theory he has developed.

31. In chap. 13 of *Fundamental Formation* (New York: Crossroad, 1983) van Kaam speaks of the pneumatic dimension of Christian life as it unfolds. The Holy Spirit, present in baptized persons, influences this unfolding via graced influencing of the stage in which people find themselves, creating an awareness of sinfulness and impotence, of the necessity of grace to realize transcendent aspirations.

32. In *Fundamental Formation*, ibid., van Kaam speaks of the dynamic capacity or potency that humans are to give and to receive form in relation to all dimensions of their life fields. See particularly chap. 13 on the central dynamic of transcendent form potency.

33. Chap. 1, n. 4 above, contains sources on this understanding of grace as the presence of the Holy Spirit, the transforming power of God's love to which we are capable of responding and by which our restless hearts are fulfilled and transformed. This gift is present as a preformative reality to which we can consent and to which we owe respect as the basis for each person's unique path to the Mystery. In *A World of Grace* (New York: Seabury, 1980), Leo O'Donovan edits commentaries on Karl Rahner's theology. Other authors consulted regarding the relationship between grace and guidance are Brian McDermott, *What Are They Saying about the Grace of Christ?* (New York: Paulist, 1984), and Gerald May, *Addiction and Grace* (San Francisco: Harper & Row, 1988).

34. Here we find it helpful to look again at the difference van Kaam sees between formative spiritual counseling and formative spiritual direction. In both, attention is focused on human spirit as central in the whole person's entire life field. In spiritual counseling the guide and the seeker need not work from the same underlying faith tradition — although the guide's use of psychology must be governed by a working image of the human person (an "anthropology" in the sense used above) that is open to the transcendent dimensions of reality. In formative spiritual direction, however, both the guide and the person guided would normally share a commitment to a specific faith and form tradition, as well as to the principles of counseling.

35. Again, as in the chapters to come, we are indebted to the formulations of formative spirituality for this understanding of Christian anthropology. See chap. 4 for more on this subject.

36. See again n. 15 above on one's felt sense of the Mystery. Also see Charles Davis, *Body as Spirit: The Nature of Religious Feeling* (New York: Seabury, 1966), and Corbin Carnell, *Bright Shadow of Reality: C.S. Lewis and the Feeling Intellect* (Grand Rapids: Eerdmans, 1974).

37. Alice Walker, *The Color Purple* (New York: Pocket Books, 1982).

38. Ibid., 202 and 203.

39. This expression is implied in a chapter by Paul Ricoeur entitled "Listening to the Parables of Jesus" in Charles Reagan and David Stewart, eds., *The Philosophy of Paul Ricoeur* (Boston: Beacon Press, 1978).

40. Ibid.

41. Once that attachment is felt, once our hearts are attracted and our minds and wills are put in motion by some aspect of the Mystery's dynamic attractiveness, then we actually find ourselves moving away from other things that no longer exercise a hold over us. Accretions may even cease to bother us as much; we find we can put up with the church's human limitations.

Chapter 3: Life Keeps Happening

1. Chinua Achebe, *Things Fall Apart* (London: Heinemann Educational Books, 1958), and *No Longer at Ease* (London: Heinemann Educational Books, 1960). These titles are found in W. B. Yeats, "The Second Coming," and T. S. Eliot, "The Journey of the Magi."

2. See chap. 1 for incidents from Judith Guest, *Ordinary People* (New York: Ballantine, 1976); Norman Cousins, *The Healing Heart* (New York: Avon, 1983); Etty Hillesum, *An Interrupted Life* (New York: Pantheon, 1983); and in the same vein, S. Vanauken, *A Severe Mercy* (New York: Bantam, 1977).

3. In his *Religion and Personality* (Denville, N.J.: Dimension Books, 1964), Adrian van Kaam speaks of two basic polarities of our existence, the simultaneous movement in our lives of the differentiating and integrating modes of presence. It is the times of differentiation or change, whether formative, deformative, reformative, or transformative, that can challenge our desire for the feeling of integration.

4. This underlying dialogue with the world is simply a given of our life that is assumed as a substructure in this book. The term encounter also speaks to this underlying reciprocal relationship of subject and world as proposed by adherents of the movement in philosophy labelled existential phenomenology. They have shown us that the unity of person and world is a dialectical unity, the unity of a dialogue which human persons are within their fields of presence. See William Luijpen, *Existential Phenomenology* (Pittsburgh: Duquesne University Press, 1960), chap. 1.

5. John Shea, *Stories of God* (Chicago: Thomas More Press, 1978), 27–28. Shea speaks in the first chapter of "contingency experiences" both positive and negative that bring us to the point of stopping and thinking, of reflecting on changes that interrupt the flow of our experience.

6. At such moments, for example, are we moving toward, against, away from, or with the mystery as it is present in our lives?

7. "Synchronicity" is a term that C. G. Jung puts forward for the connection he sees between psyche and event in a meaningful coincidence. Many people today seem fascinated with the discovery of such meaningful coincidences like "chance" meetings or stumbling upon just the right poem or text. They talk about life events that seem to point to an underlying connecting principle. The unexpected phone call when we are feeling lonely, for example, or similar events that evoke an intuitively felt sense of being cared for and no longer isolated are somehow tied in here. Popular interest in synchronicity points to the longing of each one of us for a felt sense of spiritual reality present in the seemingly unmeaningful and therefore random experiences of everyday life. For more on this experience of desiring to live more in harmony with the universe, see Jean Bolen, *The Tao of Psychology* (San Francisco: Harper & Row, 1979).

8. Gerald May, *Care of Mind, Care of Spirit* (San Francisco: Harper & Row, 1982).

9. Thomas Green, *Darkness in the Marketplace* (Notre Dame: Ave Maria Press, 1981), a meditation on the relationship between prayer and service based on Luke 10:38–41.

10. Some women complain about this passage as a way of putting women down by portraying Martha as always "in the kitchen." It must be remembered, however, that

Martha is also one of the first to put her faith in Jesus as the one who would rise again (John 11:27).

11. Like many of us, Martha may have been afraid that her energetic self would not be able to function with its former efficiency if she changed her inner disposition. She also may have wondered how such a change would affect her outer appearance or the quality of the meal she could produce.

12. The notion of "receptive volition" is found in the address "Philosophy of Will and Action" given by Paul Ricoeur and reprinted in E. W. Straus, ed., *Phenomenology of Will and Action* (Pittsburgh: Duquesne University Press, 1967), 7–33.

13. See Leslie Farber, *The Ways of the Will* (New York: Basic Books, 1966), and Paul Ricoeur, *Freedom and Nature: The Voluntary and the Involuntary* (Evanston, Ill.: Northwestern University Press, 1966).

14. These disruptions take on a variety of forms, all the way from mundane crises like losing a button or forgetting to bring our lunch, to middle-size transitions like leaving high school or starting a new job, to major ones like being fired from a lifetime job, having a child convicted for dealing in drugs, or discovering that we have a terminal illness. Each interruption of our plans for the day or for our life, whether it be the transition from breast to bottle, from early to late adolescence, or the discovery that one is a middle-aged person on the way to retirement, has the power to shake us up, to move us beyond where we were, and to represent a call to transcendence.

15. Adult life in particular is open to crises, especially those that break up earlier life patterns. See Bernard Boelen, *Personal Maturity* (New York: Seabury, 1978); Matthew Fox, *Breakthrough* (New York: Doubleday, 1980); Charles Gerkin, *The Living Human Document* (Nashville: Abingdon, 1984); George Maloney, *Nesting in the Rock: Finding the Father in Each Event* (Denville, N.J.: Dimension Books, 1977); Anita Spencer, *Crises and Growth* (New York: Paulist, 1989); and Evelyn and James Whitehead, *Christian Life Patterns* (New York: Doubleday, 1979).

16. For more on what Bernard Boelen calls "crises of limits" see Eugene Bianchi, *Aging as Spiritual Journey* (New York: Crossroad, 1985); Anne Brennan and Janice Brewi, *Mid-Life Directions* (New York: Paulist, 1985); Patrick Carroll and Katherine Dyckman, *Chaos or Creation: Spirituality in Mid-Life* (New York: Paulist, 1986); Daniel Helminiak, *Spiritual Development* (Chicago: Loyola University Press, 1987); Carol Lubering, *Brokenness: The Stories of Six Women Whose Faith Grew in Crises* (Cincinnati: St. Anthony Messenger Press); Sheila Murphy, *Mid-Life Wanderer* (Whitinsville, Mass.: Affirmation Books, 1983); Gerald O'Collins, *The Second Journey* (New York: Paulist, 1978); and Adrian van Kaam, *The Transcendent Self* (Denville, N.J.: Dimension Books, 1979).

17. In his *Fire Within* (San Francisco: Ignatius Press, 1989), Thomas Dubay takes issue with guides who confuse mental and emotional problems with the purifying experience of an authentic "dark night" (163) or who misinterpret "ordinary human sufferings as cases of the dark nights" (295).

18. For more on the "turn to transcendence" see especially Adrian van Kaam, *The Transcendent Self*. See also Daniel Helminiak, *Spiritual Development,* and the authors listed in n. 17.

19. See Ilya Prigogine, *From Being to Becoming* (San Francisco: Freeman, 1980).

20. One way of looking at the parable of the farmer plowing up the treasure in the field (Matt. 13:44) is to see that experience as a "dissipative structure" in that farmer's life. His responses could include trying to ignore it, as if nothing out of the ordinary had happened; worrying about how to integrate this new find into his old life; wondering who was responsible for burying the box in his field in the first place; mentally recalling ways in which he might have avoided the disruption; looking around for someone who would help him to cope with the situation; or perhaps consulting bygone wisdom of past generations who have lived through like situations. Here we have the familiar tension between feeling secure and undisturbed and reaching out for the new and unpredictable. We wonder, following her shocked moment of distancing, just how Martha perceived her self, her role, her style of carrying it out and her motivation as well.

21. In the Foreword to *I Ching: The Book of Change* (London: Unwin, 1976), John Blofeld maintains that this conception of the world uses divinization not for determining the future, but for raising the already present tendencies of the human mind into the light of conscious awareness, in order to give individuals a glimpse of the various possibilities before them and a chance to choose the best course of action according to circumstances.

22. A perception that resonates with the Sufi legend of the fish who must discover they are already in the water.

23. In the terminology of formative spirituality developed by Adrian van Kaam and his associates, the formation field of a Christian man or woman would be influenced in its preformative polarity by the givens of his or her biogenetic life, which are in turn rooted in inherited influences from the socio-historical context into which they were born and the potential for participating in the Trinitarian life into which they were baptized. What the person as spirit does under the impact of all the other factors in that field, how the powers of his or her mind, will, and imagination co-form encountered people, events, and things, all of this inner activity belongs to the intraformative pole. As between poles of an electric current, life energy flows from this pole to what van Kaam calls the interformative or relational sphere, where we give form to and receive form from other people. The field also is influenced by the atmosphere or immediate environing situation and wider culture within which each person's life develops. Guides will recognize that although foundationally the life field is the same for everyone, concretely it is filled out differently for each one.

24. The challenge of the interwovenness of contemporary form fields with one another, of not finding a more or less uniform Christian formation field underlying people's individual life fields, is one that must be taken into consideration by all spiritual guides and directors without exception.

25. Remember the parable of the weeds and the wheat (Matt. 13:24–30). There are some helpful books and articles on the topic of personal relationships and sexuality, for example, that represent a balanced viewpoint. See William Kraft, *Whole and Holy Sexuality* (St. Meinrad, Ind.: Abbey Press, 1989); James Nelson, *Embodiment* (Minneapolis: Augsburg, 1978); James Hannigan, *What Are They Saying about Sexual Morality?* (New York: Paulist, 1982); Jean Vanier, *Man and Woman He Made Them* (New York: Paulist, 1985); Thomas Tyrrell, *Urgent Longings* (Whitinsville, Mass.: Affirmation Books, 1980); James and Evelyn Whitehead, *A Sense of Sexuality* (New York: Doubleday, 1990); and the chapter on spirituality and sexuality in Adrian van Kaam, *Fundamental Formation* (New York: Crossroad, 1983).

26. See Robert Bellah et al., *Habits of the Heart: Individualism and Commitment in American Life* (Berkeley: University of California Press, 1985) for a convincing portrayal of the co-formative influence of a culture as the central place where "habits of the heart" originally emerge. See chap. 2 above, where we introduce the notion of "form tradition" in relation to faith tradition, explaining that founding generations of the latter tend to hand on more than just dogmas and doctrine based on a specific revelation of the Mystery. Inevitably they also hand on a set of customs, ways of doing and being, ways of thinking about life that become that group's "form tradition," to use the words of Adrian van Kaam.

27. The depth of conviction growing out of a particular form tradition is illustrated whenever students from African and Asian as well as European and North American form traditions are together in a spiritual guidance class and the discussion moves, for example, to issues that call into question the importance of autonomy versus belonging to a group. It is these differing, sometimes scarcely articulated but nevertheless strong guidelines from our various cultures that we tend to call upon as life challenges us to deal with critical events, with burdens of time and limitation, and with social questions of peace and justice that are lived avenues of intouchness with the Mystery for us here and now. Moreover, when we look at an issue of *Time* or *Newsweek* from five years ago, we are amazed to see that most of the problems and social and moral questions that

occupied center stage then, are no longer "in" the news or on the minds of readers in the 1990s.

28. In the following paragraphs, we will refer to several of these books that represent the multitude of titles that can increase awareness of our "second body" as it affects our spiritual and physical and psychic health. Robert Bellah et al., *Individualism and Commitment in American Life* (San Francisco: Harper & Row, 1987); Harriet Braiker, *The Type E Woman* (New York: Dodd, Mead, 1986); Joann Conn Wolski, *Women's Spirituality* (New York: Paulist, 1986); H. J. Freudenberger, *Burnout: The High Cost of High Achievement* (New York: Bantam, 1980); Meyer Freedman and Ray Rosenman, *Type A Behavior and Your Heart* (New York: Knopf, 1974); E. T. Hall, *The Silent Language* (New York: Doubleday, 1959), and *Beyond Culture* (New York: Doubleday, 1977); Christopher Lasch, *The Culture of Narcissism* (New York: Warner Books, 1979); and Paul Vitz, *Psychology as Religion* (Grand Rapids: Eerdmans, 1977).

29. See Introduction, n. 9, for a brief listing of books dealing with women's developing awareness of the psychic weave between themselves and others, of their growing awareness of themselves and the sacred dimensions of their experience as they welcome the return of feminine archetypes and celebrate the genius of female sensibility and potential.

30. See for example, Reginald Bibby, *Fragmented Gods* (Toronto: Irwin Publishing, 1987). Spiritual masters from the East as well as from the West have labelled the willful illusory rationalistic approach to the spiritual journey he describes as "spiritual materialism." See Chogyam Trungpa, *Cutting through Spiritual Materialism* (Berkeley, Calif.: Shambhala, 1973).

31. This quotation from 12:2 of Paul's letter to the Romans is taken from the translation of *The New Testament in Modern English* by J. B. Phillips (London: Geoffrey Bles, 1960).

32. Since the dialogue itself is usually outside of the person's conscious awareness, it is helpful but not always necessary to have another person present as they reflect together on what has been happening to one of them. However, keeping a journal is another practice that fills something of the same function of bringing what is really happening in one's life to focal consciousness.

33. A principle from the educational science of andragogy is that adults learn best by listening to their own experience rather than from the pedagogical approach in which children are required to listen to what has been learned from the experience of other people.

34. See n. 23, above, for polarities of the life field.

35. For the event-centered approach of pastoral counseling, see Robert Wicks, Richard Parsons, and Donald Capps, eds., *Clinical Handbook of Pastoral Counseling* (New York: Paulist, 1985). Kenneth Leech, in *Spirituality and Pastoral Care* (Cambridge, Mass.: Cowley Publications, 1989), has managed to keep in touch with spiritual direction at the same time as he writes about pastoral care.

36. In this paragraph we find references to situations that reach beyond what the spiritual guide may be equal to or trained for. Here is the point where the guide does not try to do what he or she cannot do, but rather becomes responsible for tapping into other sources in the community for referral. Many spiritual guides are equipped to deal with neurotic disorders and serious sexual problems, but most are not. It is often advisable, when directees have to seek therapeutic help, to assure them of support via spiritual guidance during that time of their life as well.

37. See chaps. 4 and 6 for more on the importance of the religious imagination as basis for forming the infrastructure of spiritual life.

38. Alice Walker, *The Color Purple* (New York: Pocket Books, 1982), 292.

Chapter 4: Guiding the Human Spirit

1. See chap. 2, section entitled "The Human Person in a Christian Worldview," for more on specifically Christian anthropology. Also see Adrian van Kaam, *Traditional Formation*, vol. 5 in the formative spirituality series published by Crossroad.

2. After earning a doctorate in phenomenological psychology, I have been teaching at Duquesne University's Institute of Formative Spirituality for over twenty years. I find that the gradually developing foundational anthropology provides a hermeneutic for contextualizing my work as both therapist and spiritual director. For a Christian guide, this approach provides an interpretive stance, a view of director and directee as always already in substantial union with the Divine, and seeking to participate in the life of the Trinitarian mystery through changes or conversions of the heart's inner intentionality. For more on this dynamic, see chap. 8, "Life Emerging from Death."

3. In chap. 1, in the section "How We Co-form Our Experience," I introduced the concept of co-formation. The following are suggestions for further reading from a variety of sources on how, in the process of human experiencing, body, mind, and spirit are interrelated: See David Burns, *Feeling Good* (New York: New American Library, 1980); Albert Ellis, *Reason and Emotion in Psychotherapy* (New York: Lyle Stuart, 1962); Martin Heidegger, *Discourse on Thinking* (New York: Harper & Row, 1966); Jolande Jacobi, *The Psychology of C. G. Jung* (New Haven: Yale University, 1962); Laurence LeShan, *Alternate Realities* (New York: Evans, 1976); Gerald May, *Care of Mind, Care of Spirit* (San Francisco: Harper & Row, 1982); R. Pirsig, *Zen and the Art of Motorcycle Maintenance* (New York: Bantam, 1974); E. Schachtel, *Metamorphosis* (New York: Basic Books, 1959); and Michael Talbot, *Mysticism and the New Physics* (New York: Bantam, 1980).

4. An example of reflection in action. Suppose in the midst of their daily routine, people meet what we have been calling a "dissipative structure" (see chap. 3, the section entitle "Other Ways of Looking at Change"), a new element or ambiguous event that gives them a bit of a jolt, that makes them stop and think. When we find these persons reflectively bending back on a certain event and on its impact in their life field even long after it is over and life has moved on to still other situations and ambiguities, we recognize that it is the aspect of their human spirit labelled "mind" that has been perceiving and processing this particular bit of experience.

5. For more on van Kaam's distinction between functional and transcendent mind and will, see *Fundamental Formation* (New York: Crossroad, 1983), especially chart 11 on p. 289.

6. It is beyond the province of this book to deal with hysterical and other manifestations of the religious infraconscious, but the spiritual guide often detects and has to deal with such manifestations. In his *Care of Mind, Care of Spirit*, Gerald May speaks to some of the psychiatric dimensions of spiritual direction. As was mentioned in chap. 3, n. 36, a guide is responsible to make wise referrals rather than thoughtlessly attempt to handle more than he or she can manage.

7. Perhaps now it is clearer why we began in chap. 1 with two sections on the questions that arise from people's experience of living and how these are often the point where spiritual guidance can begin.

8. In an analysis reminiscent of the bio-spiritual approach, where one uses the mind to focus attention on the body and thus get "out of the mind," Kenneth Pelletier in *Mind as Healer, Mind as Slayer: A Holistic Approach to Preventing Stress Disorders* (New York: Dell, 1977) explores the mind/body relationship.

9. Besides Burns, *Feeling Good* (see n. 3 above), other books on the mind/body relation are Norman Cousins, *The Healing Heart* (New York: Avon, 1984); Laurence LeShan, *You Can Fight for Your Life: Emotional Factors in the Causation of Cancer* (New York: Harcourt, Brace, Jovanovich, 1977); Bernie Siegel, *Love, Medicine and Miracles* (New York: Harper & Row, 1986); and Carl Simonton, *Getting Well Again* (Los Angeles: Tarcher, 1978).

10. See Introduction, the section entitled "As We Are Today."

11. A friend commented, "That would be sort of like canonizing Ben Franklin as a spiritual master." In any case, we are aware that some disastrous errors crept in to the formation (or training programs as they were often called) of those preparing for commitment in religious life as a result of this erroneous type of thinking. Here also is the general origin of the "willpower Christian," the person whose orientation toward salvation is one of self-sufficiency to the exclusion almost of the need of a savior.

12. Martin Heidegger's small book *Discourse on Thinking* is a fine introduction to meditative thinking. This mode of thinking continues to inform the reflective stance of guides and the quest of those who come to them seeking forms of meditative self-presence. See Carolyn Gratton, *Guidelines for Spiritual Direction* (Denville, N.J.: Dimension Books, 1980), chap. 5, "A Natural Foundation for Spiritual Direction."

13. Actually the mind of a healthy and whole human being is a mixture of both functional efficiency and the ability at times to dream like the poet, painter, musician, or philosopher he or she is potentially if not in everyday actuality. Some people are noticeably better in one approach than in the other. Experienced guides have a term for men and women whose thinking never comes down to the earth of everyday practicalities. They are the "holy floaters" among us — disincarnate dreamers whose ideals are never tested by the pragmatic demands of real life. People of the opposite persuasion, by the way, might be labelled "pious pushers."

14. See Norman Cousins, *The Healing Heart* (New York: Avon, 1983).

15. From my own experience trying to help people reflect on the clashes of commitment in their lives, I know how easy it is to remain in the problem-solving mindset. It can be threatening to encounter the kind of self-knowledge available when one moves beyond a merely psychological analysis of how one reacts or responds to a commitment clash. It is more comfortable to stay in the safe confines of knowing oneself as a certain personality type who copes with conflict in a certain style.

16. The power of the human spirit to co-form the self and others in its field is demonstrated daily as we observe people who begin to question the "shoulds" of their life and imaginatively alter their ideas about what others and the transcendent expect of them, or as we see teachers who have either negatively or positively predetermined the achievement levels of different classes and reap the results of their co-formative imaginings. For more on the power of the imagination as well as memory and anticipation, see Adrian van Kaam, *Human Formation* (New York: Crossroad, 1985), chaps. 7 and 8. Other suggested readings are from Joseph Campbell, *The Power of Myth* (New York: Doubleday, 1989); Roberto Assagioli, *Psychosynthesis* (New York: Viking Press, 1965); Kathleen Fischer, *The Inner Rainbow* (New York: Paulist, 1983); Jean Huston, *The Possible Human* (Los Angeles: Tarcher, 1982); Ira Progoff, *The Symbolic and the Real* (New York: Julian Press, 1963); Gerard Hughes, *God of Surprises* (London: Darton, Longman and Todd, 1986); and David Tracy, *The Analogical Imagination* (New York: Crossroad, 1981).

17. In *The TV Ritual: Worship at the Video Altar* (Boston: Beacon Press, 1981), Gregor Goethals looks at the national obsession with TV and how it gives us information, entertains us, and in the process profoundly affects our social, religious, and political beliefs.

18. This area of discipline of the imagination fascinates many of our functionally minded contemporaries — like sports psychologists, for instance. In some approaches, the deliberate control of one's fantasy life is a goal as measurable as muscle-building. It shades into self-hypnosis and is not the type of discipline meant here.

19. Karen Horney, *Neurosis and Human Growth* (New York: W. W. Norton, 1950), particularly 31–32.

20. A reference to "The Man with the Blue Guitar," a poem by Wallace Stevens in which the people ask for a song that transcends them and yet is faithful to their reality as it is.

21. James Lynch, *Images of Hope* (New York: New American Library, 1965), 35.

22. Roberto Assagioli, *The Act of Will* (Harmondsworth, Eng.: Penguin, 1973), 194. Guides in the Christian tradition from Ignatius of Loyola to Anthony de Mello have rec-

ognized in the imagination an undeniable power for enriching the prayer life of many. They too realize that the cultivation of good, positive imagery through watching worthwhile films and TV, by reading biographies and fairy tales, and by refusing to limit imaginative flights into the future, is an important asset for spiritual guidance.

23. See Andrew Greeley, *The Religious Imagination* (New York: Sadlier, 1981), 10–17. See also J. B. Phillips, *Your God Is Too Small* (New York: Macmillan, 1961); Garrett Green, *Imagining God* (San Francisco: Harper & Row, 1989); James Mackey, *Religious Imagination* (Edinburgh: Edinburgh University Press, 1986); and Raymond Studzinski, *Spiritual Direction and Midlife Development* (Chicago: Loyola University Press, 1985), with an interesting chapter, "Images and Stories at Midlife."

24. *The Cloud of Unknowing* (New York: Doubleday, 1973). Like the anonymous author of the *Cloud*, present-day instructors in the art of meditative presence advise would-be meditators in the way of nonpossessive, nongreedy letting go of thoughts, feelings, and effort. Returning gently to the heart's intentions, they are to rest trustingly in the presence of God. For more on trust and abandonment as basis of this approach to contemplative presence, see Jean Pierre de Caussade, *Abandonment to Divine Providence* (Exeter: Catholic Records Press, 1921); Kitty Muggeridge, *The Sacrament of the Present Moment* (London: Fount, 1981); and Carolyn Gratton, *Trusting* (New York: Crossroad, 1982).

25. One example of how expectations of anticipated failure or success can move us into the future or block access to it can be found in the following: You go into a job interview convinced that they won't hire you. It turns out to be a self-fulfilling prophecy. You don't get the job. This typical manner of anticipating may reflect a hidden feeling of having been abandoned, of not having been able to trust, of not having been able, period. Those of us who have overpositive, even idolatrous expectations of others will also inevitably be disappointed, and perhaps react by demonizing our former idol. Life has a way of killing our unrealistic expectations, and our disappointments will not be helpful if we don't learn from them.

26. Here again we come up against the problem posed by the "willpower" Christian who, not having been moved by the dynamics of delight, relies on the effortful striving of the secondary will to carry him or her through life. See Alan Jones's chapter "Spiritual Direction as a Work of the Imagination," in his *Exploring Spiritual Direction* (New York: Seabury, 1982).

27. For an examination of the Christian heart's dynamic, the longing for heaven, see Peter Kreeft, *Heaven* (San Francisco: Ignatius Press, 1989).

28. Memory, a related given-in-creation power, will be treated in chap. 5 in the section, "Memory: Formative and Deformative."

29. In chap. 2, in the section "The Human Person in the Christian Worldview," we introduced the need for a Christian anthropology. Here we reach the heart of the task of guiding the human spirit — the bringing into focused consciousness one's relation to transcendent Mystery, which for Christians is the Trinitarian God revealed by Jesus Christ.

30. As tradition puts it, for all Christians, vocation precedes and underlies mission. Thus lay people in the church are called first to the discovery of their "vocation" and then to express that call in a variety of missions.

31. In chap. 2, n. 31, we encountered this term as applied in van Kaam's theory to the deepest dimension of the human heart, to that sphere in us that is open and receptive to the inspirations of the Holy Spirit. Another approach to this dimension might be to see it as Providence, as a hermeneutic or meaning-giving framework that permeates the entirety of a human life. Naturally it appears and is named differently in different cultures and traditions.

32. Paul Ricoeur, *Fallible Man* (Chicago: Regnery, 1965).

33. In chap. 2 in the section "The Related Problem of 'Blockages'" we spoke of blockages that screen out the divine radiance from our lives; those can serve as an introduction to the "trouble at the root of our being" that blocks us from participating fully

in the pneumatic dimension of our life. In a variety of ways, the following authors have attempted to approach the topic of sinful resistance to the Mystery. Maria Beesing, et al., *The Enneagram* (Denville, N.J.: Dimension Books, 1984); Ruth Burrows, *Guidelines for Mystical Prayer* (Denville, N.J.: Dimension Books, 1980); John English, *Spiritual Freedom* (Guelph, Ontario: Loyola House, 1975); Henry Fairlie, *The Seven Deadly Sins* (Washington, D.C.: New Republic Books, 1978); Jean LaPlace, *An Experience of Life in the Spirit* (Chicago: Franciscan Herald Press, 1973); Karl Menninger, *Whatever Became of Sin?* (New York: Hawthorne Books, 1973); Patrick McCormick, *Sin As Addiction* (New York: Paulist, 1989); Louis Monden, *Sin, Liberty and Law* (New York: Sheed and Ward, 1965); Scott Peck, *People of the Lie* (New York: Simon and Schuster, 1983); Paul Ricoeur, *The Symbolism of Evil* (Boston: Beacon, 1967); and Don Riso, *Personality Types* (Boston: Houghton Mifflin, 1987).

34. In chap. 3 of *Asking the Fathers* (New York: Paulist, 1976), Aelred Squire refers to the recognition of our sinfulness as a moment of finding ourselves in a situation of disharmony, a land of unlikeness in which we may also become aware of our true possibilities, our true selves. In other words, it is only after we actually begin to experience ourselves as being pulled apart by various drives and passions and needs, as we catch ourselves compulsively exaggerating our own importance, talents, work, financial assets, power, sexuality, or status, or even after we begin somewhat neurotically to absolutize our need for success, approval, order, domination of others, mastery, control or whatever, that we are forced to acknowledge our inability to handle the disharmony of inner dispositions and drives alone. This is the point where spiritual guidance can begin, when people realize their sinfulness and their inability to deal with it alone.

35. Henry Fairlie, *The Seven Deadly Sins* (Washington, D.C.: New Republic Books, 1978).

36. Refer to the first section of chap. 3, "When Life Patterns Break Up," for the human security drive that tempts us to avoid differentiation and change.

37. In this short space we could not attempt to explore neurotic guilt, nor the ramifications of ego and spiritual guilt. There are many writers who do deal with these issues, one of the earliest being Edward Stein in his *Guilt: Theory and Therapy* (Philadelphia: Westminster Press, 1967). In chap. 4 of his *Dynamics of Spiritual Self Direction* (Denville, N.J.: Dimension Books, 1976), Adrian van Kaam describes spiritual conscience and transcendent guilt in their relation to life direction.

38. Everyone's thinking is implicitly if not explicitly informed by a theoretical anthropology or image of the human person. Some guides regard human beings as limited yet free spirits destined for God and inhabited in this life by God's spirit. So the questions that emerge for them tend to point toward a reality beyond both question and questioner. Other guides confine their guidance and suggestions to possible vital libidinal and ego functional disturbances that may or may not be at the root of a seeker's uneasiness and questions.

39. Sometimes the smallest details of the way people get up in the morning through the way they do or do not negotiate the day's "dissipative structures," to the final spirit in which they take leave of the day at night can reveal spiritually significant patterns that the guide can notice and appreciate.

40. From the opening words of The Pastoral Constitution on the Church in the Modern World (*Gaudium et Spes*) in Austin Flannery, *Vatican Council II* (Collegeville, Minn.: Liturgical Press, 1975), 903.

41. In all of these, the uncreated power of the Mystery is continually pushing to be released in the universe and in fruitful whole human lives. People's fundamental option, the underlying yes or no in regard to the Mystery's presence in their lives, their deepest trusting willingness or mistrustful willfulness, is what is at stake here. This is the reason for undertaking the task of confronting the lived obstacles of mastery and control and fear that are keeping what van Kaam calls the "Christ form" from emerging in people's lives. Tilden Edwards speaks to this sense of the Mystery's presence when he writes: "Spiritual guidance in its many groping ways, now and in the past, exists to help us see,

trust and allow this hidden force in and around us, and not in fear or pretense mistake some back eddy for it" (*Spiritual Friend* [New York: Paulist, 1980], 68).

42. See Karen Horney, *Neurosis and Human Growth* (New York: W. W. Norton, 1950).

43. See chap. 5, "Challenges and Practices for Today's Spiritual Guides."

44. The spiritual guide has more to offer than the spiritual counselor in some respects, but he or she also has much to learn from contemporary therapeutic practice. The following list contains examples from both disciplines, especially regarding spiritual direction as a process of co-listening, or of learning to listen with the "third ear": David Augsburger, *Caring Enough to Hear and Be Heard* (Scottdale, Pa.: Herald Press, 1982); Robin Baird-Smith, *Living Waters: An Anthology of Letters of Direction* (London: Fount, 1987); Hilde Bruche, *Learning Psychotherapy* (Cambridge, Mass.: Harvard University Press, 1974); Martin Buber, *I and Thou* (New York: Scribner, 1970); Louis Fierman, *Effective Psychotherapy* (New York: The Free Press, 1965); Richard Foster, *Celebration of Discipline* (San Francisco: Harper & Row, 1978); Thomas Hart, *The Art of Christian Listening* (New York: Paulist, 1980); Jean LaPlace, *Preparing for Spiritual Direction* (Chicago: Franciscan Herald Press, 1975); Francis Nemeck and Maria Coombs, *The Way of Spiritual Direction* (Wilmington, Del.: Michael Glazier, 1985); Frederick Perls et al., *Gestalt Therapy* (New York: Dell, 1951); Mark Stern, *Psychotherapy and the Religiously Committed Patient* (New York: Haworth Press, 1985); and Adrian van Kaam, *The Art of Existential Counseling* (Wilkes-Barre, Pa.: Dimension Books, 1966).

Chapter 5: Challenges and Practices for Today's Spiritual Guides

1. For a few recent books that make the "mix" at once attractive and confusing, see Jacob Needleman, *The New Religions* (New York: Doubleday, 1970); David Toolan, *Facing West from California's Shores* (New York: Crossroad, 1987); Marilyn Ferguson, *The Aquarian Conspiracy* (Los Angeles: Tarcher, 1980); Douglas Groothius, *Unmasking the New Age* (Downers Grove, Ill.: Intervarsity Press, 1986); Dave Hunt and T. A. McMahon, *The Seduction of Christianity* (Eugene, Ore.: Harvest House, 1985); Kirk Kirkpatrick, *The Emperor's New Clothes* (Westchester, Ill.: Crossway Books, 1985); Ronald Knox, *Enthusiasm* (London: Oxford University Press, 1950); Wayne Oates, *When Religion Gets Sick* (Philadelphia: Westminster Press, 1970); Marsha Sinetar, *Ordinary People as Monks and Mystics* (Mahwah, N.J.: Paulist, 1986); and George Trevelyan, *A Vision of the Aquarian Age* (Walpole, N.H.: Stillpoint Press, 1984).

2. See Carl Raschke's excellent *The Interruption of Eternity: Modern Gnosticism and the Origins of the New Religious Consciousness* (Chicago: Nelson, Hall, 1980).

3. Otto Friedrich, "New Age Horizons," *Time* (December 7, 1987): 62–72.

4. In my own experience, the work of the following writers, though not all are popularly recognized as addiction counselors, has been useful, especially when they have helped me see the relationship of neurotic attachments and other troubling emotional problems with addiction: Andras Angyal, *Neurosis and Treatment* (New York: Viking, 1965); Richard Berg and Christine McCartney, *Depression and the Integrated Life* (New York: Alba House, 1981); Margaretta Bowers, *Conflicts of the Clergy* (New York: Nelson, 1963); Leslie Farber, *Lying, Despair, Jealousy, Envy, Sex, Suicide, Drugs and the Good Life* (New York: Basic Books, 1976); Karen Horney, *Our Inner Conflicts* (New York: W. W. Norton, 1945, 1972); William Kraft, *Normal Modes of Madness* (New York: Alba House, 1978); Alice Miller, *The Drama of the Gifted Child* (New York: Basic Books, 1981); Hugh Missildine, *Your Inner Child of the Past* (New York: Simon and Schuster, 1963); Martin Padovani, *Healing Wounded Emotions* (Mystic, Conn.: Twenty-Third Publications, 1987); Anne Wilson Schaef, *Co-dependence: Misunderstood, Mistreated* (San Francisco: Harper & Row, 1986); Bernard Tyrrell, *Christotherapy II* (New York: Paulist, 1982); and Charles Whitfield, *Healing the Child Within* (Deerfield Beach, Fla.: Health Communications, 1987).

5. See, for example, Gerald May, *Addiction and Grace* (San Francisco: Harper & Row, 1988), or an older book, Joseph Rudin, *Psychotherapy and Religion* (Notre Dame: University of Notre Dame Press, 1968). See also *The Big Book* published by Alcoholics Anonymous, as well as their *Twelve Steps — Twelve Traditions*.

6. Thomas Keating, founder of the contemplative outreach movement suggests in his guide for tapes about *The Spiritual Journey* that human beings are addicted to certain emotional programs that gravitate to false centers of pre-rational energy. Contemplative prayer becomes a means of dismantling these programs of the false self according to different temperamental preferences.

7. There are many ways of approaching the reality of differences in people and thus of the different emphases their spiritual path may take. In chap. 6, n. 5, there are references to a variety of bio-spiritual types. Also the section "Processing a Critical Point" in this chapter is about some of the ways today's guides are helping people of different psychological types to know themselves.

8. Fritz Kunkel, *How Character Develops* (New York: Charles Scribner's, 1946).

9. See Helen Palmer, *The Enneagram* (New York: Harper & Row, 1988), as well as Don Riso, *Personality Types* (Boston: Houghton, Mifflin, 1987), and Maria Beesing et al., *The Enneagram* (Denville, N.J.: Dimension Books, 1984).

10. For more on this tool see the upcoming section entitled "Processing a Critical Point."

11. When we center our love on ourselves or on conformity to some aspect of the culture or only on some limited person or thing outside ourselves even if it be on one partial aspect or attribute of the Wholeness that is God, or if we begin to operate out of an idealized and partial image of ourselves and end up channeling most of our energy according to that hidden directive, we find ourselves compelled to act in certain ways even when we feel in reflective moments that we might well have preferred to choose another way. Like the spontaneous coping mechanisms revealed in confrontation with any disruptive life event (see chap. 3), these natural coping attitudes serve as protective security, as an unfree but nevertheless self-chosen way of avoiding their opposite which we fear would be antithetical to our idealized image of ourselves.

12. Even seemingly unnoticed details can usually be dredged up again when necessary. Witnesses apparently unable to recall details surrounding a murder, for example, are questioned carefully and sometimes put under hypnosis in order to bring to mind bits and pieces of what happened that they did not even realize they had noticed. Everyone we speak with drags behind an invisible comet's tail of remembered people, events, and things from past years.

13. On the other hand, the entire enterprise of the therapeutic effort known as "family systems" centers around the impact that past family patterns of interaction are having on the person's present behavior. Family therapists contend that the power of personal remembered stories, especially when these are negative, unless they are worked through to some extent, continues to form and deform us even when we repress and deny the stories. Among the many volumes related to this system are Murray Bowen, *Family Therapy and Clinical Practice* (New York: Jason Aronson, 1978); Jay Haley, *Uncommon Therapy* (New York: W. W. Norton, 1973); and John Bradshaw, *Bradshaw On: The Family* (Deerfield Beach, Fla.: Health Communications, 1988).

14. After a stroke or a brain injury, however, we can "forget" how to walk, eat, etc.

15. In our heart, the core where all experiences and memories come together and are integrated, these more or less enduring attitudes, dispositions, and inclinations continue to operate throughout our lives. Even the intuitive sense that there is a part of us that is made in God's image and likeness has been described as the haunting memory of God with which human beings are born.

16. Routine memories of the foods we prefer, where we work, the names of people we love, how to drive and do our work, even of our own names, are what make ordinary daily life possible. Destroy memory and we destroy the person along with it.

17. See chap. 2, "Inheriting Names for the Mystery."

18. In *Uncovering Stories of Faith* (New York: Paulist, 1989), Janet Ruffing looks at spiritual direction from a narrative perspective, seeing this faith conversation as a hermeneutic process of understanding and interpreting the verbal and nonverbal discourse of the person seeking direction. John English, in *Choosing Life* (New York: Paulist, 1978), sees the narration of personal history as significant for future decision making; Carol Christ, in *Diving Deep and Surfacing* (Boston: Beacon Press, 1986), shows how the telling of women's stories has the power to transform their lives; and Denis and Matthew Lynn describe, as in their other books about the healing of memories, how one goes about *Healing the Eight Stages of Life* (with Sheila Fabricant, New York: Paulist, 1988).

19. See upcoming chaps. 7, 8, and 9 for more on how the liturgy nourishes the transcendent memory of individual members of Christ's body, and in so doing provides a daily means of spiritual direction that is both personal and communal.

20. See Susan Muto, *A Practical Guide to Spiritual Reading* (Denville, N.J.: Dimension Books, 1976).

21. In *Stories of Paradise* (New York: Paulist, 1978), Louis Cameli describes spiritual direction as "ministering to stories of faith." In the questions that guide his reflective reading of autobiographies (a species of journal or diary) he suggests what the guide might be looking for as he or she listens to people or asks them to keep a journal. He maintains that if people are to grow in spiritual vision, they must learn to focus on what has been happening; on how they have been co-forming their experience; on how the central project of their heart is, with or without their conscious assent, giving shape to the future. Their inner images of self and God are products of the history of their spiritual journey so far. How they feel, hope, think, imagine, remember, and anticipate calls them forward to or holds them back from, what they really want, from the treasure of their hearts. For many, the practice of keeping a journal over the years can capture the sense of grace working in their lives as nothing else can.

22. See Ira Progoff, *At a Journal Workshop* (New York: Dialogue House, 1975), and *The Practice of Process Meditation* (New York: Dialogue House, 1980). Others along the same line are Harry Cargas and Roger Radley, *Keeping a Spiritual Journal* (New York: Doubleday, 1981); Ronald Klug, *How to Keep a Spiritual Journal* (New York: Nelson, 1982); Elizabeth O'Connor, *Letters to Scattered Pilgrims* (New York: Harper & Row, 1979); and George Simon, *Keeping Your Personal Journal* (New York: Paulist, 1978).

23. Refer back to chap. 3 and also forward to chap. 6, particularly the section "Moving Towards Reassessment and Handing On," for more on the mid-life transition and the second half of life.

24. In the next four chapters of this book, the reader will find discussions of the changes that are to be expected and promoted as people move through these normal stages of the life journey in a formative way in a transcendent direction.

25. It is possible to obtain this test from Isabel Myers-Briggs and the Consulting Psychologists Press, Palo Alto, Calif. Three books helpful in applying the test results are David Kiersey and Marilyn Bates, *Please Understand Me: Character and Temperament Types* (Del Mar, Calif.: Prometheus Nemesis Books, 1978); Harold Grant et al., *From Image to Likeness* (Ramsey, N.J.: Paulist Press, 1983); and Chester Michael and Marie Norrisey, *Prayer and Temperament* (Charlottesville, Va.: The Open Door, 1984). Also in chap. 6, n. 5, there is a listing of sources regarding human biospiritual origins and the differing typologies that are the result.

26. See Antoine de Saint-Exupery, *The Little Prince* (New York: Harcourt Brace, 1943), 70.

27. Some schools of therapy count on and foster transference reactions, since they can be very revealing in the quest to find out what psychic issues the client is dealing with. Rollo May ("On the Phenomenological Bases of Psychotherapy," in Ervin Straus, ed., *Phenomenology Pure and Applied* [Pittsburgh: Duquesne University Press, 1964], 166–84), speaks to the relevance of transference for the therapy project, and Gerald May in *Care of Mind, Care of Spirit* (San Francisco: Harper & Row, 1982), and William

Barry and William Connolly in *The Practice of Spiritual Direction* (New York: Seabury, 1982) have chapters on the dynamics of this interpersonal encounter in relation to the spiritual direction meeting. Lillian Rubin, *Intimate Strangers* (New York: Harper & Row, 1983) deals in a more general way with the dynamics at play in the relational encounters between contemporary men and women. Other volumes dealing with the dynamics of human interaction include The Counseling Psychologist, *The Relationship in Counseling and Psychotherapy* 13, no. 2 (April 1985); Gerard Egan, *The Skilled Helper* (Belmont, Calif.: Brooks/Cole, 1986); Constance Fischer, *Individualizing Psychological Assessment* (Monterey, Calif.: Brooks/Cole, 1985); Thomas Hart, *The Art of Christian Listening* (New York: Paulist, 1980); Rollo May, *The Art of Counseling* (New York: Abingdon, 1939); and Thomas Oden, *Game Free: The Meaning of Intimacy* (New York: Dell, 1974).

28. The suggestions prompted by these examples do not in any way exhaust the possible influence and handling of transferential/countertransferential feelings and responses. They do, however, indicate one more challenge to the aims and possibilities of the interhuman situation known as spiritual guidance. Although we cannot cover the area of supervision in depth, it is important to recognize that the guide also is a human being, both gifted and broken. He or she is more or less interiorly free or unfree, capable of attending to some feelings and inner dispositions and in denial of others. Guides are affected by both their own and the other's resistance to God and self-knowledge. Their own unresolved issues can prevent them from being more helpful to those who come seeking guidance. Supervision with an experienced and knowledgeable guide is recommended especially at the beginning of this work.

29. Referral is a major topic in itself and very much related to the actual situation of both guide and person being guided. We can only point to the responsibility of making competent referrals as one deeply embedded in the guidance process.

Chapter 6: A Guide's View of the Human Journey

1. See the four volumes of Adrian van Kaam, *Formative Spirituality* (New York: Crossroad, 1983–89), for this characterization of the situated aspects of human life in its socio–historical dimension.

2. See Psalm 139:13–15, *The New American Bible* (New York: Kenedy, 1970):
> Truly you have formed my inmost being;
> you knit me in my mother's womb.
> I give you thanks that I am fearfully, wonderfully made;
> my soul also you knew full well;
> nor was my frame unknown to you
> when I was made in secret,
> when I was fashioned in the depths of the earth.

3. Of course, the sociohistorical dimension of people's affectivity is also rooted in what happened to them as they were growing up, how the people, customs, and prejudices of the surrounding culture influenced the sensitivity of their hearts.

4. Guides may find it useful to read studies of typical neuroses based on the movements "toward," "away from," "against," and "with" of the sensing heart. Methods of prayer are now being linked to temperamental preferences: Ignatian discernment has always counseled alertness regarding feelings of desolation and consolation, and for many years now medical studies have linked certain diseases like cancer and hypertension and coronary disease to emotional stresses on the sensitive heart.

5. Contemporary interest in human biospiritual origins and the different typologies and spiritual paths that emerge as a result are reflected in the following: Richard Bandler and John Grinder, *Frogs into Princes* (Moab, Utah: Real People Press, 1979); Peter Campbell and Edwin McMahon, *Bio-Spirituality: Focusing as a Way to Grow* (Chicago: Loyola University Press, 1985); Eugene Gendlin, *Focusing* (New York: Bantam, 1981); Harold Grant et al., *From Image to Likeness* (New York: Paulist, 1983); Samuel Green-

berg, *Neurosis Is a Painful Style of Living* (New York: New American Library, 1971); Karen Horney, *Neurosis and Human Growth* (New York: W. W. Norton, 1950); C. G. Jung, *Psychological Types* (Princeton, N.J.: Princeton University Press, 1971); Morton Kelsey, *Companions on the Inner Way* (New York: Crossroad, 1983); Claudio Naranjo and Robert Ornstein, *On the Psychology of Meditation* (New York: Viking, 1971); and D. Shapiro, *Neurotic Styles* (New York: Basic Books, 1965). The concern for spiritual guidance in all this is how this primitive bio-spiritual sense of the invisible mystery that permeates the infant's atmosphere will develop. Will this child grow into a sense that life and therefore the Mystery are to be trusted or not? Trust in the Mystery provides a formative infrastructure on which not only natural faith, hope, and love, but also the suprastructure of intimate relationship with this Invisible Presence can unfold.

6. References here are to *The Complete Chronicles of Narnia* (Harmondsworth, Eng.: Puffin, 1959–75), a series of six books for children by C. S. Lewis, and the trilogy *The Lord of the Rings* (New York: Ballantine Books, 1960) by J. R. R. Tolkien. Bruno Bettelheim, *The Uses of Enchantment* (New York: Knopf, 1976); the collection of readings on children's literature entitled *Only Connect*, eds. Sheila Egoff, G. T. Stubbs and L. F. Ashley (Toronto: Oxford University Press, 1980); and Marie-Louise von Franz, *Interpretation of Fairy Tales* (Dallas: Spring Publications, 1982), are useful guides to the field of children's literature.

7. Much of the developmental research for this necessarily brief overview of childhood was found in James Fowler, *Stages of Faith* (New York: Harper & Row, 1981). Other sources consulted include Robert Kegan, *The Evolving Self: Problem and Process in Human Development* (Cambridge, Mass.: Harvard University Press, 1982); Richard Knowles, *Human Development and Human Possibility* (Lanham, Md.: University Press of America, 1986); Francis Nemeck and Maria Coombs, *The Spiritual Journey* (Wilmington, Del.: Michael Glazier, 1987); and Adrian van Kaam, *Fundamental Formation* (New York: Crossroad, 1983).

8. For material in this section I am relying on the work of Erik Erikson, particularly *Identity, Youth and Crisis* (New York: W. W. Norton, 1968), and *Gandhi's Truth* (New York: W. W. Norton, 1969), as well as on the insights of James Fowler, *Becoming Adult, Becoming Christian* (New York: Harper & Row, 1984), and D. Levinson, *The Seasons of a Man's Life* (New York: Ballantine, 1978).

9. Thus the guide should be aware that with all its confusion and changes, its agonies and peer pressures and uncertainties, it probably signals the life stage that St. Paul would characterize as the phase of "newborn spirituality." This does not imply that children do not also have a spiritual life, but only that it comes to consciousness in a new way during the adolescent years.

10. There are many exceptions to this rather general statement, particularly in our present society where teens seem inundated by fear of failure and other negative thoughts about the future. Such young people may have repressed ideals beneath a lack of confidence in their (or anyone else's) future and find it very difficult if not impossible to launch out into the deep of adult life.

11. A few references for sexuality regarding its effect on relationship with God: Esther Harding, *The Way of All Women* (New York: Harper & Row, 1970); Rosemary Haughton, *The Mystery of Sexuality* (London: Darton, Longman and Todd, 1970), and *Love* (Baltimore: Penguin Books, 1970); William Kraft, *Whole and Holy Sexuality* (St. Meinrad, Ind.: Abbey Press, 1989); Una Koll, *Sexual Counselling* (London: SPCK, 1980); Fritz Kunkel, *In Search of Maturity* (New York: Scribner's, 1943); William McNamara, *Mystical Passion* (New York: Paulist, 1977); James Nelson, *Embodiment* (Minneapolis: Augsburg, 1978); Marc Oraison, *The Human Mystery of Sexuality* (New York: Sheed and Ward, 1967); Yves Raguin, *Celibacy for Our Times* (St. Meinrad, Ind.: Abbey Press, 1975); Thomas Tyrrell, *Urgent Longings* (Whitinsville, Mass.: Affirmation Books, 1980); and Jean Vanier, *Man and Woman He Made Them* (New York: Paulist, 1985).

12. I have found this to be true in many of the countries where I have done research on the topic of commitment — in China and Australia in particular. The situation of

women is particularly difficult because, in terms of the marriage commitment, women are always operating under pressure from the biological time clock that governs their childbearing years.

13. In *Spirituality and Human Emotion* (Grand Rapids: Eerdmans, 1982), Robert Roberts speaks to the dialogue between subjective desire, whose dynamics in terms of feelings, emotion, interest, concern or passion motivate people, and the object of preoccupation that evokes their passionate concern and drives them into action. He suggests that people need to look carefully for what in life they really care about, for what expresses their true self and for how it is connected with the larger reality for them of the reign of God. People want to choose a way they can feel is intuitively right for them. They seek guidance in order to learn how to choose what for them will be "a path with a heart."

14. In *Fundamental Formation* (New York: Crossroad, 1983), 299 and 303, Adrian van Kaam speaks of the apparent or manifest form life assumes in reaction and response to real or imagined expectations of others, and of the foundational formation principle of human life with which empirical forms such as the apparent are meant to be congenial and compatible.

15. Meyer Friedman and Ray Rosenman, the authors of *Type A Behavior and Your Heart* (New York: Alfred A. Knopf, 1974), 4, describe this complex of personality traits as including excessive competitive drive, aggressiveness, impatience, and a harrying sense of time urgency.

16. Much has been written recently about the attraction for young people of fundamentalist groups or cults that assure them of the certainty, providing answers sometimes before they have even asked questions of life.

17. Ernest Becker, *The Denial of Death* (New York: Free Press, 1973).

18. See chap. 3, where we discuss how each time there is a major change in a person's life field, whether it comes in the form of a fresh awareness, a new self-understanding, another person's love, a demand from home, family, work, recreation, or from the wider needs of the community in the form of cries for justice and equality, or of ecological and other human disasters and suffering, there is an opportunity for new forms of reflective questioning.

19. Much has been written about this phase of social responsibility and control called young adulthood by writers who both see and fail to see its relation to the life of the spirit. See Joann Conn, ed., *Women's Spirituality* (New York: Paulist, 1986); Erik Erikson, ed., *Adulthood* (New York: W. W. Norton, 1978); Roger Gould, *Transformations: Growth and Change in Adult Life* (New York: Simon and Schuster, 1978); William Kraft, *Achieving Promises* (Philadelphia: Westminster Press, 1981); Scott Peck, *The Road Less Travelled* (New York: Simon and Schuster, 1978); Walter Conn, *Conversion* (Mahwah, N.J.: Paulist, 1986); and Gail Sheehy, *Passages* (New York: Bantam, 1978), and *Pathfinders* (New York: Bantam, 1981).

20. See Judith Viorst, *Necessary Losses* (New York: Fawcett, 1987), as well as Patrick Carroll and Katherine Dyckman, *Chaos or Creation* (New York: Paulist, 1986) for more on the growing resistance to losses as we move through adulthood.

21. Anyone who has attempted to bring to the fore these questions about the changing nature of human commitments or the blockages to growth that mid-age people experience will attest to how difficult such conversations can be.

22. I think here of two young couples where the husbands are from the same family. Both men left their faith tradition in their late teens and did not marry in the church. However, when the time came for their first children to be baptized, both couples reconsidered and returned to their original faith tradition because they realized that without a community of faith they could not hand on the wisdom of their tradition to the next generation.

23. For an excellent description of this process, see Adrian van Kaam, *The Transcendent Self* (Denville, N.J.: Dimension Books, 1979).

24. Ibid., 107.

25. Carl Jung, *Modern Man in Search of a Soul* (New York: Harcourt, Brace and Co., 1934), 125.

26. This rediscovery of the pneumatic dimension of the human heart must be the guiding motif throughout the whole of life. In the final chapters we will look again at this goal ultimately aimed at in spiritual guidance — the goal of putting people back in touch with their rootedness not only in humanity but also in the divine source of life. Thus, it is urgent that guides understand the deepest capacities of human existence and remain in touch not only with transcendent aspirations for "more" in this life, but also with the divine image that opens men and women to receive God's self-communication.

27. Some authors who are thinking about this phase of reassessment and handing on are Eugene Bianchi, *Aging as Spiritual Journey* (New York: Crossroad, 1986); Ruth Burrows, *Guidelines for Mystical Prayer* (Denville, N.J.: Dimension Books, 1980); Joan Wolski Conn, *Spirituality and Personal Maturity* (New York: Paulist, 1989); Benedict Groeschel, *Spiritual Passages* (New York: Crossroad, 1983); Raymond Studzinski, *Spiritual Direction and Mid-Life Development* (Chicago: Loyola University Press, 1985); Teresa of Avila, *The Interior Castle* (New York: Paulist, 1979); and Evelyn and James Whitehead, *Seasons of Strength: New Visions of Adult Christian Maturing* (New York: Doubleday, 1986).

28. Anne Brennan and Janice Brewi, authors of *Mid-Life Directions: Praying and Playing Sources of New Dynamism* (New York: Paulist, 1985), are adult educators who believe firmly that people in the second half of life need to learn to relax and let go in order to enter into both prayer and the playfulness required for entering into the reign of God.

29. To say it technically: when the fully aware, concentrated attentiveness that guides and controls conscious presence is somewhat stilled, one's preconscious presence, the bridge between consciousness, infraconscious drives, and transconscious aspirations, can emerge. Mystics witness to the further fact that when the preconscious is stilled, the barrier between transconscious and preconscious can open so that the preconscious, ultimately the heart, can be flooded with the energy of divine love, at the initiative of the Mystery.

30. The following list gives merely a glimpse of the wide field that encompasses bodily disciplines, meditative consciousness, and contemplative modes. Spiritual guides can avail themselves of these resources in service of their art. Donald Ardell, *High Level Wellness* (Emmaus, Pa.: Rodale Press, 1977); H. Benson, *The Relaxation Response* (New York: Bantam, 1975); Martin Ebon, *The Relaxation Controversy: Can You Have Relaxation without Meditation?* (New York: New American Library, 1976); Patricia Carrington, *Freedom in Meditation* (New York: Doubleday, 1978); Karlfried Graf von Durckheim, *Daily Life as Spiritual Exercise* (New York: Harper & Row, 1971), and *The Call of the Master* (New York: E. P. Dutton, 1989); Eugen Herrigel, *Zen in the Art of Archery* (New York: Random House, 1971); Willigis Jager, *The Way to Contemplation* (New York: Paulist, 1982); Thomas Merton, *The Way of Chuang Tzu* (New York: New Directions, 1965); Annie Dillard, *Pilgrim at Tinker Creek* (New York: Bantam, 1975); and Keith Sehnert, *Stress/Unstress* (Minneapolis: Augsburg, 1981).

Chapter 7: On Being a Wise Fish

1. Thomas Dubay precedes this comment by speaking of "...the widespread trend whereby men and women with meager training have been assuming the guidance of others in their spiritual lives. Veteran directors are likely to have encountered the endless variety and complexity of problems and questions that arise in the concrete circumstances of the human pursuit of the divine. Naive neophytes seem to suppose that taking a few courses in scripture, theology and psychology amply qualifies a person as an adept tutor in the life of prayer and equips one to deal with the vast ramifications that can arise. In other fields such as medicine or law, amateurism is not tolerated for a moment, and laws are framed to prevent and to punish incompetence. Yet, in the matter of guiding

immortal souls, the barest background preparation is presented and popularly accepted as normal, indeed, even advocated as being a healthy approach" (*Fire Within* [San Francisco: Ignatius Press, 1989], 289).

2. In *The Dynamics of Spiritual Self Direction* (Denville, N.J.: Dimension Books, 1976), Adrian van Kaam points to a variety of ways, including one-to-one direction, in which the search for the divine direction of one's life may be carried out as that life unfolds.

3. Dealing with one's sinful resistance to such participation calls for a unique type of trusted guide and guidance even outside of what some traditions would see as confession or the sacrament of reconciliation.

4. A descriptive expression from van Kaam's *Fundamental Formation* (New York: Crossroad, 1983) that refers to the provisional integrational form our life assumes in reaction and response to each new disclosure of our unique potential. In view of the constant flow of change in our lives, we are always moving from one current life form through some sort of changing circumstance and inner disposition to a new current life form or self.

5. In the introduction to chap. 1, "Waking Up to Freedom and Wholeness," we saw how the "current selves" of these three persons were restructured by significant life events, so that they moved from a certain shape of life through a series of life events to a new shape or form, to a new "current self."

6. People seem to feel the need for spiritual change when they become fragmented by events, when they get in touch with "unfinished business" from past years, when they recognize they have been stagnating for some time in one stage of their development, when in an insightful moment they see what an unthinking product of the culture they have become, or when they are confronted with the seaminess of their motivations or the meanness and pettiness of their sinful nature.

7. See chap. 3, section titled "Formative and Transformative Change."

8. In his *Flowers in the Desert* (New York: Paulist, 1987), Demetrius Dumm provides an interesting parallel to our discussion of the patterns of the awakening heart when he speaks of the "genetic code" of the Bible that summarizes the biblical meaning of conversion, growth, and journeying, the movement *from, through*, and *to* that characterizes the pattern of the shift we have been describing in relation to spiritual life. "This movement from presence on our terms, through apparent absence, to presence on God's terms is so all-pervasive in the Scriptures that it could be called the 'genetic code' of the Bible, by which all biblical realities are identified.... If we can live in trust and struggle through the time of darkness we will emerge into a new world of far better and more real presence and awareness" (81). In the Christian tradition of conversion also this pattern invariably appears. Augustine, for instance, feels profoundly dissatisfied with his life, but is unable to let go of his current mode until he reads in Scripture a passage that touches his heart, a message encountered at the right moment; see *The Confessions of St. Augustine* (New York: Doubleday, 1960). And Saul needs to be knocked down and blinded before he allows himself to be converted into Paul (see the Acts of the Apostles). In our day, many business executives like Norman Cousins have to hear the message contained in a heart attack before they will thoughtfully reconsider the lifestyle that is killing them.

9. Frederick Buechner describes vocation: "the place God calls you to is the place where your deep gladness and the world's deep hunger meet" (*Wishful Thinking* [New York: Harper & Row, 1972], 95).

10. These words from Psalm 95 draw attention to the voice of the Other as it appeals daily through new insights, a compelling text, an attractive person, or a significant event. Even though the insight be disconcerting, the text personally upsetting, the other person challenging, or the event have all the earmarks of a crisis, we are advised not to harden our hearts, but let them be touched "today."

11. Mystics like John of the Cross, for example, have tended to describe the response to this love as the quiet movement in the depth of one's being of a living flame of love whose inner light is the Holy Spirit.

12. See chap. 3, especially "The Challenge of Openness to One's Whole Context," for some of the obstacles that make receptive presence feel so alienating for men and women brought up to believe that success and achievement are to be measured in quite other terms.

13. See the final section of this chapter entitled "The Shift to a More Meditative Style."

14. See Thomas Merton, *The Way of Chuang Tzu* (New York: New Directions, 1965), 65.

15. See Rom. 5:5. We are ready to give up the old way that keeps us from this dialogue only when that willful, controlling way is no longer working well for us, when we catch sight of the new way glimmering before us and are moved in spite of hesitation by "dynamics of delight" in its attractiveness and personal appeal.

16. A reference to John the Baptist, who in his final witness to Christ found his joy, according to John 3:29–30, in stepping aside once the true bridegroom had appeared. Here we have a model of the spiritual director who is willing to move aside once the seeker meets the One his or her soul seeks.

17. See Carolyn Gratton, *Trusting: Theory and Practice* (New York: Crossroad, 1982). This section is based on chap. 4, "The To-Be-Trusted Others"; chap. 9, "Appraising the Other as To-Be-Trusted," and chap. 16, "Trust in Self, Others and the Holy Other" from that book.

18. The trust research revealed that we trust others who represent for us a horizon of values, an invisible context of meaning that we ourselves value and are seeking to connect with. Thus, in the direction process it would seem that the trusted guide would be one who lives in faithful presence to a way of naming the Mystery that is congenial with the deepest desires of the seeker.

19. The guide for a person seeking faith, then, must be a person of faith, aware of the presence of the Other in all that is and co-listening with the seeker for any directives that Other may initiate. Thus Christian direction is rooted in Christ as revelation of the Mystery, as being himself the way, truth, and life, the ultimate Source of spiritualization, interiorization, and sanctification, the one who from his fullness pours God's love into human hearts by giving us the Holy Spirit. Hence the thrust of this book, indicating that both guide and person guided are co-listeners to the Holy Spirit who continually provides providential direction in the life field of each man or woman whether they are aware of it or not.

20. The research also indicated that persons whom one can trust as spiritual guides might have much in common with those who are trusted by clients in therapy, an inexpressible "something" that is not necessarily external. See Carolyn Gratton, "Phenomenological and Traditional Views of Trust between Clients and Therapists," in *Duquesne Studies in Phenomenological Psychology*, eds A. Giorgi, A. Barton, and C. Maes (Pittsburgh: Duquesne University Press, 1983), 4:90–104.

21. In a section entitled "Discovering the Other 'For Me' " in *Trusting* I have applied the criteria of trustworthiness uncovered in the research to the way in which the trustable "something" about the other leads to a trust in Jesus Christ that is unique for each individual.

22. Throughout the discourse on life and Eucharist found in the sixth chapter of the Gospel of St. John, we find Christ making continual reference to the One who sent him as the ground for people's trust in himself as the bread of life. Jesus points to the attractiveness and drawing power of this invisible horizon or ground as the adequate foundation for their faith assent — adequate in a way that the figure he presents in isolation from that ground could never be.

23. Here we see again how important it is that the guide be "coming from," be grounded in, that same Mystery if he or she is to be trusted. In his *Spiritual Friend* (New York: Paulist, 1980), Tilden Edwards remarks that "when someone comes to you and asks for help in his relation to God, that person has already stepped to the threshold between the sacred and the profane, and you are needed to represent the sacred. Thus,

you do not seek to be a 'pal' or a therapist; you accept the responsibility of your symbolic position" (84).

24. Far from seeing herself as a spiritual director, my friend had no idea of applying the label "spiritual friendship" to our relationship. In fact, it was an unexpected moment for both of us. Yet it was her simple willingness to be an open channel of grace for me that day, to not try to make anything happen but simply to listen to what was happening within me, that made her presence so helpful to me. She had the gift of co-listening. Additional help for becoming a co-listener can be found in Aelred of Rievaulx, *On Spiritual Friendship* (Washington, D.C.: Consortium Press, 1974); Robin Baird-Smith, *Living Water: An Anthology of Letters of Direction* (London: Fount, 1987); Father Gabriel, *The Spiritual Director according to the Principles of St. John of the Cross* (Westminster, Md.: Newman, 1951); Thomas Hart, *The Art of Christian Listening* (New York: Paulist, 1980); William McNamara, *Christian Mysticism* (Chicago: Franciscan Herald Press, 1981); Francis Nemeck and Maria Coombs, *The Way of Spiritual Direction* (Wilmington, Del.: Michael Glazier, 1985); Jerome Neufelder and Mary Coelho, eds., *Writings on Spiritual Direction by Great Christian Masters* (New York: Seabury, 1982); and Henri Nouwen, *The Wounded Healer* (New York: Doubleday, 1979).

25. See *The Rite of Christian Initiation of Adults* (New York: Catholic Book Publishing Co., 1988). The following outline in the study text gives the reader some idea of what is involved in this initial formation program: Period of *evangelization* and *precatechumenate*; First step: acceptance into the order of catechumens; Period of *catechumenate*; Second step: election and enrollment of names; Period of *purification* and *enlightenment*; Third step: celebration of the sacraments of initiation; Period of *postbaptismal catechesis* or mystagogy (16). There are many fine texts that can help guide one through these steps. See, for example, James Dunning, *New Wine: New Wineskins* (New York: Sadlier, n.d.); Mary Malone, *Step by Step: A Handbook for the RCIA* (Dubuque, Ia: Wm. C. Brown, 1986); Karen Hinman and Joseph Sinwell, eds., *Breaking Open the Word of God* (New York: Paulist, 1986), and National Conference of Catholic Bishops, *Study Text #10, Christian Initiation of Adults* (Washington, D.C.: U.S. Catholic Conference, 1988). Other useful background texts include Maria Boulding, *The Coming of God* (Collegeville, Minn.: The Liturgical Press, 1982); Gabriel Braso, *Liturgy and Spirituality* (Collegeville, Minn.: Liturgical Press, 1971); Jean Corbon, *The Wellspring of Worship* (New York: Paulist, 1988); Tad Guzie, *The Book of Sacramental Basics* (New York: Paulist, 1981); Aiden Kavanagh, *The Shape of Baptism* (New York: Pueblo, 1978); Thomas Keating, *The Mystery of Christ* (Warwick, N.Y.: Amity House, 1987); Joseph Martos, *Doors to the Sacred* (New York: Doubleday, 1981); Adrian Nocent, *The Liturgical Year*, 4 vols. (Collegeville, Minn.: Liturgical Press, 1977); Michael Warren, *Faith, Culture and the Worshipping Community* (New York: Paulist, 1989); and James White, *Introduction to Christian Worship* (Nashville: Abingdon, 1980).

26. In working with students who are expected to return to their various communities with some idea of how to implement a formation program for a parish, university community, novitiate, or committed lay group, I have frequently used the RCIA as a formative model for such programs. Each student adapts it to his or her actual life situation, whether that be a large university campus or a small parish in a declining Pennsylvania mill town. The combined formative effect of living and worshipping in the same community of faith cannot be overemphasized, as we found in evaluating these programs.

27. As defined in the rite of Christian initiation, this time, usually the Easter season, is a time when the newly initiated experience being fully part of the Christian community by means of pertinent catechesis and particularly by participation with all the faithful in the Sunday eucharistic celebration. See Mark Boyer, *Mystagogy* (New York: Alba House, 1990). It is certainly a time for spiritual guidance, whether in a group or one-to-one setting. Also there are many occasions when a faith group asks for a special retreat or leading in contemplative practice (see Gerald May, *Pilgrimage Home* [New York: Paulist, 1979]) or for help from a spiritual guide in making a decision.

28. Chap. 8 will take up in more detail the topic of conversion, particularly in its relation to baptism and the transformative process that is the essence of Christian life and prayer.

29. More on this in the following section titled "What Guides Must Be Ready to Offer."

30. Damien Isabell, *The Spiritual Director* (Chicago: Franciscan Herald Press, 1976), 12–18. Isabell sees the "general direction of the Church" as one of the four basic models of direction operative within the church.

31. Drawing from my courses that used the RCIA as a formative model (see n. 26) I presented papers at the National Meeting of the Federation of Diocesan Liturgical Commissions (October 9 and 11, 1989) on "Liturgy as Spiritual Direction." Also, for a course dealing with Christian commitment, I am pursuing the ways in which liturgical formation can prepare and strengthen people for the various commitments they are led to embrace in the course of a lifetime.

32. Here again we meet the figure/ground paradigm noted in chaps. 1 and 2. The liturgical celebrations point to the deeper divine ground (or salvific plan) of the figure that is a person's life. Liturgical ritual from another faith tradition would offer a different ground and thus a different meaning for the event being celebrated, e.g., see Kenneth Kramer, *The Sacred Art of Dying* (New York: Paulist, 1988), in which he explores the various meanings, physical, psychological, and spiritual, that inform the attitudes toward death of members of eleven great religious faith traditions.

33. See chap. 5, section titled "Guides and 'Transference.'" Obviously this problem is more avoidable in group direction and in the other types of direction in common that we find outside the one-to-one situation.

34. See the upcoming section entitled "The Shift to a More Meditative Style" and also chap. 6, n. 30, for related bibliography.

35. For a thorough treatment of expectations of the director from the works of St. John of the Cross and St. Teresa of Avila, see chap. 16, "Spiritual Direction" in Thomas Dubay, *Fire Within* (San Francisco: Ignatius Press, 1989).

36. Appraisal is the main topic of chap. 11, "Guidelines for Appraisal."

37. See Adrian van Kaam, *Human Formation* (New York: Crossroad, 1985), especially chaps. 5 and 6.

38. Some of the more popular guides to meditation include the following: David Brandon, *Zen in the Art of Helping* (London: Routledge and Kegan Paul, 1976); Patricia Carrington, *Freedom in Meditation* (New York: Doubleday, 1978); Anthony de Mello, *Sadhana: A Way to God* (New York: Doubleday, 1984); Tilden Edwards, *Living Simply through the Day* (New York: Paulist, 1977); Lawrence Freeman, *Light Within: The Inner Path of Meditation* (London: Darton, Longman and Todd, 1986); Joseph Goldstein, *The Experience of Insight* (London: Shambhala, 1983); Thomas Green, *A Vacation with the Lord* (Notre Dame: Ave Maria Press, 1986); William Johnston, *Silent Music* (New York: Harper & Row, 1974); Lawrence LeShan, *How to Meditate* (Boston: Little, Brown, 1974); Bruce McClellan, *Waters of Life* (London: Mowbray, 1985); John Main, *Talks on Meditation* (Montreal: Benedictine Community, 1979); Joseph Pieper, *Leisure the Basis of Culture* (New York: Pantheon, 1952); and Chogyam Trungpa, *Meditation in Action* (Boulder, Colo.: Shambhala, 1969).

Chapter 8: Life Emerging From Death

1. For more scriptural texts regarding this change of mind and heart, see "Repentance/conversion" in Xavier Leon-Dufour, *Dictionary of Biblical Theology* (New York: Seabury Press, 1973), 486–91.

2. Here the reader may want to return to the section in chap. 7 "A Liturgical Model of Group Direction" to make once again the connection between the Rite of Christian

Initiation of Adults and its possibility as a pattern for spiritual guidance that aims toward change of heart and commitment.

3. See Robert Duggan, ed., *Conversion and the Catechumenate* (New York: Paulist, 1984) and Regis Duffy, *On Becoming a Catholic: The Challenge of Christian Initiation* (San Francisco: Harper & Row, 1984).

4. In chap. 5 of *The Shape of Baptism* (New York: Pueblo, 1978), Aiden Kavanagh refers to the catechumenate as "an ecclesial and liturgical structure within which conversion therapy is carried on" (128). Catechesis is understood to be concerned with conversion in Christ and with how to live continuously in such a manner not only prior to but after initiation as well. See also *The Awe-Inspiring Rites of Initiation* (Slough, Eng.: St. Paul Publications, 1971) by Edward Yarnold for baptismal homilies of the fourth century.

5. In chap. 6, in the section entitled "Foundations of Personality," we noted that the ceremony of baptism marks the day when the child is first honored by the community as a spiritual being with a mysterious vocation that will conform this child to the "Firstborn" child of God, Jesus the Christ. Thus, each Christian celebrates this invitation to respond to the same call that Jesus responded to when he or she recalls the reality of his or her own baptism.

6. In his book *Christian Conversion* (New York: Paulist, 1986), Walter Conn, citing the contemporary wisdom of philosophers and theologians like Reinhold Niebuhr, Paul Tillich, Karl Rahner, Bernard Lonergan, John Macquarrie, and David Tracy, points to this universally experienced "dynamic exigence of self-transcendence," capable of responding to invitations from a larger life. As human spirits we are compelled to aspire to these appeals. We have to want to find fulfillment in what is "more than" ourselves. And because as Christians we dare to believe that Christ embodies in himself these life-enhancing values, we are not surprised to find that fidelity to the law of our human spirit demands that sometime or other we answer for ourselves the question: Who am I? What do I really want? What in the last analysis am I called to commit myself to in love? Fidelity to ourselves as spirit may also demand that throughout our lives we undergo a gradual process of conversion begun at baptism and leading to fuller participation in that abundant life.

7. In his developmental analysis of the conversion process, Walter Conn (ibid.) uses Bernard Lonergan's categories of affective, cognitive, moral, and faith conversion to illustrate the transformational aspects of conversion. After describing Thomas Merton's conversion as a response to God's call, he links it with commitment to concrete loving actions for others in the world. He concludes that truly Christian conversion demands not only an all-encompassing story or overarching meaning context, but it also demands that one see, feel, and act in a completely new way.

8. The themes of relationship, grace, conversion, and love return here as we begin to grasp the link between conversion and transformation of heart. Some books that touch on these themes include Tad Dunne, *Lonergan and Spirituality* (Chicago: Loyola University Press, 1985); Thomas Green, *Darkness in the Marketplace* (Notre Dame: Ave Maria Press, 1981); Emily Griffin, *Turning: Reflections on the Experience of Conversion* (New York: Doubleday, 1982); William Johnston, *The Inner Eye of Love* (New York: Harper & Row, 1978); Brian McDermott, *What Are They Saying About the Grace of Christ?* (New York: Paulist, 1984); David O'Rourke, *A Process Called Conversion* (New York: Doubleday, 1985); Adrian van Kaam, *The Transcendent Self* (Denville, N.J.: Dimension Books, 1979); and Dietrich von Hildebrand, *Transformation in Christ* (Manchester, N.H.: Sophia Institute Press, 1948, 1990).

9. See Mark 8:35 or John 12:25. A cross comes into being when a horizontal thrust (one's human life) is interrupted by a vertical thrust (for the sake of Christ and the Gospel).

10. See chap. 3, the section "Formative and Transformative Change," for Martha's story. At the heart of the notion of Christian conversion lies an appeal to the capacity for freedom of mind and will that comprise the human spirit. In order, for example, to

carry an appraisal through willing affirmation into decisive choice and action, we need to be able to exert our freedom to take a distance from overwhelming feelings that may not convey the whole truth. We need to delay the instant gratification of certain satisfactions, to postpone though not ignore, the immediate fulfillment of our desires and to take time out for a reflective weighing of pro's and con's so that the decision, when finally made, will be a personal act of a truly whole and spiritual being responding not only to our own will, but receptive also to the work of grace in our lives.

11. See the last section in this chapter, "Prayer as Nourishing Compassionate Vision."

12. In chap. 7, n. 8, I noted that Demetrius Dumm has already characterized this pattern as the "genetic code" of the Bible that summarizes the meaning of conversion, and in this chapter so far we have looked at its profound connection with baptism and the conversion aimed at by the rites surrounding Christian initiation. The pattern of from–through–to seems to be a constant in all cases of *metanoia*.

13. The students at the Institute of Formative Spirituality at Duquesne University are an international graduate grouping of Catholic priests and religious, Protestant ministers from many denominations, and a growing number of lay leaders, many of them doctoral students who build entire dissertations around the formative, reformative, and transformative possibilities inherent in this lived pattern.

14. Most of us know from personal experience the sometimes costly battle involved in giving up certain accustomed sinful attitudes and dispositions. And although we do not often openly discuss our interior progress from despair to hopefulness, we know or intuit how agonizing that road can be. It is not always easy to talk freely of the painful moments we went through as we grew up, exchanging the narrow safe world of childhood for the unfamiliar territory of school and wider neighborhood, or as we gave up the security of our family's way of defining things for the many ways the others see and define that same reality in a pluralistic and sometimes hostile world.

15. See Etty Hillesum, *Letters from Westerbork* (New York: Pantheon, 1986). In *Hunger of Memory* (New York: Bantam Books, 1982) Richard Rodriguez documents the long labor of change in order to "make it" in America; and Robert Mulholland speaks of conversion from informative to formative thinking in *Shaped by the Word* (Nashville: Upper Room, 1985), to mention only three of the many books available on this subject.

16. See Judith Guest, *Ordinary People* (New York: Ballantine, 1976).

17. See chap. 6, the section "Relaxing and Letting Go," and chap. 7, the section "The Shift to a More Meditative Style."

18. Here we find the most compelling reason for recognizing the liturgical model of spiritual direction. It, too, every day of the year, centers the Christian possibility of conversion in the Paschal Mystery. It is, according to the Constitution on the Sacred Liturgy "the summit toward which the activity of the Church is directed: it is also the fount from which all her power flows.... From the liturgy, therefore... grace is poured forth upon us as from a fountain... [when]... the faithful come to it with proper dispositions" (Austin Flannery, ed., *Vatican Council II* [Collegeville, Minn.: Liturgical Press, 1975], 6). Thomas Keating, *The Mystery of Christ* (Warwick, N.Y.: Amity House, 1987), adds, "When those who participate in the liturgy are disposed by adequate preparation and understanding, [the] experience of God, in ever increasing degrees, is transmitted" (1).

19. Some of the earliest literature on spiritual direction speaks of bringing to the surface abiding tendencies and dispositions of heart. In bringing about a transformation of outlook, the Holy Spirit also brought about a transformation of the heart's desires and emotions as well as inspiring the virtues in what was seen as an inner revolution akin to the deep self-knowledge and conversion sought in spiritual direction. In *Human Formation* (New York: Crossroad, 1985) Adrian van Kaam approaches the topic of disposition formation and reformation from a contemporary viewpoint, explaining that in view of the routine and mechanistic connotations that now adhere to the term habit, he prefers to use the term "disposition," which allows for spiritual connotations as well.

20. There are also dispositions that are gratuitously given such as the gift of contemplative prayer or the gifts of the Holy Spirit, like wisdom, strength, perseverance, and compassion.

21. A most effective aid to conversion of dispositions, according to reputable spiritual guides, is humility. In humility we have a disposition that acknowledges virtues as well as limitations, and in giving up mastery and control opens us to let go of our fixed "spiritual" image of ourselves. According to Maria Beesing et al., *The Enneagram: A Journey of Self Discovery* (Denville, N.J.: Dimension Books, 1984), a shift to more humble virtues or dispositions is the way to conversion of mistaken ways of acting compelled by gut, head, or heart.

22. Paul Ricoeur's structural analysis of the brief New Testament parable about the farmer who discovers treasure hidden in a field and sells all that he has in order to buy that field, in Charles Regans, *The Philosophy of Paul Ricoeur* (Boston: Beacon Press, 1978), provided the underlying basis for this paragraph.

23. It is not surprising, in view of the former, that the majority of us prefer to embed ourselves in "little beyonds" of family, home, work, and religious duties in ways that will shelter us from the unpredictable presence in our lives of what Ernest Becker (*The Denial of Death* [New York: Free Press, 1973]) calls the Great Beyond (chap. 7, n. 17). The movement of conversion, of returning to the deepest truth of our being is what can save us from this desperate clinging to the false "homes" we construct for our anxious selves in order to avoid being disturbed by the unpredictable otherness of God.

24. In fact, the positive face of detachment lies in trusting abandonment to divine providence, in the ability to confidently flow with instead of resisting the unexpected and often unwanted impingements of Mystery in one's life. One study of Thérèse of Lisieux that brings this out strongly is Bernard Bro's *The Little Way* (London: Darton, Longman and Todd, 1979). For Thérèse conversion meant learning to shift our fulcrum from self to God. She did not have to wait for middle age in order to know and understand this secret of Christian conversion.

25. See chap. 3, the section "The Classic Crisis: Mid-Life Transition," especially n. 17 for a list of books on the subject, as well as sections in chap. 6 that pertain to this stage of the human journey. Demetrius Dumm puts his finger on the flavor of guidance during the mid-age period when he compares this life interval to the transfiguration moment when Jesus finally became aware of the divine way of love and sacrifice that was to be his. Dumm writes that the typical Christian, having recognized a "Galilean" period in life when he or she was young and strong, discovering new worlds, earning degrees, winning battles, driving out demons of fear and low self-esteem, working the "miracles" of begetting children and buying or building a house, must in mid-life begin to sense the onset of physical and mental decline, the frequently traumatic interruption of retirement and being left with too much time to think about the unpromising future. Often the guide needs to move the person out of regarding mid-age as a time to live in reveries about the nostalgic past while fearing the future that looms ahead. The man or woman seeking guidance needs to be shown that where they are now can be a fruitful time to walk with Jesus as he becomes ever more aware of the pain and suffering that await him in Judea.

26. Teilhard de Chardin, *The Divine Milieu* (New York: Harper and Brothers, 1960), 52.

27. Maria Boulding (see *The Coming of God* [London: SPCK, 1982], 98) is one person to whom I am indebted for these thoughts on prayer. Other sources include Thomas Green, *When the Well Runs Dry* (Notre Dame: Ave Maria Press, 1979); Henri Nouwen, *The Way of the Heart* (New York: Ballantine, 1981); Yves Raguin, *How to Pray Today* (Wheathampstead, Hertfordshire: Anthony Clarke Books, 1975); Karl Rahner, *On Prayer* (New York: Paulist, 1958); Adrian van Kaam, *The Woman at the Well* (Denville, N.J.: Dimension Books, 1976); and Hans urs von Balthasar, *Prayer* (San Francisco: Ignatius Press, 1986).

28. For a very helpful description of the development of prayer, see chap. 6, "The Teresian Mansions" in Thomas Dubay's study *Fire Within* (San Francisco: Ignatius Press, 1989). This entire book, subtitled "St. Teresa of Avila, St. John of the Cross and the Gospel — On Prayer," is to be recommended for guides looking for an authoritative work on Christian prayer in the Carmelite tradition.

29. Along with Dubay, contemporary writers on contemplation include Ruth Burrows, *Guidelines for Mystical Prayer* (Denville, N.J.: Dimension Books, 1980); John Gorsuch, *Invitation to the Spiritual Journey* (New York: Paulist, 1990); Thomas Keating, *Open Mind, Open Heart: The Contemplative Dimension of the Gospel* (Warwick, N.Y.: Amity House, 1986); Thomas Merton, *Contemplative Prayer* (New York: Doubleday, 1969); Francis Nemeck and Maria Coombs, *Contemplation* (Wilmington, Del.: Michael Glazier, 1982); and Peggy Wilkinson, *Finding the Mystic Within You* (Locust Valley, N.Y.: Living Flame Press, 1986).

30. For more on John's thoughts about inept directors, see Dubay *Fire Within*, 290–97. The guide is there to help people recognize the genuine prayer of darkness and not to confuse it with the ordinary trauma and turmoil that may accompany midlife or other types of transition. Currently there seems to be a number of guides who are confusing the dark night that purifies with mental or emotional problems like depression, chronic fatigue, or distraction. This is why John of the Cross insists that authenticating an individual's life of prayer requires an extensive background in Scripture, in doctrinal, moral, and mystical theology, and in the lives and teachings of the saints.

31. St. Thérèse of Lisieux, *The Story of a Soul*, John Beevers, trans. (New York: Doubleday, 1957).

32. Ibid., 50.

33. Ibid., 62. Another translation of her life is John Clarke, *The Story of a Soul* (Washington, D.C.: ICS Publications, 1976). There are also many commentaries, among them François Jamart, *Complete Spiritual Doctrine of St. Thérèse of Lisieux* (New York: Alba House, 1961).

34. *The Story of a Soul*, John Beevers, 132. In chap. 10 of this translation there are some helpful pages from Thérèse on her method of guiding the novices.

35. See this chapter, n. 23.

36. One final note on conversion from the point of view of the RCIA as a journey in faith: In *New Wine, New Wineskins* (Chicago: Sadlier, n.d.), James Dunning points to the dramatic moment when, according to Bernard Lonergan, the radical shift to "religious conversion" is made (23). Prior to that moment there may have been affective, intellectual, and moral conversions, and after may flow changes on the theistic, Christian, and ecclesial levels that continue to touch and heal and release ever-deepening levels of our person. Guides would do well to begin seeing the liturgy as a model not only for direction but for conversion and transformation as well.

37. See Charles Reagan and David Stewart, *The Philosophy of Paul Ricoeur* (Boston: Beacon Press, 1978), 241.

38. Merton spoke of being born of the Spirit, of the transformation of one's whole life. "It is not enough to remain the same 'self,' the same individual ego, with a new set of activities and a new lot of religious practices. One must be born of the Spirit, who is free, and who reaches the inmost depths of the heart by taking that heart to Himself, by making Himself one with our heart, by creating for us, invisibly, a new identity; by being Himself that identity"(*Loving and Living* [London: Sheldon Press, 1979], 200).

39. As Henri Nouwen says, we are all "wounded healers," and because suffering and helplessness and vulnerability are a necessary part of life, perhaps guides need most of all to learn to just stay with the suffering of the other without trying to solve it. Maybe that is what prayer has to teach us about a life lived in compassion.

Chapter 9: Belonging and Communion

1. For more on the autonomy-homonomy pattern of human organisms, see the first two chapters of Andras Angyal, *Neurosis and Treatment: A Holistic Theory* (New York: Viking, 1965).

2. In working with students from African, Asian, and European traditions, I have observed that even though all may adhere to the Christian faith tradition, they in no way share a common conviction about the importance of autonomy vs. belonging to a communal group. Cultural differences on this question come through clearly in class discussions as well as in written papers.

3. Some suggestions for further reading about compassion and community: Matthew Fox, *Compassion* (Minneapolis, Minn.: Winston Press, 1979); David Hassle, *Searching the Limits of Love* (Chicago: Loyola University Press, 1985); Remy Kwant, *Phenomenology of Social Existence* (Pittsburgh: Duquesne University Press, 1965); Donald McNeill, et al., *Compassion: A Reflection on Christian Life* (New York: Doubleday, 1983); Parker Palmer, *The Promise of Paradox* (Notre Dame: Ave Maria Press, 1980); Scott Peck, *The Different Drum* (New York: Simon and Schuster, 1987); Karl Rahner, *The Love of Jesus and the Love of Neighbor* (New York: Crossroad, 1983); Jean Vanier, *Community and Growth* (Toronto: Griffin House, 1979); and Stephen Verney, *Into the New Age* (London: Collins, 1976).

4. In speaking of Bernard Lonergan's approach to religious conversion, various commentators see it as growth in four levels of loving, starting with seeing God as a loving other person, then moving from perceiving God's loving presence to us now in the risen Christ through living in solidarity as a communal "we" or church, to having as one's overwhelming concern not one's own selfish aims, but the reign of God. A specifically Christian understanding of the already there others would include perceiving the entire tradition as a supportive communal web of interconnections that faith describes as the "body of Christ." Solidarity could be found in accepting the tradition as a valid source of directives for life, as a carrier of the best of the communal wisdom of Christian faith as it expresses itself socially in compassion and love.

5. Dietrich Bonhoeffer, *Life Together* (London: SCM Press, 1954).

6. Spiritual life vibrates to the heart's intentionality, which, in seeking satisfaction of the longing for homonomy, at the same time pursues harmony with its own uniqueness.

7. In order to avoid getting drawn into an alien project of life, the man or woman seeking like-minded others needs to be firmly aware of who he or she really is and of what he or she really wants out of life. Guidance will be helpful as long as a person has not arrived at the knowledge of self that is beyond the apparent or social self, at the degree of personal freedom that will allow the person to confront inevitable intra-group differences creatively without being tempted too strongly to use strategies of either fusion or withdrawal corresponding to their temperamental preferences.

8. See chap. 5, the section "False and Compulsive Types of Attachment."

9. In discussing the demands on time and energy made on us in young adulthood, Adrian van Kaam labelled them "intermediate wholes" because they mediate the energy of love (that aims at loving the Whole) in concrete and thus partial ways. Intermediate wholes almost always involve taking on some responsibility for others.

10. This perception of the communal nature of most commitments points also to the need to check out our private illuminations and commitment choices with other human beings. If this kind of "direction in common" could be a real possibility for more people, we would not need so much private direction, nor would there be such an orientation toward isolated self-sufficiency that currently seems to prevail even among people who want to live a life of faith. Some authors have approached this question of the communal nature of commitments in faith, including Walter Brueggeman, "Covenanting as a Human Vocation," in *Interpretation* 33, no. 2: 126; Margaret Farley, *Personal Commitments* (San Francisco: Harper & Row, 1986); Rosemary Haughton, *Act of Love*

(New York: J. B. Lippincott, 1968); Thomas Kelly, *A Testament of Devotion* (New York: Harper & Row, 1941); Sandra Schneiders, *New Wineskins* (New York: Paulist, 1986); and Laughlin Sofield and Carroll Juliano, *Collaborative Ministry* (Notre Dame: Ave Maria Press, 1987).

11. As we noted in chap. 2, shared faith and form traditions are ways for "inheriting names for the Mystery" as the meaning giving context for life. In our current society there is no substitute for learning to appraise one's thoughts and actions in the context of a life-giving shared tradition. Such a tradition could contextualize meaningful listening to reality (or obedience) for all members of a group or community.

12. Although drawn together in a context of faith, membership of such an intentional group may still range all the way from contract to covenant in the expectations of the members. In *Becoming Adult, Becoming Christian* (San Francisco: Harper & Row, 1984), James Fowler suggests the importance for group members of having a collective vision, a collective intentionality, deep emotions and convictions, a good number of the virtues (from 1 Cor. 13) required in communal living, and a discernment process that calls forth people's giftedness.

13. The unconscious evaluation process applying to membership in a group may focus on one's being or on one's performance, and it may emphasize either commitment to the public realm of concern for the reign of God, or the more private realm of personal strengths and community virtues. It helps someone seeking membership in a community to have some idea of how he or she will fit into this environment with these people by asking about these issues.

14. See Walter Brueggeman, "Covenanting as Human Vocation" in *Interpretation* 33, no. 2: 126.

15. In distinguishing between motivations centered in destiny and those centered in vocation or call, James Fowler, *Becoming Adult, Becoming Christian*, comments, "There is likely no area of potential self-knowledge where we are more subject to self-deception and more tempted to resort to self-serving rationalization than in accounting for our efforts to influence and determine the social collectivities of which we are a part and lives of those involved in them. Likewise, there are few areas in which it matters more to us that we create a good impression on others than regarding the motives for our claims for special privilege, for unusual institutional or moral leeway, or for their respect" (109). If this statement is true, then questions must be asked about the social dimension of our presence, as well as about the communal nature of our commitments.

16. See Margaret Farley, *Personal Commitments* (San Francisco: Harper & Row, 1986), 40.

17. See chap. 7, n. 25, for references dealing with all stages of this early Christian formation program. The intentions of the catechumens were challenged by the meanings of Christ. Their motivations were confronted by the priorities of God within the course of a radical interior revolution involving the major choices and directions of their lives.

18. The writer is possibly David Knight, author of *Cloud by Day, Fire by Night* (Denville, N.J.: Dimension Books, 1985).

19. Ibid.

20. In *Teach Us to Pray* (London: Darton, Longman and Todd, 1974), André Louf says that in spiritual direction, the Tradition reaches its culminating point, becoming once again an existential process of handing on (41). He claims that the spiritual guide forms a living bond with the faith and form tradition and it is the responsibility of the spiritual father or mother, member of the living band of brothers and sisters born of the same Word, to form a living bond with the faith and form tradition by handing it on to others.

21. Ibid., 41. Throughout this prayerful book, Louf speaks of the Word as it touches the heart, especially in the communal celebration of the liturgy, when the vision it reveals is handed on from one person to the next.

22. Walter Conn, *Christian Conversion* (New York: Paulist, 1986), 125.

23. We come to the liturgy as members of a worldwide body for whom the basic pattern of readings, homily, intercessions, and Eucharist can be a truly objective form of life direction. The liturgy incorporates various external standards above and beyond the passing whims of the congregation. It thus extends beyond the personal devotional style of any one individual, preserving what Gabriel Braso, *Liturgy and Spirituality* (Collegeville, Minn.: Liturgical Press, 1971) calls the objective, ontological, collective elements that support the communitarian and ecclesial character of the divine economy of salvation (232). It is in the liturgy that the Source of living water unites the participants in the supernatural solidarity of the "communion of saints," as liturgical prayer points us beyond ourselves to the contemplation of God and the corporate goal of the eschaton. Writers like Romano Guardini, *The Lord* (Chicago: Regnery, 1954); André Louf, *Teach Us to Pray*; Adrian Nocent, *The Liturgical Year*, 4 vols. (Collegeville, Minn.: The Liturgical Press, 1977) and Hans urs von Balthasar, *Prayer* (New York: Sheed and Ward, 1961) concur in seeing liturgical prayer as a way of handing on the Christian vision of faith.

24. All people have agreed upon rituals for celebrating key events like birth and death, marriage and ordination to priesthood, communal anniversaries and commemorations of various kinds. Often the people involved do not have enough instruction to really understand much of what is going on. Nevertheless, through the effective symbolism of the ritual, whether it be the Fourth of July, a fiftieth wedding anniversary, the Easter vigil, or a burial service, the gathered community is made aware through symbols, speeches, and gestures, of the lived aspects of wisdom handed down from previous generations. The rites of baptismal initiation that incorporate new members into the Christian faith, for example, are suffused with meanings that can unite those who share the vision of reality these rites symbolize. See chap. 2, which explains how one's sense of the Mystery offers an interpretive frame for the life experiences of an individual or a group.

25. See chap. 8 on conversion as necessarily involving a shift from "I" to "we." The liturgical life of the church is thus a communal and an ecclesial model for spiritual direction. At this point, although it seems to have been obscured by the one-to-one model, there are signs that the resurgence of participation by entire parishes in the Rite of Christian Initiation of Adults plus the dearth of competent directors is once again bringing the more communal liturgical model of direction to the fore.

26. In his *In Search of Maturity* (New York: Scribner's, 1943), psychologist Fritz Kunkel describes what he calls the "we-experience." See also Mary Jo Leddy, *Reweaving Religious Life* (Mystic, Conn.: Twenty-Third Publications, 1990). Sociologically speaking, it is the rare community that does not founder in its action or service to the human community at a certain point because of not being clear about what "we want."

27. Although not necessarily writing from a communal perspective, in chap. 5 of *Personal Commitments*, Margaret Farley speaks most helpfully of the conditions for remaining connected with, present to, the objects of our committed love. In doing so she points to the intuitive knowledge spiritual guides have of the necessity of plumbing the heart's intentionality in the midst of its communal commitments.

28. Ibid., 62.

29. In n. 1 of the introductory chapter, "Looking for Connections," as well as in its final section "Encountering 'otherness'," I have referred to the Sufi legend that gives us a guiding image for the spiritual guide as a "wise fish." At the risk of projecting even more meaning into that simple story, I have ventured to build further on that image, both here and chap. 7, "On Being a Wise Fish."

30. See chap. 1, "Waking Up to Freedom and Wholeness," the section entitled "How We Co-form Our Experience," for a reminder about how this approach to the task of spiritual guidance relies on a lived understanding of the dialogue "between" the person and the person's life field or world. So, for example, for the guide who works in a socio-economic and cultural situation where the outer reality seems at times almost totally devoid of spiritual awareness in the deepest sense, the inner lived meaning of that universally depressing situation varies according to the interior meanings alive in each unique and individual heart.

31. Sometimes the psychological techniques and labelling offered in the name of spiritual guidance these days actually make this problem worse.

32. See the remarks about the Type-A personality and our "second body" in chap. 3 the section "The Challenge of Openness to One's Whole Context," as well as n. 29.

33. See chap. 3, the section "When Life Patterns Break Up," and notes 20 and 21 for reference to dissipative structures.

Chapter 10: Vocation: Finding The Work Of Love

1. From an article entitled "Covenanting as Human Vocation," in *Interpretation* 33, no. 2: 115–129.

2. Among the many volumes one might choose as references for developing vocational commitments, the following have been found helpful: Donal Dorr, *Spirituality and Justice* (Maryknoll, N.Y.: Orbis, 1984); Katherine Dyckman and Patrick Carroll, *Inviting the Mystic, Supporting the Prophet* (New York: Paulist, 1981); James Dunning, *Sharing God's Gifts* (Winona, Minn.: Saint Mary's Press, 1982); John Haughey, *Converting 9 to 5: A Spirituality of Daily Work* (New York: Crossroad, 1989); Kenneth Leech, *Spirituality and Pastoral Care* (Cambridge, Mass.: Cowley Publications, 1989); Karl Rahner, *Christian at the Crossroads* (New York: Seabury, 1975); and James and Evelyn Whitehead, *Method in Ministry* (New York: Seabury, 1981); and *The Emerging Laity: Returning Leadership to the Community of Faith* (New York: Doubleday, 1986).

3. *Becoming Adult, Becoming Christian* (San Francisco: Harper & Row, 1984).

4. The guide may find some of the following helpful: Jesse Bernard, *The Future of Marriage* (New York: World Books, 1972); Stephanie Covington and Liana Beckett, *Leaving the Enchanted Forest* (San Francisco: Harper & Row, 1988); Rosemary Haughton, "The Meaning of Marriage in Women's New Consciousness," in William Roberts ed., *Commitment to Partnership* (New York: Paulist, 1987); Chuck Gallagher, *The Marriage Encounter* (New York: Doubleday, 1975); Andrew Greeley, *The Young Catholic Family* (Chicago: Thomas More Press, 1980); Bernard Haring, *Marriage in the Modern World* (New York: Newman Press, 1965); Thomas Hart, *Living Happily Ever After* (New York: Paulist, 1979); Rosemary Haughton, *The Theology of Marriage* (New York: Fides, 1977); Walter Kasper, *Theology of Christian Marriage* (New York: Seabury, 1980); Kenneth Kenniston, *All Our Children* (New York: Harcourt, Brace, Jovanovich, 1977); Lillian Rubin, *Women of a Certain Age* (New York: Harper & Row, 1979); and *Intimate Strangers* (New York: Harper & Row, 1983); Edward Schillebeeckx, *Marriage* (New York: Sheed and Ward, 1965); Virginia Tufte and Barbara Myerhoff, eds., *Changing Images of the Family* (New Haven, Conn.: Yale University Press, 1979); and James and Evelyn Whitehead, *Marrying Well* (New York: Doubleday, 1983).

5. *Converting 9 to 5* (New York: Crossroad, 1989), 127.

6. See the description of that dynamic in the last section of chap. 2, entitled "Joy in the Mystery."

7. It is also a fact that most people do not seem to be doing the work they want to do or can do best. Forced usually by economic circumstances, they hate the way they spend their "9 to 5" hours each day, and frequently are not able to achieve anything close to their heart's desire. For such people, coming to self-knowledge through an appraisal of attractive commitments that carry value for them in their work does not seem possible or even desirable. In the upcoming section entitled "Work: Source of Self-knowledge and Pain" some of the problems emerging from an uncongenial and incompatible work will be considered.

8. See J. D. Salinger, *Franny and Zooey* (New York: Bantam, 1955).

9. Ibid., 201–2.

10. In chap. 2 of *Spirituality and Human Emotion* (Grand Rapids: Eerdmans, 1982), Robert Roberts mentions a variegated list of people's specific interests, concerns, and

preoccupations that may or may not indicate where their emotional passions are to be found.

11. See chap. 1, n. 23. On this question of the spiritual dimension of one's work, it may be helpful to add Adrian van Kaam's *On Being Involved: The Rhythm of Involvement and Detachment in Daily Life* (Denville, N.J.: Dimension Books, 1970), and Evelyn and James Whitehead's *Seasons of Strength* (New York: Doubleday, 1986), to the list begun in n. 2 of this chapter.

12. A few more suggestions of books on the topic of work: Martin Helldorfer, *The Work Trap* (Whitinsville, Mass.: Affirmation Books, 1983); Oscar Lewis, *Five Families* (New York: New American Library, 1959); Gabriel Marcel, *Man Against Mass Society* (Chicago: Regnery, 1965); Lillian Rubin, *Worlds of Pain* (New York: Basic Books, 1976); and Studs Terkel, *Working* (New York: Pantheon, 1974).

13. Guides familiar with the RCIA plan of formation will recognize that the time in the liturgical year called the *mystagogia* is patterned to deal directly with the newly baptized person's appraisal of how he or she will live and act as a member of the Christian community. The neophyte will be introduced over the course of the seven weeks leading to Pentecost to the various forms of work or ministry that exist in that particular community. Appraisal of how one may be called to serve in the parish or wider society can be guided not only by the newly acquired self-knowledge of one's wants and desires but also by a fresh perception of the needs of neighbors who, in this new horizon, evoke their committed love.

14. See Sidney Callahan, *With All Our Heart and Mind: The Spiritual Works of Mercy in a Psychological Age* (New York: Crossroad, 1988), 21.

15. Here again we come up against the need for a deep spiritual understanding of the faith story that is the context for the lives of both guide and person seeking guidance. For Christians, this means that the guide at least must have a loving and sympathetic grasp of the major mysteries of the Christian Story of Salvation in and through God's revealing self-communication in Christ. Otherwise, it maybe difficult for the guide to get his or her own small plan for them out of the way so that they may freely live and act in harmony with the larger plan that contains the design of God's heart for them. See also chap. 2 for more on the relation between spiritual guidance and faith tradition.

16. Lives that lack such direction are experienced as meaningless, absurd, lacking in direction. Ignatius of Loyola points to this inner awareness of meaningful direction when he speaks of the possibility of living in "indifference" to small disappointments once one's transcendent destiny has been disclosed.

17. See chap. 3, section titled "Two Dimensions of Human Willing" for the difference between primary and secondary willing.

18. See T. S. Eliot, *Murder in the Cathedral* (New York: Harcourt, Brace and World, 1963). The question of the ambiguity of motivation becomes even more complex in cases where people confuse their own personal and confused impulses with the voice of God, but these and other more complex issues cannot be treated here.

19. It is also possible, of course, to say no and to find oneself resisting the call of the Mystery and feeling more isolated and alone than ever before.

20. See Wallace Stevens's poem "The Man with the Blue Guitar."

21. By "irresistible" we refer to the fact that through revelation we are aware that not only human beings, but all of creation is being drawn in a spiritual direction that has but one term — God. In their study of the critical thresholds and stages of adult spiritual genesis in *The Spiritual Journey* (Wilmington, Del.: Michael Glazier, 1987), Francis Nemeck and Maria Coombs draw on the visions of St. Paul, Pierre Teilhard de Chardin, and St. John of the Cross for their account of spiritual genesis and its different stages of diminishment and growth until a natural and spiritual apex is reached in personal death.

22. Ibid. In their work, as in the writing of spiritual leaders like John of the Cross and Teresa of Avila, these authors go further along the route of the spiritual journey.

They move beyond personal conversion to the classic stages of spiritual espousal and spiritual marriage that are beyond the scope of this book.

23. David Steindl-Rast, *Gratefulness, the Heart of Prayer* (New York: Paulist, 1984), 34–35. Suggestions for guides and others interested in connecting with the Source: Ruth Burrows, *Guidelines for Mystical Prayer* (Denville, N.J.: Dimension Books, 1980); Jean Corbon, *The Wellspring of Worship* (New York: Paulist, 1980); Jean Pierre de Caussade, *Abandonment to Divine Providence* (New York: Doubleday, 1975); Michael Crosby, *Spirituality of the Beatitudes* (Maryknoll, N.Y.: Orbis, 1982); Thomas Green, *Opening to God* (Metro Manila: St. Paul Publications, 1971); John Main, *Word into Silence* (New York: Paulist, 1980); Yves Raguin, *Attention to the Mystery* (New York: Paulist, 1979); Alexis Riaud, *The Holy Spirit Acting in Our Souls* (New York: Alba House, 1978); Dietrich von Hildebrand, *Transformation in Christ* (Baltimore: Helicon Press, 1960); Hans urs von Balthasar, *Prayer* (San Francisco: Ignatius Press, 1986); and Adrian van Kaam and Susan Muto, *Practicing the Prayer of Presence* (Denville, N.J.: Dimension Books, 1980).

Chapter 11: Guidelines for Appraisal

1. Derived from the Latin *ad + pretium* (to + price), to "appraise" means to evaluate or (literally) set a price on some aspect of reality, some person, event, or thing, some choice or action, usually in the light of a meaning-giving transcendent context. Appraisal is above all a spiritual capacity of the whole person, revealing the current inner dispositions of his or her responsible heart. Much has been written about this spiritual capacity in the Christian tradition, including the following: Piet Penning De Vries, *Discernment of Spirits* (New York: Exposition Press, 1973); Lewis Delmage, *The Spiritual Exercises of St. Ignatius of Loyola* (Hawthorne, N.J.: Joseph F. Wagner, 1968); Thomas Dubay, *Authenticity: A Biblical Theology of Discernment* (Denville, N.J.: Dimension Books, 1977); Thomas Green, *Weeds among the Wheat* (Notre Dame: Ave Maria Press, 1984), and *A Vacation with the Lord* (Notre Dame: Ave Maria Press, 1986); Jacques Guillet et al., *Discernment of Spirits* (Collegeville, Minn.: Liturgical Press, 1970); Ignatius of Loyola, *Modern Spiritual Exercises* (New York: Doubleday, 1978); Morton Kelsey, *Discernment* (New York: Paulist, 1978); Ernest Larkin, *Silent Presence* (Denville, N.J.: Dimension Books, 1981); and Adrian van Kaam in whose series on *Formative Spirituality* (New York: Crossroad, 1983–88) the word "appraisal" is used almost exclusively to indicate this human spiritual capacity.

2. In 1 Corinthians 2, Paul speaks of a "certain wisdom" that he experiences among those who are spiritually mature. He locates this wisdom as being hidden from all ages in the plan of God. It is the Holy Spirit and not mere human intelligence that is able to understand or discern this hidden teaching that must be "appraised in a spiritual way" by those who have "the mind of Christ."

3. See Carolyn Gratton, *Trusting: Theory and Practice* (New York: Crossroad, 1982), 219. Part 4 of this book, "Trust and the Christian Mystery," reiterates many of the more empirical themes of the research in terms of their contextualization by the Christian faith and the way its ever-spiralling effect is mirrored in the church's liturgical cycle.

4. See n. 1 for a few of the many volumes dedicated particularly to the study of discernment in the writings of these masters of spiritual living.

5. Gerard Egan, *The Skilled Helper* (Monterey, Calif.: Brooks/Cole, 1986), is a helpful text that could profitably be read by most spiritual guides. It does not, however, purport to be a text for spiritual guides. Rather it deals with helping clients from a problem-management model, a cognitive-behavioral approach to counseling and psychotherapy whose focus is human problem solving rather than attempting to co-listen with another for the presence and action of the Mystery in their lives.

6. In chap. 5 of his *Human Formation* (New York: Crossroad, 1985), Adrian van Kaam sets forth guidelines for appraisal, including the following eight criteria: open-

ness, appreciation, congeniality, compatibility, compassion, joyousness, competence, and effectiveness (67).

7. See chap. 4, the section "How Our Minds Deal with What Happens," for the difference between functional and transcendent mind.

8. Both Eugene Bianchi, author of *Aging as Spiritual Journey* (New York: Crossroad, 1986), and Paul Tournier, author of *Learn and Grow Old* (New York: Harper and Row, 1983), would dispute this last judgment on old age. It is precisely in circumstances like old age that the Gospel offers a liberating perspective on cultural appraisals.

9. We have moved here to an explicit awareness of the presence of a Holy Otherness in her life as well as in mine. A more technical way of expressing this new level of discourse would be to say that we have moved from pre-presence to presence to the sacred horizon or Ground of both our lives. We have moved from the contract of spiritual counseling to the contract of spiritual guidance or direction.

10. See chap. 2, the section "Traditions in Today's Pluralistic Context," for reference to these ways of facilitating openness toward the Mystery on all dimensions and in the entire surrounding field of the human heart.

11. See Adrian van Kaam, *Fundamental Formation* (New York: Crossroad, 1983), 264–65.

12. In Isaiah 55:8 we find the words:
> For my thoughts are not your thoughts,
> Nor are your ways my ways, says the Lord.

13. At this level of appraisal, Shellie may also begin to understand that there is something radically wrong with the situation itself, especially where she is concerned, and she may leave or decide she is called to put effort into changing it as well as herself.

14. See chap. 3, the section "Formative and Transformative Change."

15. Jean Pierre de Caussade, *Abandonment to Divine Providence* (Exeter: Catholic Records Press, 1921), 71.

16. The point here is that one of the aims of the guides is to foster self-direction so that people who come will soon be able to do without them. They will have worked themselves out of a job.

17. For example, Shellie might be taken by a friend to visit a L'Arche home. She would meet there a small enthusiastic group, some of them near her own age, sharing their lives in a family-style residence with an equal or larger number of mentally handicapped persons. Everyone in the residence shares meals, work, celebrations, prayer, and personal care of each other. It is hard work. There is not much private space. There is not much money around. Some of the handicapped people cannot speak or cannot feed themselves. But there is a wonderful spirit.

18. Recall how the questions emerging from life itself provided the "starting points for direction" in chap. 1.

19. For example, if Shellie is a New Yorker who has always had a high standard of living and who has acquired some pretty rooted habits from her wealthy environment, maybe her choice of the L'Arche community might be unrealistic, a too exalted choice that is not compatible with her real-life circumstances.

20. The choice here could be living in a L'Arche community or it could involve choosing a life of celibate commitment or of committing oneself to another in marriage.

21. Although not formally functioning as confessors, Christian guides might ask themselves why more good fruits of the Spirit are not being produced in the lives of the people they are guiding. Questions of sin and judgment are outside the scope of these considerations, but guides must be aware that each person lives out of a unique sinful profile that may be cutting him or her off from the flow of divine energy in and throughout their life fields. Certainly Christian appraisal tends to disclose the blocks to grace in a person's life.

22. See chap. 3, n. 16, for references regarding the second half of life. See also chap. 3, "The Classic Crisis: Mid-Life Transition"; chap. 5, "Processing a Critical Point";

chap. 6, "Moving Towards Reassessment and Handing On," and chap. 8, "Dynamics of Detachment and Second Conversion."

23. See Adrian van Kaam, *Dynamics of Spiritual Self Direction* (Denville, N.J.: Dimension Books, 1976), 209, where he describes emergence by transcendent participation. Quotations that follow are from p. 209. Van Kaam notes that "... for the Christian today who wants to live a spiritual life, it is more necessary than ever to learn the art of effective spiritual self direction" (224).

24. See suggestions in chap. 6, "Relaxing and Letting Go"; chap. 7, "The Shift to a More Meditative Style"; chap. 8, "Prayer Guidance for a New Stage in Life"; and chap. 10, "Connecting with the Source."

25. See William Johnston, *The Inner Eye of Love* (San Francisco: Harper & Row, 1982), chap. 18, "Mysticism in Action." Ignatius of Loyola and John of the Cross both saw appraisal as central to the mystical life, the former intent on tracing the origin of intentionality and feelings appraised as from the spirit of evil or the spirit of love, the latter claiming that the living flame of love that obscurely sensed the Spirit's presence in the midst of conflict and suffering would also tell us what to do in daily life.

26. For books already noted on contemplation and prayer, the reader is referred to chap. 4, n. 24, chap. 7, n. 38, and chap. 8, n. 27 and 29.

27. See Gerald May, *Will and Spirit* (San Francisco: Harper & Row, 1982), 315.

28. See the Appendix for a summary of how the elements of appraisal are spelled out in each chapter of this book.

29. Jean-Pierre de Caussade, *Abandonment to Divine Providence, Abandonment to Divine Providence*, 5.

BIBLIOGRAPHY

Abhishiktananda. *Prayer*. London: SPCK, 1967 (1972).

Achebe, Chinua. *Things Fall Apart*. London: Heinemann Educational Books, 1958.

Aelred of Rievaulx. *On Spiritual Friendship*. Washington, D.C.: Consortium Press, 1974.

Angyal, Andras. *Neurosis and Treatment: A Holistic Theory*. New York: Viking, 1965.

Anonymous. *The Cloud of Unknowing*. New York: Doubleday, 1973.

Ardell, Donald B. *High Level Wellness an Alternative to Doctors, Drugs and Disease*. Emmaus, Pa.: Rodale Press, 1977.

Aschenbrenner, George A. *A God for a Dark Journey*. Denville, N.J.: Dimension Books, 1984.

Assagioli, Roberto. *Psychosynthesis*. New York: Viking, 1965.

——. *The Act of Will*. Harmondsworth, Eng.: Penguin, 1973.

Augsburger, David. *Caring Enough to Hear and Be Heard*. Scottdale, Pa.: Herald Press, 1982.

Augustine, St. *Confessions*. New York: Doubleday, 1960.

Aumann, Jordan. *Christian Spirituality in the Catholic Tradition*. San Francisco: Ignatius Press, 1986.

Baars, Conrad W. *Feeling and Healing Your Emotions*. Plainfield, N.J.: Logos, 1970.

Baird-Smith, Robin. *Living Water: An Anthology of Letters of Direction*. London: Fount, 1987.

Bandler, Richard and John Grinder. *Frogs into Princes*. Moab, Utah: Real People Press, 1979.

Barry, William A., and William J. Connolly. *The Practice of Spiritual Direction*. New York: Seabury, 1982.

Barton, Anthony. *Three Worlds of Therapy*. Palo Alto, Calif.: National Press Books, 1974.

Becker, E. *The Denial of Death*. New York: Free Press, 1973.

Beesing, Maria et al. *The Enneagram*. Denville, N.J.: Dimension Books, 1984.

Belenky, Mary Field, et al. *Women's Ways of Knowing. The Development of Self, Voice and Mind*. New York: Basic Books, 1986.

Bellah, Robert. *The Broken Covenant*. New York: Seabury, 1975.

Bellah, Robert et al. *Habits of the Heart: Individualism and Commitment in American Life*. Los Angeles: University of California Press, 1985.

——. *Individualism and Commitment in American Life*. San Francisco: Harper & Row, 1987.

Benson, H. *The Relaxation Response*. New York: Avon, 1975.

Berg, Richard R., and Christine McCartney. *Depression and the Integrated Life*. New York: Alba House, 1981.

Berger, Peter L., and Thomas Luckman. *The Social Construction of Reality*. New York: Doubleday, 1966.

Berman, Morris. *The Reenchantment of the World*. Ithaca: Cornell University Press, 1981.

Bernard, Jesse. *The Future of Marriage*. New York: World Books, 1972.

Berry, Thomas. *The New Story*. Chambersburg, Pa.: Anima Publications, 1978.

————. *Dream of the Earth*. Nature and Natural Philosophy Library, 1988.

Bettelheim, Bruno. *The Uses of Enchantment*. New York: Knopf, 1976.

Bianchi, Eugene. *Aging as a Spiritual Journey*. New York: Crossroad, 1986.

Bibby, Reginald W. *Fragmented Gods*. Toronto: Irwin, 1987.

Blofeld, John. *I Ching: The Book of Change*. London: Unwin, 1976.

Boelen, Bernard. *Personal Maturity*. New York: Seabury, 1978.

Bolen, Jean Shimoda. *The Tao of Psychology: Synchronicity and the Self*. San Francisco: Harper & Row, 1982.

Bonhoeffer, Dietrich. *Life Together*. London: SCM Press, 1956.

Boulding, Maria. *The Coming of God*. Collegeville, Minn.: Liturgical Press, 1982.

Bouyer, Louis. *Introduction to Spirituality*. New York: Desclee, 1961.

————. *A History of Christian Spirituality*. 3 vols. New York: Seabury, 1969.

Bowen, Murray. *Family Therapy and Clinical Practice*. New York: Jason Aronson, 1978.

Bowers, Margaretta. *Conflicts of the Clergy: A Psychodynamic Study with Case Histories*. New York: Nelson, 1963.

Bradbury, Ray. *Dandelion Wine*. New York: Bantam, 1959.

Bradshaw, John. *Bradshaw on: The Family*. Deerfield Beach, Fla.: Health Communications Inc., 1988.

Braiker, Harriet B. *The Type E Woman; How to Overcome the Stress of Being Everything to Everybody*. New York: Dodd, Mead, 1986.

Brandon, David. *Zen in the Art of Helping*. London: Routledge and Kegan Paul, 1976.

Braso, Gabriel. *Liturgy and Spirituality*. Collegeville, Minn.: Liturgical Press, 1988.

Brennan, Anne, and Janice Brewi. *Mid-Life Directions: Praying and Playing Sources of New Dynamism*. New York: Paulist, 1985.

Bro, Bernard. *The Little Way*. London: Darton, Longman and Todd, 1979.

Bruche, Hilde. *Learning Psychotherapy: Rationale and Ground Rules*. Cambridge, Mass.: Harvard University Press, 1974.

Brueggeman, Walter. "Covenanting as a Human Vocation," in *Interpretation* 33, no. 2: 126.

Bryant, M. Carrol, and Frank Flynn, eds. *Interreligious Dialogue*. New York: Paragon House, 1989.

Buber, Martin. *I and Thou*. New York: Charles Scribner's, 1970.

Buechner, Frederick. *Wishful Thinking*. San Francisco: Harper & Row, 1973.

Burns, David D. *Feeling Good*. New York: New American Library, 1980.

Burrows, Ruth. *Guidelines for Mystical Prayer*. Denville, N.J.: Dimension Books, 1980.

————. *Fire upon the Earth*. Denville, N.J.: Dimension Books, 1981.

————. *Ascent to Love: The Spiritual Teachings of St. John of the Cross*. London: Darton, Longman and Todd, 1987.

Callahan, Sidney. *With All Our Heart and Mind: The Spiritual Works of Mercy in a Psychological Age*. New York: Crossroad, 1988.

Cameli, Louis John. *Stories of Paradise: Classical and Modern Autobiographies of Faith*. New York: Paulist, 1978.

Campbell, Joseph. *The Power of Myth*. New York: Doubleday, 1988.

Campbell, Peter A., and Edwin M. McMahon. *Bio-Spirituality: Focusing as a Way to Grow*. Chicago: Loyola University Press, 1985.

Capra, Fritjof. *The Tao of Physics: An Exploration of the Parallels between Modern Physics and Eastern Mysticism*. New York: Bantam, 1977.

————. *The Turning Point: Science, Society and the Rising Culture*. New York: Bantam, 1982.

Cargas, Harry J., and Roger J. Radley. *Keeping a Spiritual Journal*. New York: Doubleday, 1981.

Carmody, Denise Lardner, and John Carmody. *Religion: The Great Questions*. New York: Seabury, 1983.

Carnell, Corbin Scott. *Bright Shadow of Reality: C. S. Lewis and the Feeling Intellect*. Grand Rapids: Eerdmans, 1974.

Carrington, P. *Freedom in Meditation*. New York: Doubleday, 1978.

Carroll, L. Patrick and Katherine M. Dyckman. *Chaos or Creation: Spirituality in Mid-Life*. New York: Paulist, 1986.

Chicago Studies. *Spiritual Life Handbook*, 1976.

――――. *Christian Symbols and Human Experience* 19, no. 1 (Spring 1980).

Christ, Carol P. *Diving Deep and Surfacing*. 2d ed. Boston: Beacon Press, 1986.

Christian Initiation of Adults. Washington, D.C.: U.S. Catholic Conference, 1988.

Cobb, John B. *The Structure of Christian Existence*. New York: Seabury, 1979.

Congar, Yves M. *Tradition and Traditions*. London: Burns and Oates, 1966.

Conn, Joann Wolski. *Women's Spirituality: Resources for Christian Development*. New York: Paulist, 1986.

――――. *Spirituality and Personal Maturity*. New York: Paulist, 1989.

Conn, Walter. *Christian Conversion*. New York: Paulist, 1986.

The Counseling Psychologist. *The Relationship in Counseling and Psychotherapy*. 13, no. 2 (April 1985).

Corbon, Jean. *The Wellspring of Worship*. New York: Paulist, 1980.

Cousins, Norman. *Anatomy of an Illness*. New York: W. W. Norton, 1979.

――――. *The Healing Heart*. New York: Avon, 1984.

Crosby, Michael H. *Spirituality of the Beatitudes: Matthew's Challenge for First World Christians*. Maryknoll, N.Y.: Orbis, 1982.

Culligan, Kevin G. *Saint John of the Cross and Spiritual Direction*. Dublin: Carmelite Centre of Spirituality, 1983.

――――. *Spiritual Direction: Contemporary Readings*. Covent Valley, N.Y.: Living Flame Press, 1983.

Cummings, Charles. *The Mystery of the Ordinary*. San Francisco: Harper & Row, 1982.

Davis, Charles. *Body as Spirit: The Nature of Religious Feeling*. New York: Seabury, 1976.

de Castillejo, Irene Claremont. *Knowing Woman*. New York: Harper & Row, 1973.

de Caussade, J. P. *Abandonment to Divine Providence*. Exeter: Catholic Records Press, 1921; New York: Doubleday (Image), 1975.

de Chardin, Pierre Teilhard. *The Divine Milieu*. New York: Harper, 1960.

Delmage, Lewis. *The Spiritual Exercises of St. Ignatius of Loyola*. Hawthorne, N.J.: Joseph F. Wagner, 1968.

de Sales, St. Francis. *Treatise on the Love of God*. New York; Doubleday, 1963.

de Mello, Anthony. *Sadhana: A Way to God*. New York: Image Books, 1984.

de Vries, Piet Penning. *Discernment of Spirits*. New York: Exposition Press, 1973.

Dillard, Annie. *Pilgrim at Tinker Creek*. New York: Bantam, 1975.

"Direction spirituelle," in *Dictionnaire de Spiritualité*. Beauchesne, 1957, pp. 1002-1214.

Dorr, Donal. *Spirituality and Justice*. Maryknoll, N.Y.: Orbis, 1984.

Dorsey, Larry. *Space, Time and Medicine*. Boulder, Colo.: Shambhala, 1982.

Dubay, Thomas. *Authenticity: A Biblical Theology of Discernment*. Denville, N.J.: Dimension Books, 1977.

――――. *Fire Within*. San Francisco: Ignatius Press, 1989.

Duffy, Regis. *On Becoming a Catholic; A Challenge of Christian Initiation*. San Francisco: Harper & Row. 1984.

Dufour, Leon. *Dictionary of Biblical Theology*. New York: Seabury Press, 1973.

Duggan, Robert, ed. *Conversion and the Catechumenate*. New York: Paulist, 1984.

Dumm, Demetrius. *Flowers in the Desert*. New York: Paulist, 1987.

Dunne, J. *A Search for God in Time and Memory*. London: Macmillan, 1967.

Dunne, Tad. *Lonergan and Spirituality*. Chicago: Loyola University Press, 1985.

Dunning, James B. *New Wine, New Wineskins*. New York: Sadlier, n.d.

――――. *Sharing God's Gifts*. Winona, Minn.: Saint Mary's Press, 1982.

Dyckman, Katherine Marie, and L. Patrick Carroll. *Inviting the Mystic, Supporting the Prophet*. New York: Paulist, 1981.

Ebon, Martin. *The Relaxation Controversy: Can You Have Relaxation without Meditation*. New York: New American Library, 1976.

Edwards, Dennis. *The Human Experience of God*. New York: Paulist, 1984.

Edwards, Tilden. *Living Simply through the Day*. New York: Paulist, 1977.

——. *Spiritual Friend*. New York: Paulist, 1980.

Egan, Gerard. *The Skilled Helper*. Belmont, Calif.: Brooks/Cole, 1986.

Egoff, Sheila, et al., eds. *Only Connect*. Toronto: Oxford University Press, 1980.

Eliade, Mircea, and David Tracy, eds. *What Is Religion?* New York: Seabury, 1980.

Ellis, Albert. *Reason and Emotion in Psychotherapy*. New York: Lyle Stuart, 1962.

Ellwood, Robert S. *Many Peoples, Many Faiths: An Introduction to the Religious Life of Mankind*. Englewood Cliffs, N.J.: Prentice-Hall, 1976.

English, John. *Spiritual Freedom*. Guelph, Ontario: Loyola House, 1975.

——. *Choosing Life: Significance of Personal History in Decision-Making*. New York: Paulist, 1978.

Erikson, Erik H. *Identity, Youth and Crisis*. New York: W. W. Norton, 1968.

Erikson, Erik H., ed. *Adulthood*. New York: W. W. Norton, 1978.

Fairlie, H. *The Seven Deadly Sins Today*. Washington, D.C.: New Republic Books, 1978.

Farber, Leslie. *The Ways of the Will*. New York: Basic Books, 1966.

——. *Lying, Despair, Jealousy, Envy, Sex, Suicide, Drugs, and the Good Life*. New York: Basic Books, 1976.

Faricy, Robert. *The Spirituality of Teilhard de Chardin*. Minneapolis: Winston Press, 1981.

Farley, Margaret. *Personal Commitments*. San Francisco: Harper & Row, 1986.

Ferguson, Marilyn. *The Aquarian Conspiracy*. Los Angeles: J. P. Tarcher, 1980.

Fenhagen, James C. *Invitation to Holiness*. San Francisco: Harper & Row, 1985.

Ferman, Louis B., ed. *Effective Psychotherapy: The Contribution of Hellmuth Kaiser*. New York: Free Press, 1965.

Fiorenza, Elizabeth Schüssler. *In Memory of Her*. New York: Crossroad, 1983.

Fischer, Constance T. *Individualizing Psychological Assessment*. Monterey, Calif.: Brooks, Cole, 1985.

Fischer, Kathleen R. *The Inner Rainbow: The Imagination in Christian Life*. New York: Paulist, 1983.

——. *Reclaiming the Connections*. Kansas City: Sheed and Ward, 1990.

Fleming, David A., ed. *The Fire and the Cloud*. New York: Paulist, 1978.

Foster, Richard J. *Celebration of Discipline*. San Francisco: Harper & Row, 1978.

Fowler, James W. *Stages of Faith: The Psychology of Human Development and the Quest for Meaning*. New York: Harper & Row, 1981.

——. *Becoming Adult, Becoming Christian*. New York: Harper & Row, 1984.

Fox, M. *A Spirituality Named Compassion*. Minneapolis: Winston Press, 1979.

——. *Breakthrough: The Creation Centered Spirituality of Meister Eckhart*. New York: Doubleday, 1980.

Freeman, Lawrence. *Light Within*. London: Darton, Longman and Todd, 1986.

Fremantle, Anne, ed. *The Protestant Mystics: An Anthology of Spiritual Experience*. New York: New American Library, 1964.

Freudenberger, H. *Burnout: The High Cost of High Achievement*. New York: Doubleday, 1980.

Friedman, Meyer, and Ray H. Rosenman. *Type A Behavior and Your Heart*. New York: Knopf, 1974.

Gabriel, F. *The Spiritual Director: According to Principles of St. John of the Cross*. Westminster, Md.: Newman, 1951.

Gannon, Thomas H., and George W. Traub. *The Desert and the City*. New York: Macmillan, 1969.

Gendlin, Eugene. *Focusing*. New York: Bantam, 1981.

Gerkin, Charles V. *The Living Human Document: Revisioning Pastoral Counseling in a Hermeneutical Mode*. Nashville: Abingdon, 1984.

Gilligan, Carol. *In a Different Voice: Psychological Theory and Women's Development*. Cambridge, Mass.: Harvard University Press, 1982.

Goethals, Gregor. *The TV Ritual*. Boston: Beacon Press, 1981.

Goldstein, Joseph. *The Experience of Insight*. London: Shambhala, 1983.

Gorsuch, John. *Invitation to the Spiritual Journey*. New York: Paulist, 1990.

Gould, Roger L. *Transformations: Growth and Change in Adult Life*. New York: Simon and Schuster, 1978.

Graf von Durckheim, Karlfried. *Daily Life as Spiritual Exercise: The Way of Transformation*. New York: Harper & Row, 1971.

————. *The Call for the Master*. New York: E. P. Dutton, 1989.

Grant, Harold W. et al. *From Image to Likeness*. New York: Paulist, 1983.

Gratton, Carolyn. *Guidelines for Spiritual Direction*. Denville, N.J.: Dimension Books, 1980.

————. *Trusting: Theory and Practice*. New York: Crossroad, 1982.

————. "Phenomenological and Traditional Views of Trust Between Clients and Therapists," in *Duquesne Studies in Phenomenological Psychology* 4, 1983.

Gray, Elizabeth Dodson, ed. *Sacred Dimensions of Women's Experience*. Wellesley, Mass.: Roundtable Press, 1988.

Greeley, Andrew. *Ecstasy: A Way of Knowing*. Englewood Cliffs, N.J.: Prentice-Hall, 1974.

————. *The Religious Imagination*. New York: Sadlier, 1981.

————. *God and American Culture*. Chicago: Thomas More, 1989.

Green, Thomas. *Opening to God*. Metro Manila: St. Paul Publications, 1971.

————. *When the Well Runs Dry*. Notre Dame: Ave Maria, 1979.

————. *Darkness in the Market Place*. Notre Dame: Ave Maria Press, 1981.

————. *Weeds Among the Wheat*. Notre Dame: Ave Maria Press, 1984.

————. *A Vacation with the Lord*. Notre Dame: Ave Maria, 1986.

Greenberg, Samuel L. *Neurosis Is a Painful Style of Living*. New York: New American Library, 1971.

Griffin, Emily. *Turning: Reflections on the Experience of Conversion*. New York: Doubleday, 1982.

Groeschel, Benedict J. *Spiritual Passages: The Psychology of Spiritual Development*. New York: Crossroad, 1983.

Groome, Thomas H. *Christian Religious Education: Sharing Our Story and Vision*. San Francisco: Harper & Row, 1980.

Groothuis, Douglas R. *Unmasking the New Age*. Downers Grove, Ill.: Intervarsity Press, 1986.

Guardini, Romano. *The Lord*. Chicago: Henry Regnery, 1954.

Guest, Judith. *Ordinary People*. New York: Ballantine, 1976.

Guillet, J., et al. *Discernment of Spirits*. Collegeville, Minn.: Liturgical Press, 1970.

Gutiérrez, Gustavo. *We Drink From Our Own Wells: The Spiritual Journey of a People*. Maryknoll, N.Y.: Orbis, 1984.

Haley, Jay. *Uncommon Therapy*. New York: W. W. Norton, 1973.

Hall, E. T. *The Silent Language*. New York: Doubleday, 1959.

————. *Beyond Culture*. New York: Doubleday, 1977.

Hannigan, James. *What Are They Saying About Sexual Morality?* New York: Paulist, 1980.

Harding, M. Esther. *The Way of All Women*. New York: Harper & Row, 1970.

Haring, Bernard. *Marriage in the Modern World*. New York: Newman, 1965.

Hart, Thomas W. *The Art of Christian Listening*. New York: Paulist, 1980.

————. *Living Happily Ever After*. New York: Paulist, 1979.

Hassle, David. *Searching the Limits of Love*. Chicago: Loyola University Press, 1985.

Haughey, John C. *Converting 9 to 5: A Spirituality of Daily Work*. New York: Crossroad, 1989.

Haughton, Rosemary. *Act of Love*. New York: J. B. Lippincott, 1968.

————. *The Mystery of Sexuality*. London: Darton, Longman and Todd, 1970.

————. *The Catholic Thing*. Springfield, Ill.: Templegate, 1979.

Heidegger, Martin. *Discourse on Thinking*. New York: Harper Torchbooks, 1966.

Hellwig, Monika. *Tradition: The Catholic Story*. Dayton, Oh.: Pflaum Press, 1974.

Helminiak, Daniel A. *Spiritual Development: An Interdisciplinary Study*. Chicago: Loyola University Press, 1987.

Herrigel, Eugen. *Zen in the Art of Archery*. New York: Random House, 1971.

Hillesum, Etty. *An Interrupted Life*. New York: Pantheon, 1983.

——. *Letters from Westerbork*. New York: Pantheon, 1986

Holmes, Urban T. *A History of Christian Spirituality*. New York: Seabury, 1980.

Horner, Michael. *The Way of the Shaman: A Guide to Power and Healing*. New York: Bantam, 1982.

Horney, Karen. *Our Inner Conflicts*. New York: W. W. Norton, 1945 (1972).

——. *Neurosis and Human Growth*. New York: W. W. Norton, 1950.

Houston, Jean. *The Possible Human: A Course in Enhancing Your Physical, Mental and Creative Abilities*. Los Angeles: Tarcher, 1982.

Hughes, G. *God of Surprises*. London: Darton, Longman and Todd, 1986.

Hunt, Dave, and T. A. McMahon. *The Seduction of Christianity*. Eugene, Ore.: Harvest House, 1985.

Hurding, Roger. *Roots and Shoots: A Guide to Counseling and Psychotherapy*. London: Hodder and Stoughton, 1985.

Ignatius of Loyola. *The Spiritual Exercises of St. Ignatius*. New York: Doubleday, 1964.

——. *Modern Spiritual Exercises*. New York: Doubleday, 1978.

Isabell, Damien. *The Spiritual Director*. Chicago: Franciscan Herald Press, 1976.

Jacobi, Jolande. *The Psychology of C. G. Jung*. New Haven: Yale University Press, 1962.

Jager, Willigis. *The Way to Contemplation*. New York: Paulist Press, 1987.

Jamart, François. *Complete Spiritual Doctrine of St. Thérèse of Lisieux*. New York: Alba House, 1961.

James, W. *The Varieties of Religious Experience*. New York: Longman, 1982.

Janis, Irving, and Leon Mann. *Decision Making: A Psychological Analysis of Conflict, Choice and Commitment*. New York: Free Press, 1977.

John of the Cross, St. *The Living Flame of Love* in Kieran Kavanaugh and Otilio Rodriguez. *The Collected Works of St. John of the Cross*. Washington, D.C.: Institute of Carmelite Studies, 1973.

Johnston, William. *Silent Music: The Science of Meditation*. New York: Harper & Row, 1974.

——. *The Inner Eye of Love*. New York: Harper & Row, 1978.

Jones, Alan. *Exploring Spiritual Direction*. New York: Seabury, 1982.

Jones, Cheslyn, Geoffrey Wainwright, and Edward Yarnold, eds. *The Study of Spirituality*. New York: Oxford University Press, 1986.

Jung, C. G. *Modern Man in Search of a Soul*. New York: Harcourt, Brace, 1933.

——. *Psychological Types*. Princeton, N.J.: Princeton University Press, 1971.

Kasper, Walter. *Theology of Christian Marriage*. New York: Seabury, 1980.

Kavanagh, Aiden. *The Shape of Baptism*. New York: Pueblo, 1978.

Kavanaugh, Kieran, and Otilio Rodriguez, trans. *The Collected Works of St. John of the Cross*. Washington, D.C.: Institute of Carmelite Studies, 1973.

Kavanaugh, Robert E. *Facing Death*. Middlesex, Eng.: Penguin, 1972.

Keating, Thomas. *Open Mind, Open Heart*. Warwick, N.Y.: Amity House, 1986.

——. *The Mystery of Christ*. Warwick, N.Y.: Amity House, 1987.

Kegan, Robert. *The Evolving Self: Problem and Process in Human Development*. Cambridge, Mass.: Harvard University Press, 1982.

Keirsey, David, and Marilyn Bates. *Please Understand Me: Character and Temperament Types*. Del Mar, Calif.: Prometheus Nemesis Books, 1978.

Kelly, Thomas R. *A Testament of Devotion*. New York: Harper & Row, 1941.

Kelsey, Morton T. *Companions on the Inner Way: The Art of Spiritual Guidance*. New York: Crossroad, 1983.

Kilpatrick, W. K. *Psychological Seduction*. Nashville: T. Nelson, 1983.

——. *The Emperor's New Clothes*. Westchester, Ill.: Crossway Books, 1985.

Klug, Ronald. *How to Keep a Spiritual Journal*. New York: Nelson, 1982.

Knitter, Paul. *No Other Name?* Maryknoll, N.Y.: Orbis Books, 1985.

Knowles, Richard T. *Human Development and Human Possibility*. New York: University Press of America, 1986.

Knox, Ronald. *Enthusiasm*. New York: Oxford University Press, 1950.

Kopp, Sheldon B. *If You Meet the Buddha on the Road, Kill Him!* New York: Bantam, 1972.

Kraft, William F. *Normal Modes of Madness*. New York: Alba House, 1978.

————. *Achieving Promises: A Spiritual Guide for the Transitions of Life*. Philadelphia: Westminster Press, 1981.

————. *Whole and Holy Sexuality*. St. Meinrad, Ind.: St. Meinrad Press, 1989.

Kramer, Kenneth. *The Social Art of Dying*. New York: Paulist, 1988.

Kreeft, Peter. *Heaven: The Heart's Deepest Longing*. San Francisco: Ignatius Press, 1980.

Kroll, Una. *Sexual Counseling*. London: SPCK, 1980.

Kunkel, Fritz. *In Search of Maturity. An Inquiry into Psychology, Religion and Self-Education*. New York: Scribner's, 1943.

————. *How Character Develops*. New York: Charles Scribner's, 1946.

Kwant, Remy C. *Phenomenology of Social Existence*. Pittsburgh, Pa.: Duquesne University, 1965.

Labat, Elisabeth-Paule. *The Presence of God*. New York: Paulist Press, 1980.

LaPlace, Jean. *An Experience of Life in the Spirit*. Chicago: Franciscan Herald Press, 1973.

————. *Preparing for Spiritual Direction*. Chicago: Franciscan Herald Press, 1975.

Lasch, Christopher. *Culture of Narcissism*. New York: Warner Books, 1979.

Larkin, Ernest. *Silent Presence: Discernment as Process and Problem*. Denville, N.J.: Dimension Books, 1981.

Leddy, Mary Jo. *Reweaving Religious Life*. Mystic, Conn.: Twenty-Third Publications, 1990.

Leech, Kenneth. *Soul Friend: A Study of Spirituality*. San Francisco: Harper & Row, 1977.

————. *Spirituality and Pastoral Care*. Cambridge, Mass.: Cowley Publications, 1989.

LeShan, Lawrence. *How to Meditate: A Guide to Self-Discovery*. Boston: Little, Brown, 1974.

————. *Alternate Realities: The Search for the Full Human Being*. New York: Evans, 1976.

————. *You Can Fight for Your Life: Emotional Factors in the Causation of Cancer*. New York: Harcourt, Brace, Jovanovich, 1977.

————. *Cancer as a Turning Point*. New York: Dutton, 1989.

Levinson, D. *The Seasons of a Man's Life*. New York: Ballantine, 1978.

Lewis, C. S. *The Complete Chronicles of Narnia*. Harmondsworth, Eng.: Puffin, 1959–75.

Liderbach, Daniel. *The Numinous Universe*. New York: Paulist, 1989.

Linn, Matthew, et al. *Healing the Eight Stages of Life*. New York: Paulist, 1988.

Loder, James. *The Transforming Moment*. San Francisco: Harper & Row, 1981.

Lonergan, Bernard. *Method in Theology*. London: Darton, Longman and Todd, 1972.

Louf, Andre. *Teach Us to Pray*. London: Darton, Longman and Todd, 1974.

Luijpen, William. *Existential Phenomenology*. Pittsburgh, Pa.: Duquesne University Press, 1960.

Lynch, William. *Images of Hope*. New York: New American Library, 1965.

McAllister, Robert J. *Living the Vows: The Emotional Conflicts of Celibate Religious*. San Francisco: Harper & Row, 1986.

McClellan, Bruce. *Waters of Life: A Guide to Spiritual Reading*. London: Mowbray, 1985.

McCormick, Patrick. *Sin as Addiction*. New York: Paulist, 1989.

McDermott, Brian O. *What Are They Saying About the Grace of Christ?* New York: Paulist, 1984.

McNamara, William. *Mystical Passion*. New York: Paulist, 1977.

————. *Christian Mysticism: A Psychological Theology*. Chicago: Franciscan Herald Press, 1981.

McNeill, Donald P. et al. *Compassion: A Reflection on Christian Life*. New York: Doubleday, 1983.

McNeill, John T. *A History of the Cure of Souls*. New York: Harper & Row, 1951.
McQuarrie, John. *In Search of Humanity*. New York: Crossroad, 1983.
Main, John. *The Christian Mysteries*. Montreal: Benedictine Priory, 1979.
———. *Talks on Meditation*. Montreal: Benedictine Community, 1979.
———. *Word into Silence*. New York: Paulist, 1980.
Maloney, George A. *Nesting in the Rock: Finding the Father in Each Event*. Denville, N.J.: Dimension Books, 1977.
———. *A Theology of Uncreated Energies*. Milwaukee: Marquette University Press, 1978.
Marcel, Gabriel. *Being and Having*. New York: Harper Torchbooks, 1965.
———. *Man Against Mass Society*. Chicago: Regnery, 1965.
Martos, Joseph. *Doors to the Sacred*. New York: Doubleday, 1981.
May, Gerald C. *Pilgrimage Home: The Conduct of Contemplative Practice in Groups*. New York: Paulist, 1979.
———. *Care of Mind, Care of Spirit*. San Francisco: Harper & Row, 1982.
———. *Will and Spirit*. New York: Harper & Row, 1982.
———. *Addiction and Grace*. San Francisco: Harper & Row, 1988.
May, Rollo. *The Art of Counseling*. New York: Abingdon, 1939.
———. "On the Phenomenological Bases of Psychotherapy." In Erwin W. Straus, ed. *Phenomenology: Pure and Applied*. Pittsburgh: Duquesne University Press, 1964, 166–84.
Menninger, Karl. *Whatever Became of Sin?* New York: Hawthorne Books, 1973.
Merton, Thomas. *Spiritual Direction and Meditation*. Collegeville, Minn.: Liturgical Press, 1960.
———. *The Way of Chuang Tzu*. New York: New Directions, 1965.
———. *Contemplative Prayer*. New York: Doubleday, 1971.
———. *Loving and Living*. London: Sheldon Press, 1979.
Michael, Chester P., and Marie C. Norrisey. *Prayer and Temperament*. Charlottesville, Va.: Open Door, 1984.
Miller, Alice. *The Drama of the Gifted Child*. New York: Basic Books, 1981.
Miller, Jean Baker. *Toward a New Psychology of Women*. Boston: Beacon Press, 1976.
Missildine, Hugh. *Your Inner Child of the Past*. New York: Simon and Schuster, 1963.
Monden, Louis. *Sin, Liberty and Law*. New York: Sheed and Ward, 1965.
Muggeridge, Kitty. *The Sacrament of the Present Moment*. London: Fount, 1981.
Mulholland, M. Robert. *Shaped by the Word: The Power of Scripture in Spiritual Formation*. Nashville: Upper Room, 1985.
Murphy, Sheila. *Mid-Life Wanderer*. Whitinsville, Mass.: Affirmation Books, 1983.
Muto, Susan. *A Practical Guide to Spiritual Reading*. Denville, N.J.: Dimension Books, 1976.
———. *St. John of the Cross Today: The Ascent*. Notre Dame: Ave Maria Press, 1991.
Myers-Briggs. Isabel Briggs Myers and the Consulting Psychologists Press. Palo Alto, Calif.
Naisbett, John. *Megatrends: Ten New Directions Transforming Our Lives*. New York: Warner Books, 1984.
Naranjo, Claudio, and Robert E. Ornstein. *On the Psychology of Meditation*. New York: Viking, 1971.
Needleman, Jacob. *A Sense of the Cosmos: The Encounter of Modern Science and Ancient Truth*. New York: E. P. Dutton, 1965.
———. *The New Religions*. New York: Doubleday, 1970.
Needleman, Jacob, and Dennis Lewis, eds. *On the Way to Self Knowledge: The Aims and Disciplines of Sacred Tradition and Psychotherapy*. New York: Knopf, 1976.
Nellas, Panayiotis. *Deification in Christ*. Crestwood, N.Y.: St. Vladimir's Seminary Press, 1987.
Nelson, James B. *Embodiment: An Approach to Sexuality and Christian Theology*. Minneapolis: Augsburg, 1978.

Nemeck, Francis K., and Maria Theresa Coombs. *The Way of Spiritual Direction.* Wilmington, Del.: Michael Glazier, 1985.

———. *Contemplation.* Wilmington, Del: Michael Glazier, 1987.

———. *The Spiritual Journey.* Wilmington, Del: Michael Glazier, 1987.

Neufelder, Jerome M., and Mary C. Coelho, eds. *Writings on Spiritual Direction by Great Christian Masters.* New York: Seabury, 1982.

Nocent, Adrian. *The Liturgical Year.* 4 vols. Collegeville, Minn.: Liturgical Press, 1977.

Nouwen, Henri J. *Intimacy: Essays in Pastoral Psychology.* Notre Dame: Fides, 1969.

———. *The Wounded Healer.* New York: Doubleday, 1979.

———. *The Way of the Heart.* New York: Ballantine Books, 1981.

O'Collins, Gerald. *The Second Journey: Spiritual Awareness and the Mid-Life Crisis.* New York: Paulist, 1978.

O'Connor, Elizabeth. *Letters to Scattered Pilgrims.* New York: Harper & Row, 1979.

Oden, Thomas C. *Game Free: The Meaning of Intimacy.* New York: Dell, 1974.

———. *Agenda for Theology.* San Francisco: Harper & Row, 1979.

O'Donovan, Leo J., ed. *A World of Grace.* New York: Seabury, 1980.

Oraison, Marc. *The Human Mystery of Sexuality.* New York: Sheed and Ward, 1967.

O'Rourke, David K. *A Process Called Conversion.* New York: Doubleday, 1985.

O'Shaughnessy, Mary Michael. *Feelings and Emotions in Christian Living.* New York: Alba House, 1988.

Otto, R. *The Idea of the Holy.* London: Oxford University Press, 1932.

Palmer, Helen. *The Enneagram.* San Francisco: Harper & Row, 1988.

Palmer, Parker J. *The Promise of Paradox: A Celebration of Contradictions in the Christian Life.* Notre Dame: Ave Maria Press, 1980.

Payne, Richard J., ed. *Classics of Western Spirituality.* New York: Paulist Press.

Peck, M. Scott. *The Road Less Traveled.* New York: Simon and Schuster, 1978.

———. *The People of the Lie.* New York: Simon and Schuster, 1983.

———. *The Different Drum.* New York: Simon and Schuster, 1987.

Pelletier, Kenneth R. *Mind as Healer, Mind as Slayer.* New York: Delta, 1977.

Perls, Frederick, et al. *Gestalt Therapy.* New York: Dell Publishing, 1951.

Phillips, J. B. *The New Testament in Modern English.* London: Geoffrey Bles, 1960.

———. *Your God Is Too Small.* New York: Macmillan, 1961.

Pieper, J. *Leisure: The Basis of Culture.* New York: New American Library, 1963.

Pirsig, R. *Zen and the Art of Motorcycle Maintenance.* New York: Bantam, 1974.

Prigogine, Ilya. *From Being to Becoming.* San Francisco: Freeman, 1980.

———. *Order Out of Chaos.* New York: Bantam, 1984.

Progoff, Ira. *The Symbolic and the Real.* New York: Julian Press, 1963.

———. *At a Journal Workshop.* New York: Dialogue House, 1975.

———. *The Practice of Process Meditation.* New York: Dialogue House, 1980.

Raguin, Yves. *Celibacy for Our Times.* St. Meinrad, Ind.: Abbey Presss, 1975.

———. *How to Pray Today: A Book of Spiritual Reflections.* Hertfordshire: Anthony Clarke, 1975.

———. *Attention to the Mystery.* New York: Paulist, 1979.

Rahner, Karl. *On Prayer.* New York: Paulist, 1958.

———. *Christian at the Crossroads.* New York: Seabury, 1975.

———. *Foundations of Christian Faith.* New York: Seabury, 1978.

———. *The Love of Jesus and the Love of Neighbor.* New York: Crossroad, 1983.

———. *Encounters with Silence.* Westminster, Md.: Christian Classics, 1984.

Raschke, Carl A. *The Interruption of Eternity: Modern Gnosticism and the Origin of the New Religious Consciousness.* Chicago: Nelson-Hall, 1980.

Reagan, Charles E., and David Stewart. *The Philosophy of Paul Ricoeur.* Boston: Beacon Press, 1978.

Riaud, Alexis. *The Holy Spirit Acting in Our Souls.* New York: Alba House, 1978.

Richards, Innocentia, trans. *Discernment of Spirits.* Collegeville: Liturgical Press, 1970.

Ricoeur, Paul. *Fallible Man.* Chicago: Regnery, 1965.

———. *Freedom and Nature*. Evanston, Ill.: Northwestern University Press, 1966.
———. *The Symbolism of Evil*. Boston: Beacon Press, 1967.
Riso, Don Richard. *Personality Types*. Boston: Houghton Mifflin, 1987.
Rite of Christian Initiation of Adults. New York: Catholic Book Publishing Co., 1988.
Roberts, Robert C. *Spirituality and Human Emotion*. Grand Rapids: Eerdmans, 1982.
Rodriguez, Richard. *Hunger of Memory*. New York: Bantam Books, 1982.
Rubin, Lillian. *Worlds of Pain*. New York: Basic Books, 1976.
———. *Intimate Strangers*. New York: Harper & Row, 1983.
Rudin, Josef. *Psychotherapy and Religion*. Notre Dame: University of Notre Dame Press, 1968.
Ruffing, Janet. *Uncovering Stories of Faith*. New York: Paulist, 1989.
St. Exupery, Antoine de. *The Little Prince*. New York: Harcourt Brace, 1943.
Salinger, J. D. *Franny and Zooey*. New York: Bantam, 1955.
Schachtel, E. *Metamorphosis*. New York: Basic Books, 1959.
Schaef, Anne Wilson. *Co-dependence: Misunderstood-Mistreated*. San Francisco: Harper & Row, 1986.
Schillebeeckx, Edward. *Marriage*. New York: Sheed and Ward, 1965.
Schmidt, Joseph. *Praying Our Experiences*. Winona, Minn.: Saint Mary's Press, 1980.
Schneiders, Sandra M. *New Wineskins*. New York: Paulist, 1986.
———. *Women and the Word*. New York: Paulist, 1986.
Schutz, Alfred. *Collected Papers*. The Hague: Martinus Nijhoff, 1964.
Sehnert, Keith W. *Stress/Unstress*. Minneapolis: Augsburg, 1981.
Selye, Hans. *Stress without Distress*. New York: New American Library, 1975.
Shah, Idries. *The Sufis*. New York: Doubleday, 1971.
Shapiro, D. *Neurotic Styles*. New York: Basic Books, 1965.
Shea, John. *Stories of God*. Chicago: Thomas More Press, 1978.
Sheehy, Gail. *Passages: Predictable Crises of Adult Life*. New York: Bantam, 1976.
Siegel, Bernard. *Love, Medicine and Miracles*. New York: Harper & Row, 1987.
Simon, George F. *Keeping Your Personal Journal*. New York: Paulist, 1978.
Simonton, O. Carl. *Getting Well Again*. Los Angeles: Tarcher, 1978.
Sinetar, Marsha. *Ordinary People as Monks and Mystics*. Mahwah, N.J.: Paulist, 1986.
Smart, Ninian. *Worldviews: Crosscultural Explorations of Christian Beliefs*. New York: Scribner's, 1983.
Smith, Huston. *The Religions of Man*. New York: Harper & Row, 1958.
Sofield, Loughlan, and Carroll Juliano. *Collaborative Ministry*. Notre Dame: Ave Maria Press, 1987.
Sommerfeldt, John R., ed.. *Abba: Guides to Wholeness and Holiness, East and West*. Kalamazoo, Mich.: Cistercian Publications, 1982.
Spencer, Anita L. *Crises and Growth*. New York: Paulist, 1989.
Squire, Aelred. *Asking the Fathers*. New York: Paulist Press, 1973.
Steindl-Rast, David. *Gratefulness, the Heart of Prayer*. New York: Paulist, 1984.
Stern, E. Mark. *Psychotherapy and the Religiously Committed Patient*. New York: Haworth Press, 1985.
Straus, Ervin, ed. *Phenomenology Pure and Applied*. Pittsburgh: Duquesne University Press, 1964.
Studzinski, Raymond. *Spiritual Direction and Mid-Life Development*. Chicago: Loyola University Press, 1985.
Sudbrack, Josef. *Spiritual Guidance*. New York: Paulist, 1983.
Sullivan, John. *Spiritual Direction*. Washington, D.C.: ICS Publications, 1980.
Talbot, Michael. *Mysticism and the New Physics*. New York: Bantam, 1980.
Teresa of Avila. *The Way of Perfection*. New York: Doubleday, 1964.
———. *The Interior Castle*. New York: Paulist, 1979.
Terkel, Studs. *Working*. New York: Pantheon, 1974.
Thérèse of Lisieux, St. *The Story of a Soul*. John Beevers, ed. New York: Doubleday, 1957.
Toffler, Alvin. *The Third Wave*. New York: Bantam, 1980.

Tolkien, J. R. R. *The Lord of the Rings*. New York: Ballantine Books, 1960.

Toolan, David. *Facing West from California's Shores*. New York: Crossroad, 1987.

Toor, Djohariah. *The Road by the River*. San Francisco: Harper & Row, 1987.

Tracy, D. *The Analogical Imagination*. New York: Crossroad, 1981.

Trevelyan, George. *A Vision of the Aquarian Age*. Walpole, N.H.: Stillpoint Press, 1984.

Trungpa, Chogyam. *Cutting through Spiritual Materialism*. Berkeley: Shambhala, 1973.

——. *Meditation in Action*. Boulder, Colo.: Shambhala, 1969.

Tyrrell, Bernard J. *Christotherapy II: The Fasting and Feasting Heart*. New York: Paulist, 1982.

Tyrrell, Thomas J. *Urgent Longings: Reflections on the Experience of Infatuation, Human Intimacy and Contemplative Love*. Whitinsville, Mass.: Affirmation Books, 1980.

Underhill, Evelyn. *Mysticism*. New York: Meridian, 1967.

Van den Berg, J. H. *Divided Existence and Complex Society*. Pittsburgh: Duquesne University Press, 1974.

van Kaam, Adrian. *The Art of Existential Counseling*. Wilkes-Barre, Pa.: Dimension Books, 1966.

——. *On Being Involved: The Rhythm of Involvement and Detachment in Daily Life*. Denville, N.J.: Dimension Books, 1970.

——. *On Being Yourself*. Denville, N.J.: Dimension Books, 1972.

——. *In Search of Spiritual Identity*. Denville, N.J.: Dimension Books, 1975.

——. *The Dynamics of Spiritual Self-Direction*. Denville, N.J.: Dimension Books, 1976.

——. *The Transcendent Self*. Denville, N.J.: Dimension Books, 1979.

——. *Religion and Personality*. Denville, N.J.: Dimension Books, 1980.

——. *Fundamental Formation*. Vol. 1, Formative Spirituality series. New York: Crossroad, 1983.

——. *Human Formation*. Vol. 2, Formative Spirituality series. New York: Crossroad, 1985.

——. *Formation of the Heart*. Vol. 3, Formative Spirituality series. New York: Crossroad, 1986.

——. *Scientific Formation*. Vol. 4, Formative Spirituality series. New York: Crossroad, 1987.

van Kaam, Adrian, and Susan Muto. *Practicing the Prayer of Presence*. Denville, N.J.: Dimension Books, 1980.

Vanauken, S. *A Severe Mercy*. New York: Harper & Row, 1977.

Vanier, Jean. *Man and Woman He Made Them*. New York: Paulist, 1985.

——. *Community and Growth*. London: Darton, Longman and Todd, 1989.

Verney, Stephen. *Into the New Age*. London: Collins, 1976.

Viorst, Judith. *Necessary Losses*. New York: Fawcett, 1987.

Vitz, Paul C. *Psychology as Religion: The Cult of Self-Worship*. Grand Rapids: Eerdmans, 1977.

Von Balthasar, Hans urs. *Prayer*. New York: Sheed and Ward, 1961.

Von Franz, Marie-Louise. *Interpretation of Fairy Tales*. Dallas: Spring Publications, 1982.

Von Hildebrand, Dietrich. *Transformation in Christ*. New York: Doubleday, 1963.

Walker, Alice. *The Color Purple*. New York: Pocket Books, 1982.

Wallis, J. *The Call to Conversion*. San Francisco: Harper & Row, 1982.

Warren, Michael. *Faith, Culture and the Worshipping Community*. New York: Paulist, 1989.

"Ways of Human Direction." In *Studies in Formative Spirituality* 7, no. 2: (May 1986).

White, James. *Introduction to Christian Worship*. Nashville: Abingdon, 1980.

Whitehead, E., and J. Whitehead. *Christian Life Patterns*. New York: Doubleday, 1979.

——. *Method in Ministry*. New York: Seabury, 1981.

——. *Marrying Well*. New York: Doubleday, 1983.

——. *The Emerging Laity: Returning Leadership to the Community of Faith*. New York: Doubleday, 1986.

————. *Seasons of Strength: New Visions of Adult Christian Maturing.* New York: Doubleday, 1986.

————. *A Sense of Sexuality.* New York: Doubleday, 1990.

Whitfield, Charles L. *Healing the Child Within.* Deerfield Beach, Fla.: Health Communications Inc., 1987.

Wicks, Robert. *Christian Introspection: Self-Ministry through Self-Understanding.* New York: Crossroad, 1983.

Wicks, Robert., et al., eds. *Clinical Handbook of Pastoral Counseling.* New York: Paulist, 1985.

Wilkinson, Peggy. *Finding the Mystic Within You.* Locust Valley, N.Y.: Living Flame Press, 1986.

Wilder, Thornton. *Our Town.* New York: Coward-McCann, 1938.

Woods, Richard. *Mysterion.* Chicago: Thomas More, 1981.

Yankelovich, David. *New Rules: Searching for Self Fulfillment in a World Turned Upside Down.* New York: Bantam: 1981.

Yarnold, Edward. *The Awe-Inspiring Rites of Initiation.* Slough, Eng.: St. Paul Publications, 1971.

Youngblut, John R. *The Gentle Art of Spiritual Guidance.* Warwick, N.Y.: Amity House, 1988.

Zukav, Gary. *The Dancing Wu Li Masters.* New York: Bantam, 1979.